A CONCISE HISTORY OF SPORT IN CANADA

Don Morrow and Mary Keyes
Wayne Simpson
Frank Cosentino
Ron Lappage

TORONTO
Oxford University Press
1989

Oxford University Press, 70 Wynford Drive, Don Mills, Ontario, M3C 1J9

Toronto   Oxford   New York   Delhi   Bombay   Calcutta   Madras   Karachi
Petaling Jaya   Singapore   Hong Kong   Tokyo   Nairobi   Dar es Salaam
Cape Town   Melbourne   Auckland

and associated companies in
Berlin   Ibadan

To
MAXWELL L. HOWELL
For his leadership and pioneer efforts
in Canadian sport history

Canadian Cataloguing in Publication Data
Main entry under title:
A Concise history of sport in Canada
Includes bibliographical references.
ISBN 0-19-540693-1
1. Sports—Canada—History.   I. Morrow, Don.
GV585.C66 1989   796'.0971   C89-094796-1

Contents

Preface

'My country has no history, only a past.'—ALDEN NOWLAN

Play, said Johan Huizingua, is both anterior and superior to culture. Sport is (or should be) a specialized form of play that has a significant role in the process that binds the elements of a culture. As immortalized in Homer's *Iliad* and *Odyssey,* sport is a form of behaviour and an attitude of life-celebration that can speak volumes about the values of a culture and what it lived for—unlike more orthodox subjects of history that tend to focus on what cultures died for.

A Concise History of Sport in Canada has been written in the belief that more people should know about those sporting activities that provided meaning and enjoyment to our ancestors, and how these sports acquired their current place in Canadian life. Our heritage in sport is both rich and enriching. While there have been many books by outstanding journalists about the great moments and heroes of Canadian sport, and several limited academic treatments of the subject, there has been no book that attempts an intensive thematic approach to sport in Canada from its beginnings to the present. The perspective of the sport historian is not well known. Indeed, sport history is a relatively new subject in Canadian universities.

As its title implies, this book is not exhaustive or encyclopedic. Countless other topics might also have been discussed (some of which were prepared for inclusion), but could not be given a place in the text for reasons of space. Nevertheless, the chapters that follow embrace a multitude of subjects. They collectively offer wide-ranging discussions, and descriptions, of many important aspects of sport in Canada, and the concerns that affect it. Besides describing the significance of Montreal in its early development, and examining such themes as sport between the wars, women in sport, sport and technological change, the Olympics, and government involvement, this book emphasizes major changes in selected sports—notably hockey, football, baseball, and lacrosse—

along with the signal achievements in their chosen sport of men and women from the nineteenth century to the present.

Only organized competitive sport is discussed; apart from the subject of fitness, patterns of leisure and recreational activity are noticed only in passing—they await further study. From the beginning of this project it was our intention to use, and to quote from, primary source material wherever possible, as well as to draw upon—and draw attention to, in the extensive endnotes—a small but impressive collection of graduate theses and dissertations that lie, virtually unnoticed, in university libraries. The product of our collaborative effort is, we hope, a readable history of selected facets of sport that will give form and meaning to many of its most important manifestations. Inevitably multi-authorship means a multi-dimensional history, but we feel this a strength, not a limitation. It is also our hope that others will build upon and extend the work that has gone into this book. The authors believe, and our texts surely reveal, that—if not with this book—with a fuller treatment sport can be assigned a significant and well-deserved place in the social history of Canada.

We would like to acknowledge with gratitude the contribution of John Dewar, who originally conceived the project and got it started, and of our editor, William Toye, whose inexhaustible efforts on behalf of this book have been much appreciated.

London, Ontario
July 1989   DON MORROW

1

Montreal:
The Cradle of Organized Sport

Most sporting activities in British North America before the middle of the nineteenth century were prompted by impulse. Pioneer sports associated with such social occasions as work bees and with taverns were spontaneous and loosely organized. Very few of the structures and necessities of organized sport that we take for granted today—clubs, teams, budgets, commercial support, leagues, playing schedules, facilities, and so forth—were present or established in Canadian sport before 1850. It was in Montreal that the first and most significant changes took place in a distinct incubation of organized Canadian sport.

That Montreal became a kind of mecca for Canadian sport in the nineteenth century was logical in view of its geographical, economic, cultural, and commercial advantages.[1] The city was the metropolitan nexus of a vast Canadian hinterland that had once made Montreal the great outlet for the fur trade and for which the city was now a railway terminal, a maritime port, and a manufacturing and financial centre. The population of 58,000 in 1851 increased to over a quarter of a million fifty years later. Though English-speaking Montrealers outnumbered French-speaking citizens for only the forty years before Confederation, the development and organization of sport, and its spread beyond the Montreal region, were due mostly to the efforts of Anglophones.

The first event in Canada that signified organization in any sport was the formation of the Montreal Curling Club in 1807 by twenty élite citizens of Montreal, all of them Scottish. This is the oldest sport club in continuous existence in Canada,[2] a record that is a tribute to the energetic efforts of the Scots as well as to Canada's many successes in international curling events for well over a century and a half. There has been considerable debate about the origins of the 'roarin' game'. Pieter Bruegel's 1565 painting, 'Hunters in the Snow', clearly depicts curling in the foreground, an indication that the game was commonplace in Bruegel's native Holland. Nevertheless Scotland has argued vehemently for recognition as the birthplace of curling, and the game was well enough established in that country by the end of the eighteenth century that a small group of its emigrants in Montreal—who had become civic leaders, most of them wealthy merchants who were members of the North West Company of fur traders—met at Gillis's Tavern to establish officers and draw up club 'rules'. In the early nineteenth century several societies and clubs had been formed by Montreal's élite. The St Andrew's Society, the Natural History Society, the Horticultural Society, the Theatre Society, and the Beaver Club for men connected with the fur trade had each been formed around a common interest. In the first half of the nineteenth century sporting clubs in Canada were primarily social. The earliest (1807) rules of the Montreal Curling Club reflected social concerns, and exclusivity, more than playing procedures:

> 1st. The Club is to meet every Wednesday at 12 o'clock to play till 3 and no member shall absent himself, without giving a sufficient excuse one day before, to the Secretary of the Club, that the party may otherwise be made up under the penalty of Two Clubs. [Two club dinners?]
>
> 2nd. The Club shall meet at Gillis on Wednesday every fortnight at 4 o'clock to dine on *Salt Beef and Greens*. The club *Dinner and Wine* shall not exceed seven shillings and six pence a head and any member infringing on this rule under any pretext whatever shall be liable to a fine of Four Clubs.
>
> 3rd. Each absent member shall pay his proportion of the Dinner only, and each member shall preside at table in rotation.
>
> 4th. No member shall ask a friend to dinner except the President and Vice President for the day, who may ask two each, but it is understood that gentlemen assisting in the game may be asked to dine at the expense of the Club.
>
> 5th. The Club shall not consist of more than twenty members, and in case of any member leaving the country, or wishing to retire from the Club, another may be elected by a majority of the other members.
>
> 6th. The Loosing [sic] Party of the day shall pay for a Bowl of *Whisky Toddy* to be placed in the middle of the table, for those who may chuse [sic] it.
>
> Montreal, 22 January 1807[3]

These stipulations, preceded by a four-line club motto, were followed by twenty-one signatures, but nowhere were there any playing rules for the game of curling. Fraternizing and dining were uppermost; in fact there is evidence that only two or three of the original members even knew how to curl, or had curled prior to 1807.

From such inauspicious beginnings—and in spite of the severity of

Curling on the St Lawrence River, Montreal, 1878—a Notman composite showing the Governor General, the Marquis of Lorne, and his wife in the middle foreground, and seated across the ice, wearing a top hat, Sir John A. Macdonald. (Notman Photographic Archives 48,781-II, courtesy the McCord Museum of McGill University.)

Montreal winters and of outdoor playing conditions on the St Lawrence River ('sheds' were occasionally made and rented out for shelter), interruptions from the War of 1812 and the 1837–8 Rebellion in Lower Canada, and the 1849 Montreal Riots—great strides were later made in the development of the sport in Montreal. Rules and playing regulations were codified by the MCC in 1820, complete with restrictions concerning the use of the club's stock of stones—very likely natural boulders or 'irons' (granites cracked in the intense cold) of various shapes and sizes fitted with makeshift handles or crude finger-holes. One can envision the club secretary and a hired hand, or even 'ice managers', carting the stones and brooms ('besoms') by sled to the river on a frosty Wednesday afternoon in February. Laboriously they would clear a thirty- or forty-metre strip of ice, etch the necessary markings, and prepare the stones for the six or eight curlers. Often MCC members had to compete with the ice harvesters, whose job it was to cut blocks of ice to supply to the hotels and taverns of Montreal. (Conflicting encounters between the two groups—curlers and cutters—must have been frequent and perhaps sometimes comical.) Dressed warmly, the curlers would arrive at the appointed place of meeting on the ice, form two teams of, say, bachelors versus benedicts, and proceed to curl. Three hours later they would retreat to their favourite tavern to engage in whisky toasts ('bumpers'). While it appears that actual games were not all that frequent, the MCC's existence was continuous and its members met regularly, if only to socialize and to conduct the affairs of the Club.

Maintaining its social and ethnic exclusivity, the MCC played a leadership role in the formation of other curling clubs, especially new ones created during the 1830s in such southern-Ontario towns as Guelph, Fergus, and Galt, where Scottish immigrants had settled. Rules and regulations, codes of conduct deemed appropriate to the game's adherents, club-members' moral and financial obligations, as well as refined aspects of the method of play—all developed by the MCC during the 1820s and early 1830s—were passed along to the new 'brothers of the stone' in Ontario. By the end of the 1840s the MCC had lent some of its stones to rinks outside Montreal, had affiliated with the Grand Caledonian Curling Club in Scotland to maintain cultural ties and to participate in the standardization of curling rules, had stimulated two new curling clubs in the city—the Thistle (1843) and the Caledonia (1850)—and had come to be recognized generally as Canada's senior curling society. Although exclusive and restrictive, the formation and development of the MCC represented a major first step towards, and a strong precedent for, the creation of other sport clubs in Montreal.

The MCC exemplified the fact that before sport became organized it was the exclusive preserve of a small select segment of Montreal society.[4] Organization and growth were brought to sport by the officers of the garrisoned regiments in Montreal and other cities in British North America prior to 1850. After 1814 Montreal became the headquarters of the British imperial forces in Canada. The officers were well educated and imbued with the sporting experiences and traditions of Rugby, Eton, Chester, and Harrow. Via such British public schools modern sport was organized, codified, and disseminated to the Empire as cricket, rugby-football, soccer, track and field, and so forth. Equally important was their code of conduct of gentlemanly behaviour and 'manliness', and the vaunted character development that was assumed to flow automatically from participation in the great public-school games. This cult of athleticism, as it was labelled near the end of the nineteenth century, was glorified in the famous epigram, 'The battle of Waterloo was won on the playing fields of Eton' and in the ringing verse from Sir Henry Newbolt's 'Vitai Lampada:'

> There's a breathless hush in the Close tonight
> Ten to make and the match to win
> A bumping pitch and a blinding light,
> An hour to play and the last man in.
> And it's not for the sake of a ribboned coat,

> Or the selfish hope of a season's fame
> But his captain's hand on his shoulder smote—
> Play up! Play up! and play the game.[5]

A belief in the supremacy of 'games' in the building of men's characters was zealously carried to British North America by military personnel.

Garrison officers possessed the leisure time, the money, and the administrative skills to impose some organization on the sporting activity of their choice.[6] The Hunt (1829), Cricket (1829), Tandem (1837), and Racquet (1839) Clubs were all formed by the officers of the Montreal garrison, along with like-minded members of the social élite in the city. The Montreal Hunt Club kept and trained a kennel of hounds and engaged in fox-hunting by 'riding to hounds' on horseback. Equally exclusive was the Racket Club at the corner of Craig and St Peter Streets, which was used for early forms of handball, tennis, and squash and is regarded as the first club of its kind in North America. But cricket, the sport of the British gentleman, and horseracing, the revered 'sport of kings', seemed to be the most favoured activities. Tandem clubs were merely ostentatious winter displays of military colour, horses, and sleighs. Meetings and contests were sporadic, entirely dependent on the whim of the officers, who of course also decided on venue, equipment, rules, prizes, and so forth. When troops were withdrawn from Canada for the Crimean War during the 1850s, there was a dramatic decline in Montreal sporting events—strong evidence of the garrison officers' importance in Montreal sports.

Two sets of events in the mid-1840s brought changes in the development of Montreal sport. The first was initiated in 1842 with the founding of the Montreal Olympic Club by the 93rd Highland Regiment. The earliest track-and-field organization in Canada, the Olympic Club staged the Montreal 'Olympic Games' in 1844. Events in these Games included practical contests, Scottish track-and-field competitions, and at least one novelty event—a game of 'La Crosse', which the officers had seen the Caughnawaga Indians play. The practical contests were in rifle-shooting, the standing high vault (a pole-vaulting event attempted from a stationary start), the running high leap, a standing leap, throwing light (3 1/2kg) and heavy (7kg) hammers, a 365-metre foot race, throwing the cricket ball for distance, and a 1 1/2-kilometre walking race rounded out the program, with most events being won by garrison officers. Significantly the games received extensive coverage in the *Montreal Gazette* on 29 August 1844. The reporting for individual events was terse:

> The race was followed by the Indian game of La Crosse much resembling
> the game in Scotland termed 'shinty.' A purse of $10 was made up for the

winners among the spectators, who appeared highly gratified by the agility displayed.

In the running leap:

> Eight competitors keenly contested this game and the leaping was admirable, exciting intense interest among the spectators. The prize was won by Mr. Augustus Lamontagne, hotly pressed by Sergeant McGillivray of the 93rd Highlanders and Private A. McPherson of the same Regiment. The winner cleared 5 ft 1/2 inch, and McGillivray 5 feet. This game was very protracted.[7]

The only descriptive commentary in the newspaper was a summary of the Games:

> This closed the amusements of the day, to be resumed today at 12 o'clock, when excellent sport is anticipated. The greatest harmony prevailed throughout, and the gentlemen who directed the games manifested much commendable urbanity in their deportment and impartiality in their decisions. The fine band of the 93rd Regiment enlivened the amusements, and contributed much to the enjoyment of the spectators; and it is due to this fine regiment to state, that in almost every game some one of their number put the skill and metal [sic] of the civilian competitors to a severe test.[8]

The tone of these descriptions indicates the interest that was taken in a sporting event organized not for social but for athletic reasons. The upper-class readership assumed by the article is apparent in the reporter's diction: 'much commendable urbanity' and 'an Indian glorying in the mellifluous name of Onasateka' (regarding a native competitor in the 400-yard foot race). The complimentary reference to the proper conduct of the gentlemen suggests that this was unexpected in a public sporting event. On 18 September 1841 the Kingston garrison officers also organized a set of track-and-field events, plus such unique 'manly exercises' as climbing a ladder with hands only, a blindfolded wheelbarrow race, and tilting at a ring with a lance while mounted on horseback.[9] Such competitions, and those in Montreal, reflect a diversification and widening of sporting interests that had begun to attract both spectators and the media.

A second series of events that provided a significant incentive to organized sport stemmed from the earliest-known gatherings of about a dozen prominent Englishmen, from the highest strata of Montreal society,[10] to engage in long-distance outings or 'tramps' on snowshoes.[11] Amerindians, *coureurs de bois*, Nor'Westers, military units, and white men living in the bush used the snowshoe to facilitate winter transport.

A snowshoe outing, c. 1878. (Courtesy the National Archives of Canada, C 22233.)

But it was not adopted for recreational and sporting use until these twelve Montreal men engaged in regular tramps and then in 1843 formalized their interest in snowshoeing by creating the Montreal Snow Shoe Club. It is not generally known that snowshoeing was the pivotal and transitional activity around and through which Montreal sport was ushered into the modern era of commercial organized sport. Proximity to the reserve at Caughnawaga provided a distinct advantage in the development of snowshoeing in Montreal because the Iroquois there were a constant source of both quality snowshoes and competition.

In the early years of the MSSC, tramping was the most common activity of members. During the winter months the snowshoers mustered twice weekly at an appointed rendezvous and time. The snowshoeing tramps were disciplined and orderly. At the rendezvous the ranking club officer was appointed leader and follow-the-leader was the protocol. An experienced snowshoer was appointed by the leader to be 'whipper-in'; that is, to bring up the rear of the file and keep the group together. Compass-in-hand, the leader took his charges on various cross-country excursions in the vicinity of Montreal. By the 1860s and 1870s new snowshoe clubs in the city—among them the Beaver, the Alexandria, and St George's—followed the example of the MSSC and adopted blanket coats, pants, sashes, and distinctive tuques to signify club affiliation. Members of the MSSC were known as the Tuques Bleues and their activities were romanticized frequently in the press, as on the occasion of an 1873 torchlight procession of snowshoers:

> Softly, silently, like the snow flakes upon which they trod, with the peculiar roll of the shoulders and jogging of the hips went the band of athletes, the livid torches illuminating their picturesque costumes, their bright turbans, their fleecy bashiliks [i.e. hoods] and their cerulean tuques. Tramp tramp like the stroke of fate went their webbed foot-falls.[12]

Sumptuous dinners and tavern stops were hallmarks of the growing snowshoeing fraternity in Montreal by 1867. At the taverns many toasts were drunk, there was dancing among the men, and self-laudatory ballads were sung to celebrate the 'manliness' of snowshoeing. Women were not allowed into snowshoe-club membership. The last verse of the 'Song of the Montreal Snow Shoe Club' exemplifies the snowshoers' prevailing perspective on women:

> All pretty girls take my advice,
> On some vain fop don't waste your 'lub,'
> But if you wish to hug something nice,
> Why marry a boy of the Snow Shoe Club.
> Then each night, with wild delight,
> You'll sing success to the Snow Shoe Club.[13]

By the mid-1870s the MSSC was frequently requested to put on musicals and concerts in Montreal and surrounding towns. These shows, featuring singing and living tableaus of the tramping, racing, and dining activities of club members, propelled the MSSC into the public spotlight, especially since all concert proceeds went to charity.

Racing was the competitive branch of snowshoeing, a complement to its more recreational tramping aspect. Once again it was owing to the MSSC's initiative that racing formats were standardized. By the mid-1860s a typical racing card listed 8 events: a race for Indians of 2 to 4 miles; an open one-mile race; a hurdle race; a half-mile boys' race; a 100-yard dash; a garrison race of half-a-mile; a club race of two miles; and a half-mile dash. The greatest test of stamina and training was the two-mile race, which was open only to members of the host club. The hurdle race also required considerable skill since only the tail of the snowshoe was allowed to touch the large wooden equestrian hurdles. Winter racing venues were horseracing tracks and lacrosse and cricket grounds. Carefully ploughed and packed quarter- and half-mile tracks provided the best racing conditions. Whenever grounds with a grandstand could be

A drawing of a mile-long snowshoe race for the Worthington Cup, Montreal, c. 1879. (From the Scrapbook of the Montreal Amateur Athletic Association, volume 14, courtesy Don Morrow.)

used, entrance fees were levied (ladies were always admitted free of charge). Bands were hired and vendors sold food and beverages. By the late 1870s winter weekends in Montreal were crowded with snowshoe-racing events hosted by different clubs. Gambling popularized the races: newspapers published betting odds and the *Montreal Gazette* actually printed race cards on which performance and betting information was listed.[14]

The calibre or rate of performance was admirable. Five-minute fifty-second miles were common by 1870. Top racers achieved 13.5 seconds in the 100-yard dash, a time that was only 3.5 seconds slower than a competitive footrace at that distance in the same period. Some racers actually drove nails through their snowshoe frames for better traction under icy conditions. In general the performance times of non-natives were surpassed by those of natives, who were nonetheless victims of social and racial discrimination—they were never assimilated into competitive snowshoeing and were never considered for membership in any snowshoe club in nineteenth-century Montreal. However, because of their perceived innate skill and demonstrated excellence in the sport, and because they were a crowd-drawing feature, the 'Indian race', varying in distance from two to four miles, was the first event on every race card. All other events were understood to be closed to natives. There was an unfortunate side to these distance races. Incentives were offered to native competitors to perform at near-maximum speed for, say, the first mile of a three-mile race, so that spectators could sadistically witness their agony in the last stages of the race while betting on individual runners. Often clubs would offer novelty events for natives that had as their objective ridicule and entertainment for the white spectators. For example, at a winter sports day in 1875, hosted by the Volunteers at Decker Park, four natives were entered in a 100-yard snowshoe-potato race in which each competitor had to pick up the potatoes placed every yard along the stretch and return them, one at a time, to a basket at the starting line. Such degrading practices were as prevalent in track and field and lacrosse. Excluded from white competitions, and held up to ridicule or induced to perform to exhaustion, natives were treated as lower-class athletes by the middle-class organizers of sport even though—perhaps because—they were perceived to have superior skill.

These snowshoeing events set the example for the organization of Montreal sport. By the later 1870s there were twenty thriving snowshoe clubs in the city. Of those, the MSSC was the 'senior' club, and also the largest, boasting 400 members. But it was its administrative efficiency and panache that played a leading role in Montreal sport. The adoption of club colours and uniforms; the discipline and ritual attached to tramping; well-organized racing events complete with natives, bands, caterers, manicured tracks for the racers and comfortable seating for spectators; the lure of gambling on racers and races; snowshoeing's association with commendable values such as manliness; and with attention paid to charity, as demonstrated by the donation of concert proceeds—all these traditions of the MSSC influenced and shaped the conduct of sport generally in Montreal.

Ice-skating was a complementary and at times rival sport to snow-shoeing. During the 1860s an ice-skating mania enveloped eastern Canada at all levels of society. Like snowshoeing, ice-skating could be practised for its own sake as a pastime or it could be organized into competitions for speed or skill. Most public skating was relegated to natural ice on rivers and ponds, but the sport's popularity, the indoor sheds of Montreal's three curling clubs, and the increasing tendency towards 'clubbing' in Montreal sport combined to prompt well-to-do citizens in the west end of the city to proffer shares for the building of the magnificent Victoria Skating Rink on Drummond Street. Completed in 1863, the red-brick rink was spanned by a semi-circular framed roof that rose to a height of 16 metres and was supported on the inside by huge wooden arches that were anchored in the ground. Around the perimeter of the

A Notman composite of a skating carnival in the Victoria Rink, Montreal, 1870. (Courtesy the National Archives of Canada, C 15302.)

1,350 square metres of ice was a 3-metre-wide raised platform for promenading. Above this, in a horseshoe shape on three sides of the rink, was a gallery with enough space to seat 700 people. At the west end over the entrance was a bandstand and a private gallery for the rink's directors. Fifty large windows lighted the interior by day, and by night 'six pendant stars, each having about 50 gas burners', or about 300 jets of gas, illuminated the rink. Its elaborate design was paralleled by its exclusiveness: membership was restricted to, and carefully controlled by, Montreal's social élite in a 'blackball' voting system.[15]

Nevertheless the Victoria Rink became *the* fashionable winter meeting-place in Montreal during the 1860s and 1870s. It was not unusual for spectators and skaters to be served 5 o'clock tea. Moreover, the fancy-dress carnivals and masquerade skating events staged frequently each winter were popular and colourful pageants of winter recreation in the city. Hundreds of skaters came to the Rink dressed as Marie Antoinette, Henry VIII, or as a pirate or princess. The next day the Montreal papers would publish a complete list of those in attendance and the characters they represented or the costumes they wore. So renowned were these skating masquerades that the world-famous Notman photographic firm completed a beautiful composite picture of one such occasion entitled 'The Skating Carnival, 1870', which conveys both the spectacular aspect and the social cachet of skating in nineteenth-century Montreal. Notman's composites used huge painted backgrounds on canvas—in this case the interior of the rink—on which individual hand-painted photographs of hundreds of characters taken in the studio in pre-planned poses were superimposed. The entire process for such a composite took about a year and a half to complete.[16] The final product was a coloured, framed photograph/painting that measured approximately 1 1/2 by 2 metres. The sale of smaller black-and-white photographs of both the composite and the individual staged portraits provided the funding for the composite production.

Until the 1890s, however, ice-skating in its recreational figure- and speed-skating forms was overshadowed by snowshoeing in Montreal. In fact, as other indoor and outdoor rinks were gradually constructed during the 1870s and 1880s, their proprietors would often advertise a snowshoe race on the ice surfaces to attract paying crowds to skating and racing events. But eventually the various kinds of ice-skating were developed into popular competitive sport forms, and the Victoria Rink was at the forefront of this development. For example, Montreal's Louis Rubenstein trained at the Victoria Rink and went on to capture the Canadian, American, and world figure-skating championships by 1890 (see Chapter 2). Similarly the first Stanley Cup hockey game in 1893 at the Victoria Rink was contested between two Montreal teams; the dimensions of the rink, 56 by 24 metres, provided the standard for North American ice-hockey rinks for decades. The impact of this one facility in Montreal, then, was widely felt in the development of organized winter sports.

Summer sports were also fuelled by Montreal's prominence and its sportsmen. Snowshoeing's summer counterpart was lacrosse, and the overlap between these two sports accounts for the growth and development of lacrosse in its early years. Impromptu games among natives, and between native and white teams, led in 1856 to the formation of Canada's first lacrosse organization, the Montreal Lacrosse Club, by several of the members of the Montreal Snow Shoe Club. Lacrosse grew slowly in Montreal, and until the 1860s only a few other clubs were formed. But during that decade zealous promotion by MLC member Dr W. George Beers, a dentist, accelerated the development of the sport. Called a 'flaming lacrosse evangelist',[17] Beers argued the merits of lacrosse over cricket as a symbol of national identity in the Montreal press throughout the 1860s. As a direct result of Beers' campaigning, and the

A hockey match in the Victoria Rink, Montreal, 1893—possibly the Stanley Cup game. (Courtesy Don Morrow.)

leadership of Beers and the MLC in drawing up the first rules early in the decade, the representatives of twenty-seven clubs in Ontario and Quebec met in Kingston in 1867 to form Canada's first sport governing body, the National Lacrosse Association.[18] By the end of Confederation year there were eighty clubs in the two provinces and lacrosse went on to flourish as one of the most widespread and popular sports in Canada. It is noteworthy that the impetus that made lacrosse tremendously popular throughout the country arose from one body, the Montreal Lacrosse Club. The belief still lingers that lacrosse was officially named—by Parliamentary decree—Canada's national sport, but this is only a myth. (See Chapter 3.)

Other summer sports existed in Montreal by the 1870s, but not with the popularity, prominence, or frequency of participation of lacrosse. Although the Montreal Cricket Club was formed in 1843, cricket remained a closed sport, devoid of any concerted overt attempts to popularize it in Montreal. Even when the 'Gentlemen of England' played the Montreal Cricket Club in 1872, their appeal seemed to be confined to upper-class cricket aficionados—even though in London, Ontario, they attracted some 3,000 spectators. Baseball, by contrast, seemed to draw its adherents from among the lower classes of society and was not very well developed in Montreal until the end of the nineteenth century. In essence, baseball was an industrial sport played by factory workers, or rude 'mechanicals', as they were sometimes called. It gained its first foothold in southern Ontario through a reliance on industrial communities that were linked by railways. Toronto, in fact, was the site for the initial efforts towards the organization of baseball when the Canadian Base Ball Association was formed in 1876 in that city.[19]

Like baseball, sailing or yachting received its organizational impetus outside Montreal. The Maritimes—especially Halifax—and Kingston and Toronto were instrumental in the development of yachting, although the formation in 1888 of the Royal St Lawrence Yacht Club in Montreal signifies an early degree of interest in the sport there.[20] The organizational genesis of golf, however, was directly attributable to the influence of Scots in Montreal. The first golf club created in North America was the Montreal Golf Club, formed in 1873,[21] but there is some evidence of golf-like activities taking place on commons or farms by the mid-nineteenth century, and even of some three-hole courses in Quebec City and Montreal during the 1860s. The lack of specialized clubs, suitable playing areas, and the necessary leisure time prevented earlier development of the game. Granted the prefix 'Royal' in 1884, the Montreal Golf Club set the pattern for the development of clubs in Quebec, Toronto, Hamilton, and other areas, as well as for inter-club competitions. As curious to the French Canadians as the Scottish curlers rolling balls of iron down the ice and crying, 'Soop, soop', the dress of early golfers must have drawn bewildered gazes from the uninitiated. Club members were required to wear

> red coats, white flannel trousers, and caps of the 'fore-and-aft' style. Rules stipulated that opposing captains made the initial drives for their teams wearing white gloves, after which they were removed. Ties were also worn, and severe fines were imposed upon any members who were improperly dressed.[22]

Such conventions and traditions, as well as the facility and equipment requirements of golf, prohibited its popularization in the nineteenth century. Nevertheless the Royal Montreal Golf Club played a significant founding role in the early history of organized Canadian golf.

Leadership, initiative, and success in sports escalated in Montreal throughout the 1860s and 1870s. Billiards was so notorious and popular as a public-house amusement in Montreal that the provincial government in 1801 enacted a licence fee to be imposed on billiard-parlour owners. The game prospered, and sixty years later, in abject fear for the morality of youth, the same act was bolstered by another act to limit clientele to mature players and to prohibit anyone from playing for money.[23] During the same decade, in 1865, Cyrille Dion of Montreal won the title of champion of Canada in Toronto. Yet Cyrille's brother Joseph, who competed only for money, was the more talented player. Gaining his victories after a series of published challenges in the newspapers, Joseph Dion won the title of billiard champion of America from John Deery in New York. The *Montreal Gazette* dramatized the event on 11 June 1867:

> Notwithstanding that the Hall, at New York, was packed with bullies and sharpers, bound to defeat by fraud and force, the attempt to carry away the champion's laurels from New York; in spite of shouts and threats, attempted personal violence and cowardly interruption, our Canadian champion played on steadily and patiently without a tremor of the nerves or a quiver of the lip.[24]

Joseph Dion defended his title at least twelve times, occasionally in Montreal and always for a wager. It is significant that the government legislation against playing billiards for money was overlooked as the Dion brothers' success garnered fame for Montreal; in fact the city council profited by the increased popularity and visibility of the game when it imposed an amusement tax on billiard establishments.[25]

In the 1870s direction and structure were needed to promote and develop clubs, facilities, participants, and events. Unquestionably the greatest change in the organization of competitive sport was ushered in by the bicycle. Originally confined to individual wealthy enthusiasts, the velocipede or bicycle came into prominence in Canada as the penny-farthing or boneshaker. On 1 July 1874 a Montreal resident, A.T. Lane, rode through the streets of Montreal the first such machine ever seen in North America. It was a 'plain-bearing, socket steering high wheeler', or a penny-farthing style of bicycle with a front wheel of 127 centimetres and a diminutive rear wheel. As the penny-farthing became mass-produced in Britain and France, other Montreal citizens acquired the vehicle and, under Lane's initiative, formed the Montreal Bicycle Club in 1878. It was only the third bicycle club in North America, the other two being in Boston and Bangor, Maine.

Although roads in the nineteenth century were never clear of broken glass, wire, garbage, horse dung, and potholes, by 1881 MBC cyclists were organizing 'outings' or rides into the country after the fashion of the Montreal Snow Shoe Club tramps. They wore dark-blue braided patrol jackets and knee breeches, fore-and-aft peaked caps with a tiny gold winged wheel at the front, blue-ribbed stockings, and blue canvas shoes. In this costume twenty to fifty men would ride in paramilitary formation through the Montreal countryside. Club rides were mustered by the MBC bugler and occasionally twelve men were picked to perform

A Notman composite of the Montreal Amateur Athletic Association Bicycle Club, 1885. (Notman Photographic Archives, 26,273 view, courtesy the McCord Museum of McGill University.)

manoeuvres—marching drills on high-wheel bicycles—at public gatherings, exhibitions, track-and-field meets, and lacrosse contests. Cycle races on dirt, cinder, or board tracks as well as on open roads were quickly popularized as the competitive focus of bicyclists in urban areas. The MBC was instrumental in the formation and development in 1882 of a national body—the Canadian Wheelmen's Association—to govern, regulate, and promote competitive cycling. With the invention and mass-production in the late 1880s of the 'safety' bicycle, which had two wheels of equal size propelled by a chain to the back wheel, the MBC rode the crest of public popularity in cycling and promoted racing and cyclists' rights within the city and throughout the province.[26]

The Montreal Bicycle Club was the third club in the triumvirate that in 1881 formed Canada's first multi-sport club, the Montreal Amateur Athletic Association. In essence the MAAA brought order to the random development of sport in Montreal when the prestigious Montreal Snow Shoe Club amalgamated with the Montreal Lacrosse and Montreal Bicycle Clubs in order to acquire grounds and a club facility. It was incorporated by an act of Quebec Parliament, but this was merely a legal necessity for property acquisition. There was no grand design for the development that would give the MAAA a leadership position in Montreal, as well as in Canadian sport.[27]

Yet the timing and the foresight of the members of the three founding clubs were fortunate. In 1881 the MAAA acquired the former Montreal Gymnasium, located at what is now the northwest corner of Mansfield and Maisonneuve. Early gymnastic enthusiasts in the city—perhaps inspired by the interest in physical fitness engendered by the American Civil War—had formed a joint stock company in 1867 with members subscribing as shareholders. Within one year the Montreal Gymnasium was built and equipped for $13,800. Complete with all forms of gymnastic apparatus, a billiard room, and two bowling alleys, the Gymnasium was run as a non-profit business and for a while was financially successful. But within two years it was in difficulty, owing to its inability to collect the shareholders' promised subscriptions and to attract new members from a public more interested in lacrosse, ice skating, and snowshoeing than in physical culture alone. In a last attempt at solvency the Gymnasium merged with the Mercantile Library Association in 1874. Given suitable accommodation for its books, periodicals, and reading facilities, and a few other concessions of usage, the Library in return assumed the Company's $4,000 debt; the union provided only temporary relief, however. Interest in use of the facility dwindled and the debt continued to increase.

In terms of success, renown, and growth the Snow Shoeing and Lacrosse Clubs overshadowed the Gymnasium Company during the 1870s. The two sporting clubs required permanent club quarters and Angus Grant, a notable snowshoer, was the guiding force in the eventual amalgamation of the three clubs. In 1877 Grant was a director of the Gymnasium Company and president of both the MSSC and the MLC. The two clubs made arrangements to rent space from the Gymnasium Company in order to conduct business affairs, and when the MSSC and the MLC united from 1878 to 1881, they were referred to only as 'the associated clubs' in the Montreal press—the meaning of the term was clear to all. Members of the associated clubs enjoyed their preferred activities as well as gymnastics, boxing, fencing, single sticks, billiards, shooting, and bowling, which were also available within the Gymnasium building. Grant was instrumental in inviting the members of the Montreal Bicycle Club to confederate with the other clubs to buy the Gymnasium by assuming all liabilities and the mortgage on the building at a total cost of $13,000. Thus the Montreal Amateur Athletic Association was formed in 1881. The bicycle wheel became the basis of the MAAA's emblem— a winged wheel, the Canadian counterpart to the New York Athletic Club's winged foot. Symbolically the wheel signified that the MAAA was the hub of the organization, with the various recreational and sporting branches representing the spokes. In the rim of the wheel was cast the Association's motto: *jungor ut implear*, 'I am joined that I may be complete.'[28]

With an initial base of some 600 people, the MAAA membership increased threefold within three years. By the end of the century total membership was 2,600. In 1888 outdoor grounds were acquired in West-mount, at the junction of St Catherine Street and Hallowell Avenue, where for $70,000 the MAAA built a pavilion, grandstands, a cinder track surrounding a large outdoor playing field, and acquired a second clubhouse. All outdoor team events and most recreational activities were conducted at the Westmount Grounds. Financially the Association was successful. Owing to its tax-free status as a non-profit organization, it was able to rely on only two sources of income: membership fees set at $10 annually, $100 life-membership fees, and gate receipts from events held in its outdoor grounds. The Association's board of directors, elected from the major sporting clubs, administered all activities, and this was the key to the MAAA's quickly acquired position of power in Montreal and in Canadian sport. The officers of the Association were middle-class businessmen, many of whom were managers of various businesses, and they were well able to conduct the affairs of the MAAA. Indeed, they became highly qualified professional administrators of sport.

The directors skilfully built a pyramidal sport structure. At the base was mass recreation for its members (bowling, billiards, tobogganing, ice skating, etc.) and an ascending hierarchy of team sport through junior, intermediate, and senior levels was maintained, to be conducted intramurally, municipally, provincially, nationally, and internationally. Meticulous attention to detail—such as the early adoption of new equip-ment and devices to enhance sport—attracted members and events to the Association. A revolutionary electric timer was purchased for the track, along with brass distance markers installed on the inner rim; the latest pulley-weight apparatus was placed in the gym; a 'home trainer' or stationary bicycle was purchased for off-season cycle practice as early as 1883; gym cleats for tug-of-war practice were installed in the late 1880s; and a rowing machine was set up near the bowling alleys for training purposes. In addition to hosting popular local spring track-and-field championships, the MAAA's annual Fall Games attracted the best athletes from the Manhattan and New York athletic clubs, and prior to 1909 the Canadian track-and-field championships were repeatedly held on the MAAA grounds.

In the late 1870s there began to be an increasing emphasis on sport outcome and on winning championships and trophies. This led to dis-honest practices among teams, athletes, and clubs in Montreal and else-where. For example, teams were enlarged by the tacit importation of paid players to supplement club players, so that the amateur ideology of the clubs was corrupted by what came to be called, pejoratively, professionalism. Fixed outcomes, widespread unregulated gambling, and lack of standardized codified rules created unfair conditions in sport. To correct them, the MAAA actively sought involvement and control in competitive sports. From its inception it advocated the ideal of nine-teenth-century amateurism. This British-based value system in sport emphasized the virtues of character-building through sport, of fair play and adherence to rules, and most of all the notion of playing solely for the joy of contest. Amateur purists saw money as the root of all evil in sport; professionalism, with some justification, was considered the pros-titution of sport. To remedy the increasing trend towards an unofficial, corrupt 'professionalism', the MAAA followed the lead of British and American sport systems and organized the Canadian Amateur Athletic Association in 1884. MAAA executives dominated the affairs of this national amateur-sport governing body until well into the twentieth century.

The MAAA's winged-wheel emblem became synonymous with effi-ciency in the organization of, and success in, sport on national and international levels. Appropriately the MAAA held the Canadian Wheel-men's Association's national cycling championships in 1886 and again in 1894. Five years later the Association hosted the World Bicycle Meet. Cycling fever in Montreal, fanned by MAAA initiative, was celebrated when an entire issue of the *Montreal Daily Star* (2 May 1896) was devoted to the bicycle.

Members of the MAAA conceived and became the principal organizers of the world-famous Montreal Winter Carnivals that were staged an-nually between 1883 and 1889. Propelled and financed by civic boost-erism, the carnivals were effective lures to the tourist industry—even more than festivals of winter sport. Notwithstanding any underlying motives, the carnivals featured week-long activities in ice-skating, mas-querade balls on skates, tobogganing, snowshoeing, and ice-hockey con-tests. The crowning event each year was a fireworks display at the ice palace constructed in Dominion Square. For the 1883 Carnival:

> The palace will consist of nearly 10,000 blocks of ice, each about 40 × 20 inches in size, and will cost about $3,200. It will face on Dorchester Street, the façade being 160 feet and the greatest depth 65 feet. The walls will be castellated and of different elevations, and three thick partitions of ice will trisect the building. Doors, however, will be cut in these walls so that the public can roam about the interior at will. The main tower standing about 76 feet in height will be a marvel of frozen architecture . . . . Numerous windows will be left at intervals in the walls of the structure which will be filled in with thin ice afterwards.[29]

City clubs and businesses decorated 'cars' or horsedrawn floats to be paraded around Montreal during Carnival week and driven to the ice palace for the big evening. When the crowd of 50,000 had gathered, 1,500 snowshoers representing every club in Montreal, and each carrying a lighted torch, marched eight abreast down Peel Street to surround the castle and initiate a mock battle with a spectacular 'pyrotechnic display'. This winter jollification always ended with hundreds of musical instruments and thousands of voices mingling in the strains of God Save the Queen. But the great Montreal Winter Carnivals of the 1880s became too big too quickly and were halted in 1889.

The Winter Carnivals represented only one facet of the MAAA's influence. Its members were instrumental in the formation and administration of at least ten national governing bodies in rugby-football, hockey, cycling, baseball, figure-skating, bowling, and water polo between 1882 and 1906. During the 1890s the MAAA hosted the Amateur Skating Association of Canada's championships, and in 1897 this 'powerhouse' of Canadian sport staged the world speed-skating championships. Numerous Canadian titles were won by MAAA athletes in lacrosse, snowshoe races, cycling, steeplechases, track and field, figure-skating, ice-hockey (including the championships of seven consecutive Amateur Hockey Association of Canada victories and four Stanley Cup victories between 1886 and 1902), bowling, billiards, football, fencing, speed-skating, and boxing between 1881 and 1909. Even Canada's first Olympic gold medallist, Étienne Desmarteau (the champion 56-pound hammer-thrower in the 1904 St Louis Olympic Games) was a product of MAAA training. Through meticulous administration and the prestige achieved through success and reputation, the MAAA gained power and influence in the organization of Canadian sport. The Notman firm took hundreds of photographs of MAAA events and preserved them in splendid composite photographs that were displayed at exhibitions around the world. Sporting clubs from all over the continent wrote to the MAAA for copies of its constitution, and modelled their own organizations accordingly. The Hamilton Amateur Athletic Association, the St Paul Amateur Athletic Association, and the Abegweit Amateur Athletic Association were only a few of the MAAA's clones.

By 1900 there were almost 250 sport clubs in Montreal, with 24 leagues operating in seven different sports.[30] For the most part, potential chaos was averted by the MAAA, which brought sound administration and organization to this flowering of amateur sport. Most of the growth was in team sports—notably lacrosse, rugby-football, ice hockey, soccer, and baseball—and was the result of the entrance into sport of members of the working class. French Canadians were involved in lacrosse and snowshoeing, but participants in organized sport were mainly English-speaking Montrealers, whose middle-class ideology of amateurism was paramount in the structure and governance of sport. A trend towards commercialism in spectator team sports, however, was accelerating without adherence to any amateur ideals. In addition to, and complementing, this direction in team sports, recreations of the working-class—cycle races, prizefighting, cockfighting, skating, and billiards—were engaged in and enjoyed (in direct contravention, incidentally, of Sabbath laws against such activities). Gambling, swearing, and drinking were features of these commercially based activities, in contrast to the morally uplifting ideology associated with the amateur ethos.[31]

Just after the turn of the century the commercial elements in organized sport, which were virtually unchecked, created bitter feelings among athletes, clubs, and associations. In lacrosse, ice hockey, and rugby-football especially, athletes had become lionized as heroes and were covertly induced by job offers and playing bonuses to transfer to or join certain 'amateur' teams. Professional teams and leagues had not as yet been officially formed, but 'shamateur' practices corrupted the basis of competitive sport—namely, equality and fairness. In the interest of pre-serving some of the standards that had obtained when sport was an activity of the élite, the MAAA tried to persuade team-sport leagues to sanction playing with and against declared professional athletes in order to remove from sport the hypocrisy and inequality of competition that resulted from the practice of paying athletes under the table and bols-tering teams unfairly. Prevailing amateur sentiment, however, rein-forced in 1906 by the emergence of the same ideal in the revised modern Olympics, was stronger than the proposal of the MAAA, which elected to withdraw from the national amateur governing body it had created in 1884 and start a new 'Federation'. The result was a protracted 'athletic war' between the Amateur Athletic Union of Canada and the new Fed-eration that produced many conflicts between their respective teams and athletes.[32]

In the quarter-century since it was formed out of the crystallization of Montreal sport, the MAAA had been outstripped by the diffusion of sport throughout Canada. In flexing its muscle during the athletic war, the Association erred in assuming that its reputation alone would mag-netically draw sport organizations to its perspective. While Montreal had been the cradle—albeit gilt-edged—of organized sport in Canada, and it had been nurtured by the MAAA, a single association in one large city was no longer able to control sport across the country. Toronto-based sport administrators of the Amateur Athletic Union engineered the formation of a national governing body with tiers of provincial, regional, municipal, and club representation. The Federation of the MAAA was forced to amalgamate with the Union in 1909, thereby reaffirming traditional amateur ideals. Having begun in Montreal and emerged from its infancy there, and grown up under the wing of the MAAA, organized sport in Canada was now poised to embark in new directions.

2

Of Leadership and Excellence: Rubenstein, Hanlan, and Cyr

Another view of sport in nineteenth-century Canada over a period of some forty years—before and after the turn of the century—can be gleaned from examining the careers of three prominent athletes. Louis Rubenstein, Ned Hanlan, and Louis Cyr achieved not only national but world-championship status in figure-skating, rowing, and weightlifting respectively. Rubenstein was a Montreal Jew, Hanlan a Torontonian of Irish extraction, and Cyr the eldest of seventeen children of rural French-Canadian parents. These three symbolize the dispersion and democratization of Canadian sport. Moreover, an examination of their careers reveals the magnetic attraction to sport of Canadians from all walks of life.

Louis Rubenstein (1861–1931) grew up in Montreal at a time when snowshoeing, curling, and ice-skating were becoming increasingly popular.[1] Exactly who or what it was that attracted him to skating is unknown, but the Victoria Rink, with its colourful skating pageants and masquerades, must have played an important role. Perhaps the publication in 1869 and the subsequent popularity of Mary Elizabeth Mapes Dodge's *Hans Brinker or the Silver Skates* fuelled the youngster's interest in skating, but an article in the *Montreal Herald* (18 April 1891) speculates simply, and probably accurately, that Rubenstein 'loved skating' as a boy, and that with 'practice and ambition' he developed his skills. Whatever his early motivation, Rubenstein directed his attention to the sport of 'fancy' skating and in 1878, at the age of seventeen, he won the Montreal championship.[2]

The development of Rubenstein's career in skating paralleled the growth in popularity of winter sports in Montreal during the late 1870s and 1880s. He was the right person in the right place at the right time. After moderate success in sporadic competitions, he won the Canadian figure-skating championship at the Victoria Rink in 1883 and retained it for the next seven years. In this period the Montreal winter carnivals—of which ice-skating was one of the sporting competitions—were staged annually and became immensely popular as a tourist attraction of international magnitude. Rubenstein's talent was honed during the eighties by competing with skaters from Toronto; Montreal; Brooklyn; New York; Somerville, Massachusetts; and with his two brothers, Abraham and Moses. He outclassed all those skaters. The single factor in his rise to premier 'fancy-skater' lay in his unprecedented ability to trace and re-trace figures on the ice with tremendous accuracy and precision. Today compulsory figures are mundane prerequisites or warm-up manoeuvres and take second place in the public's mind to the more exuberant and popular free-skating. But 100 years ago precision skating was the only form known to North Americans. Figure-skating was—as the name implies—the tracing and retracing of figures on ice, and Rubenstein's skill was appreciated and applauded. As early as 1884, and again in 1885, he was invited 'at the request of some prominent residents', to give skating exhibitions and take part in competitions in Eastern Canada—in Saint John, St Stephen, Newcastle, Bathurst, Chatham, Moncton, and Halifax.[3] In 1884 one poster advertising Rubenstein's expected exhibition in St Stephen, New Brunswick, described his coming as 'The event of the season'.[4] By 1889 the Montreal press fairly burst with praise for Rubenstein:

> Most Montrealers are acquainted with the champion's style and he went through the list yesterday with all his wonted grace and precision, some of the figures executed being marvels of skill and patient practice while the apparent ease with which he surmounted the difficulties of the cross cut and other intricate movements was a sight worth going to see.[5]

It is difficult to appreciate Rubenstein's skill without understanding some basic elements of his sport as it was conducted during his time. Because of the lack of standardization among host clubs for skating competitions, the skaters signed 'articles of agreement', or minor contracts, that delineated the details of the events. Originating in track and field, articles of agreement were a common means of ensuring uniformity for events in a variety of sports. The articles for figure-skating stipulated the list of figures (the 'lists', as they were known) to be skated, their specific order, and the point value for each figure. The point values for judging the figures in each category varied from 2 for basic locomotive-type steps to 15 for double-eight figures skated entirely on one foot. Often the lists varied markedly from competition to competition and disputes were common. For example, in the seasons of 1883 and 1885, arguments between Rubenstein and H. Robinson, a Toronto speed-skater, over the lists were aired in the *Montreal Gazette*, a further testimony to the public's strong interest in this sport.[6]

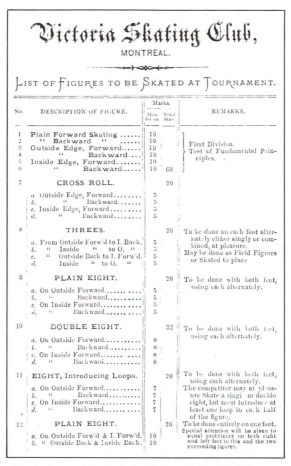

Victoria Skating Club,

MONTREAL.

List of Figures to be Skated at Tournament.

No.	DESCRIPTION OF FIGURE.	Marks. Max. for ea.	Marks. Total Max.	REMARKS.
1	Plain Forward Skating	10		First Division.
2	" Backward "	10		Test of Fundamental Prin-
3	Outside Edge, Forward......	10		ciples.
4	" " Backward....	10		
5	Inside Edge, Forward.......	10		
6	" " Backward......	10	60	
7	CROSS ROLL.		20	
	a. Outside Edge, Forward........	5		
	b. " Backward.......	5		
	c. Inside Edge, Forward........	5		
	d. " Backward........	5		
8	THREES.		20	To be done on each foot alter-
	a. From Outside Forw'd to I. Back.	5		nately either singly or com-
	b. " Inside " to O. "	5		bined, at pleasure.
	c. " Outside Back to I. Forw'd.	5		May be done as Field Figures
	d. " Inside " to O. "	5		or Skated to place
9	PLAIN EIGHT.		20	To be done with both feet,
	a. On Outside Forward.........	5		using each alternately.
	b. " Backward.........	5		
	c. On Inside Forward.........	5		
	d. " Backward.........	5		
10	DOUBLE EIGHT.		32	To be done with both feet,
	a. On Outside Forward..........	8		using each alternately.
	b. " Backward..........	8		
	c. On Inside Forward.........	8		
	d. " Backward..........	8		
11	EIGHT, Introducing Loops.		28	To be done with both feet, using each alternately.
	a. On Outside Forward...........	7		The competitor may at pleas-
	b. " Backward..........	7		ure Skate a single or double
	c. On Inside Forward..........	7		eight, but must introduce at
	d. " Backward..........	7		least one loop in each half of the figure.
12	PLAIN EIGHT.		20	To be done entirely on one foot.
	a. On Outside Forw'd & I. Forw'd.	10		Special attention will be given to equal proficiency on both right
	b. " Outside Back & Inside Back.	10		and left feet in this and the two succeeding figures.

The first page of the Victoria Skating Club's List of Figures.

As a member of the Victoria Skating Club, Rubenstein was naturally partial to its list of figures, not only because he was accustomed to them, but because the Club was 'the most important one in the Dominion, if not on the continent.'[7]Further, he noted, the Club's list had governed all the 'important competitions', such as those for the Dufferin and Bantin medals. In short, Rubenstein contended that he was advocating 'correct' lists; that is, those originating with the Victoria Club. Because of its prestige, the success of the skating competitions in the Montreal winter carnivals, and the media's description of Rubenstein's standing as 'the finest figure skater in Canada,'[8] Montreal took the leading role

Louis Rubenstein, 1890.
(Courtesy Don Morrow.)

in standardizing and organizing the sport. How they did so, to Rubenstein's advantage, provides an interesting case-history of nineteenth-century Canadian sporting politics.

On 1 November 1887 a circular was sent to all rinks in Canada giving 15 days' notice of a meeting to form a national governing body to administer both speed- and figure-skating.[9] Thanks to so little warning, the resulting Amateur Skating Association of Canada was Montreal-dominated. One of its first duties was to codify the list of figures and, of course, the list adopted was the one favoured by Rubenstein and the directors of the Victoria Rink. Regulations to govern competitions were formulated and twenty-one categories of figures for the championship list were established. Included were the use of inside and outside edges, forward and backward rolls, changes, figure eights, figure threes, rocking turns, grapevines, toe- and flat-foot spins. The Club published its 'List of Figures to be Skated at Tournament',[10] in all of which Rubenstein had become extremely skilled.

In addition to his advantage of location, Rubenstein enjoyed the distinct benefit of time—time to train, to compete and to give exhibitions—that accounts in large measure for his success in a sport demanding precision from constant repetition and practice. He was a partner in the family business of Rubenstein Brothers, a silver-, gold-, and nickel-plating and manufacturing firm in Montreal. Among nine children, Louis and his four brothers shared sporting interests and the firm donated medals for skating competitions as early as 1884.[11] A bachelor, Louis was free from the constraints of family responsibilities. In 1886 alone he spent five consecutive weeks travelling to and from Picton (Ontario), Detroit, New York, and various places in Vermont, giving skating exhibitions and engaging in competitions.[12]

By virtue of acquiring the United States championships in both 1888 and 1889,[13] Rubenstein was considered the best figure-skater in North America by the end of the decade. Recognition of his athletic excellence was widespread and he won many tributes. The *Montreal Gazette* reported that the Ottawa press referred to Louis as 'King of the Ice.'[14] After a visit to Quebec City, Rubenstein was presented with a gold pin 'set with emeralds and diamonds as a souvenir of his visit to the Ancient Capital'.[15] The ice-skate manufacturers Barney and Barry of Springfield, Massachusetts, gave Rubenstein 'a pair of the finest skates their celebrated firm can turn out . . . as a mark of appreciation and esteem of the world's fancy skater'.[16] When news of the St Petersburg (Leningrad) 'world' championship—staged to commemorate the twenty-fifth anniversary of the St Petersburg Skating Club—reached Montreal in mid-December 1889, the choice of the most appropriate and deserving representative to be sent by the Amateur Skating Association of Canada was a foregone conclusion.

Four hundred dollars was raised through private donations to defray Rubenstein's expenses. In early January 1890 he boarded the Cunard Royal Mail steamer *Etruria* in New York carrying letters of introduction from Canada's Governor General, Lord Stanley, to the Foreign Office and the British ambassador in St Petersburg. Rubenstein knowingly embarked on an adventure, for he entered Czarist Russia at the height of the pogroms and other organized anti-Semitic practices taken against Jews in that country. Prophetically (and insensitively) the Montreal press stated that 'our skaters can now wait confidently for the cablegram that shall inform us that the redoubtable Louis has either carried off the championship in triumph or is snugly incarcerated in the Trubetskoi Bastion.'[17] Indeed, Rubenstein received extensive newspaper coverage during his two-and-a-half month absence from Montreal, often in the form of his published letters home. When it was all over and Rubenstein was interviewed in Montreal's Bonaventure Station, a reporter asked him for his preconception of Russia. In jocular fashion, and with characteristic wit—surprising in view of the obstacles he faced and the discrimination he suffered in St Petersburg—he responded:

> Well, before I went there I had an idea that Russia was a country somewhere in Europe but I did not know exactly where its boundaries began or left off; that one end of it was somewhere near India and the other near Constantinople; and the principal productions of the country were Nihilists and nitroglycerine, and that it was governed by a man whose family name was Romanoff and whose business it was to get up every morning and light the sun.[18]

Upon his arrival in St Petersburg, Rubenstein registered at the Grand Hotel d'Europe. He used the four weeks available before the contest to familiarize himself with the outdoor conditions under which he would have to compete. There were no indoor rinks in the city, and wind, the glare of the sun, and extreme cold were the most common problems confronting skaters at the competition. To Louis, the ice felt 'like stone' and was very difficult to trace figures on. Above all, the skating standards were much different in St Petersburg than those under which he had gained such an advantage in Montreal:

> Instead of what we call our list in Canada there are three separate competitions in Russia. The real figure skating or what we call list skating goes under the name diagram skating in Russia. Then there are two other departments—special figures and specialties—and in these there is a tendency to acrobatic work, which would not be recognized as fine skating in Canada.[19]

In short the evolution of figure-skating in Europe was more advanced than in North America and closer to the modern form of figure-skating that has both compulsory and free-style components. Rubenstein expressed his distaste for 'acrobatics' succinctly when he commented on skaters doing a spread-eagle:

> . . . it was a physical impossibility for some men to look directly north and compel the toes of the right foot to point exactly east, and the toes of the left foot exactly west.[20]

At the time of the St Petersburg competition there was no international standardizing agency. The International Skating Union was not established until 1894.[21]

As if the pressures of different conditions and styles were not enough to challenge Rubenstein, he was not spared the effects of Russian anti-

Semitism. Within a few days of his arrival he was required to go to the municipal police office. Asked if he was a Jew, he responded affirmatively. His passport was seized and a few days later he was taken from skating practice to another police station, only to be told to leave the country within twenty-four hours. When he asked the reason, he was told:

> You are a Jew, and there is no necessity to further discuss the matter. We cannot permit Jews to remain in St. Petersburg.[22]

Rubenstein made his plight known to the British ambassador, Sir Robert Morier, who intervened on Louis's behalf. Ultimately the prefect of police had Rubenstein roused from sleep to meet with him. The skater was told the he would be allowed to compete but that he must leave Russia immediately after the contest. Rubenstein's passport was returned with the words 'British subject' crossed out and replaced by 'L. Rubenstein, Jew'.[23]

Apparently Rubenstein's skating talents quickly attracted other competitors and coaches, who came to watch him practice. Finally, on Valentine's Day 1890, the North American press announced his victory in the unofficial world-championship event. Within two days the title was rescinded—but it was finally re-awarded. In spite of disadvantages, including the alleged bias of the nine judges, Rubenstein defeated all the other skaters from Vienna, Stockholm, Norway, Finland, Moscow, and St Petersburg by securing first place in two of the three 'departments' in the competition.[24]

Rubenstein returned from St Petersburg in triumph. He was besieged by reporters in both New York and Montreal, but a death in his family subdued his homecoming welcome. He retired from competition in the sport in 1892, after finishing in a first-place tie in the 1891 United States championships.[25] His triumph in, and devotion to, skating led him to write *Lessons in Skating* (1900).[26]

It is tempting to think of Rubenstein as nothing more than a pioneer and brilliant practitioner of figure-skating. But his contribution to sport encompassed many activities as an athlete and/or administrator in other sports and sporting organizations. He also exhibited a tireless devotion to the promotion and conduct of cycling. Attracted to the prestigious Montreal Amateur Athletic Association by the lure of membership and participation in the Montreal Bicycle Club in 1882, Rubenstein showed an active interest in long-distance cycling. Between 1883 and 1886 he placed consistently among the Club's top seven cyclists, accumulating the most mileage in a given season. For example, his total in 1885 was

452 miles, and that distance was achieved at a time of high-wheelers, or penny farthings, and poor roads.[27] In competitive cycle racing he worked on committees concerned with issues of 'Cyclists' Rights' in the city, campaigned for various events, and officiated as a scorer, starter, timekeeper, handicapper, course charter, and judge. Between 1893 and 1900 he served as Montreal's delegate to the Canadian Wheelmen's Association (CWA, the national sport governing body in bicycle racing) and became its president in 1899,[28] which title, or that of honorary president, he retained for the next eighteen years. During the late 1890s he travelled all over eastern Canada to promote the formation of bicycle clubs and their affiliation with the CWA. When Montreal was awarded the World Bicycle Meet in 1899, all confidence was placed in Rubenstein for its efficient functioning. To advertise the Meet, his own bicycle club formed a group called 'Rubenstein's Greatest Canadian Bicycle Band', which travelled with him to play selections from Wagner and Beethoven at bicycle races leading up to the world championship.[29] The World Bicycle Meet itself, and its races, were conducted on a special third-of-a-mile board track constructed at Queen's Park.Together with its masquerade bicycle parades, moonlight tours, and banquets, the Meet was a tremendous success and Rubenstein was involved in every phase of it.

Rubenstein was most interested in sports that required precision, patience, and practice. During the winter in the 1890s he played billiards and bowled (ten-pins) at the Montreal Amateur Athletic Association and curled at the St Andrew's Curling Club. He was elected president of the Canadian Bowling Association in 1895, the same year he was made honorary secretary of the Amateur Skating Association of Canada.[30] In the latter capacity he 'pulled the labouring oar' for the World Speed-skating Championships held at the MAAA Grounds in 1897 and was presented with a handsome diamond pin for his efforts.[31] In 1907 he was instrumental in forming the International Skating Union of America, in opposition to the strictures imposed on amateur skaters in both the United States and Canada. Two years later he became its president.[32] It is clear that his administrative abilities were much in demand. In 1911 he was elected president of the Montreal branch of the Royal Life Saving Society,[33] and two years later he became president of the MAAA.[34] Throughout his life he maintained some kind of involvement in sport. During the First World War he campaigned for and worked hard to complete an indoor swimming pool in Montreal. In tribute to his efforts the $50,000 'Rubenstein Baths' was officially opened in 1916.[35] At the end of the war he was elected president of the Young Men's Hebrew

Association and retained the post until his death in 1931. For a similar period Rubenstein represented the St Louis ward in Montreal as alderman.[36]

People who knew Rubenstein in his later years remarked on his selfless devotion to serving others and on his affable personality.[37] At social gatherings or 'smokers' he was noted for his recitations and his renditions of favourite comic songs, such as 'McCracken's Dancing School', 'Only a Cat', and 'Pay no Rent'.[38] He was inducted posthumously into both the Canadian Sports Hall of Fame and the Jewish Sports Hall of Fame in Israel. His penny-farthing bicycle is preserved in the Château de Ramezay in Montreal, where in 1939 a drinking fountain was erected in his honour at the corner of Mount Royal and Park Avenue. And a 1960 publication, Frank Andrews' *Rejoice We Conquer*, contains a poetic tribute to, and an account of, his 1890 world championship.[39] Thousands of mourners witnessed his funeral cortège in January 1931.[40]

A fascinating contrast to Louis Rubenstein in athletic distinction was **Edward (Ned) Hanlan** (1855–1908), Canada's first individual world champion in sport. Hanlan's sport—single-sculls rowing—was one of the most popular spectator sports in Canada during the last half of the nineteenth century. In fact if public interest, press coverage, international success, and numbers of clubs are criteria, rowing may well have been the major sport at the time.[41] The earliest-known regatta took place in 1820 at Quidi Vidi Lake, Newfoundland. Fishing skiffs were the boats used at early regattas in the Maritimes. Garrison officers in the eastern provinces provided the competitive impetus in the sport by importing racing shells from England and Scotland and by organizing clubs and regattas in major cities. There were at least six rowing clubs in Saint John, New Brunswick, during the 1840s.[42] By mid-century a boat-building rivalry developed between Saint John and Halifax that led quickly to standardization in the sport as well as to rivalries among various eastern cities. In Ontario, Barrie and Toronto supported a large number of rowing clubs and numerous regattas by the late 1850s. Four-oared crews were the popular form of racing prior to 1860 and no crews were more famed than that of Saint John, which won many events in the United States and Canada during the fifties and sixties.[43] In Confederation year a four-oared crew from that city won the world amateur rowing championships held on the Seine in Paris, thereby earning the title 'Paris Crew', which stuck with them in competitions over the ensuing four years.

The popularity of rowing had more than a little to do with gambling and lucrative prizes. Without stringent amateur distinctions, the Saint

John crews commonly won $2,000 per race, plus undisclosed amounts in side-bets.[44] In any sport there is always an urge to find the best or the fastest person, and in rowing this led naturally to the evolution of a popular trend towards single sculling. George Brown of Herring Cove, Nova Scotia, was one of Canada's most prominent early scullers. Five times between 1864 and 1875 Brown won the Cogswell Belt, one of the most coveted prizes in North American rowing. In Toronto, Thomas Tinning, hailed as the 'father' of modern rowing because of his mastery of the sleek shell, 'The Cigarette', won the prestigious Toronto Bay Rowing Regatta many times during the late 1850s and early 1860s. Eventually Tinning sold his 13-kilogram craft to Ned Hanlan, who was world-single-sculls champion from 1880 to 1884.

Hanlan's Irish lower-class family background did not endear him to Toronto's snobbish upper- or middle-class British sportsmen who were dominant in the organization of rowing. Ned's father was a fisherman who also ran a hotel on Toronto Island, and Ned gained his early rowing practice in a fishing skiff, either in the pursuit of angling or in the business of illegally smuggling rum across Lake Ontario to his father's hotel.[45] He won several four-oared and singles sculling races as a teenager in the early 1870s, and won the Ontario singles championship in 1875. Shortly afterwards he came close to being caught by the police for illegally supplying liquor to his father's hotel; Hanlan left Toronto in late May 1876 and carried out his plans to race at the Centennial Regatta in Philadelphia on the Schuylkill River. After he won the regatta the City of Toronto, overlooking his indiscretion, received him with a tumultuous welcome. No doubt the adulation directed at Hanlan was fuelled by major media attention that focused on the events of the American centenary celebrations.[46]

At this moment Hanlan was an athlete who had broken the law, won a sporting competition, and was fêted as a hero—a combination that would be repeated again and again and would lend a rather shadowy character to the triumphant rowing career that followed.

Hanlan's external advantages in his sport were two: his backers, and his mastery of the technological innovation of the sliding seat. Five Toronto businessmen—Dave Ward, Col. Albert Shaw, J. Rogers, Jack Davis, and H.P. Good—recognized the lucrative potential of 'handling' Hanlan as a promising rower if he were backed by a small consortium. Some time between 1875 and 1876 these men formed the Hanlan Club, which managed all negotiations and arrangements, leaving Ned free to train and row.[47] At a time when the professional athlete was regarded as something of an athletic prostitute because of fixed contests in several

Ned Hanlan, c. 1876. (Courtesy Metropolitan Toronto Library, T 32165.)

sports, Hanlan competed only for money, usually $200 to $1,000 a side before 1878. His Club set up all contests and even had Hanlan and his opponents advertise an upcoming race by making whistle-stop tours between Toronto and Barrie. Hanlan reportedly accepted $3,900 from various railroad companies after an 1878 train tour to promote a race with the champion oarsman from Saint John, New Brunswick, Wallace Ross.[48]

Hanlan was apparently the first sculler to master the use of the sliding seat, which his backers had imported for him from England. It was a form-fitting wooden seat fixed to wheels that rolled back and forth in parallel tracks with the oarsman's stroke and recovery motions. Hanlan was diminutive compared to most scullers, weighing only 70 kilograms, and standing 175 centimetres high. Perhaps that was part of his appeal; his small size made him appear to be the underdog. He needed the added leverage the sliding seat gave him and he trained and worked hard to perfect his technique because it made possible a longer stroke, a longer lever arm, and a much more efficient sculling motion. Other oarsmen, wearing slippery chamois-padded shorts and committed to catching the blade in the water and then prying against a fixed foothold with tremendous upper-arm strength, could not see the logic behind

A composite of photographs and painting (the painting by Frederic Marlett Bell-Smith) of Ned Hanlan racing Fred Plaistad, Toronto Bay, 15 May 1878. (Courtesy the Metropolitan Toronto Library, T 13375.)

Hanlan's up-and-back motion in the boat—nor, it seems, could they manage his technique. Some newspaper reports suggested that Hanlan must have had some kind of blacksmith's bellows propelling his craft underneath the keel. It is to Hanlan's credit that he was able to surmount the intricacies of the sliding seat; already blessed with natural talent, it made him a formidable opponent.

In 1878 Hanlan engaged in a series of races with Charles Courtney, the American amateur champion from the Philadelphia races—Hanlan had won the professional championship in the same set of races—at Lachine, Quebec. The three races were well publicized and extremely popular, but they were marked by controversy. There is a strong possibility that the backers of the two athletes 'arranged' to have Hanlan win the first, lose the second, and win the third race in order to profit by a dramatic series of contests.[49] Given ensuing events, and Hanlan's frequently questionable behaviour throughout his career, a fixed set of races seems highly probable.

The twelve articles of agreement signed by Hanlan and Courtney for their race on 3 October 1878 stated that they were to row 'a 5 mile race with turn'; the race was to be for $2,500 a side; 'the referee, after preliminary warning, shall start the race by the word "go"'; the race was to be rowed in smooth water, otherwise there would be a postponement; and it was to be governed by the laws of boat racing as adopted by the National Association of Amateur Oarsmen. The last two articles read:

11th. This race is not to be rowed for, and is not to involve or affect, the championship of either the United States or the Dominion of Canada, now held by the said Edward Hanlan.

12th. It is hereby further mutually agreed that the said Edward Hanlan or his representatives do hereby guarantee the sum of $5,000 in the form of a purse, and as much more as may be raised for the purposes of the said match.

The main concerns were as far as possible to ensure equality in the racing conditions and payment procedures for the stakes. Before 20,000 spectators, Hanlan won the first match by a small margin of one-and-a-quarter boat lengths, thereby leaving some doubt about the superiority of one oarsman over the other.

Hanlan's backers did an admirable job, producing the 37-page *Sketches of the Champion Oarsmen: Hanlan and Courtney,*[50] financed by advertising revenue from Montreal businesses. It included an account of Canadian rowing successes, early life stories of each athlete, their records to date, the articles of agreement, and preliminary comments on race conditions. The publication was not merely good advertising; it also gave the conduct of the races an aura of legitimacy and business acumen. Further dignity was added to the event with the distribution of an Official Programme of the 'Championship Boat Race', which featured handsome sketches of the competitors, a full list of the officials, and advertised prices for spectators that ranged from 50 cents for a grandstand seat to ten dollars for a place on the press steamer that would follow the boats with the referee. Preceding the main event was an Indian war-canoe race of three miles, with a thirty-dollar first prize, and a 'squaw race' with 'not less than 12 squaws in each canoe' for a fifteen-dollar first prize. Over the five-mile course of the main event, flags were hoisted on the judges' barge to give information to the public on the progress of the race at every half-mile—and incidentally providing good betting information. If Hanlan was ahead, a red flag was raised; if Courtney was in the lead, a white flag was raised; a blue flag indicated the race was in suspense. Overall it was a masterfully orchestrated piece of entertainment.

Hanlan's narrow margin of victory at Lachine was characteristic of his entire career. Some have thought that Hanlan 'refused to row away from his victims and allow them to suffer an ignominious defeat.'[51] But it is more likely that Hanlan, for whom rowing provided his livelihood, won his races by narrow margins to maintain uncertainty about the outcome, which is the very foundation of all professional sport and its attendant gambling. His technical advantage and talent made him so much better than his opponents that it would have been career suicide always to

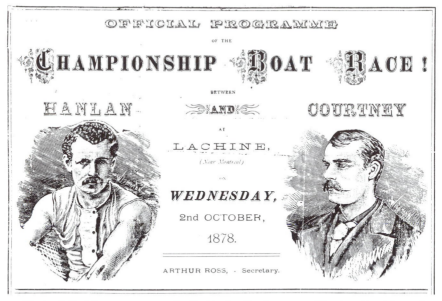

The top half of the program cover for the Hanlan-Courtenay race. (Courtesy Don Morrow.)

pull ahead of them at the outset of a race and to stay ahead—as he could have done. Hanlan and his backers were much too clever to have him go all-out in any single event for fear of losing the element of betting speculation.[52]

Betting on horse-racing events, snowshoeing contests, and matched rowing events was the addiction of the era. Odds were published in the newspapers before every one of Hanlan's races, and gambling outlets and pool-selling ventures were widely available at the contest sites. In selling pools, the operator ran an auction on the athletes. The highest bidder selected his favourite athlete, established odds on him, and the operator then auctioned the odds on the second athlete. Bids on the second athlete had to be close to the odds established by the original highest bidder. Pool-selling worked best when the outcome was uncertain. Front-page headlines were blatant in providing gambling information. For example: 'Toronto Men Putting Their All on Hanlan' (Toronto *Mail*, 2 October 1878). For the Lachine race 'pools were sold . . . in the Windsor Hotel which presented the appearance of an exchange in one of the Metropolitan Cities of the world.'[53]

For the third Hanlan-Courtney race near Washington D.C. in 1880: 'The city swarmed with strangers. In pool rooms, at hotels, even on the streets, rolls of money were waved by persons who sought wagers.'[54] During the race, hawkers and speculators alike ran along the shores shouting, 'Five hundred to three hundred on Hanlan!' or, 'Two to one or any amount on the Torontonian!'[55] Such was the lure of matched rowing races. If the published stakes in Hanlan's races were lucrative, they were minor compared with spectator and gambling revenues.

Preparations were elaborate for the second Hanlan-Courtney match at Chatauqua, New York, in 1879. In the months following the Lachine race, a great deal of newspaper controversy over Hanlan's and his backers' tactics was aired in the *American Spirit of the Times* and the Toronto *Globe*.[56] In the midst of the disputes Hanlan was shipped to England, where he defeated John Hawdon and William Elliott and added the English championship to his Canadian and American titles.[57] Uncharacteristically, Hanlan won the English contest by ten lengths. Very likely he performed to capacity solely to annex a title; he was now rowing to establish gambling opportunities in his own country. Again, Hanlan was the toast of the town when he returned to Toronto. A three-mile flotilla followed Hanlan's steamer into Toronto harbour. One editorial in the Ottawa *Citizen* proclaimed that Hanlan should be knighted for his British victory![58] The Toronto *Globe* heavily advertised a 'Hanlan Gala Day', during which Hanlan would be presented in full racing costume to the audience attending the performance of *HMS Pinafore* at the Horticulture Gardens.[59] Meanwhile, at Chatauqua a grandstand for 50,000 spectators was erected and a stomach-tonic manufacturer, Hop Bitters of Rochester, provided a $6,000 purse in exchange for five per cent of the gate. A special railway spur-line was constructed into the rowing venue to carry a half-mile-long observation train; steamers sold tickets for $5 per person and hotel rates skyrocketed from $1 to $12 per day.[60] But the race never took place. The night before the contest, 15 October 1879, Courtney's boat was sawed in half. Hanlan rowed the course alone, but the incident was regarded as scandalous in sporting circles. All manner of accusations were made against Hanlan, Courtney, their sponsor and backers, but no resolution of the 'greatest sports crime ever committed' was found.[61]

Controversy and intrigue seemed inextricably united to Hanlan's athletic career. For one encounter in 1879, against the American Jimmy Riley on Kempenfelt Bay (near Barrie, Ontario), Hanlan was described as 'fat as a bullock' and 'unfit' when the two finished the four-mile race tied for first:

> . . . of course it is just possible that his miserable condition may have something to do with this . . . it is more than possible that he threw away

what ought to have been a very easy victory by trifling with Riley for the sake of making it a close finish. But if, as some appear to think, the Champion of Canada, the United States and England has descended to the practices of crooked sprint runners [fixed foot races], it will be some time before the people of Canada will go wild over another aquatic hero.[62]

On the contrary, the Hanlan 'mania' never seemed to abate. There was an inevitable backlash, however. In letters to the editor of the *Globe*, disgruntled critics of the 'betting fraternity' associated with Hanlan's races and those who favoured more 'noble' and 'manly' sports such as cricket, shooting contests, and yacht races, were vituperative in their summation of Hanlan's impact. For example:

The fever that has fairly seized the feeble-minded portion of the masses has now been raging for several months past. Column after column has been and is still being devoted to it, until great numbers of people have become so surfeited with what are termed 'aquatics' that they begin to loathe them as Jews do swine. It is said that enough is as good as a feast, but it is very evident that some of the journals labour under the impression that the reading public can never have too much of this simple boat race, where one professional proved himself faster than the other, a fact that is weighing upon some minds so much that they are actually led to make the ludicrous declaration that the honour of nations hung upon this sculling contest.[63]

Perhaps Hanlan's fans were mainly drawn from the working-class and gambling elements whose values were different from those of the upper- and middle-classes, who espoused sport for sport's sake.

Some 100,000 spectators were drawn to the third Hanlan-Courtney race in 1880 on the Potomac River in Washington. Both Houses of Congress adjourned; businesses closed; hats, shoes, and cigars named after the oarsmen were on sale everywhere; pickpockets disguised as clergymen roamed the crowds; partisan spectators wore the colours of their favoured oarsman; a system of coloured balloons and rockets was set up to provide spectators with information on the progress of the scullers; and gambling was as rampant as ever. Courtney folded early in the race and Hanlan won easily, thereby satisfying his Canadian public and quieting detractors of his racing prowess. Only one title remained to be won.

In November 1880 Hanlan defeated the 198-centimetres-tall Edward A. Trickett for the championship of the world in the Oxford-Cambridge boat-race on the Thames. The race drew as many spectators along the course as had attended the Hanlan-Courtney encounter on the Potomac. Never in doubt, Hanlan's win is less revealing of his prowess in this particular case than of his grandstanding conduct. Adorned with a broad moustache, he was always regarded as a handsome man and a crowd favourite, and in this race with Trickett he was the consummate showman. His behaviour—described on other occasions as 'clowning,' 'harlequinading', and 'gamesmanship'—amounted to nothing short of sideshow entertainment and the complete humiliation of his opponent. At various points over the course Hanlan blew kisses to the crowd, stopped to chat or wipe his brow or fan himself. Once he feigned fatigue and slumped over in his boat. As Trickett pulled alongside, Hanlan smiled to the crowd, who went wild with appreciation, and he rowed away from his opponent using alternate strokes of each oar.[64] Unsportsmanlike and technically unethical, such behaviour was nevertheless part and parcel of Hanlan's cockiness and irresistible fan appeal.

Ned Hanlan defended his world title six times before relinquishing it in 1884 to Australia's William Beach, a physically powerful blacksmith who had learned the sliding-seat technique.[65] Because of his renown, Hanlan was unable to profit financially by matched races during his reign as world champion. For income-producing events he was relegated for the most part to staging rowing exhibitions and performing 'trickster' feats, such as rowing in a straight line using only a single oar.[66] On his tours of Australia he was honoured, wined, and dined, and his commercial interests were not readily obvious to many Australian sportsmen and reporters. Hanlan also hypnotized much of the rowing public in that country. Diamond rings, pins, buttons, and bracelets were presented to him as gifts in Australia even after his loss to Beach.[67] Hanlan stayed in Australia for over half a year, hoping to regain his title in 1885, but in that he did not succeed. He even returned to Australia in 1887. In the interim, and while on this second tour, he frequently failed to show up for arranged races, made excuses for losing, and fouled his opponents during races.[68] True to form, he turned his trips to Australia into commercial exhibitions, putting on aquatic displays and rowing in exhibitions anywhere he could command spectators and a significant gate.[69]

Hanlan eventually coached oarsmen at two universities, Columbia and Toronto; operated for a while his father's hotel on Toronto Island; and, like Rubenstein in Montreal, was a city alderman for Ward 4 in the late 1880s. In addition to dazzling the world with his talent and showmanship in rowing in the decade prior to 1884, he was regarded personally as a friendly, attractive, humorous man. The Toronto *Globe* claimed that he was singlehandedly the greatest immigration agent for Canada in the last third of the nineteenth century.[70] In spite of the shadow cast on his reputation by manipulative tactics and unethical practices, he was a classic sports hero whose character flaws were overlooked in deference to the perceived significance of his athletic prowess. At his death he was given a civic funeral in St Andrews Presbyterian Church and 10,000 people filed past his bier.[71] In 1926 the City of Toronto spent $17,000 to erect a commissioned bronze statue of Hanlan near the Princes' Gates of the Canadian National Exhibition Grounds in Toronto, and he was enshrined in a six-verse poem published in the Toronto *Telegram*.[72] Less altruistic than his fellow world sport champion, Louis Rubenstein, Hanlan is no less significant as a symbol of Canadian leadership and excellence in sport.

Montreal and Toronto were the recognized centres of Canadian sport in the nineteenth century and Rubenstein and Hanlan were their much-vaunted English-speaking world-champion heroes. But Montreal could also boast of a French-speaking hero, Neo-Cyprien Cyr, or **Louis Cyr** (1863–1912). Born in Saint Cyprien de Napierville, Quebec, Cyr is often remembered, or billed in contemporary accounts of weightlifting, as the 'strongest man who ever lived.' (His biographer, Ben Weider, entitled his book *The Strongest Man in History: Louis Cyr*.)[73] Unlike the activities of Rubenstein and Hanlan, Cyr's were not well publicized during his lifetime, partly because weightlifting was in its infancy. It was not standardized into formal competitions, with uniform weights or weight classes. As a result some of the information about Cyr's life and athletic career is shrouded in myth or has become legendary. At the same time his achievements, renown, and impact on his sport, and on French Canadians, and his early leadership in weightlifting, have ensured his place in the pantheon of great Canadian athletes.

Eight kilograms at birth, Cyr inherited his adult size from his mother. She was reputed to be 183 centimetres tall and weighed over 114 kilograms, while his father, a farmer-butcher, was of normal size. In his prime, Louis's vital statistics were:

Weight:	144 kg
Height:	179 cm.
Biceps:	61 cm.
Neck:	56 cm.
Forearms:	48 cm.
Chest:	152 cm.
Waist:	114 cm.
Thighs:	84 cm.
Calves:	71 cm.

Cyr was only 5 centimetres taller than Ned Hanlan but his weight was more than double Hanlan's. Apparently his paternal grandfather, himself a village strongman, was a primary influence, encouraging Cyr as a growing boy to develop his strength.[74] Strength was a coveted virtue in French-Canadian culture, especially since the economy of most of Quebec was based on hard physical work in lumber and associated industries.[75] Cyr's inherited physique and his environment combined to shape his physical development and interest in weightlifting.

Undocumented stories abound concerning the adolescent Cyr's feats of strength in arm-wrestling and lifting heavy loads. At fifteen, having quit school three years before, Cyr moved with his family to Lowell, Massachusetts, where he lived for four years and worked at odd jobs in the area. During that time he became proficient in English, an advantage and facility that would work in his favour as a public performer. Married to Melina Comtois when he was nineteen, he moved back to Quebec and worked as a lumberman in the backwoods. Accounts of his feats of strength spread by word of mouth. Finally in 1885 the reigning strongman, David Michaud, challenged Louis to a boulder-lifting competition. Cyr won the contest by successfully raising one end of a boulder, thought to weigh some 226 kg, and became the unofficial champion strongman of Canada.[76] Following his victory he made a brief tour of the province, giving demonstrations of his prowess.

Near the end of 1885, having saved some money from his tour and after putting in a short stint as a policeman in Montreal, Cyr purchased a tavern called Carré Chaboillex and used it as both a stable economic base and a stage from which to demonstrate his strength and attract paying customers.[77] From there he toured parts of Canada and the United States as a weightlifter for the remainder of the 1880s. During this time he learned to do something that Hanlan had honed to an art; he realized that it was wise to outlift an opponent by only the smallest margin necessary to win. Cyr's tactic, in the absence of organized competitions, was to issue newspaper-published or word-of-mouth challenges to strongmen, wherever he was visiting, to test their strength against his. For example, Cyr published a declaration in the *Montreal Gazette* on 24 June 1885:

> I hereby challenge any man in the world, bar none, to a heavy weightlifting contest, without harness, for any sum from one hundred dollars to five hundred dollars a side. Yours truly, Louis Cyr.

By 1889 he had achieved enough distinction and fame to be invited to perform before the Prince of Wales in London's Royal Aquarium Theatre.

Louis Cyr in the 1890s. (Courtesy Don Morrow.)

Cyr reportedly astounded a crowd of 5,000 by raising a 250-kilogram weight off the floor with a one-finger hold on a hook attached to the top of the weight. At the same event he pressed a 124-kilogram barbell from his shoulder with one arm, and after backing under a platform loaded with verified weights totalling 1,864 kilograms, raised the plat-form on his back by straightening at the knees.[78] Such uncommon lifts became trademarks of Cyr's skill and talent.

Throughout his career Cyr controlled and entertained his audiences both by his impressive demonstrations and by allowing anyone to verify any of the weights he used. For a while he fancied himself a modern Sampson, wore a tight-fitting costume and grew his hair long after the fashion of the Biblical character; he even used his hair to twirl people around while they held onto his locks.[79] One of his more dramatic exhibitions was to have harnesses strapped to his arms, bent at the elbow in a muscleman pose. The other ends of the harnesses were attached to two pairs of horses that, on a given signal, pulled away from either side. In reality, the pairs were actually pulling against each other through Cyr's shoulders: the signal to the horses was precisely timed or Cyr would have been injured for life. Still, from his first performance of this act in 1891 at Sohmer Park, Montreal, it became a favourite.[80] It was re-enacted on TV in the late 1980s in an American Express Card commercial.

During the 1890s Louis Cyr toured Europe and the United States, putting on exhibitions and meeting challenges wherever and whenever he could. Without standardization in his sport, and with no agency of organization, his weightlifting bordered on a circus-like performance. In fact he occasionally travelled with the Ringling Brothers and Barnum and Bailey. Yet his weightlifting records were documented. Probably the most impressive of these were established in 1896 in Chicago's St Louis Arena:[81]

1. right and left arm, 85 kg.
2. left shoulder lift with arm 70 kg.
3. iron cross with 44 kg. in right hand, 40 kg. in left
4. 35 consecutive right arm presses with 74 kg.
5. 251 kg. one finger lift
6. lifted 86 kg. with 2 arms straight in front of his body
7. lifted 448 kg. with one hand
8. lifted 197 kg. from right shoulder without use of knees
9. restrained 4 horses for 55 seconds.
10. in one motion, raised or snatched 158 kg. over his head.

Since many of these feats are unorthodox by modern standards and technique, it is difficult to make contemporary comparisons. More significant is the fact that during his lifetime no one could equal Cyr's feats or best him in his self-proclaimed billing as the world's strongest man. He was in a class by himself—as exceptional in his skill, in his way, as were Rubenstein and Hanlan in theirs.

Cyr's appeal was not merely confined to, or defined, by his absolute strength. To complement his talent he nurtured a flair for theatrics, making spectacular and unforgettable entrances.[82] Often when he appeared on stage the curtain was drawn to reveal Louis, wearing a tight-fitting costume that accentuated his physique, spotlighted in erect stance, arms akimbo. He learned to manipulate the collective emotions of his audiences by building tension before a stunt, or by delaying a difficult lift to the very edge of audience patience. In addition, he frequently used members of the crowd in his feats: twirling people from his hair; loading a platform with all the fat men in the audience for his famous backlift; or lifting up a woman seated in the palm of his hand. Once he balanced on his chin a ladder, at the top of which his wife was seated.[83]

Such show-business tactics had a magnetic appeal to audiences. So popular was Cyr during his twenty-three week tour of Europe in 1889 that his originally scheduled two-week booking in the South London Music Hall was extended to a full month.[84]

In declining health by 1906, and aged 43, Cyr performed his last competition in Montreal against Hector Decarie, twelve years his junior. Although victorious, Cyr announced that he was relinquishing his title to Decarie and retired from weightlifting.[85] Over-indulgence in food and liquor had left him with heart ailments. An asthmatic, Cyr died of Bright's disease on 10 November 1912; his funeral in Montreal was attended by thousands.[86]

In their abundance of talent, and in their approaches to sport as entertainment, Cyr and Hanlan were similar. Cyr's career, however, had the added dimension of becoming part of Quebec folklore in his lifetime. One researcher found, in sampling 84 Canadian newspapers on dates coincident with significant performances by Cyr, that he was not at all known across Canada; his Canadian renown was apparently confined to Montreal and vicinity.[87] He was not the celebrated hero Hanlan was, but his historical reputation approaches legendary proportions, especially among French Canadians.

The careers of these three famous sports figures—Rubenstein, Hanlan, and Cyr—not only represent exceptional athletic achievement but also illuminate the enthusiasm for, and the significance of, sport in nineteenth-century Canada: they provide early evidence in Canadian sports history of the impact athletic heroes have on their society in any era. Finally, they mark the early entrance of Canadian sportsmen into the international arena.

3
Lacrosse as the National Game

There is a powerful depiction by the American artist George Catlin (1796–1872) of Amerindian lacrosse in the early nineteenth century that conveys a distinct and profound image of the aboriginal origins of the game. Catlin's painting shows hundreds of athletic-looking natives engaging in a ball-and-stick game; but more significantly it evokes the motion and struggle of these early contestants. There were some forty variations of lacrosse—also known as or *baggataway* or *tewaarathon*—that were engaged in by Ojibwa, Choctaw, Mohawk, Seneca, Cherokee, Huron, Iroquois, and other tribes at least as early as the first North American explorers observed them. The best evidence indicates that inter-tribal contests were rare, perhaps because of the subtle differences in playing forms, but more likely because of the purpose of aboriginal lacrosse: the games were ritual affairs.[1] Ceremoniously dressed in colourful plumed head-dresses, decorated with irridescent paint, and wearing elaborate bead-work belts, native players contested to honour a fallen warrior[2]—paralleling in purpose the funeral games for Patroclus in Homer's *The Iliad*—or for medicinal purposes, to bring a sick person back to health. The games often lasted for days and required tremendous skill and endurance.

Although lacrosse was perceived by early missionaries and travellers to be crude and dangerous, and despite the seemingly chaotic appearance of the game, modern research has emphasized the ritualistic nature of the contests, the skills required, and the emphasis on values such as discipline, leadership, physical skill, physical conditioning, and tribal unity.[3] Most often a single racket about one metre long was used, but in a few tribes the contestants carried one stick in each hand. In either case the top end of these hickory sticks was bent over to form a small hoop or crook that was netted with leather thongs. The hoop of the stick was only large enough to hold the ball, which was made of wood or buckskin and stuffed with hair. The Indian name of the game alluded to the ball, but the Europeans in Canada named it for the stick, calling it 'la crosse' because the stick resembled a bishop's crozier.[4]

The form of the early stick suggests that lacrosse as played by the natives must have been more of a running than a passing game. The object was to drive the ball through two sets of poles or posts erected at each end of the field, affording prime occasions for wagering on the outcome[5]—a significant aspect of the sport that was inherited by white settlers in the nineteenth century. By far the most notorious and most repeated account of early lacrosse concerns a contest witnessed by Alexander Henry doing the Pontiac Rebellion and described in his *Travels and Adventures in Canada* (1809). The game in question was played between the Chippewa and the Sauk at Fort Michilimackinac on the occasion of George the Third's birthday, 4 June 1763. The two teams conspired to use the contest to mask an intended attack on the British fort. Having drawn the officers out of the fort to view the game, at a prearranged signal Ojibwa charged the fort, killed over seventy soldiers, and took many others—including Alexander Henry—prisoner.[6] The massacre and capture of the fort are a major feature of the folklore and history of lacrosse, and very likely perpetuated the idea that Indian lacrosse was brutal.

Early Indian lacrosse holds a significant place in sports history. Having originated as an important activity in the cultures of the Algonkians and Iroquoians of the Atlantic seaboard and Great Lakes regions, with spiritualistic and ritualistic emphases that were central to the contests, it evolved by the late eighteenth century as more of a sporting contest among tribes. As winning became important, so did training methods and diet and other restrictions, such as the following:

> . . . a player should abstain from touching a woman for seven days before a game and seven days after a game. The violation of this rule would weaken the player and subject him to the powers of the players of the opposing team. Even if a woman were to touch a player's stick on the eve of the game, the stick would be rendered unfit for use.[7]

At first heralded in adoption, then transformed in nature, the Indian origins of the game were finally shunned by nineteenth-century white promoters and players.

The *Montreal Gazette*, on 1 August 1833, carries the earliest newspaper reference to lacrosse in a report on an all-Indian game that represented merely one element of an initiation ceremony for five new chiefs.[8] The best-known and most visible native centres of lacrosse in British North America were the Caughnawaga (Iroquois) reserve near Montreal and the St Regis (Mohawk) reserve near Cornwall. Although there were some attempts to package the Indian sport for white spectatorship in the mid-

1830s, there are no records of non-natives playing lacrosse until the Montreal Olympic Games match discussed in Chapter 1.[9] The major thrust to competitive lacrosse came with the formation of the Montreal Lacrosse Club (MLC) in 1856.

In the early years of the MLC members met in the field behind St James the Apostle Church, piled their surplus clothes in a heap, and played a lacrosse match among themselves—before breakfast. The bond linking the men was their joint membership in, and enthusiasm for, the activities of both the Montreal Snow Shoe Club (MSSC, also discussed in Chapter 1) and the MLC.[10] Although there are no formal records of matches, it seems likely that the formation of the MLC was prompted by sporadic games during the 1840s and 1850s between MSSC members and the Caughnawagas. The MLC's leadership in the game is evident in an 1858 photograph, the first one taken of a white lacrosse team.[11] The stick is seen to be of floor-to-shoulder length, but the major change from the Indians' style of racket was a much larger hoop or crook at the top and a greatly increased expanse of interwoven thongs (made from rawhide, gut, or clock strings) to form a flat surface of stringing some twenty centimetres wide at the top and tapering down to the shaft about one-third of the length of the stick. Clearly this transformed lacrosse stick signalled major changes—increased emphasis on passing the ball, for example—in the game itself.

Before 1860 there were no established playing rules. Instead, rules were understood among devotees; playing conditions and standards of acceptable conduct were mutually agreed upon by participants before a match. With only three non-Indian clubs in Montreal—the MLC, the Hochelaga (1858), and the Beaver (1859)[12]—rule formalization was not deemed necessary. In fact the social aspect of getting together and play-ing the early games seemed to be stronger than the interest in winning.[13] A noticeable injection of enthusiasm for the game and its standardization resulted from the visit to Canada of the Prince of Wales and his entourage in August 1860. Newspapers followed his every move. Upon his arrival in Montreal he was ushered into the grounds shared by the Montreal Cricket and Lacrosse Clubs to witness a 'Grand Display of Indian Games'.[14] The 'games' were actually two lacrosse contests sandwiched between an introductory Indian war dance and a concluding Indian foot-race. Featured in the first lacrosse match were an Iroquois team and an Al-gonkian team, with 30 players a side. But the special event of the day—for which the Prince asked that the first contest be halted!—was a game between 25 selected natives and 25 'gentlemen players of Montreal'. The Prince of Wales medal was eventually awarded to the native team.[15]

More important than the event itself was the subsequent publication of the first lacrosse rules in a brochure entitled 'The Game of Lacrosse'.[16]

Advertised in Montreal newspapers, beginning on 15 September 1860,[17] it contained notes on the construction of a stick, sketches on methods of throwing and catching the ball, tactical points on checking, dodging, and goal-keeping, and a set of eight playing rules set out as follows:

1. No *swiping* is allowed.
2. No *tripping*, *holding*, or any such unfair play is allowed.
3. Throwing the ball with the hand is prohibited, though if in a struggle, and opponents around, it may sometimes be kicked with the foot.
4. *Picking up the ball with the hand* is not allowed, except in extreme cases, where the Crosse cannot get it, such as in a hole, etc.
5. After every game the players change *sides*, unless the players who tossed up agree otherwise.
6. If a ball flung at the goal is caught by the 'goal-keeper' but breaks through his Crosse and enters the goal, it is *in*. Or, if a player of either side puts the ball in by accident, it is game for the party who were attacking that goal.
7. In facing, neither of the 'facers' shall attempt to gain the ball till 'three' is counted.
8. When a player is posted in a certain position, he must remain there, unless a favourable chance presents itself for him to leave it, and then he should return to his former position.[18]

These 'rules', which obviously left a great deal to the imagination, reflect not only an initial attempt to formalize the sport but an embryonic stage of lacrosse development.

Before 1867 lacrosse was played on fields of varying dimensions (some were almost a kilometre in length) with teams that fluctuated between 10 and 60 players. Goal-posts with no cross-bar or net, often surmounted with a single pennant or 'flag', were planted in the ground at either end. With the transformation of the stick in the 1850s, lacrosse moved away from the mass attacks of the Indian running game and became more of a passing game that emphasized team-work and positional play. Goals were likely infrequent since a match was won when the first goal was scored. (A goal in the terminology of the time was a 'game'.) From all accounts spectator interest was minimal and the sport was confined to a triangular region bounded by Montreal, Cornwall, and Ottawa.

Expansion of the sport was inspired almost singlehandedly by a Montreal dentist, Dr William George Beers. In 1861 lacrosse boasted nine clubs in Montreal, but the American Civil War dampened the spread and development of the game until Beers undertook the task himself.

Born in Montreal in 1843, he attended Phillips School and Lower Canada College and was apprenticed to Dr Dickenson to complete his formal education in dentistry.[19] A product of Montreal's burgeoning sport environment during the 1840s and 1850s, Beers was picked as one of the goalkeepers for the match played before the Prince of Wales, and under the pseudonym 'Goal-keeper' he wrote the 1860 brochure. An ardent patriot, he was one of the founders of the Victoria Rifles Volunteers militia unit, formed during the Fenian Raids of the early 1860s, and recruited members of the Montreal and Beaver lacrosse clubs. He retired from military service in 1881 with the rank of Captain.[20]

George Beers' propagandizing of things Canadian was clearly in evidence during the decade of Confederation. By 1865 he had published three articles in popular magazines—'A Rival to Cricket', 'The Voyageurs of Canada', and 'Canada in Winter'—all with distinct national themes.[21] Within the dental profession he founded and published the *Canadian Journal of Dental Science*, the first attempt at dental journalism in Canada. Unquestionably George Beers adopted a leadership posture in his vocation and avocation, and in the latter respect he was nothing short of a 'flaming lacrosse evangelist'.[22] Capitalizing on the nationalistic fervour of Confederation year, Beers provided several stimuli towards the expansion of lacrosse. In Montreal newspapers, for example, he wrote several articles under the banner 'The National Game', in which he argued the merits of lacrosse over the imported, revered sport of cricket:

> As cricket, wherever played by Britons, is a link of loyalty to bind them to their home so may Lacrosse be to Canadians. We may yet find it will do as much for our young Dominion as the Olympian games did for Greece or cricket for our Motherland.[23]

This excerpt is part of a reply to an article published one day earlier under the pseudonym 'Stumps'. It had argued that cricket alone, an established sport of the British upper classes in Canada, deserved to be heralded as the new Dominion's national game. Beers' lengthy response was uncharacteristically mild, very likely because he was in the throes of attempting to nationalize lacrosse by riding the crest of pro-Confederation enthusiasm.

In the spring of 1867 there were about ten lacrosse clubs in Canada; by the end of October there were eighty with some 2,000 members, and Beers was the catalyst for this expansion. On 1 July 1867 the MLC adopted 17 rules as the official 'Laws of Lacrosse'; drawn up by Beers and published in the *Montreal Gazette* on 17 July 1867, they were made available for sale through that newspaper's offices:

1. The *Crosse* may be of any given size to suit the players, but the woven network must not be bagged.

2. The ball shall be india rubber sponge, not less than eight, and not more than nine inches in circumference. In all matches it shall be furnished by the challenging party.

3. The *Goals* may be placed at any distance from each other and in any position agreed upon by the Captains of both sides. The Flag Poles of each goal shall be six feet above the ground, and seven feet apart. They shall be furnished by the challenging party.

4. The *Players* shall be designated as follows:
   1st—*Goalkeepers*, who defend the goal.
   2nd—*Point*, who is the first man out from the goal.
   3rd—*Cover Point*, who is in front of the Point.
   4th—*Centre*—who faces in the centre of the field.
   5th—*Home*—who is nearest the opponents' goal.
   The remaining players shall be termed fielders.

5. There shall be two Umpires at each goal, one for each side to be selected by the Captains. Unless otherwise agreed upon, they shall not be members of either of the Clubs engaged in the match. They must be thoroughly acquainted with the game. It shall be their duty before a match to see that all the regulations respecting the Crosse, Balls, Goals, etc., are strictly complied with; during the game they shall stand behind the Flags and shall have the power to decide all disputes and suspend from playing any player infringing these laws. No Umpire shall either directly or indirectly be interested in any bet upon the result of the match. No person shall be permitted to speak to the umpire when the ball is near or nearing their goal.

6. *Captains* may be appointed by each side previous to a match, whose duty shall be to toss up for a choice of goal and superintend the play. They may not be players in the match.

7. No player may wear spiked soles.

8. The ball must not be caught, thrown, or picked up with the hand, save in the case of Rules IX and X, but a ball coming in the air may be blocked or patted away with the hand to *protect the face or body*, otherwise it must not be touched.

9. Goalkeeper while defending the goal may stop balls in any manner.

10. Should the ball lodge in any spot inaccessible to the 'crosse' it may be taken out by the hand and immediately placed on the 'crosse' but should an opponent be checking and cry 'face' it must be faced for.

11. Should the ball be accidentally put through a goal by one of the players defending it—it is the game for the side attacking that goal. Should the ball be put through a goal by one not actually a player it does not count for or against either side.

12. Players shall not hold each other nor grasp an opponent's 'crosse', neither shall they deliberately trip or strike each other.

13. After each game the players shall change goals, unless otherwise agreed upon.
14. A match shall be decided by winning three games out of five, unless otherwise specially agreed upon. The refusal of one side to proceed with a match deemed fair by the umpire shall be equivalent to a defeat.
15. Twelve players on a side shall constitute a full field, and they must have been regular members of the club they represent and no other, for 30 days prior to the match.
16. No change of players after a match has commenced except by reason of accident or injury during the match. When a match has been agreed upon and a side is deficient in the number of players, their opponents at their option may either limit their own numbers to equal them or select men to fill up the complement.
17. Any amendment, revision or alteration proposed to be made in any part of these laws shall be made only to a Committee of the MON-TREAL LACROSSE CLUB, specially appointed and a delegate from every other club in Canada. All clubs shall receive due notice of such a Committee meeting and should they not be represented at the time appointed, the business will be proceeded with and the decisions become law without the concurrence of absentees.

The publication and dissemination of these rules was a crucial factor in the evolution of the sport. Uniformity of playing regulations is a hallmark of modern competitive sport, and rules are the very foundation on which the spread of any sport depends. Beers' new 'Laws of Lacrosse' standardized the number of players (12), the nature of the ball (India rubber), playing positions, the use of umpires (quasi-referees), and the method for determining the outcome of a match (best 3 out of 5 'games' or goals, instead of the previously unpredictable system of 'first goal wins'). Beers' rules provided an instant recipe for competition; all that was lacking was a competitive structure.

Beers and the members of the MLC prompted lacrossists in the Montreal, Cornwall, Ottawa, and Toronto areas to attend in 1867 a lacrosse convention's in Kingston, Ontario,[24] in order to adopt formally a common code of playing rules and to organize a national association to promote and perpetuate lacrosse as the national sport of Canada. Kingston, a central location, was strategic in Beers' conscious effort to expand the sport outside Montreal; it was also the site of the Provincial Exhibition. The Kingston Lacrosse Club issued an official invitation and 52 delegates representing 27 clubs assembled in Kingston's Temperance Hall on 26 and 27 September 1867. One of the major outcomes of this convention was the formation of Canada's first sport governing body, the National Lacrosse Association (NLA), with a mandate to administer the sport by codifying and enforcing rules, and to encourage all clubs to join the Association.[25] A detailed constitution was drafted and published verbatim in several newspapers, including the *Montreal Gazette* on 15 October 1867.

Without question the formation of the NLA was a brilliant stroke of promotional strategy that resulted almost immediately in the proliferation of lacrosse clubs in Quebec and Ontario. In Toronto alone 13 new clubs—the Maple Leaf, the Osgoode, the Toronto, the Ontario, and several military teams—were formed and playing within one month of the convention.[26] Thus the two major urban centres in Canada embraced lacrosse and effectively secured its future. Montrealers figured prominently in the executive of the NLA since the inveterate snowshoer, Nicholas 'Evergreen' Hughes (a founding member of the MSSC in 1843), was elected president and Beers was elected to the central administrative position of secretary-treasurer. Another testament to Beers' recognized organizational efficiency was the virtual adoption of his 'Laws of Lacrosse' with only minor modifications, such as the appointment of a referee in matches and the standardization of field length to a minimum of 150 yards.

The creation of the NLA was a landmark in the history of Canadian sport. No other national sport governing body was organized until 1880, when the Canadian Association of Amateur Oarsmen was formed to govern rowing at a national level. In effect the establishment of the NLA constituted an overt attempt to popularize a particular sport, at a time when sport in general was the preserve of the upper classes. Moreover, the NLA was part of Beers' drive to enshrine lacrosse as Canada's national game. He claimed repeatedly that lacrosse had been sanctified as Canada's national game by an Act of Parliament, and this came to be believed. Henry Roxborough in *The Story of Nineteenth-Century Canadian Sport* (1966) declared: 'Lacrosse is especially linked with Confederation Year, for the Dominion's first parliament had proclaimed it to be Canada's national game.'[27] Nowhere in the Dominion's first parliamentary session, however, is lacrosse even mentioned—and no Montreal or Toronto newspaper in 1867 reports such a proclamation or enactment. The 1894 edition of the *Dictionnaire Canadien-Français* stated that lacrosse became the national game of Canada on 1 January 1859.[28] Beers wrote a book on the sport, entitled *Lacrosse: The National Game of Canada* (1869),[29] in which he made the following claim:

> I believe that I was the first to propose the game of lacrosse as the national game of Canada in 1859; and a few months preceding the proclamation of Her Majesty, uniting the Provinces of Canada, Nova Scotia and New

The Shamrock Lacrosse Club, 1867. (Courtesy the National Archives of Canada, C 5567.)

Brunswick, into one Dominion, a letter headed 'Lacrosse—Our National Field Game', published by me in the *Montreal Daily News*, in April, 1867, was printed off and distributed throughout the whole Dominion, and was copied into many of the public papers.[30]

Beers was only sixteen years old in 1859. Furthermore, in a year when only three lacrosse clubs, all in Montreal, were known to exist, it seems unlikely that such an Act would have been considered. The *Canadian Parliamentary Proceedings and Sessional Papers* and the *Journals of the Legislative Council of the Province of Canada* reveal that Parliament was not even in session in either January or July 1859 and that no mention of lacrosse was made in those publications during the entire year. As for the 1867 letter, only selected issues of the April 1867 editions of the *Daily News* could be located; but every April and May issue of the *Montreal Gazette*, the *Montreal Herald*, the Ottawa *Citizen*, and the Toronto *Globe* were combed to ferret out Beers' letter—to no avail. No sporting contests at all were mentioned by the *Globe* and the *Gazette* in April 1867. Considering that the British Parliament passed the Act to create the Dominion of Canada on 29 March 1867, April would have been a good month

A lacrosse match on the Shamrock Grounds, Montreal, 1867. (Courtesy the National Archives of Canada, C 87235.)

to begin such a publicity campaign. All research[31] suggests that any such campaign must have been by word-of-mouth only, or was a figment of Beers' imagination.

Beers, it would seem, invented the whole national-game concept, which nevertheless managed to gain acceptance by a kind of consensual validity: if something is claimed to be true enough times, it is often accepted as truth—then and now. By late 1867 the sport was indeed surrounded by a 'national' aura; for example, the formation and acceptance of the name National Lacrosse Association had its own connotation; and the Association's provision of a banner for 'championship' play bore the slogan '*Our* Country and *Our* Game'.[32]

Where the national-game concept does emerge is in the columns of the *Montreal Gazette*, beginning in late July and early August 1867. Under the banner 'Sporting Intelligence' was the subheading 'The National Game' and the newspaper pronounced in a 1 August 1867 editorial: 'Let it [lacrosse] be our national game.' One week later there occurred the 'Stumps' versus 'W.G.B.' letters arguing the merits of cricket versus lacrosse as the national game. In fact a letter from Beers dated 8 August 1867 offered a lengthy and well-constructed case for lacrosse as the national game: it is 'peculiar' to our country; it is simple, yet scientific; every man 'has his innings . . . at the same time', that is, unlike cricket, it enables everyone to be on the field at the same time; the ground needs no particular preparation as cricket does; and the materials for play are very cheap.[33] If the game had been accepted by an Act of Parliament in either 1860 or 1867, why did Beers take the trouble to argue his case in such a detailed and thorough manner in this column? The fact remains, however, that the myth of the national game was eagerly accepted. Other newspapers in Montreal, Toronto, and Ottawa echoed the *Gazette's* example and reported lacrosse under the headline 'The National Pastime' or 'The National Game'. George Beers was certainly at the centre of the movement that propelled the game into unprecedented prominence and popularity.

Lacrosse was a featured event in many Dominion Day celebrations. Five thousand Montreal spectators watched the Caughnawagas defeat the Montreal Lacrosse Club, whose members wore white caps, white jackets with red cuffs, grey knickerbockers with a red sash, and black stockings.[34] These costumes promoted the rise of lacrosse over cricket; lacrosse was all colour and rapid motion whereas—to all but devout cricketers—cricket was cream in colour and almost slow-motion. In late October the *Gazette* stated:

> Every Saturday afternoon particularly, the Parks and Commons are crowded with Lacrosse players, from the Professor who doffs the gown for the occasion, to the little urchin who can barely scrape together 50 cents to purchase a Crosse.[35]

In November T. James Claxton, the millionaire head of a Montreal wholesale dry-goods company,[36] donated four championship 'flags' (poles topped with banners in goal-flag style and valued at over $250) for challenge competition in the city.[37] Together with the NLA's banner, 'Our Country and Our Game', and the City of Toronto championship medal, the emphasis in lacrosse had shifted from social conviviality to competition.

The years between 1868 and 1885 were pivotal in the development and growth of lacrosse in Canada. With an established set of rules, a governing agency, 'championship' incentives, such as the Claxton flags and the NLA banner, and the promotion of the national-game concept, lacrosse behaviour was funnelled more and more into a competitive win-emphasis mode. Moreover, as skills were refined the game increasingly became a drawing-card. In 1876, for example, 8,000 spectators attended a game in Toronto between the Montreal Shamrocks and the Toronto Lacrosse Club.[38] The Shamrocks embodied the spiralling emphasis on winning lacrosse games.[39] Formed in Griffintown along the Lachine Canal in 1867, the Shamrock Lacrosse Club was composed of Irish-Roman-Catholic working-class members in an era when the playing-fields were dominated by middle-class Protestants. In 1876 when the Shamrocks met the Toronto club, which had an Irish-Protestant membership, there was a built-in rivalry that could only enhance the emphasis on winning from a spectator point of view. Although lacrosse and other team sports were slowly evolving towards an emphasis on winning and its attendant behaviours, the Shamrocks were ahead of their time in their total dedication to winning first and foremost: constantly accused of dirty play and ungentlemanly conduct, and subjected to media attributions such as the 'unwashed' and 'denizens of Griffintown' (insulting allusions to the Shamrocks' working-class origins and to the district of Montreal in which they and their supporters lived), they won three times as many championship matches as the Toronto club, their closest rival, between Confederation and 1885.[40]

The Shamrocks represented only the tip of the iceberg of the lacrosse phenomenon that was crystallizing. Protests and disputes over game outcomes among 'crack' or first-class teams were common during the 1870s. As early as 1867 natives were barred from playing for white clubs in 'championship' matches, which operated on a challenge basis before 1885, rather than through the league structure that is common in modern sport. The ban against natives in such competitions was due both to social exclusivity and to a perception that they naturally possessed superior skills in lacrosse. Meanwhile commercialism first crept, then galloped, into lacrosse as it became a gate-taking sport in the 1870s. For example, $100 was offered as top prize for the winning team at a Paris, Ontario, lacrosse tournament in 1868,[41] and in 1875 the Shamrocks played the Caughnawagas for the 'championship of the world' and a $500 cash prize.[42]

The expense of maintaining high-calibre lacrosse clubs escalated in the 1870s. Teams and their organizers had to contend with rising costs in between-city transportation, in facility lease or purchase and maintenance, and in spectator attractions—hiring bands to play at the matches, printing programs, installing telegraph connections to cater for fan interest and media demands, and hiring groups or vendors to sell refreshments. Clubs became heavily dependent on admission revenues—about 25¢, plus 10¢ more for a grandstand seat at most matches before 1885—despite initial newspaper criticism that this practice smacked of professionalism. But the emphasis on winning, and the commercialization, necessitated professional practices. Skilled lacrosse players were offered inducements—cash bonuses and job placements—by teams recruiting non-local talent. Lacrosse clubs and the NLA were actually run by professional administrators, middle-class businessmen who had an interest in sport but seemingly possessed a rigorous loyalty to pristine amateurism. The only way the NLA could control player inducements was to institute in 1877 a residence rule to prevent 'tourist' lacrosse players from jumping from team to team.[43] It was a band-aid measure that did not stop the flow of commercialism in lacrosse. As had been the case with the Indian brand of lacrosse, gambling was entrenched in the sport by the 1870s. At various venues of the clubs in Ontario and Quebec as early as 1870, the NLA put up posters prohibiting gambling on site, and threatened to expel violators. Yet both the Toronto *Globe* and the *Montreal Gazette* frequently reported betting information throughout the 1870s. Moreover, the Shamrocks actually promoted betting. One of the club's officers, the owner of the Tansey House, sold pools at his tavern. After one victory over Toronto in 1881 the *Star* estimated that Shamrock supporters collected over $15,000 in bets.[44] The *Montreal Gazette* in 1869 and 1876 also reported pool-selling at Tansey's.[45]

Lacrosse was being propelled against the grain of an idealistic value system—amateurism—that was used as a policy and a means of regulating the sport. Although commercialism and gambling were natural by-products of the 1870s, emphasis on winning, rumours of scandals in other sports, such as 'pedestrianism' (any foot race) and rowing, made organizations like the NLA wary of the 'intrusion' of professionalism; it was a canker to be eradicated. At first the link between money and professionalism was subjected to minor control. In 1876 Article IX of the revised NLA Constitution stated:

> No club in the Association shall play for a money challenge except with Indians. Any club playing for money (except as aforesaid) shall be suspended from membership in the Association.[46]

But playing for a stake or wager apparently continued to be a problem. Natives, however, were almost axiomatically labelled professional by virtue of their skill. By 1880 Indian teams were excluded from NLA championship games on the basis of race and perceived skill advantage and were assigned (by the NLA) professional status. In the same year the NLA changed its name to the National Amateur Lacrosse Association and adopted a formal policy of strict amateur membership (i.e. non-native players and no monetary connections to players except travel and accommodation expenses) and enforcement.[47] This was a futile effort to throw a wet blanket over the wildfire of commercialism. Frustrated by their inability to control semi-professional and professional practices—such as direct payments to players by clubs—the MLC actually withdrew from the NALA between 1880 and 1882.

By the late 1870s and early 1880s the popularity and dispersion of lacrosse had outstripped the most optimistic dreams of that eccentric lacrosse salesman, George W. Beers. Competitive levels of organized lacrosse were categorized, on the basis of proficiency, into junior, intermediate, and senior divisions. Although Ontario was the 'hotbed' of the sport, by 1881 Manitoba—whose first lacrosse club, the Prince Rupert, was established in 1871—had two clubs affiliated with the NLA: the Garry and the Winnipeg.

A major contributor to the widespread and rapid rise to popularity of lacrosse was its spectator appeal. Not only was it fast-paced, colourful, and easy to understand, but it was a rugged body-contact sport that by nature led to disputes and rough or violent play. Since the goals were only two sticks placed about two metres apart, the players, umpires, and spectators were often in dispute about whether the ball had passed inside, outside, or over the top of the goals. By the mid-1870s lacrosse reports in the newspapers were filled with descriptions of game delays over the alleged incompetency of officials and of excessively rough and even violent behaviour (slashing, fouling, fighting). Between 1867 and 1885 the incidence of disputes and rough play during championship matches was more than double that of exhibition or regular games.[48] Rules against foul play, crosse-checking, deliberate charging, interfering, and threatening to strike, which appeared as early as 1878, reflected the spread of such behaviours. But they were very likely crowd-drawing features; rough sport is irresistible to many.

There were more positive aspects to lacrosse, however. Skill levels accelerated from 1867 to 1885. As the game progressed and players became more experienced, they refined positional play and offensive and defensive tactics. Basic skills of throwing and catching evolved from clumsy underarm patterns to sidearm and overhand techniques. Beers' *Lacrosse: The National Game of Canada*, which was filled with lacrosse mechanics, was widely sold in 1869, and again in 1879 when it was reprinted. Two publications that were virtual plagiarisms—'Hints to Players by a Native' printed in an 1871 issue of *Canadian Magazine*[49] and W.K. McNaught's *Lacrosse and How to Play It*[50]—served to disseminate and enhance playing skills and thereby advanced the sport.

Perhaps one of the strongest unifying factors in the spread and acceptance of lacrosse was its export as a showcase activity and as a symbol of Canada to Great Britain in 1867, in 1876, and again in 1883. Nineteenth-century Canadian sport thrived on cordial sporting ties with England, and British North America had imported most of its sport, as well as its traditions and values, from English and Scottish immigrants. A precedent for international tours was established in the late 1850s when an English cricket 'eleven' toured British North America. Canada, in turn, sent teams of marksmen to the world-famous annual rifle cham-

A Notman photograph of the Caughnawaga Lacrosse Club, Montreal, 1867. (Notman Photographic Archives, 29,099 BI, courtesy the McCord Museum of McGill University.)

pionships at Wimbledon. Acting on an offhand suggestion, Captain W.B. Johnson of the Montreal Lacrosse Club engaged sixteen Caughnawagas to leave Canada on 12 July 1867 and tour England to demonstrate lacrosse. But Johnson was mainly interested in the financial prospects of the venture; the visit was not publicized and was short-lived and of little consequence.[51]

In the mid-1870s another MLC member, Dr Thomas Archer, moved to London, England, and persuaded the Thames Hare and Hounds Club to form a lacrosse club. Subsequently Archer corresponded with Beers to explore the possibilities of a tour. Beers persuaded Mr Charles Rose to visit Britain in 1875 to solicit support for a lacrosse trip. With the verbal and financial encouragement of the celebrated Hurlingham Polo Club, it was decided that lacrosse teams would be sent to Britain. Public subscriptions were sought in Montreal, a Committee of Management of the MLC was struck, and discussions about ensuring success were predicated on sending one team of natives along with a white team.[52] The trip was at least partially envisaged as a Canadian image-builder: 'Thousands will go to see Canada's game to one who would go to hear Canada's immigration agents.'[53]

Beers, of course, primarily desired to sell lacrosse to Great Britain not only as a game but also as a symbol of Canada. Before the teams' departure the Montreal press gave details of the trip under the banner 'Young Canada'. In Britain the press used material from Beers' book to educate its readers on the nature of the game, but the real media emphasis was laid on its Indian origins, including the 1763 Fort Michilimackinac incident (although the press was careful to point out that Iroquois were not involved in that massacre). The fact that this native historical build-up in all the British papers ran parallel to the games suggests that it was pre-packaged and pre-released by Beers. The tour was drenched in Indian imagery; the natives themselves were Beers' advertising gimmick and his drawing-card for the British.

At Montreal's Bonaventure Station, on 29 April 1876, 3,000 people and a large band bade farewell to the 'European team', composed of 13 members of the MLC and 13 Caughnawagas. One can visualize George Beers, puffed up with pride as he stood on the deck of the *S.S. Moravian*, contemplating his arrival in Ireland to begin the dissemination of Canadian culture via lacrosse. A well-meaning Irish hotelkeeper burst Beers' bubble by hoisting the 'Stars and Stripes' in welcome tribute. In a frenzy of nationalistic fervour Beers rushed out to purchase a Dominion flag and personally raised it at each and every game.

The teams played sixteen games during their month-and-a-half swing through Ireland, Scotland, and England. The order of ceremonies was repeated for each match. The natives were escorted to centre-field in their playing costumes, which consisted of red-and-white striped 'guernseys' (jerseys, or tunics) and knickers, with white hose (or red-and-yellow striped knickers); blue velvet caps overlaid with much ornamental bead work and topped by two or three scarlet feathers; and tight-fitting sashes and waist belts of blue velvet with a large letter C (for Caughnawaga) on the front. In addition all the natives wore earrings and many silver-coloured finger rings. Against the stark green backdrop of the cricket grounds on which they played, and the creams of the cricket players, they were vivid to say the least. Next the 13-member MLC team came onto the grounds wearing white guernseys, grey tweed knickers, and dark brown hose. After brief introductions to the chief dignitary present, the match commenced.

The British reaction was most favourable and 3,000 to 5,000 spectators attended the games. Enthusiastic descriptions of the natives and the equipment used in lacrosse were plentiful in the British press. The most eloquent characterization of a lacrosse stick was rendered in the London *Daily Telegraph*: 'a spoon of Brobdingnagian size and Filigree pattern.'[54] Both teams had been carefully coached to be above reproach; the players were repeatedly commended for their exemplary behaviour in the intervals between matches, whether touring cairns, castles, or collieries. Always on such occasions, away from the playing-fields, the natives were asked to wear their lacrosse outfits. Between games they were urged to hold snowshoe races on the grass, to dance 'war dances' or the 'green corn dance', or to hold mock 'pow-wows'. During the contests Keraronwe, who spoke English very well, made 'wild verbal ejaculations' and frantic gestures to his team-mates. James Fenimore Cooper could not have contrived a more colourful image of stereotypical Indianness for these early 'Harlem Globetrotters' of lacrosse.

Although the Indian hype predominated, some perceptive journalism crept into the media. The *London and Provincial News* remarked that natives might be Indians at lacrosse matches but:

> At home they are staunch Conservatives, devout Roman Catholics, sit on Windsor chairs, and are more addicted to smoking bird's eye tobacco than to brandishing tomahawks.[55]

The *Glasgow Baillie* quipped sarcastically:

> Get out of my sight with your redskins and your war-paint and your thousand miles in a thousand hours, and all such tomfoolery! At my time of life a man can find his amusements in his own hemisphere without importing them like wooden nutmegs from the other side of the Atlantic.[56]

If the British 'went in' for lacrosse, the *Newcastle Daily Journal* pondered rhetorically:

> Would war paint and feathers become de rigueur? Would a complete mastery of the art of scalping be indispensable?[57]

In the United States the New York *Herald* carried all the lacrosse news sent by a special correspondent to that newspaper, and the Toronto *Globe* reprinted the *Herald*'s stories by special permission.[58] Perhaps the *Globe*'s third-hand coverage reflected Toronto's dissatisfaction with the Montreal-monopolized lacrosse tour, as well as the city's rivalry with Montreal teams.

Near-sanctification came to the tour when Queen Victoria requested that a private game be played before her at Windsor Castle on 25 June 1876. This audience was interpreted even in Toronto as indicative of 'the estimation in which this country is held by the highest person in the

Empire'.[59] Before the game Keraronwe read the Queen a speech—inscribed on a colourfully decorated piece of birchbark—in his native tongue. The irony was that both the speech and the artwork on the birchbark were fashioned by Mrs H. W. Becket, the wife of one of the MLC players.[60] After the match and the usual snowshoeing displays, the monarch presented each player with an autographed picture of herself.

Back in Montreal the teams were extolled as 'representatives of the young manhood of Canada' at a civic reception in the Victoria Rink (heavily decorated with lacrosse sticks and snowshoes).[61] Financially the trip broke even, with its nearly $12,000 cost; its success, however, must be measured in terms of the lacrosse-Canada-Indian symbolism that was promoted to the British. Seven years later, in 1883, a more up-scale tour was organized, specifically to use the lacrosse-Indian image to sell Canada to potential British immigrants. George Beers, the organizer once again, had written in his book:

> Lacrosse dislikes fellows who 'spree,' who make syphons of their oeso-phagi, and who cannot make better use of their leisure than to suck mint juleps through straws. . . The game dislikes all hypocrisy, unnaturalness, and assumption, and it is the very thing to knock all such out of a man.[62]

Notwithstanding this rejection of hypocrisy, both the 1883 tour and the earlier one effectively *used* natives to showcase lacrosse at a time when they were being gradually excluded from major lacrosse competitions in their own country.

Two teams of Caughnawagas and MLC players combined with six Toronto LC players for the 1883 tour. Glowing tributes to, and expansive coverage of, Ned Hanlan's triumphs in Great Britain gave firm evidence that the link between sporting prowess and Canadian nationhood had developed greatly since the 1876 tour. This was Beers' chance to exert the lacrosse muscle of Canada. Furthermore there had been only two lacrosse clubs in Britain before the 1876 tour, but in 1883 it was estimated that there were around 150.[63] In some ways this meant that the teams faced a stronger challenge than they had had in 1876. Beers made all the pre-trip organizational arrangements through a London journalist, E.T. Sachs.

The tour was frantic; 62 matches were played in 41 different cities in just over two months—a heavier schedule than that of most modern professional baseball teams. It is notable that no member of the Shamrocks was invited to go on the tour, even though the team was the most successful in Canada by 1883. Were the working-class Shamrocks not the 'proper' group to build a Canadian image? (Several references in the

The Canadian lacrosse team that toured England and Ireland in 1883; Dr Beers is in the centre. (Courtesy Don Morrow.)

Montreal press during the tour forecast an 1884 Shamrocks tour of the British Isles—perhaps an indication of ruffled feathers.) The players docked in Liverpool and the tour started in Scotland. The teams went on to London for games in its vicinity, then to the southwest coast of England, followed by games in the southeast. They then ventured into the Midlands and the manufacturing towns before touring northern cities and, finally, municipalities in Ireland. In all they travelled over 9,000 kilometres by train in Britain, mostly at night. Extracts from British press accounts that were republished in the Toronto *Globe* and the *Montreal Gazette* indicate that the dominant image was exactly the same as that of the 1876 tour; the Indians—dressed in scarlet this time—predominated. The 'Canadian Gentlemen' (were natives not Canadian gentlemen?) were dressed in bright blue with a white maple-leaf crest—the first used in association with Canadian sport—encasing the letter 'C' emblazoned on their jerseys.

The 1883 tour went well beyond the subtle advertising of its 1876 counterpart. The distinct role of both teams was to act as a collective immigration agent. With the co-operation and financial support of the federal Department of Agriculture, team members distributed 150,000 immigration fly-sheets certified by the Governor General, and a total of

120 cases, each weighing 660 kilograms, containing copies of a special supplement of the *Canadian Illustrated News* that described Canada's resources in words and pictures.[64] Beginning in the 1870s Canada had stepped up its immigration methods—in fierce competition with those used by the United States, Australia, and Africa[65]—and the 1883 tour was a state-driven propaganda compaign that used lacrosse as the delivery system.

As if the written barrage was not enough to saturate British lacrosse audiences, Beers arranged to have lectures or speeches about Canada's resources given in every city. An MP and two ordained ministers accompanied the teams for this purpose, and their messages were often reprinted in the British press.[66] The valuable work of the lacrosse players in bringing the country into greater prominence was applauded by the federal government,[67] and Beers was acclaimed for writing some 300 letters in answer to immigration queries while in Britain.[68] The dominant image portrayed to the British public during the 1883 tour was that of a young, resourceful nation that had carried on the sporting tradition of Great Britain through its national Indian game of lacrosse. The entire tour must have been an endurance contest for the players. The fact that they did not rebel, and that public reaction to the games was excellent (if judged by glowing letters written home by the players and by crowds that numbered up to 8,000 per game), is a tribute to the organizational prowess of Beers and the players' devotion to him, and to the immigration device.

By the mid-1880s lacrosse was a major, perhaps *the* major popular team sport in Canada. Undoubtedly the fame of the lacrosse tours enhanced the attraction to the sport for both players and spectators. The British blessing on lacrosse combined with the forces of commercialization, professionalism (in the true sense of the word), and organizational changes to develop the game. For example, at the 1885 NALA convention a league or series system of matches was adopted for senior lacrosse competition.[69] That is, instead of a challenge system of games a league schedule for the season was created and a play-off format was pre-established. The initiation of the league system launched lacrosse into the format of modern sport and provided an organizational framework that triggered considerable change and growth in the sport. Next to Beers' contributions to the image of lacrosse as the national game, this development was the most important change in the game's history.

In the thirty-year period preceding the First World War lacrosse activity intensified in Quebec, and especially in Ontario. Although the game was launched in the major cities of the Maritimes during the 1880s and 1890s,[70] it never gained a firm, established acceptance there. Saint John, Halifax, Pictou, Windsor, Springhill, and other centres formed clubs, played sporadically, and disbanded. It seems that in the Maritimes the British sports of cricket and rugby-football, as well as the American pastime of baseball, were of more interest than lacrosse.[71] By contrast, rivalries among cities in Ontario and Quebec were so intense, and the emphasis\ on winning so strong, that disputes over the league system plagued the NALA constantly for three years after its implementation. Toronto clubs rebelled in 1887 and formed a rival second league, the Canadian Lacrosse Association (CLA). Most Ontario clubs became af-filiated with the CLA while Quebec and eastern Ontario clubs remained loyal to the NALA. By 1889 the CLA established some eleven geograph-ical districts in order to provide manageable leagues for the various levels of play. The two associations actually had to agree to draw a boundary-line at Peterborough for recruitment of top players for the senior cham-pionship series. Fractionalization increased in 1889 when the Shamrocks, the MLC, the Toronto LC, the Cornwall LC, and the Ottawa LC broke off all affiliation and created a Senior League with 'home-and-home' matches (one home and one away game for each pair of teams).[72]

All these organizational changes in the late 1880s resulted in a dilution of lacrosse management and inconsistent administrative direction in the development of the sport. When the Senior League became an élite league in its own right, the governing bodies were severely weakened and were left to organize junior and intermediate levels of lacrosse dur-ing the 1890s. The CLA became the largest association, governing rural lacrosse strongholds within a 160-kilometre radius of Toronto (southern Ontario was a baseball Mecca).[73] Recognition of the Toronto heartland of lacrosse—although the Athletics of St Catharines were the most suc-cessful club between 1885 and 1914[74]—was demonstrated in 1901 when the *Globe* Publishing Company donated the Globe Shield for senior CLA supremacy (thereby replacing the CLA banner).[75] Presumably the *Globe* felt that lacrosse promotion was a significant campaign tool to increase newspaper sales, but the existence of a major trophy also enhanced championship prestige.

In the two decades surrounding 1900 lacrosse developed rapidly in the western provinces. Manitoba and British Columbia in particular be-came major centres of the sport. With a precedent for the structural system having been established in Ontario and Quebec, lacrosse was able to progress very quickly from intra-club matches to challenges to championship play to league structures in Winnipeg, Brandon, Portage La Prairie, Vancouver, Victoria, and New Westminster. The change in

1887 from the best 2 of 3—or 3 of 5—goal systems in the East[76] to a 2-or 2 1/2-hour time limit was easily adopted in the West. The New West-minster Salmonbellies emerged from its late 1880s triangle of competi-tions with Vancouver and Victoria and travelled east in 1890 to play the best teams in Toronto and Montreal. With a 5-to-1 win-loss record, the Salmonbellies returned to a tumultuous reception in their home town: 'The Royal City stood on its head to welcome home the conquering heroes, and they hung a gold locket around the scarred neck of each player.'[77]

By the mid-1890s the CLA and the NALA were geographic misnomers because they were regional sport governing bodies. The British Columbia Amateur Lacrosse Association (BCALA) governed the sport in that prov-ince, while most major prairie-city lacrosse clubs were under the um-brella of the Western Canadian Lacrosse Association (WCLA). In fact by 1900 the WCLA boasted club memberships from Fort William and Port Arthur (now Thunder Bay), through Minneapolis and St Paul, to cities in southern Alberta. All sport governing bodies relied on and adopted the rules and constitution of the established NALA. Although leadership in lacrosse generally flowed from east to west, major inno-vations, such as the use of goal nets in the BCALA in 1897, did affect the game across the country.[78] Lacrosse became a truly national cham-pionship sport in 1901 when the Governor General, the Earl of Minto, donated a cup for challenge competition among the champions of the senior lacrosse leagues in Canada.[79] As the emblem of national suprem-acy the Minto Cup engendered intense competition over the next thir-teen years. Significantly, British Columbia teams held the Minto Cup without a loss between 1908 and 1914. In fact they dominated early-twentieth-century lacrosse at the élite level, stimulated by the Salmon-bellies' new style of lacrosse tactics—they turned from methodical po-sitional play using long passes towards free-flowing, shorter passes, hitting the open man and a run-run-run offence.[80]

Rough play increased during the nineties and the early years of the twentieth century. Violent play was repeatedly blamed on incompetent referees, whose powers were extended beyond ejecting players from contests to imposing heavy fines. But the referees were merely scape-goats for the competitive emphasis in lacrosse, especially élite lacrosse, that persisted despite the pretense of amateurism. Indian 'ringers' or skilled Indian players who spoke perfect English and had few strong native facial features were imported for teams in the east and west, and the recruitment of outstanding white players for financial inducements was prevalent in amateur circles. Hypocritical and inconsistent enforcement of amateur regulations was at the root of the strife that existed among the NALA, the CLA, and the Senior League during the 1890s.[81]

Although commercialism was basic to élite lacrosse, it was discountenanced at least publicly—as if an admission that money was a critical factor in the health of the sport would somehow destroy it. Suspensions of entire lacrosse teams from competitions were frequent, as when a trial in 1898 disclosed that each member of the Capital Lacrosse Club of Ottawa had accepted a $100 bonus.[82] The whole conflict between amateurism and professionalism/commercialism reached a chaotic crescendo in 1904. In an effort to deal openly with the situation, the founding lacrosse club of Canada, the MLC, petitioned its governing body to allow known professionals to play with and/or against amateurs.[83] Although this was a significant and viable request and offered a workable solution, it was directly antithetical to strict amateur regulations. Within two years this initiative resulted in a protracted athletic war over the concession to professionals implemented by the MLC. Its resolution—a return to strict amateur regulations—was a giant step backward. Meanwhile gambling and pool-selling on lacrosse matches continued unabated. In spite of the 1910 donation of the Mann Cup, by railway magnate Sir Donald Mann, to stimulate amateur lacrosse competition at the élite levels, and despite the formation in 1912 of a truly national governing body, the Canadian Amateur Lacrosse Association, commercialism remained fundamental to élite lacrosse. In fact two of the professional associations, the National Lacrosse Union and the Dominion Lacrosse Association, had become joint stock companies, with capital stock of $14,000 and $20,000 respectively.[84]

By 1914 the glorious years of the heyday of lacrosse were drawing to a close. The tug-of-war between amateur ideology and commercial forces interfered with the consistent promotion and development of the sport. The raiding of players was widespread at the professional level; amateur leagues were weakened because the best players were siphoned off from them. Salary wars were common among élite teams, and clauses were implemented in player-owner agreements to bind players to specific teams. Lacrosse moguls placed their emphasis on élite lacrosse and did not take sufficient measures to stimulate the sport in school or church leagues.[85] Lacking strong grass-roots player development, and with amateur-professional-commercial fragmentation at the top levels, lacrosse fell into decline. On the commercial side the sport faced the geographical dilemma that still plagues Canadian professional sports: a huge country with a small population. Spectators were the only source of revenue, and there just weren't enough of them. Although the game could not sustain itself commercially, amateur lacrosse was mired in commercial trends. Newspapers had great difficulty keeping track of the various leagues, divisions, clubs, and levels and gradually reduced their coverage of the sport. Meanwhile media and public attention turned to the emerging and increasingly popular team sports of baseball, football, and ice hockey.[86]

The halcyon days of lacrosse were the years between 1867 and 1885 when George Beers and the great tours brought the game into prominence as a national symbol of Canada. That symbol, however, was tarnished, since lacrosse originated with Canada's natives, who were shamefully used in the transformation of the sport from its aboriginal to its modern form. Although lacrosse re-emerged during the Depression as box lacrosse (boxla) and has been promoted in that form at various times over the past fifty years, interest in this sport has been confined to pockets of southern Ontario.

4

Sport and Physical Education
in Schools and Universities

Sport has only recently become a significant part of the curriculum in Canadian schools and universities. Whereas educational institutions in the United States have long regarded sports and games in physical-education classes as legitimate components of the curriculum, schools in Canada have relegated sport instruction to extra-curricular status. In fact physical education as a branch of instruction in Canadian schools, considered historically, is rooted in activities such as military drill, rifle shooting, calisthenics, and gymnastics. This chapter will examine the origins of this two-pronged development of physical education and sport. Because the British North America Act placed education under provincial jurisdiction, and because Ontario's system of education was one of the first to become organized, the focus here will be mainly on Ontario schools and universities.

Norman O. Brown, in his classic psychoanalytic study of history, *Life Against Death*, stated that western civilization has come through '2000 years of higher education based on the notion that [the human being] is essentially a soul for mysterious accidental reasons imprisoned in a body.'[1] Since education in Canada conformed to a religion that placed primary emphasis on the mind and the spirit, it was little concerned with development of the body, or indeed with the integration of body and spirit. Moreover, as educational systems developed first at the apex of the institutional pyramid—in universities and private colleges—public education in Ontario before the mid-nineteenth century was abysmal by any standard. The first educational act, passed in 1807, concerned itself solely with secondary or 'grammar' schools. Nine years later elementary or 'common' schools were officially recognized, although responsibility for them was entrusted to individual communities that could erect a schoolhouse and pay for the teacher.[2]

Before 1850 pioneer settlement conditions, prevailing social mores that favoured the élite (sons of the élite especially), and public apathy were major deterrents to a strong educational system in Ontario. Teaching was not regarded as a noble profession; the typical teacher was male and British-born, often an ex-soldier.[3] Rural schools were crude and curriculum quality varied widely. Few teachers or administrators in a rural-agrarian society were concerned with the nature of the physical activity of their pupils (unless they were inconvenienced by it). 'There were no playgrounds nor Closets—the Highway was occupied for the Former and the adjoining woods for the latter.'[4] Play was equated with idleness and was therefore not viewed by educators as an agent of the child's physical or moral development:

> Schools were the right arm of the churches in the moral and ethical training of the young. Children were regarded as basically evil and depraved creatures whose salvation depended on their being disciplined severely.[5]

If a 'common' school had any facility for play or games it was purely the result of the whim of a particular teacher or community. In 1826, opposite a schoolhouse in Bertie Township, '. . . fastened to the boughs of lofty beech and maple trees are placed two swings, made of the bark of the elm and basswood . . . one for the boys and one for the girls.'[6] Similarly grammar schools, which emphasized the classics, seldom offered pupils physical education. An exception was Upper Canada's earliest school, the 'Old Blue School' in York (Toronto). It was opened in 1807 as the Home District Grammar School, and eighteen years later acquired the Reverend Dr Thomas Philips as headmaster:

> The ground surrounding the School, which in primitive times was slightly undulating, had been cleared of the stumps, and a space of a few hundred square feet was selected for the good old English sport of Cricket, which was cultivated from 1825 under the enthusiastic direction of Mr. George Anthony Barber who accompanied Dr. Phillips to York as his principal Assistant in the School.[7]

Barber is the acknowledged 'father' of cricket in Ontario, owing to his involvement with Upper Canada College in later years.[8] The provision he made for cricket at the Home District School was decidedly unusual. In most schools marbles and peg-tops were the common amusements for pupils, and fighting was probably the only kind of vigorous physical activity indulged in. Physical education, either as systematized physical training or as sports and games, was non-existent. The only official nod to the importance of physical fitness before 1840 appeared in the *Report on Education* prepared by Doctor Charles Duncombe and submitted to the House of Assembly in 1836:

An education should be such as to give energy and enterprise to the mind, and activity to the whole man. This depends, in part, upon the physical constitution. Hence the necessity of preserving a sound state of bodily health. To secure this, temperance and proper exercise are requisite. But what exercise is best, as part of a student's education, is still unsettled. Without stopping to discuss that point at large here, in my opinion, the best kind of gymnastics are the exercises of the field and of the shop, in some kind of useful labour.

That Duncombe should associate 'gymnastics' with manual labour, the better to enhance the productivity of society, was quite in keeping with the prevailing view that education was properly an instrument of social policy.[9]

Into this educational wasteland came Dr Egerton Ryerson, who is generally recognized as the founder of the provincial and national systems of education. A Methodist itinerant or 'saddle-bag' preacher until he was 41 years old, he was appointed Ontario's first superintendent of education in 1844.[10] He remained throughout his career and his life a living embodiment of the Protestant work ethic. While a practising minister, he had been extremely self-disciplined and ascetic—an unlikely candidate to champion the cause of physical education, as he did many years later. Ryerson's first known exposure to a sporting event was when he attended a horserace—a sport that was least likely to appeal to him because of the atmosphere it created. All social classes were lured to the races by prospects of gambling. Tents were set up on the hills surrounding the open race-track, where roulette wheels and other betting contrivances and quantities of drink were the main attractions. While the élite wagered money, the lower classes made their bets in goods such as salt pork, cedar shingles, pork sausage, tanned leather, blacksmiths' bellows, and so forth. Pickpockets and swindling were rampant, a general rowdyism took over, and smaller communities suffered the loss of workers for two or three days. Because of the 'demoralizing activities surrounding the events' Halifax abolished horseracing by municipal enactment for over a decade before mid-century.[11] Little wonder, then, that in his diary entry for 4 May 1824 Ryerson recorded his aversion:

I watched today a large concourse of people assembled to witness horseracing. I stood at a distance that I might observe an illustration of human nature. Curiosity and excitement were depicted in every countenance. What is to become of this thoughtless multitude? Is there no mercy for them. Surely there is. Why will they not be saved? Because they will not come to Him.[12]

Thirty-five years later, however, Ryerson would boast of his new-found pleasure in rowing a skiff to Toronto Island and back, in walking long distances, in riding, hunting, and swimming.[13] By the 1860s he was converted to seeing the value of physical exercise for its own sake:

> I feel better than at any time during my tour. All who have known me and seen me in former years say how well and healthy I look. I owe this in a great degree to my boating and riding.[14]

In fairness, sport was more ingrained in the social landscape by the 1860s, and at the 1824 horserace Ryerson may have been repelled not by the sport itself but by the gambling, drinking, and rowdyism that accompanied it.

Ryerson was impressed by the work of the great English educator Dr Thomas Arnold, headmaster of Rugby (1828–42).[15] In the light of this interest he probably read *Tom Brown's Schooldays* (1857), a novel about Rugby by one of Arnold's pupils, Thomas Hughes, who advocated what later became known as 'muscular Christianity', a combination of Christian principles and physical courage, self-reliance, love of sport, and school loyalty. This book had a great impact on English public schools and helped to create the 'cult of athleticism'—an over-emphasis on sports and games in schools and universities throughout the British Empire.[16] Ryerson's efforts to reform the school system in Ontario, however, focused on mass rather than élite education, and he garnered his information and ideals for education in general, and physical education in particular, from a European tour to study systems of instruction on the Continent. His *Report on a System of Public Elementary Instruction for Upper Canada*, published in 1846, was based on observations he had made in Holland, Belgium, Germany, Switzerland, and Britain in 1844–5, and in the United States, where various systems of physical education already existed.[17] In it he included physical training among the many subjects he recommended to supplement the study of the three R's.

> On the development of the physical powers I need but say a few words. A system of instruction making no provision for those exercises which contribute to health and vigour of body, and to agreeableness of manners, must necessarily be imperfect. The active pursuits of most of those pupils who attend the public Schools, require the exercise necessary to bodily health; but the gymnastics, regularly taught as a recreation, and with a view to the future pursuits of the pupil, and to which so much importance is attached in the best British Schools and in the Schools of Germany and France, are advantageous in various respects,-promote not only physical health and vigour, but social cheerfulness, active, easy and graceful movements. They strengthen and give the pupil a perfect command over all the members of his body. Like the art of writing, they proceed from the

simplest movement, to the most complex and difficult exercises—imparting a bodily activity and skill scarcely credible to those who have not witnessed them.

To the culture and command of all the faculties of the mind, a corresponding exercise and control of all the members of the body is next in importance. It was young men thus trained that composed the vanguard of Blutcher's army; and much of the activity, enthusiasm and energy, which distinguished them, was attributed to their gymnastic training at school. A training which gives superiority in one department of active life, must be beneficial in another . . . .

The youth of Canada are designed for active, and most of them for laborious occupations; exercises which strengthen not one class of muscles, or the muscles of certain members only, but which develop the whole physical system, cannot fail to be beneficial.

The application of these remarks to Common Day Schools must be very limited. They are designed to apply chiefly to boarding and training, to Industrial and Grammar Schools—to those Schools to the Masters of which the prolonged and thorough educational instruction of youth is entrusted.[17]

He advocated physical training for its health benefits, although under prevailing conditions—lack of facilities and a general lack of interest— few teachers or pupils at the time were actually affected by his plea.

Recognizing that the key ingredient in quality education was teacher-training and the establishment of a profession, Ryerson brought to fruition in 1853 the construction of the first teacher-training institution in the province: the Toronto Normal and Model School. Significantly the original buildings included two 'Play Sheds', similar in appearance to two roofed railway platforms set back-to-back, and two acres of 'Grounds for Gymnastic Exercises of Students and Pupils'.[18] Ryerson also appointed Mr Henry Goodwin as 'gymnastic master'of the Normal and Model School, at a salary of £50 per annum.[19] Goodwin was an Irish-born soldier who had fought at the Battle of Waterloo. When he received his discharge in 1818 he enlisted in the King's Light Infantry and was made head drill-instructor. Recognized and honoured in five European countries for his proficiency in gymnastics and fencing, he immigrated to Canada at the age of 55 and opened a school to teach calisthenics and riding. Two years later Lord Elgin recommended Goodwin to Ryerson. Canada's first instructor of physical education was 57 when he was hired; surprisingly, at age 77 Goodwin was still the gymnastic master at the Normal School, and at Upper Canada College, Bishop Strachan's Ladies School, and Mrs Nixon's Ladies School as well. He also tutored privately! (Goodwin's widespread employment may have resulted from necessity—he fathered sixteen children by two wives.)[20] Goodwin was respected for his skills, if judged by the number of Toronto families who hired him for private instruction.

Ryerson made provision for teachers to receive instruction in physical training—likely in military drill, light apparatus gymnastics (vaulting benches, parallel bars), calisthenics, and fencing. Ryerson's reports in the 1850s and 1860s included references to the Normal School timetable, which incorporated drill for men and calisthenics for women for two hours per week.[21] (One wonders what adjustments in instruction, if any, Goodwin made for female teachers-in-training.) But Goodwin's impact on physical education in Ontario seems to have been slight; as late as 1877 only seventeen per cent of the province's teachers had any professional teacher-training whatsoever.[22]

The only two authorized texts for physical training within Ryerson's Department of Education were Charles Spencer's *Field Exercises and Evolutions of Infantry Drill* and *Modern Gymnast*.[23] Both were published in Britain and both were geared to adult readership and use—with no provisions for the instruction of children. The training of teachers in military drill suggests that physical training in the schools during Ryerson's tenure (1844 to 1876) was mainly valued as a means of instilling discipline in pupils.

Through his monthly *Journal of Education for Upper Canada* (first issued in 1848), an official publication, Ryerson did his utmost to have apparatus gymnastics inaugurated in Ontario schools. There is considerable doubt, however, that his *Journal*—intended as a disseminator of information to all levels, from education administrators to the teachers—was even picked up by school trustees, let alone passed on from them to teachers. Nevertheless it reflects Ryerson's early enthusiasm for physical training and a sincere desire to promote the subject in his quest for ways to improve practical education. Between January and September 1852 Ryerson published in the *Journal* a series of articles entitled 'Physical Training in Schools'.[24] Intriguing as the engravings of gymnasts performing elaborate exercises on novel pieces of apparatus may have been to readers, they provided little benefit to teacher or pupil. Nevertheless Ryerson made an important start in educating the new teaching profession about physical exercise.

A few articles during the 1850s continued to advocate apparatus gymnastics for males and light calisthenics for female students. In the latter regard, an article in 1857 strongly advocated the use of a 'backboard', literally a board strapped to the back, as a postural exercise device for girls.[25] During the 1860s the articles became decidedly militaristic in nature,[26] possibly owing to the influence and proximity of the Civil War to the south. The actual introduction of drill into schools led to consid-erable controversy, especially over its inclusion in elementary schools; as a result Ryerson devoted ten pages in 1866 to various articles that stressed the necessity and importance of military drill in the schools.[27] His efforts to vindicate drill were predictable, since he was a social conservative. By the end of his term he was casually advocating this favoured form of physical training for public schools:

> The Boys to be arranged in companies, sized from both flanks, numbered and told off in half-companies and sections. To be put through the for-mations, Right, Left and Right and Left About as a Company. To increase and diminish the Front. To form a company Square, Fours, Right, Left, Deep. Calisthenics for Girls.[28]

Military drill was convenient; instructors—often discharged military personnel—were abundant; equipment was inexpensive and minimal; it could be conducted outside; and it fostered, or exemplified, prompt obedience by 'miniature adults', who were of course males. Military drill—which Ryerson called military gymnastics and was taught throughout the 1860s in many elementary and secondary schools, es-pecially in cities and the larger towns of Ontario—reinforced the pe-dagogical emphasis on educating boys, with a resulting neglect of curriculum development for girls. The subject was optional in the ele-mentary schools and was at the discretion of the trustees. In 1876 Toronto became the first city to introduce a regular system of military training into public schools.[29] In the rest of the province the fledgling educational system and its slow rate of development prevented many of Ryerson's ideas on physical training from being realized until late in the century.

Despite Ryerson's efforts, actual physical-training programs in the schools during his tenure were minimal. Although playground devel-opment around schoolhouses increased, play and games were relegated to recess. But even then: 'When admonition, remonstrance and reproof fail in securing proper attention, the offender is required to stand on the floor during a part or the whole of the playtime.'[30] Before 1876 the only evidence of curricular physical training at the secondary-school level was at the Galt Grammar School and the Hamilton Central School.[31] As for facilities, public opinion would not permit school boards to spend taxpayers' money on 'frills' such as gymnasiums or playgrounds.

Any sports that did occur in the schools up to the 1870s were organized under the teachers' own initiative—as in the case of George Barber's promotion of cricket at the Old Blue School.[32] By the late 1860s sporadic contests in track and field, cricket,[33] lacrosse, and rugby-football took place at some secondary and private schools, but always as extra-curricular activities outside regular classroom instruction. Prior to Confederation the private schools—in keeping with the precedents and traditions of the vaunted British public schools—were at the forefront of any sporting developments in educational institutions.

Between 1868 and 1900 schools and universities 'were often the nurseries in which new games were practised and then spread into the community'.[34] In 1887, when the first Canadian cricket 'Eleven' visited England, five of the team members were Upper Canada College 'old boys'. Contemporary newspaper accounts reveal a pattern of carrying sport into society at large via former student-athletes who continued to play rugby-football and association football (soccer) in the 1870s and 1880s, and ice hockey in the 1890s. Sport dispersion occurred to a certain extent within Ontario's secondary schools, with soccer becoming the most widespread secondary-school sport before 1900.

Emerging sports, such as baseball and lacrosse, and even cricket, were not prominent among institutes of higher education—perhaps owing to their being played mainly in the summer when universities were not in session and schools were closed. By contrast track and field was nurtured in the universities and was promoted strongly by the Canadian Amateur Athletic Association as well as by the numerous Scottish Caledonian societies.[35] Thus universities and private schools were significant contributors to the emergence of organized competitive sport in the late nineteenth century. Their contribution, however, was élitist—in the sense that a university education was a privilege available to a very small minority—and it was unsystematic, because sport activities were energized in a haphazard fashion by interested people outside the formal framework of education.

Sports and games were never included in the nineteenth-century physical-education curriculum, in spite of the emergence of two general trends in educational philosophy: a new recognition of the importance of childhood and of child-centred activities, along with the recommended inclusion of practical subjects into the school curriculum, such as bookkeeping, drawing, music, health, temperance—and physical education.[36] Still, before 1908 the only exercise facility that any elementary school could boast of was the great outdoors. The use of gymnasiums began at the secondary level. In order to become a collegiate institute in 1882 any one of Ontario's 104 high schools was required to have 'suitable buildings, outbuildings, grounds and appliances for physical training'.[37] Thereafter Department of Education 'circulars' were distributed widely and frequently to induce and to police curricular change in physical training. Although more indicative of intent than actual practice, such circulars provide clues to prevailing ideals about physical training. For example, an 1885 circular recommended the following equipment for a high-school gymnasium (with the usual dismissal of the needs of girls):

Dumb Bells	Fixed Parallel Bars
Bar Bells	Trapezium
Leaping Rope	Pair of Rings
Leaping Pole	Row of Rings
Horizontal Beam	Elastic Ladder
Vaulting Bar	Ladder Plank
Vaulting Horse	Inclined Ladder
Vertical Rope	Rosary or Knotted Rope
Vertical Pole	Mast

For girls a suitable supply of Indian Clubs should be provided.[38]

Drafted directly from the British book, *The Modern Gymnast*, the list was premature: it was a long time before schools wanted, could afford to buy or in some cases accommodate such elaborate equipment.

More significant incentives to curricular physical training in secondary schools occurred in 1886 and 1887, when regulations for upgrading existing facilities and equipment were tied to increased government grants. Though drill, gymnastics, and calisthenics were made 'obligatory' subjects, the teaching of physical training continued to have a subsidiary role in the curriculum:

> Now that the Collegiate Institutes have gymnasia, and Regulation 50 is explicit as to the requirements, there will probably be an improvement; but so long as the July examinations are so vitally important to both teacher and pupil, physical education will, in many cases, be subordinated to even the least important of the examination subjects.[39]

In fact, where gymnasiums were constructed—in Guelph, Hamilton, Lindsay, and elsewhere—they were more often used as auditoriums, assembly halls, or even as extra classroom space.[40] When they *were* used for physical-education classes—it never occured to anyone to permit games to be played in them—the prevailing viewpoint was a holdover from Ryerson's era. Sports and games in public education were 'rational amusements', best left to informal organization by students themselves, and drill, gymnastics, and calisthenics were tolerated as adjuncts to more academic pursuits. Furthermore, teachers could not teach what they did not know: without lesson plans, nineteenth-century teachers could not instruct in any subject, let alone a new one. The first important and useful guide for physical-training instruction was a small book published in 1879 by the foremost educator of the period, James L. Hughes: *Manual of Drill and Calisthenics: Containing Squad Drill, Calisthenics, Free Gymnastics, Vocal Exercise, German Calisthenics, Movement Songs, The Pocket Gymnasium, and Kindergarten Games and Songs.*[41] Hughes (1846–1935) was appointed inspector of public schools in Toronto in 1874. He was 'an Orangeman, a Mason, an athlete, and unquestionably an administrative success'.[42] An ardent patriot, he focused mainly on military drill in his manual—which caused it to be harshly reviewed in an 1880 issue of the *Canadian Education Monthly*. Nevertheless the drill content was in keeping with the precedent Ryerson had set and conformed to the equipment, facilities, and teacher competence of the era. If any educator had enough sporting background and expertise to develop sports and games in the curriculum, it was Hughes. Yet his training for 'proper' education was steeped in discipline and obedience. Furthermore, his three brothers were all high-ranking military officers,[43] a fact that must have reinforced his tendency to stress military drill in the schools. Ratified by the Ontario Teachers Association, Hughes' manual advocated teaching proper form in saluting, marking time and marching, squad formations, and so forth. Though there was some public opposition to treating children in elementary schools as 'little soldiers', drill was entrenched as the proper 'system' of physical instruction in secondary schools, and even at the University of Toronto. Hughes' manual, which excluded any concept of curricular instruction in sports and games, simply consolidated its presence.

In 1886 E.B. Houghton, a retired physical-training instructor from Chatham, wrote a book that did advocate important changes in physical education. Authorized by the Minister of Education and available to teachers for 50 cents, *Physical Culture*[44] became the recommended textbook on physical training in the Toronto and Ottawa Normal schools.[45] It was useful, popular, and a harbinger of landmark transitions in the concept of physical training for students. First and foremost, it was suited to actual school conditions and teacher preparation. Drill was included (but only occupied 20 per cent of the book) to uphold prevailing practice:

> That the drill may assimilate with that in use by the volunteers and regulars, so that if at any future time the pupil should join the volunteers or Military School, he will have nothing to learn or unlearn as far as Squad Drill is concerned.[46]

The second section, 'Calisthenics', which advocated the use of straight lines and squads after the military fashion—every schoolchild from then until now has been subjected to squads, straight lines, and precision in physical-education classes—was organized from simple to complex exercises. Free exercises, the use of climbing and skipping ropes, stretching and flexibility exercises were all illustrated with sketches of the movements for teachers, and the section on 'gymnastics' described different exercise series for dumb-bells and stationary ropes—far more practical than the apparatus gymnastics advocated earlier by Ryerson and others. As Ontario education in general was male-oriented—the government grant for educating girls in high school was exactly half that for boys— the most progressive aspect of Houghton's book was that nearly half of it was devoted to physical training for girls. *Physical Culture* offered girls basic exercises containing elementary movements that resembled dance or postural positions; dumb-bell exercises, which were almost the same as those for men; and 50 pages devoted to Indian-club exercises. The origin of the name 'Indian club' is obscure, but it resembled a wooden bowling pin and weighed one to one-and-a-half pounds. (The largest mass-producer of Indian clubs was the American sporting-goods manufacturer A.G. Spalding.) Houghton was full of admiration for them as exercise tools for women:

> The illimitable number of combinations that may be effected in Artistic Indian Club swinging, the exceeding grace and beauty of the movements, the poetry and rhythm of motion, especially when accompanied by music, the operation of the mental faculties in conjunction with the physical, the splendid exercise which it gives to the body, especially the upper portion, the fact of both sides being equally employed, the great ease and freedom of carriage acquired through its practice, mark it as being pre-eminently adapted as an exercise for ladies.[47]

Indian-club movements were made in positions—circles and 'ellipses' of various combinations—and mainly involved the arms, with some trunk twisting. Still, girls were finally involved in physical training, and Houghton's text was a reservoir of practical information for teachers.

Finally, *Physical Culture* provides the most detailed description of state-of-the-art gymnasiums for high schools late in the last century:

> The three sizes best adapted for gymnasia according to the capacity required are: 1st 80 × 40, 2nd 70 × 35, 3rd 60 × 30 [feet], the last size given being the smallest that can be recommended.
> The windows in the sides of the building should be placed as high as possible; they should be about three feet high and about six feet wide; there should be as many of them on both sides as can be put in; there should be a large window or several windows in one end of the building,

the other end being a dead wall. The windows should all work on pivots. The doors should be placed at the end of the building containing the window or windows. A large door for bringing in sawdust, etc., may be placed at one side. The end of the building having the dead wall should have a plank floor for about twenty feet from the wall, so that it can be used, if necessary, for the purpose of school entertainments, gymnasium choral society, hand ball, etc., and it should be entirely free from apparatus. The trapeze and flying rings should be in the central portion of the building, the point from which they are suspended being sixteen feet from the ground; the point of suspension for the row of side rings can be any height from thirteen to sixteen feet from the ground. The building must be properly heated and ventilated; if heated with stove, it and the stationary gymnastic apparatus should be properly placed at the end of the building containing the doors and windows. The flooring, except at the dead wall end of the building, should consist of sawdust or sand, about one foot and a half deep; this should be sprinkled with water every morning, about an hour before the first class commences to exercise, and again at noon if necessary. A locker should be provided, where the movable appliances can be securely kept when not used by the class.

Concurrent with the publication of Houghton's work were major curricular changes directed at education in health ('hygiene') and at the kindergarten movement. Increasing social sensitivity to sanitary living conditions resulted in the creation in 1882 of the Provincial Board of Health and the subsequent release into the schools of a spate of books on health, physiology, temperance, and hygiene. These books, such as *Public School Physiology and Temperance* (1893), dealt with the treatment and prevention of illnesses, the dangers of alcohol abuse, and bodily functions. They went through multiple editions, evidence that they were widely distributed and used in the schools. Some of the books even contained small chapters proclaiming, briefly, the benefits of physical exercise. By 1893 hygiene was a compulsory subject on the high-school entrance examination,[48] and throughout the 1890s the Ontario Education Association's annual meetings were flooded with speeches on the topic of health practices.[49]

Both health teaching and kindergartens in the 1880s created a favourable environment for the development of physical-training courses. Kindergartens, and the international kindergarten movement, were predicated on the concept of the importance of play to childhood learning. Play had previously been considered antithetical to 'real' intellectual education; but kindergartens literally brought it inside the school walls from the playground outside. James L. Hughes was most responsible for implementing the kindergarten movement in Ontario.[50] Opposition—based on objections to expensive fads in education—was strong and rural schools in particular had difficulty in developing kindergartens, but by 1900 there were well over 100 kindergarten classes in the province. It was the kindergarten movement of the 1880s and 1890s that laid the foundation for the acceptance of child-centred physical activity (play). The concept, however, was not extended so that play could be valued and taught at all levels of the school system. Drill and calisthenics were ingrained in teachers at normal (preparatory) schools and they were highly resistant to change.

Both Hughes' and Houghton's books had a direct impact on schools through extensive use. The Annual Reports of the Minister of Education for Ontario actually listed the numbers of elementary pupils taking each subject. If the number taking physical training is expressed as a percentage of those taking the most common school subject—spelling—the early 1870s statistics revealed that only three-and-a-half per cent received any physical-training instruction. By 1880 there was a five-fold increase to 18 per cent. Ten years later, immediately following the publication of *Physical Culture*, almost half of all Ontario elementary pupils received some instruction in curricular physical education and the trend gradually increased to 70 per cent by 1905. These figures, however, reveal nothing about the nature or the quality of instruction. Since Houghton's manual was the one used in all normal schools, it seems reasonable to assume that it was not only responsible for the increase in curricular instruction but provided the basis for teaching. At the same time there can be no doubt that drill prevailed as the main thrust of physical education for boys. Compulsory physical training was on the horizon, but at the close of the century the Dominion Education Association revealed the prevailing attitude to curricular sports and games, calling them a 'sporadic exercise', which

> cannot be called training in a proper sense—to which young men in college subject themselves in the form of boating, baseball, football, lacrosse etc., with the belief that they are doing great things for themselves, yet instead often planting in their bodies the seeds of irremediable troubles . . .[51]

Such activities were considered much inferior to calisthenics, 'the exercise that in kind and quantity is directed by the most enlightened science.' Objectives for physical training in the schools were shifting from an emphasis on discipline and obedience to more health-related concerns for bodily development. Even in primary grades, growing health awareness was evident:

Children who drill
Seldom are ill

For sinking, tiptoeing, and right and left going,
And shouting and clapping and measured out tapping,
Strengthen their limbs,
Drive away whims,
Make faces shine brightly, make spines grow uprightly;
So I suppose,
Illness all goes.[52]

In secondary schools drill remained the basis of all physical-training instruction, thanks to a close working relationship between the Department of Education and the federal Department of Militia. Public opinion and the enlightenment of some educators softened the military overtones of drill in the elementary schools, but in secondary schools military drill for young men seemed to be accepted without question. Moreover, small monetary grants ($50 to $100) were available after 1890 to secondary schools that employed a drill instructor and held regular classes in drill.[53] This inducement was apparently effective, because the mid-1890s were peak years for the numbers of secondary-school students taking drill and calisthenics.[54] But a letter written by the young Arthur Meighen (Conservative Prime Minister of Canada twice, briefly, in the 1920s), who was living and attending school in St Marys in 1892, suggests that the students were opposed to drill. Meighen and his fellow students, who believed drill to be 'practically a waste of time', pleaded with the Minister of Education to write them a note excusing them from 'this obligation so unnecessary and so embarrassing'.[55] The Minister declined to give permission. Beginning in 1898 grants had entrenched cadet corps in Canadian high schools.

By 1907 the Education Department had passed five 'regulations' concerning obligatory physical training in high schools and collegiate institutes developed around Houghton's drill and calisthenics exercises. The fourth regulation, however, provided a glimmer of hope for the future of physical-education classes and sport development within the schools: 'During the months of May, June, September, October, and November, the Principal may substitute for drill etc. such sports and games as he may approve.'[56] Although it would be some years before this regulation was sanctioned and practised, it suggests that the Education Department could no longer ignore the interests of students and the popularity of sport in society at large.

Early in the twentieth century sport was being promoted outside educational institutions by various regional, provincial, and national sport governing bodies. Team sports—such as lacrosse, football, baseball, and ice hockey—were especially popular; the modern Olympic revival began in 1896 at Athens. It was well established that sport was energized, administered, and controlled by its own devotees—no level of government and no educational or entrepreneurial agency assumed any responsibility for its development. Schools or universities that wished to become involved in sport at any level did so under their own volition. Sport remained at the periphery rather than at the core of educational environments.

Even though sport in the university remained outside the curriculum, it developed much more rapidly there than at the pre-university level. This was undoubtedly because it was entirely in the hands of students— who formed teams, challenged other university teams, created team (university) spirit, and inaugurated leagues in the 1890s. Leadership in sport development was provided by McGill University, the University of Toronto, and Queen's University. Canadian football's enduring tradition as the major sport in most contemporary Canadian universities grew out of early matches among these three institutions. Moreover, a series of games in 1874 between McGill and Harvard is thought to be the source of both Canadian-style football and the American hybrid.[57] Canadian intercollegiate football was inaugurated in 1881 with the first annual McGill-Toronto game; Queen's established its football foundation in matches against the Royal Military College during the 1880s, and in the 1890s ventured into intercollegiate competitions with Toronto and McGill.[58] Ontario university teams dominated both provincial and national football competitions during the last decade of the nineteenth century.

Although there is considerable debate about where the first game of ice hockey originated, it is well established that three McGill students devised the first modern rules for the game in the late 1870s.[59] By merging and adapting the rules from field hockey, lacrosse, and rugby-football, these students were able to bring uniformity to the game and establish it firmly within the structures of late nineteenth-century Canadian sport. The dominance of the Stanley Cup by Montreal teams during the 1890s is documented in Chapter 8; Queen's University teams were frequent challengers for the prestigious trophy throughout the decade and University of Toronto teams were competitive in provincial leagues.[60]

Universities assumed the dominant role in competitive sport development, especially in football, ice hockey, and track and field. In 1906 the Canadian Intercollegiate Athletic Union was formed as an umbrella governing body for affiliated universities and colleges.[61] Whereas students had originally been responsible for the organization of university sport, the creation of the CIAU signalled a bureaucratic structure that would increasingly wrest control of university sport from informal student organizations and transfer it to university officials and administrators. Although for many years the management of university athletics was monopolized by the University of Toronto, Queen's, and McGill,[62] and the contribution of universities to general sporting development is beyond question, the issue arising from the creation of the CIAU was the function of sport within an educational framework.

There seemed to be a 'natural adherence to the English tradition of games and sports'[63] that served to keep sport in rational perspective. But after 1910 commercial trends began to affect the function of sport, or some sports, at Canadian universities, particularly the increasingly popular sport of Canadian football, which was 'the university game' of this period, as it is today. Between 1909 and 1924 universities in central Canada dominated major football competitions, including those for the Grey Cup.[64] Football players were 'shoe-horned' into post-secondary institutions; American players were recruited; athletes were subsidized;[65] professional coaches, such as Frank Shaughnessy at McGill, were hired. Spectators flocked to the university game while 'the music of swiftly turning turnstiles [could] be heard quite clearly on the autumn air.'[66] Alma Mater became enveloped in pigskin[67] until municipal and commercial interests wrenched football away from university dominance, leaving post-secondary institutions after 1925 with a rich legacy of football traditions and the prospect of playing the game at a lower level among themselves.

The third leading sport at Canadian universities prior to 1920, track and field, was popularized throughout the school system—from grade schools to tertiary levels of education—in 'field days', 'sports days', and 'annual games'. Intra-school competitions led to interscholastic competition and, in turn, to continued participation at the intercollegiate level. The spread of track and field across all levels of ability and education ought to have triggered comparable models in a variety of sports,[68] but unfortunately this did not happen. There was always a hierarchy of sporting importance, intercollegiate sport being at the apex of a weakly developed system of school sports. Even in established universities, intramural sports of every conceivable variety were implemented by the 1920s, but their budgets were only a fraction of those devoted to the 'major' intercollegiate sports of football and hockey. Universities seemed more interested in raising the level of their intercollegiate competition from 'intermediate' designation to 'senior' than in developing curricular and extra-curricular sports opportunities for all students at all ability levels.[69]

In elementary and secondary schools sports remained decidedly extra-curricular until well into the 1930s. Strong competitive leagues existed in sports such as lacrosse, baseball, football, and track and field, and the Toronto Public Schools Amateur Athletic Association was the dominant model of interscholastic organization. With the installation of wooden-floor gymnasiums in secondary schools and universities—mostly during the 1920s—competitive sport participation in basketball, volleyball, boxing, fencing, wrestling, and apparatus gymnastics was promoted.[70] But the persistent dominance of physical education by militaristic interests continued to retard the progressive development of sport within the educational framework.

Public displays of drill work and the strutting of prestige and patriotism by cadet corps were common early in this century. The principal of Prescott High School stated in 1907:

> When cadet corps boys at target practice score bull's-eyes at 200 yards with a Lee Enfield rifle that kicks like a broncho, they've got guts. When the same boys, marching past a red-tabbed Inspecting Officer from Ottawa, give him such a snappy eyes-right that he says they are the smartest corps in the country, they've got esprit de corps. When the corps took part in such celebrations [May 24th festivities] they marched from the old High School, down Main Street, past bevies of fair damsels who waved frilly handkerchiefs, to the green expanse of the Fort Field, where a big Union Jack floated proudly under the blue Canadian sky.[71]

Mass pageants of marching, ceremonial drill, and physical exercises—conducted with and without rifles—were held frequently and publicly on the grounds of Toronto's Canadian National Exhibition.[72] The time was ripe for advancing military instruction in the schools and the Department of Militia was quick to take advantage. The success of Sir Frederick Borden, the Federal Minister of Militia, in persuading Lord Strathcona to provide funds to equip a 500-man contingent for the Boer War (the Strathcona Horse) led Borden to approach Strathcona for money again in 1909. He agreed to donate half a million dollars to 'encourage physical and military training in the schools'. Prime Minister Sir Wilfrid Laurier made a stirring acceptance speech before members of the House of Commons, lauding Strathcona's generosity.[73] The following day, 25 March 1909, the Toronto *Globe*, 'Canada's national newspaper', reacted with front-page headlines and feature articles, such as the one headed:

Physical and Military Training in the Schools
Ten Thousand Dollars Yearly
Offer Stirs the House to a Burst of Patriotism

The basic concept of the scheme, later known as the Strathcona Trust, was to invest the principal sum at 4 per cent, to yield twenty thousand dollars annually for use by elementary and secondary schools across the Dominion.

Reaction was mixed. Some school boards embraced the concept, but opposition was mounted by the executive of the Trades and Labour Congress, the Peace and Arbitration Society, a committee of the Toronto Methodist Conference, and the trustees of the Ontario Education Association.[74] A member of the last group proclaimed:

> I see designing enthusiasts aiming at a huge organization which will furnish a fresh crop of emoluments and tinsel honours at the expense of the great mass of the people, creating in time a small army of inspectors, drill-masters and officials of all kinds, added to our already costly and overgrown military establishment.[75]

The vision was not unprophetic.

The Strathcona Trust was actually two-pronged: it was meant to encourage both military *and* physical training, not merely to propagate cadet corps at all educational levels; and it was intended by both Strathcona and its architect, Borden, to be only a 'stimulus or inspiration'[76] to school boards to foster the growth of curricular physical education. Unfortunately, in spite of initial opposition, by 1911 the Trust was fully in place in all provinces except Quebec, which never did enter the agreement. As might be expected, it was administered with precision and efficiency and dominated by the Department of Militia on local, provincial, and national committees. Since the funds were available on a per-capita school-aged-child by province basis, some schools obtained only a few dollars in any given year. But instructors—drill sergeants—were donated to school boards and creative plans were effected to pool resources so that drill and exercise competitions could be held among schools and school boards. Uniform syllabuses, first published in 1911, then updated in 1919 and 1933, were used to train teachers in the Strathcona system at all teachers' colleges. The First World War likely reinforced the perceived need for drill-based programs in the schools.[77]

The Strathcona Trust may have suited the educational climate in Ontario, where mere lip-service was being paid to the importance of physical education, but it represented a giant step backward for child-centred education and for the incorporation of sports and games into the curriculum. Instead of trying to educate the whole child, body and mind, the schools were set on disciplining the body and the will into military obedience. The legacy of the Trust and the Strathcona system lingers still, both in the tedium of squads and the exaggerated emphasis on discipline in many physical-education classes, and in the designation of school sports as extra-curricular activities that are less important than intellectual pursuits. There were some vocal opponents to the system— even well-respected educators such as Ethel Mary Cartwright at McGill (and later the University of Saskatchewan)—but they were easily over-come by the large machinery of the Strathcona system in the 1920s and 1930s.[78] It was not until the 1940s—when the first degree programs for training in physical education were established at the University of To-ronto, McGill, and the Universities of Western Ontario and British Co-lumbia—that sports and games received legitimate curricular attention.[79] Although interscholastic and intercollegiate competition in every con-ceivable sport was fully established for both boys and girls during the twenties and thirties,[80] it was reserved strictly for skilled athletes.

Between 1850 and 1930 physical education and sports and games de-veloped quite separately within Ontario's (and Canada's) schools and universitites. Physical education was regimented—it had a distinctly disciplinary component—and was only loosely accepted as part of the curriculum. Sports and games were *extra*-curricular activities, open to interested and élite students or gifted athletes. It was not until the 1930s that progressive steps were taken to dovetail sports and games into the curriculum of physical education and to introduce a degree in physical education at the university level.

5

Sport Between the Wars

In the 1920s, and in the Depression years of the thirties, Canadian sport responded to numerous changes, many of which are dealt with directly or indirectly in various subject treatments elsewhere in this book. But it is worthwhile to look at some of them from the perspective of the period itself when, taken together, they can be seen to have been as transforming and influential as the changes taking place today.

The historical resentment of the West and the Maritime Provinces towards central Canada in most aspects of Canadian life—which was strengthened in the West during the Depression by the collapse of world wheat prices and the resulting unemployment—was also evident on the sports scene and provides one of the dominant themes of the period. Most of the dissatisfactions of the West centred on the Amateur Athletic Union of Canada, which was controlled by eastern officials. Alberta had advocated for some years (especially since the First World War) that amateurs be permitted to play with, and against, professionals in certain sports. As there were far fewer athletes in the West than in Ontario and Quebec, in order for Alberta, say, to have enough participants for competitive leagues, a more liberal ruling concerning eligibility was needed. The eastern-dominated AAU, however, blocked most western attempts at change and imposed even more demanding criteria of eligibility.[1]

In 1931 the British Columbia branch of the AAU considered leaving the Union because the delegates at the annual meeting in Winnipeg rescinded a promise that the Olympic trials would be held in Vancouver, and then awarded the trials to Hamilton. As trials were usually held in eastern Canada, western athletes felt they were not given an equal opportunity for international teams, and few westerners could afford to travel to the East without sponsorship.[2] For example, in 1925 a Canadian women's track-and-field team was sent to compete in the British women's championships, but the West was unable to send representatives to Hamilton for the trials because there was not enough time to select candidates and raise funds to cover expenses.[3] Even if a western athlete received funding for travel, the trip east undoubtedly affected his or her performance. Percy Williams, the Canadian gold medalist in the 100-metre and 200-metre sprints at the 1928 Olympics, indicated that western athletes were at a distinct disadvantage because they had to travel from two to four days by train to eastern Ontario or Quebec to compete in national championships for Olympic trials. More than once, Williams had to endure the long train ride from Vancouver, where he lived, to Ontario and compete almost immediately after arriving.[4]

East-West rivalry reached its peak in Canadian football. In 1921 the Edmonton Eskimos were the first team to represent the West in the Grey Cup, but it was not until 1935 that a western team, the Winnipeg Blue Bombers, fortified with several American imports, finally won the Grey Cup.[5] In the interim western teams often went down to humiliating defeats, such as Regina's 54–0 loss to Queens's in 1923. Needless to say, the victory of 1935 was cause for much rejoicing, not only in Winnipeg but throughout western Canada.

Then the Canadian Rugby Union (CRU), dominated by easterners, went into action. Meeting in Toronto on 29 February 1936, it moved to prevent further importations, denied the petition of western representatives for a western final, and drafted proposed rule changes for a considerably more conservative structure. The eastern representatives objected strenuously to the motion of the westerners that the Dominion final be played in the West in alternate years. In the end, eastern delegates partially agreed to some western demands and passed a ruling that the location of the final game should be decided each year by the executive of the CRU. The westerners, however, knew full well that eastern representatives held the balance of power and hence could control any decision made by the CRU.[6]

It had always been particularly galling to westerners that the eastern unions had more votes in the councils of the CRU than the western unions. Not until 1937 was this inequity of representation removed by affiliating the Western Interprovincial Union and the British Columbia Union directly with the national organization. Previously both had belonged to the CRU only indirectly, through their membership in the Western Canada Union.[7]

Nevertheless conflict continued between West and East over differences in rules. Joe Ryan, the Winnipeg general manager, persuaded the CRU to make the rules of eastern and western unions uniform within two years. Throughout the Depression, the East-West rivalry seemed to act as a vehicle for westerners to express their resentment towards the East for all the social ills that assailed them.

In the Maritime Provinces a similar resentment existed towards Ottawa for a tariff structure that seemed to be building up central Canada at their expense and for a general disregard of local problems. In 1925 the Canadian track-and-field championships, held on the Wanderers' grounds in Halifax, were a dismal failure because the AAU had not encouraged its athletes from central Canada to attend.[8] And at the 1928 Olympics in Amsterdam, Silas McLellan, the only Nova Scotian on the national track-and-field team, complained that he received little attention from Canadian officials—that the 'Upper Canadians' had been given all the attention. During the ocean voyage he was forced to train mainly by himself.[9]

In hockey there was little connection between the Maritimes and the rest of the country[10] until 1927, when the Maritime Amateur Hockey Association affiliated with the Canadian Amateur Hockey Association.[11] In 1935 the Halifax Wolverines defeated the Port Arthur Bearcats to win the Allan Cup and the right to represent Canada at the 1936 Winter Olympics in Berlin.[12] However, because of financial difficulties the Wolverines were unable to put a team on the ice for the 1935–6 season.[13] The CAHA then invited the Port Arthur Bearcats to represent Canada[14] and decided to bolster the team with four players from the Wolverines.[15] Maritime hockey fans became irate when the four Halifax players were dropped from the Bearcats, allegedly for demanding money to keep their families while they were away.[16] The four Wolverines maintained that they did not ask for assistance but rather that E.A. Gilroy, president of the CAHA, had approached them to find out if their families were being assisted. When they replied that they had no financial help, Gilroy said he would see what could be done for them. The next thing they knew the Olympic Committee announced that they were being dropped from the team for demanding 'broken time' payments (paying athletes for wages lost while absent from work), a violation of Olympic rules.[17] Whatever the truth was, Maritimers lay most of the blame on the CAHA, which they saw as notoriously dominated by central Canada.

It is perhaps not surprising that Ontario and Quebec assumed a condescending attitude towards other parts of Canada. Most of the star athletes came from there, where approximately three-fifths of Canada's population resided in the twenties and thirties. Ontario and Quebec had a distinct advantage simply because they produced more athletes from whom to choose—and attracted top athletes from other parts of the country. Central-Canadian athletes were frequently exposed to top-calibre competition, both within the two provinces and with the USA. More and better facilities were available to them and the climate was conducive to a long playing season in outdoor summer sports. Also, with the abundance of industry in the urban areas of central Canada, there was an extensive commercial sponsorship of sport. Finally, since most championships were held in central Canada, athletes from outside this area were at an immediate disadvantage because of the distance to travel to such centres as Toronto and Montreal, Hamilton and Ottawa. These inequities were not really resolved until after the Second World War.

However, not all was resentment and gloom in the Maritimes. The *Bluenose* exemplified the Canadian maritime sporting spirit superbly and aroused great pride. This famous schooner was launched on 26 March 1921 from the Smith and Rhuland shipyard at Lunenburg, Nova Scotia. Forty-four metres long, she was both a 'worker'—able to earn her way on the fishing grounds of Newfoundland's Grand Banks, or to haul freight—and a racing vessel. She was created specifically to be a strong contender for international races, which were becoming increasingly popular, and Angus Walters of Lunenburg was chosen to skipper her. In 1920 the promotion of racing in Halifax resulted in the Nova Scotia Fishing Fleet Race in the North Atlantic and the donation of the International Fishermen's Trophy, which the *Bluenose* won in 1921, 1922, and 1923. The races she was in were the biggest events in the Maritimes during this period and her repeated success in international races—involving other Canadian, American, and British schooners—directly stimulated the economy of host cities, particularly Halifax. The *Bluenose* also brought increased recognition to the fishing industry, and of the Maritimes' way of life generally. She hardly ever wavered in her dominance as the racing champion of sailing vessels. Civic pride and celebrations in Lunenberg and Halifax were tremendous whenever she triumphed in one of her many victories. With this past, it is ironic and tragic that Nova Scotia could not continue to finance the vessel during the war: the *Bluenose* was sold in 1942 to a West Indian company. In 1946 she struck a reef off the coast of Haiti and sank. Her sculptured image appears on the Canadian dime, and also on a beautiful stamp. In 1963 an exact replica, the *Bluenose II*, was constructed by the Smith and Rhuland shipyard.[18]

While the *Bluenose* was capturing the imagination of Maritimers and other Canadians alike, the Dominion's urban population was rapidly increasing. Between the wars this expansion led to the development of professional sport as 'big business', often to the detriment of amateur sport. As Henry Roxborough wrote in 1928, 'a medium once intended to develop physique and create social diversions has become a big business paying real salaries; organized play, once supposedly a means of recreation, is now a financial dividend-paying investment.'[19] Roxbor-

The start of the five-mile women's marathon swim, Canadian National Exhibition, Toronto, 1935. (Courtesy Don Morrow.)

ough also pointed out that during the winter of 1926–7 the National Hockey League, the major professional circuit, attracted about one-and-a-quarter-million fans. When professional Scottish soccer stars toured Canada in 1927 they were cheered by 83,000 spectators, and one professional boxing show attracted '15,000 admirers of the knights of the padded mitts'.

Swimming too was prospering commercially:

> Swimming, possibly our cleanest sport, was formerly as amateur in principle and practice as dominoes, croquet, ping-pong or marbles. But the Canadian National Exhibition Marathon, with a bait of fifty thousand dollars, so aroused the latent financial instincts of many lads and lasses that scores of former amateur, marine athletes are now out of the swim wherever simon-pure currents flow. And with so many swimmers not eligible for amateur competition it is reasonable to assume that many pro races will be arranged for their benefit during the summer of this year.[20]

The fact that professional sport was considered big business attracted to its management well-informed, respected, and experienced executives who recognized that it was necessary 'to shout your merits from the headlines'.[21] Promoters of professional sport did this very effectively.

In addition to the vast increase of publicly declared professional athletes, there was also a rapid rise in the number of pseudo-amateurs, or 'shamateurs' as sportswriters called them. Although Canadian football was lauded as an amateur sport, it was obvious to all that many of the American imports and top Canadian players were not playing merely for love of the game. In 1937 Lewis Brown, sports journalist for the *National Home Monthly*, stated that football in Canada was fast approaching the point where it would have to come out in the open and declare itself professional.[22] He went on to cite several examples of 'shamateurism': two players allegedly studying French at an Ottawa institution who failed to attend lectures; a professional baseball player who played football under an assumed name; and a group of players who refused to obey training rules at Montreal and returned to the States, 'gurgling about non-payment of salaries'.[23] Numerous other examples were given by sportswriters concerning athletes who played for industrial teams but showed up at work only to pick up their pay-cheques,[24] or junior teams that secretly received financial support from professional hockey teams.[25] In one embarrassing incident a Quebec hockey team, the Valleyfield Braves, went on strike during the 1939 Allan Cup playoffs because they wanted a guarantee that the weekly salaries they had been receiving throughout the regular season would continue as long as the team remained in the playoffs.[26] Lou Marsh summed up the situation in his own way: '. . . real amateurs among the star hockey, rugby, lacrosse, and baseball players are as scarce in Canada as skate sharpeners are in Central Africa.'[27]

This movement towards professional sport did not go unanswered. At the fourteenth annual meeting of the Amateur Athletic Union of Canada in Edmonton in 1928, the Union's new president, Dr A.S. Lamb, gave a portentous warning:

> The insidious tendencies of the present day toward commercialism and professionalism of most forms of sport are tendencies which must be combatted by all forces at our disposal . . . . In the past few years, we have witnessed a relaxation of several important principles and I have grave fears as to the outcome, should this tendency continue.[28]

The AAU imposed stringent residency and eligibility rules and enforced the amateur code strictly. But its power dwindled in the second half of the thirties. Because professionalism existed in eastern-Canadian football, in 1935 the Ottawa Branch of the AAU suspended every man who played in the Interprovincial Football Union, or who played exhibition games against a Big Four team (see page 160) that season. The Canadian Rugby Union ignored the ultimatum and proceeded with the playdowns as scheduled.[29] Then in 1937 the Canadian Amateur Hockey Association cancelled its articles of alliance with the AAU because it had adopted a policy of 'broken-time' payments.[30] By the end of the thirties professional and 'shamateur' sport were rampant in Canada. Ralph Allen commented that a cynic could tell the story in three lines:

> 1930—'What is an Amateur?'
> 1935—'Why is an Amateur?'
> 1940—'Where is an Amateur?'[31]

In no other sport was the relationship between the growth of professional sport at the big-business level and urbanization more clearly seen than in Canada's national winter sport, hockey. Professional hockey was initiated on two fronts in Canada—on the Pacific Coast and in central Canada (Ontario and Quebec), regions that boasted Canada's three largest cities. In 1912 on the west coast Frank and Lester Patrick started the Pacific Coast Hockey League with three Canadian entries: Vancouver, Victoria, and New Westminster. Of the three, Vancouver proved to be the only city large enough to support a professional team. New Westminster, a city of about 14,000, was forced to drop out in 1914,[32] while Victoria, with a population of 38,727 in 1921, managed to continue until the League was abandoned in 1924.[33] If it were not for the fact that the Patricks owned the League and operated it as a syndicate, with all teams sharing the revenues, professional hockey would have met a quicker end on the Pacific Coast. Vancouver, with a population of 246,593 in 1921, drew large crowds in the range of 8,000 to 10,000 for League games, whereas Victoria's crowds seldom exceeded around 2,000 to 3,000.[34]

In the East, professional hockey flourished after the mid-twenties. In the autumn of 1917 the National Hockey League was organized out of the National Hockey Association and by 1924 the NHL was the top league in the country, being made up of the Hamilton Tigers, the Ottawa Senators, the Toronto St Pats, the Montreal Canadiens and Wanderers, and the Boston Bruins. The best in the game flocked to the NHL and, in the competition to sign up outstanding amateurs, salaries escalated. Fred Edwards reported in 1928 that the average wage in the NHL was $5,000 a year.[35] The great Howie Morenz, however, who signed a three-year contract with the Canadiens in 1923, one season before the rush, had to put in two winters as the most brilliant youngster in the game while drawing about a third of the pay other players were getting.[36]

By 1927 ten clubs were operating in the NHL: two in New York, two in Montreal, and one each in Ottawa, Toronto, Detroit, Boston, Pittsburg, and Chicago.[37] Rising attendance figures attested to the growth of professional hockey, and the NHL reported a total increase of 22 per cent in the 1928–9 season over the previous year.[38]

Meanwhile minor leagues were organized in the wake of the NHL, with many of the teams being farms for the majors.[39] When they were formed, 'shamateur' players were reluctant to sign with a professional organization because they knew that if they failed to make the team they would still be branded as professionals and hence be unable to return to the amateur ranks, where they were already getting paid 'under the table'. The creation of minor-league teams in smaller cities provided these players with a satisfactory alternative. Near the end of the 1920s Windsor, Niagara Falls, Hamilton, London, Stratford, Kitchener, Toronto, Quebec, Winnipeg, Edmonton, Calgary, Saskatoon, Moose Jaw, and Regina all had teams in the minor leagues, which had a working agreement with the NHL that they would get players 'not yet seasoned enough for the big show'.[40] Out of the twenty largest cities in Canada in 1927, thirteen had professional hockey teams connected with the NHL, while Vancouver and Victoria were operating in a professional league separate from the NHL. Thus fifteen out of the twenty largest cities in Canada supported professional hockey teams.

It was not long before several of these centres discovered that they were not large enough to support professional hockey as a 'big business'. Top-heavy payrolls, travelling expenses, and the cost of facilities, accompanied by the devastating effects of the Depression, caused many minor clubs to fold. In 1933 the Regina Capitals were moved to Vancouver because of the poor support received in the Saskatchewan capital.[41] By 1938 only Vancouver remained on the minor professional hockey scene in the West. In the East the cities unable to handle minor professional hockey were Moncton, Syndey, Halifax, Quebec, Galt, Waterloo, Kitchener, Brantford, London, and Windsor.[42]

Even some of the NHL teams found it difficult to keep up with the rapidly increasing costs of putting on a good show. Ottawa, the smallest city in the NHL, began to be hit in this way in 1927. In 1931, after suffering a $50,000 loss the previous season, the Ottawa Senators, along with the Philadelphia Quakers, had their franchise suspended for one year—their players were distributed among the remaining eight teams of the League.[43] Finally, after the 1934 season, Ottawa, 'the home of the Silver Seven, birthplace of scores of stars, winner of more Stanley Cup titles than any other', was forced to pass from the professional hockey scene 'in a wave of red ink'.[44] The Montreal Maroons, also 'submerged in red ink', fell by the wayside after the 1937–8 season.[45] A pattern had emerged: only teams in the large urban centres made a profit. Professional hockey had become a big-city game. In Canada this meant Montreal and Toronto.

An examination of sport during the 1930s reveals that the Depression played both positive and negative roles in its development. In 1933 Ted Reeve commented: 'Sport was the last business to really suffer from the world-wide slump.'[46] He said that as long as people had a few extra quarters, they seemed willing to spend them on a game that might help them forget their troubles for a pleasant hour or so. Indeed, until the end of the 1932 season, professional hockey flourished in the NHL. The Rangers, Maple Leafs, Bruins, Maroons, and Canadiens played before packed houses, and star performers were paid from $8,000 to $10,000 for a season.[47] In 1933 the teams were able to emerge from the worst year of the Depression with a profit. But by 1939, when the only two Canadian teams in the NHL were the Toronto Maple Leafs and the Montreal Canadiens, it was evident that the Depression had shifted the top level of Canada's national winter sport across the border.[48]

Minor-league professional baseball suffered a similar fate. By 1932 both Montreal and Toronto of the International League were experiencing financial problems. The Montreal Royals, which had been revived in 1928, struggled until 1932, when a local group bought the franchise (see page 132). Although the Leafs managed to avoid losing their franchise, they continued to experience financial difficulties and in 1937 had to borrow $35,000 to keep functioning.[49] Part of the Leafs' problem centred on their reluctance to reduce admission prices. In 1933 a disturbed baseball fan wrote to the Toronto *Globe*:

> Baseball fans—and Toronto is full of them—are forced to take themselves to the various city parks, where they see mighty good baseball for five, ten, twenty-five cents, as they can afford, and if, instead of holding us up at fifty cents and a dollar twenty-five admission, they would make a general admission of twenty-five cents and fifty cents they would find the attendance running up 15,000 to 20,000 every game. And is not 15,000 at fifty cents more profitable than 400, 700, and such numbers at eighty cents and a dollar twenty-five?[50]

Football was also touched by the Depression. Bert Gibb would not attend Hamilton Tiger practices until that club bought him a new bicycle tire, while another man would not play until the Hamilton club filled his cellar with coal.[51] Sarnia, however, which had a football team sponsored by an oil company, suddenly found that it could hire top talent.

A Saturday baseball game in High Park, Toronto, 1922. (Courtesy the Metropolitan Toronto Library, T 13355.)

Unemployed American football players jumped at the chance to play for a Canadian team provided they were rewarded for their efforts. In 1935 Joe Ryan, the Winnipeg general manager, acquired the services of nine outstanding American football players for $7,500: Fritz Hanson, Bob Fritz, Bud Marquardt, Joe Perpich, Bert Oja, Herb Peschel, Nick Pagones, Russ Rebholz, and Greg Kabat.[52] With the increase of American imports made possible by their low price-tags during the Depression, Canadian football rapidly became professional, even though it continued to function under the guise of amateurism.

The Depression certainly did not dull Canadians' enthusiasm for sport. On 15 August 1938 the Halifax *Chronicle Herald* reported the desperate plight of close to 5,000 residents of Stellarton, Nova Scotia, who were pleading for food from nearby towns. There were over 300 unemployed and 1,200 miners who received pay envelopes for only one shift a week.[53] But in spite of this deplorable situation, on 5 September Stellarton's softball team played before 4,000 spectators, the largest crowd of the season.[54]

When the Winnipeg football team brought the Grey Cup to the West in 1935 for the first time, the citizens of that city went 'wild over the win':

Depression, unemployment, its railway problem, the wheat problem, all the host of troubles sent to Winnipeggers were just so much nonsense to

the citizens Saturday night as they set about the serious business of cel-
ebrating the glorious victory of their championship rugby team.

The game was over not a second when the first tidal wave of exulting
enthusiasm engulfed the city. On it rolled, touching, it seemed, everyone
from panhandler to professor, from society dowager to scrubwoman.[55]

Earlier in 1935, in Halifax, tremendous interest was aroused in the Allan
Cup series staged between the Halifax Wolverines and Port Arthur.
Weeks before the games, officials of the Halifax Forum were besieged
by ardent fans writing early to be assured of seats.

Strange as it may seem, 'the sport of kings', horse-racing, retained its
popularity during the Depression and proved to be financially successful. In 1933, the worst year of the Depression, it was reported that in
Summerside, Prince Edward Island, over 3,000 people, the largest attendance in ten years, witnessed the Dominion Day horse races.[56] At
the Mont Royal race track in Montreal approximately 9,000 attended the
last race day in 1933, and that week records were set in both attendance
and betting. More than 59,000 visited the track during the seven-day
meet, and the betting increased by $50,000 over the corresponding ses-
sion the previous year.[57] Whittier and Polo Parks in Winnipeg drew
daily crowds in the range of 8,000 during the Depression.[58] Most surprising of all was the fact that in 1932 Regina also hosted a successful
race meet. Track officials had been fearful about how things would turn
out because there had been no crops for three years and nobody seemed
to possess a nickel. As a precaution they cut the number of races from
seven to six for the first day lest the percentage would not compensate
them for the purses. Business was good, and meet officials replaced the
seventh race after the first day. The Regina meet prospered 'with a
handle that was only just 9 3/4 per cent to 10 per cent less than in 1930.'[59]
Obviously gambling instincts could not be suppressed even by the economic hardships of the Depression.

A rather low level of sport-as-entertainment during the Depression
was the fad for six-day bicycle racing, whose stellar performer was **William 'Torchy' Peden** (1906–80) of Victoria, B.C.[60] Held in arenas on
steeply angled board tracks (cycling 'saucers'), the bicycle 'grinds' featured teams of two riders (provided with sleeping areas in the middle
of the track area) who competed in amassing as many laps as possible
over a six-day period (only one rider at a time could build up laps).
Between designated laps, sprints for prizes and extra points were held
to excite the interest of spectators sitting in stands above the tracks
(women were usually admitted free). Henry Roxborough, a frequent
observer of cycle-racing, captured the arena atmosphere:

The scene of a six-day cycling race in Maple Leaf Gardens, Toronto, 1934. (Courtesy Don Morrow.)

But the real thrills, for which all the dull hours were forgiven and forgotten, came during jam sessions in a crowded arena. At a signal, the fastest partners took to the track, and plunged into the manoeuvering for position. Heads were down; legs were pumping. At speeds up to fifty miles an hour, chancing spills, taking risks that few other athletes faced, the racers streaked around the well-worn track, while spectators stood on seats and shouted encouragement . . . .

The hum of the wheels as they skimmed around the boards had an almost mesmerizing effect; if you shut your eyes and just listened, you could be soothed into a drowsiness. Yet not for very long, for in the big cities there were bands that were chosen, not for sweet tone, but rather for brassy volume.[61]

Popularized in New York's Madison Square Gardens during the 1890s and the early years of this century, the athletic grinds were refined into an exciting spectacle by the 1920s and 1930s. Competitors from many countries in Europe and from all over North America, wearing jockey-style colours, competed in a circuit: Montreal, Toronto, Vancouver, Portland, St Louis, Minneapolis, Milwaukee, Chicago, Detroit, and New York. Peden—nicknamed Torchy because of his red hair and his cycling speed—won several national titles before competing in the 1928 Am-

'Torchy' Peden, stationed behind a windscreen, about to begin his record-breaking mile race in Minneapolis, 1931. (Courtesy Don Morrow.)

sterdam Olympics. He then raced on the European circuit and turned professional in 1929. Over the next nineteen years he competed in almost 150 six-day races and won a quarter of them.[62]

Peden was a master showman who satisfied the strong need of the time for entertainment in sport, coupled with thrills. Like Ned Hanlan half a century before, he played to the crowd during races, grabbing a hat or a scarf from a spectator and wearing it for a few laps, or doing stunts on his bike. This was part and parcel of a general laxness associated with the grinds and their sponsors. Judges were omnipotent and often crooked, fixing races quite openly, juggling recorded laps at their own discretion, and creating frenzied and dangerous riding conditions, all in the interests of drawing large crowds and exciting them. Cyclists themselves were known to collude over outcomes—again, for the purpose of maximizing profits. Even organized crime touched cycling. Criminals like Al Capone became involved in persuading riders (including Peden) to obey their instructions in order to predetermine outcomes.[63] The grinds came to resemble a circus more than an athletic competition, and were therefore on the fringe of sporting entertainment.

Canadians who were unable to attend major sports events during the Depression could listen to them on the radio. Radio provided the greatest advance in the promotion of sport, and hockey broadcasts—for which Foster Hewitt's first broadcast from the Gondola of Maple Leaf Gardens, Toronto, on 12 November 1931 was a historical event—were by far the most popular form of radio entertainment, surpassing such comedy and musical programs as Jack Benny, Lawrence Tibbett, Wayne King, Frank Parker, and others. Station CJOR in Vancouver completed a hook-up with the General Motors broadcasting system and began carrying Hewitt's broadcasts on 5 January 1933. The *Vancouver Sun* called this 'the finest New Year's gift on the sports calendar'. For a few hours on Saturday evenings during the winter, Canadians seemed to forget their regional differences, and the sad inroads of the Depression, and focused their attention on hockey.

Other sports besides hockey were also delivered to Canadians over the air. In Vancouver, starting in 1933, Leo Nicholson announced box lacrosse games on the radio:

> When stacatto lacrosse reports crackle out over the air lanes this summer, direct from box-side through the vocal efforts and keen percepts of Leo Nicholson, it will be the third season of Shell sponsorship. As far as can be determined Leo Nicholson is the only sports announcer bringing the fastest game to a radio public . . . .
>
> Tuesday night's opening game in Vancouver Arena will be the 151st lacrosse broadcast by Shell. On their radio popularity survey, B.C. lacrosse broadcasts rate 99%, which is not such a bad recommend when it is considered that Al Jolson's Shell Chateau only drew 60%.[64]

The press, of course, was also highly influential. The Canadian Press and United Press International of Canada began operation in Canada in 1917 and 1922 respectively, but under different names. The Canadian Press was known as Canadian Press Limited until 1923, and United Press International began as British United Press, a subsidiary of the United Press, an American organization. Through their wire services these two agencies made it possible for Canadians in all parts of the country to be equally well-informed through fast and comprehensive news of their region, the nation, and the world.[65] Newspapers were able to provide immediate sports results to their readers from other parts of Canada, the USA, and Britain. By the 1920s Canadian newspapers contained a regular sports section reporting on local, national, and international events. Action photographs, as well as series on 'how-to-play-the-game', were often featured to increase public interest, making

CO-OPERATIVE
MILK RINK
Port Arthur Ont.

CO-OP MILK RINK

WORLD FAMOUS MILK RINK . Port Arthur Ont.

An example of recreational sport during the Depression. Once in the mid-thirties the Co-operative Dairy in Port Arthur (now Thunder Bay) flooded this rink with excess milk, giving it its present name. (Courtesy Northwestern Ontario Sports Hall of Fame, Thunder Bay.)

the names of players 'better known to thousands of Canadians than are the names of the members of the Federal Cabinet.'[66] Popular magazines, like *Maclean's* and the *National Home Monthly*, followed suit with articles by such well-known sports writers as Ted Reeve, Lou Marsh, J. Lewis Brown, Henry Roxborough, Fred Edwards, Elmer Ferguson, and Leslie Roberts. Their articles, which tended to be critical analyses of controversial sports issues, kept the public further informed about the latest developments in sport. Although amateur sport received the most attention in the early 1920s, by the latter half of the decade professional sport was receiving most of the coverage.

While communication systems such as the press and radio increased the popularity of sport during the Depression, it was enhanced by numerous other technological developments. Artificial ice, for example, was a further impetus to the growth in popularity of hockey, and also of curling, especially in those regions where ice conditions were unpredictable. The first artificial rinks in Canada were built in 1911 by the Patrick brothers in Vancouver and Victoria to house professional hockey on the Pacific Coast, where there was little or no artificial ice. By 1928 every professional hockey club had artificial ice.[67] Its installation in Winnipeg's Amphitheatre in 1922 made it the only artificial ice-plant between Toronto and Vancouver, greatly prolonging the period of play.[68] In Toronto in 1925–6 the opening of three new artificial-ice plants—the High Park and Granite Clubs for skating and curling and the Varsity Arena at the University of Toronto for skating and hockey—brought the total up to six.[69] The Toronto complement was probably more than in any other North American city at the time.[70] The Granite Curling Club built '. . . a magnificent new clubhouse on St. Clair Avenue near Yonge St., marking the opening of a new era in the winter game of Auld Scotia in Eastern Canada.'[71] Artificial ice was well in place in Maple Leaf Gardens, Toronto , when it opened on 13 November 1931 'before the largest crowd that ever attended a hockey game in Toronto, 13,542.'[72] There it was possible to remove the ice in a few hours so that boxing and wrestling matches could be held throughout the winter without interfering with the hockey games.[73] In the Maritime Provinces, where technological progress was somewhat retarded by depressed economic conditions, the Halifax Curling Club was operating the first artificial curling rink in the region.[74] The Yarmouth Curling Club followed suit in February 1932:

> The Linde Refrigerator company of Montreal has completed the installation of the artificial ice plant for the Yarmouth Curling Club, and last evening, for the first time this winter, despite the soft weather and heavy fog of the day, several members of the club enjoyed their first games of the season.[75]

Another innovation that gained widespread acceptance by the end of the thirties was the use of floodlighting for night games of baseball, softball, lacrosse, football, and soccer. Floodlit games made it possible for the public to enjoy its favourite teams not just on weekends during the day but during the week at night. The first football game played in Canada under electric lights was at Athletic Park in Vancouver on 29 September 1930 when the touring Hamilton Tigers defeated the University of British Columbia team by 38 to 1.[76] Later that season at Ulster Stadium in Toronto, Balmy Beach and the Oshawa Blue Devils played another game of night football under floodlights.[77] The installation of floodlights in Calgary, Edmonton, Regina, and Winnipeg by the 1939 season made night games possible in all four cities of the western circuit, enabling them to play a twenty-four-game schedule.[78] As a result, great increases in attendance were anticipated for the 1939 season,[79] but the war broke out before the effects could be clearly seen.

Soccer prospered from the introduction of floodlights into stadiums. For example, night soccer was introduced in Winnipeg in 1932:

All games in the Greater Winnipeg League, several games in the Winnipeg and District League and a number of Dominion Football Association and Manitoba Football Association games are being played under floodlight at both the new Osbourne stadium and the Wesley college grounds. There is no doubt that the venture proved satisfactory in many aspects. The players benefited during the hot summer months in not having to turn out to play until the cool of the late evening; the football public also benefited in being able to go home from their work, enjoy their evening meal and get down to the game by starting time.[80]

These night soccer games were also successful from a financial standpoint. In 1931 the Greater Winnipeg League had gate receipts of $1,837.20 for twenty-one games, and in 1932, for only sixteen games, the intake was $2,694.50.[81] In May 1938 the *Vancouver Province* reported a packed house for the first night softball games in the city:

Night softball made a brilliant and colorful bow last night under giant floodlights, when more than 3,000 enthusiasts in some miraculous fashion jammed their way into the newly-built Smith Park at Broadway and Fir Street for the senior league opening. The fans packed the baseline, and the fences. The stands, which seat 1,300 souls, proved totally inadequate.[82]

Progress in the construction of indoor facilities meant that tennis, badminton, curling, lacrosse, track and field, swimming, and basketball could be conducted inside newly built gymnasia, clubhouses, and arenas. Even in Vancouver, where a mild winter was conducive to outdoor sport:

Indoor playgrounds took the calendar out of the sports whirl. Summer, winter, spring, and fall, the old arbiters of our sport passed from the picture when we all got together and began building these living monuments to our worship of health and exercise.

So today [3 March 1934] in Vancouver, where there is no natural ice, this city is one of the great hockey centres of the West; where swimming records are smashed in midwinter; tennis players play all the year around, rain or shine; and probably more people per capita play badminton than in any other city on this continent.

And it's all because we brought our playgrounds indoors, and because we keep building more and more until few cities on the continent are served by such well-equipped gymnasia as is Vancouver.[83]

Similar progress was being made in producing safer sports equipment. Improvements in football padding and the safety harness decreased the risk of injury in football and skiing.[84] In racing the new Bahr starting gate, first used at Woodbine in Toronto in 1931, made the start of a horse-race much less hazardous. The fourteen padded stalls attached to an overhead superstructure could be raised and lowered at will, and the entire apparatus could be removed from the course very quickly.[85]

Other developments made sports more pleasurable for participants. Golfers gained more satisfaction from smacking livelier golf balls 'into infinite space',[86] while interest in downhill skiing was greatly enhanced by the unspectacular appearance in 1929 of a ski-tow, the first of its kind in North America, operated by Alex Foster at Shawbridge, Quebec.[87] Though pioneering groups in most ski clubs continued to extol the virtues of natural trails, the overwhelming voice of new skiing converts advocated a preference for the ski-tow and groomed hills.[88] Finally, in 1927 Fenton A. Roth, an electrical engineer at Port Arthur Shipbuilding, perfected a timing device that worked on the principle of the stop-watch. It was basically an electrical mechanism to which were connected four canvas 'clocks', four-feet square, each one facing a different part of the arena. Operated by the official time-keeper, it was placed so that hockey spectators and players alike could 'watch every minute of the game ticked off'.[89] The Montreal Forum and Maple Leaf Gardens acquired such a clock in 1931 and it was not long before every indoor rink across Canada had one. (See photograph on page 204.)

With technological advances and the rise of professional sport greatly stimulating sport activities across the country, religious restrictions still inhibited sport to some extent and were slow to break down. It was not until the late thirties that people bridled against the Lord's Day Act, which had been passed by Sir Wilfrid Laurier's government in 1907 and was intended to restrict secular activities on Sunday, particularly sport.[90] On 4 July 1938 the Toronto *Globe and Mail* complained:

> As far as civic encouragement is concerned, Sunday athletic recreation in Toronto is strictly taboo. A fine system of parks and playgrounds is open six days in the week for those fortunate enough to have time to enjoy them, but recreational facilities are padlocked on Sundays. At the same time, sporting events on private grounds go on full blast.[91]

The protests were heeded, for in August of that year the Toronto Board of Control opened the parks to the public on Sundays—but only for part of the day. They were closed in the morning 'so as not to interfere with church services'.[92] Similarly parks in Montreal were opened only after morning Mass.[93]

In the Maritimes several clergy objected in 1933 to the Sunday radio broadcast of the Hawks-Quakers Allan Cup game.[94] Then in the winter of 1936 railway authorities in Nova Scotia abandoned plans for ski trains after protests had been received about the desecration of the Sabbath by skiers. One Halifax clergyman, however, the Rev. H.I.S. Borgford, spoke out in defence of Sunday recreation:

> Outdoor activities, insofar as they serve in developing and strengthening people, can be considered as religious exercises. We in this community have recently been made aware of the fact that the ski enthusiasts have been denied special Sunday trains for the enjoyment of sport. This is not a unique problem since it is essentially the same in all sports, such as golf, tennis, swimming and so forth, here and everywhere at various seasons of the year.
>
> I don't think anyone will deny the real value of these outdoor activities, they are healthful. In a great many cases too many people would not have the benefit of them if they were denied the right to enjoy them on Sunday.
>
> To me, at any rate, insofar as they serve in developing and strengthening people, I must consider them as religious exercises. For me they are a phase of true religion.
>
> What the inhibitors of these activities hope to gain by their actions, I frankly cannot understand. Perhaps they have some hope that if the day can be kept clear of all sporting activities men and women will turn their thoughts to religion.[95]

A Sunday cricket game in 1936, played by the Army and Navy on the Garrison playing field, provided one of the first indications of a general acceptance in the Maritimes of Sunday sport. A large crowd gathered to watch it. About this break from the past, a *Chronicle Herald* reporter wrote:

> And so it went, at the grounds without exception. Twenty years ago, never. Today, most certainly yes. The new-generation growing up wants something more than staying home on a hot afternoon. Without a car the average person has little to do, it was explained.
>
> It is a strange coincidence that the Army and Navy, who were the original founders of sport in the Garrison city, should be the first to introduce the Sunday sport.[96]

A similar disregard for the Sunday observance laws spread throughout Canada in the late thirties. Most Canadians wanted Sunday sport and were willing to test the law in spite of opposition. In 1938 the Hon. Gordon D. Conant, Attorney-General of Ontario, admitted that the restrictive law was almost impossible to enforce and was not in tune with modern conditions.[97]

Churches, however, played a positive role in sport development between the wars by forming teams and even leagues, and the YMCA was also active and effective. Among the sports included in Sunday school or church leagues were hockey, basketball, baseball, softball, soccer, track and field, badminton, and tennis. Competition was provided for all age groups and skill levels, as can be seen from the fact that in 1925 the Greater Vancouver Sunday School Basketball League had a senior men's league as well as intermediate 'A' and 'B' leagues, which were further divided into divisions.[98] As eighty-six teams applied for berths in the League, fourteen divisions had to be formed.[99] The soccer league was broken down into senior, intermediate 'A' and 'B', junior 'A' and 'B', and juvenile categories.[100]

Participation in Sunday school leagues was high in most urban centres of the country. Winnipeg's Sunday School Athletic League reported a successful season in 1926 with 42 teams from 25 Sunday schools in the football league, 58 teams from 38 schools in hockey, 81 teams from 32 in basketball, and a total of 455 boys participating in the Sunday-school track-and-field meet.[101] Smaller centres also operated church leagues, but not on such a large scale as the cities. In Truro, Nova Scotia, however, a church softball league in 1926 was made up of eight teams from First United, St James Presbyterian, First Baptist, St John's, Immaculate Conception, Sacred Heart, St Andrew's United, and Brunswick Street United.[102] Such small centres were forced to form inter-denominational church leagues, whereas in the large cities each main religious denomination often had its own league, like Winnipeg's Presbyterian Football League[103] and the United Churches Football League.[104] The winners of these denominational leagues often played off for a city championship.

Although by 1920 religion had become de-emphasized in the YMCA,[105] teaching a Christian way of life was still one of its guiding principles, but this did not interfere with its belief that sport helped to instil many desirable qualities in youth. The YMCA therefore promoted a wide variety of sports, including basketball, boxing, wrestling, swimming, gymnastics, hockey, weight-lifting, badminton, baseball, softball, canoeing, rowing, water polo, track and field, soccer, rugby, and football. The Y was especially prominent in basketball, gymnastics, swimming, boxing, and wrestling.

Basketball grew rapidly in popularity in the 1920s, with the YMCA figuring prominently in this trend. The Central Y in Toronto fostered the movement for a senior men's Canadian basketball championship, which became an actuality in 1924.[106] During the twenties basketball spread out from the YMCA into athletic clubs:[107]

> Basketball is now one of the best known games in Canada today [1928]. Its rise has been remarkable in the last two or three years. The game itself is largely played in the Y.M.C.A. throughout Canada, but there are now . many private leagues throughout the Dominion. Each year at this season,

the winners of these different leagues play off, and a Dominion championship series is played to determine the team worthy of these laurels. The
first game was played in 1898 in the old 90th Drill Hall, but the Y.M.C.A.
was instrumental in bringing it to the fore during the years from 1900 to
1910.[108]

In spite of this extension of basketball outside the YMCA, the Y contin-
ued to produce top teams that frequently gained recognition at both the
provincial and national levels. Sports pages carried headlines like 'HAL-
IFAX Y.M.C.A. WINS MARITIME INTERMEDIATE TITLE AT BASKETBALL',[109] VAN-
COUVER 'Y' SQUAD CAPTURES CAGE TITLE',[110] and 'TRURO Y.M.C.A. TAKES
FIRST OF PLAYOFF FOR PROVINCIAL BASKETBALL TITLE'.[111]

In gymnastics the YMCA provided leadership, instruction, facilities,
and equipment that otherwise were not available. Throughout the twenties and thirties Y gymnasts dominated local, provincial, and national
championships.[112]

The YMCA Athletic League had been affiliated with the AAU since
1905,[113] enabling registered athletes to take part in any amateur competition in Canada. In 1926 the secretary, J.H. Crocker, reported that
among 54 associations in Canada that were members of the Amateur
Athletic Union, 1,680 YMCA members were eligible to compete in open
competitions.[114]

The twenty years between the two world wars were pivotal ones in the
process of change in Canadian sport. As more Canadians across the
country became involved, the dominance of central Canada in governing
the upper levels of sport, and national championships, was irksome to
both the western and eastern provinces. (Though the unfairnesses that
existed then were eventually corrected, the strong sense of regional
competitiveness remains.) The 1920s were a period of notable expansion—with the YM-YWCAs fostering development in sport, with churches
supporting a variety of teams and leagues, with women becoming increasingly accepted at all levels (see Chapter 9), with international distinctions (some by women) being earned in the Olympics, and with
technological advances bringing the public closer to sporting events.
This explosion of sporting development was sharply focused in the
Depression years when sport as entertainment, sport as a means of
gambling, and greater spectatorship in general prompted a shift towards
the evolution of sport-as-business. By the end of the thirties the promotion of any sport, if it would attract crowds to a paying contest—
whether it was football, baseball, ice-hockey, marathon swimming, or
six-day bicycle races—became the epitome of sport in Canada

6

Baseball

Unlike the team sports of lacrosse, football, and hockey, which originated and developed in Montreal, the Canadian origins of baseball were
in southwestern Ontario. Though profoundly American in its later development—with its star players, rules, leagues, and large financial
backing—it was not 'invented', as legend has it, by Abner Doubleday
in Cooperstown, New York, in 1839.[1] A game has been described one
year earlier in Beachville, Ontario, halfway between Woodstock and
Ingersoll. It was played in a form remarkably similar to the so-called
'New York' rules later established by the New York Knickerbrocker Club
in 1845.[2]

Baseball must have had its origin in children's ball games—throwing
and catching the ball, then batting it with a stick to a catcher. The loose
development of a team composed of pitcher, catcher, batters running
to bases, and fielders had obvious connections with the English games
of rounders and even cricket. The Beachville game of 4 June 1838 was
described by Adam E. Ford (1831–1906) in a letter that was published
in part in the Ingersoll *Chronicle* on 20 May 1886 and later appeared in
full in *Sporting Life*. The game was held on a holiday, Militia Muster Day
(this was only six months after the Mackenzie Rebellion in Toronto),
and took place in a field behind Enoch Burdick's shops, between the
Beachville Club and the Zorras, players from two neighbouring townships.

> The ball was made of double and twisted woolen yarn, a little smaller than
> the regulation ball of today and covered with good honest calf skin, sewed
> with waxed ends by Edward McNames, a shoemaker . . . . The club (we
> had bats in cricket, but we never used bats in playing baseball) was gen-
> erally made of the best cedar, blocked out with an axe and finished on a
> shaving-horse with a drawing knife. A wagon spoke, or any nice straight
> stick would do.[3]

Four bases, called 'byes', marked the infield area, and there were foul
areas—corroborating the early departure from cricket's 360-degree 'fair
territory' (the 'oval') surrounding the batsman. Hits and runs were numerous, since the real fun was in getting runners out by 'plugging'—

that is the runner, when caught between bases, could be tagged or hit (plugged) by a ball thrown at him. No one wore gloves; the score was kept by notches on a stick; and games lasted from 6 to 9 innings. Games played earlier than 1838 (so Ford suggested) were declared finished when one team reached 18 or 21 runs first. Finally the players—Ford noted that the number per team varied between 7 and 12—ranged in age from 15 to 24. Ford named them all.

His letter establishes baseball as one of the earliest team sports in Canada. Moreover, it underscores the village roots of the game. Vestiges of the 1838 rules—namely the use of 11 players and 4 bases and a common striker's box/home bye—remained in the Woodstock-Ingersoll area until at least 1860. The more popular New York game—which used 9 players and 3 bases—was in vogue in the United States and in other Ontario communities.

Generally speaking cricket and rowing were the emerging summer sports in the 1850s and 1860s. For one thing they benefited from the organizational skills and support of a local élite. Baseball was very much a working-man's sport and caught on quickly in Woodstock, Ingersoll, and even in the larger centre of Hamilton. In 1854—the year the Great Western Railway completed its main line (Niagara Falls-Hamilton-London-Windsor)—the Hamilton Young Canadians became the first known organized team, with an executive, a membership fee, and a regular place to play.[4] They played the New York game, where every player had to be put out before the side was retired. The founders of the club were William and James Shuttleworth, a clerk and a shoemaker, and the members represented a wonderful array of working-class occupations: 5 clerks, 3 shoemakers, 2 turners, 2 labourers, and a coach manufacturer, a saloon-keeper, a painter, a marblecutter, a brakeman, a tinsmith, one maker each of brooms, horsecallars, cigars, watches, carriages, and many others.[5] This overwhelming representation of the working-class at both the playing and organizational levels also characterized other clubs in nearby communities, like the Dundas Mechanics, and eventually across the country, and (at least among the players) puts a stamp on baseball today.[6] It has had the salutary effect of exempting baseball, relatively speaking, from the class manipulation prevalent in other sports.

The team of the 1860s was the Woodstock Young Canadians, who played their first match in 1861 and were undefeated by a Canadian team until 1867, when they were beaten by the Dundas Independent Club.[7] Coopers, shoemakers, a carriagemaker, a blacksmith, a painter, and a grocer made up the Woodstock club in 1862, and three-quarters of these players were Ontario-born.[8] This club was instrumental in introducing the concept of baseball 'championship' when, in 1863, they solicited subscriptions to purchase a silver ball, the winner of which would be designated the champion baseball club in Canada. It must not be assumed or implied that middle-class and professional men did not relish participating in, and watching, informal baseball games. The merchants and clerks from the 'Detroit and Windsor' sides of Ingersoll's King Street, for example, frequently challenged their business competitors from across the street.[9] Similarly players from various districts of Woostock's commercial core-area divided themselves up geographically to form teams; on one occasion employees working between 'Farrell's Hotel to Watson's Corner' played against those from 'White's to Woodroofe's blocks.'[10] It is interesting that rarely, if ever, did men from dissimilar occupational backgrounds intermingle to compete with each other. A further indication of the organization that was being brought into the sport was the formation of the Canadian Association of Baseball Players at Canada's first baseball convention held in Hamilton at the time of the Provincial Exhibition, on 30 September 1864.[11] Of course this national designation was a misnomer; only southwestern-Ontario teams were involved, although there were a few clubs in Victoria, B.C., in 1863. The only evidence of clubs outside Ontario and British Columbia is in Montreal, where there was a baseball subsidiary of the Montreal Foot Ball Club in 1865,[12] and in Halifax, where there were two clubs in 1867.[13]

By the end of the 1860s community-rooted baseball teams were playing more and more inter- rather than intra-community games. For example, several Canadian teams placed quite well in the three categories (classes) of competition in an 1867 Detroit tournament.[14] One of the most extensive reports of early Canadian baseball appeared in the *Brampton Times* on 3 July 1868 and described a contest between Streetsville and Brampton. It merits duplication in full:

A friendly game of BaseBall was played on Wednesday last (Dominion Day) between the first nine of the Union Base Ball Club, of Streetsville, and the first nine of Brampton Club, which resulted in a victory for the former by the following score:

Streetsville	Outs	Runs
Ecclestone, C.	0	11
Sanders, C.F.	1	8
Burnett, S.S.	1	8
Flumerfelt, L.F.	2	7
T. Anderson, R.F.	3	7
G. Anderson, 2nd B.	1	8

McCasker, 3rd B.	1	8
Ross, 1st B.	4	5
Cooper, P.	2	8
	15	70

Brampton	Outs	Runs
Stephens, P.	2	2
Standish, C.	3	1
Foster, S.S.	1	2
W. Tilt, 1st B.	2	0
McMurray, 2nd B.	1	0
Bunting, 3rd B.	2	1
J. Tilt, L.F.	2	1
Frank, C.F.	1	1
Elliott, R.F.	1	1
	15	9

Synopsis

	1	2	3	4	5	
Union Base Ball Club	9	12	24	16	8	Total 70
B. Base Ball Club	3	3	3	0	0	Total 9

Home Runs— Flumerfelt 1. Fly Catches—G. Anderson 3; Frank 1; Stephens 1; T. Anderson 1.

Umpire— R. B. Lewis of Mechanics' Base Ball Club, Clayville, N.Y.

Scorers— A.E. Bicknell and R.K. Smither

Time of Game— One hour and a half

The excellent fielding and prompt and decided movement which characterized the play of the Streetsville Club bore evidence of long experience in the 'Biz,' and indeed we noticed among other scienced players, R.B. Lewis, Esq., of the 'Mechanics', Clayville, N.Y. and P.H. Sanders of Rochester, N.Y., and other clubs in the United States. The Brampton Club (though not having been organized longer than two months) by their superior batting, displayed a precision seldom acquired except by long practice, and showed themselves by no means deficient in the muscle requisite to render them first-class players, while their zeal and alacrity, which, notwithstanding the intense heat of the sun, continued unabated to the end, although contending against great odds, evinced their determination to 'die game.' The general physique of the men of both sides was remarkably good, while their gentlemanly bearing could not fail to elicit the admiration of all. The decisions of the umpire were strictly impartial, and indicated a thorough acquaintance with the game. After doing ample justice to a bountiful repast provided by John Hannah, at the British Arms Hotel, the players dispersed highly satisfied with the manner in which the game had been conducted.[15]

This account—its self-satisfied tone very typical of newspapers of the time—reveals a number of things about early baseball. The ludicrously uneven score in the five-inning game, 70–9, was quite common in an era when strikers (batters) could wait for their choice of pitches, when no player wore gloves (as the game increased in speed and the ball became more resilient most players dusted rosin on their hands), and when fielders and infielders were usually quite inept at catching and throwing. 'Fly catches', or catching a fly ball, was not much practised, since a ball caught after the first bounce registered the same out. Streetsville used at least two American players in the contest and they, as the lopsided score suggests, were very likely 'crack ballists'. The players were praised for their 'gentlemanly bearing'—an expectation of the upper strata of athlete in most sports at the time—and this suggests either the desire to impose a measure of élite respectability on the working-class game, or that there were no fights among the players! The one umpire used was an American, who probably stood behind the pitcher to make all calls in the game, a custom retained by baseball until well into the twentieth century, although some umpires gravitated to a place behind the catcher during the 1880s.

In 1864 Woodstock played Guelph, beginning a rivalry in which Guelph would come out on top, becoming the leading baseball town of the 1870s. The Guelph Maple Leafs wore only their workclothes and a red maple leaf sewn onto their shirts, but within two years they had adopted a formal set of by-laws.[16] Heated games between the two teams, with fights in the bleachers, were not uncommon. For example, on 4 August 1868 in Woodstock, 'toughs' from that town roamed the stands to provoke Guelph spectators and players. The lure of competitive baseball in southwestern Ontario seemed to outweigh its more sordid characteristics. Over the Dominion Day weekend in 1869, Woodstock hosted a 3-day tournament, complete with substantial cash prizes derived from a $10 entrance fee to competing clubs and from subscriptions solicited from local businessmen. Some 5,000 people—at least a thousand in excess of Woodstock's entire population—watched Ingersoll defeat Woodstock and Guelph clubs in the first-class competition.[17] Not to be outdone by Woodstock, London, the metropolis of southwestern Ontario, held one month later a much larger 3-day tournament, involving 11 teams from 8 Ontario towns, alongside the Provincial Exhibition. The

Guelph team won and received $150 in gold.[18] Nevertheless, disagreements over the rights to the prestigious Silver Ball trophy, emblematic of the so-called Canadian championship, reached the point of threatened legal action that year.[19] These games began in earnest the fierce community rivalry/loyalty that has been so much a part of baseball to this day.

At the helm of Guelph's rise to baseball dominance was entrepreneur George S. Sleeman (1841–1926). A prominent brewer during the 1860s and 1870s, he was civic-minded and absolutely committed to promoting and developing Guelph in any way possible. He was instrumental in the construction of the Guelph Opera House, brought the Provincial Fair to Guelph, was the owner of the first street railway in the city, and eventually became mayor of Guelph for a six-year term.[20] He was astute in recognizing the potential in baseball not only to enhance community spirit but to promote the city.

Sleeman's first contact with baseball was tied to the mid-sixties' formation of his own factory team, the Silver Creeks. Games were held in the empty lot beside his brewery and Sleeman himself paid all expenses for equipment and road trips. His players were quite literally 'home brews'. The Maple Leafs, of course, were by far the better team. When Sleeman, along with 3,000 others, accompanied the Leafs to Woodstock for the 1869 Canadian championship game, the expertly played and exciting contest (which the Leafs won) must have been a revelation to the businessman.[21] He began to put money into the team and in the early seventies, when there were baseball clubs throughout Ontario,[22] the Guelph Maple Leafs were acknowledged as the best team. The Leafs, with which the Silver Creeks had merged by 1873, were employing the tactic of hiring two American players. In an era when money in almost any other sport (except professional rowing) was anathema to the conception of 'true' sport, Sleeman was investing in the Leafs, realizing that money was essential, indeed critical, to the maintenance of the game, as it is to this day.

In 1874 Sleeman was elected president of the Maple Leafs. One of the first things he did was to devise a set of club rules governing player behaviour in public.[23] Fines that ranged from $5 to $25 were deterrents. The strategy was sound. Players were often praised for their 'gentlemanly' playing and bearing . . . both on and off the field. In June 1874 Sleeman took the team at his own expense to Watertown, New York, for the 'World' semi-pro championship. The Leafs won and took the $450 First Prize. They won the Silver Ball both that year and the next. Correctly anticipating that the reputation of the Leafs would attract other

Guelph's Maple Leaf Baseball Club, 1874. (From the Montreal Amateur Athletic Association Scrapbook, volume 14, courtesy Don Morrow.)

teams, players, and fans to come to Guelph, Sleeman built the Wellington Hotel near the baseball grounds.

Sleeman worked hard to maintain Guelph's baseball pre-eminence. The Sleeman Papers at the University of Guelph are files, five centimetres thick, of correspondence to and from Sleeman for 1876 and 1877, containing letters regarding match dates, travel rates, equipment purchases, and (most abundant) player recruitment—Sleeman must have known that the continuing quality of his baseball product was dependent upon the calibre of players. In that regard alone Sleeman's talent-hunt was extraordinary. The Leafs' prowess in 1874 and 1875 was well known and candidates for his team wrote him from all over North America:

> The St. Louis Red Sox manr [manager] want me to play with them next season but I don [sic] like to stay there so I thought I would write to you and let you know that I will play with your team next season of (6) months commencing the 15th of April until the 15th of October to be paid in equal payments the first of every month. If those figures suits you let me know immediately as I would like to have my contract signed as soon as possible for if I cannot make any terms I want to answer my other letters.

This was written on 16 November 1876 by T. Dolan of St Louis, Missouri. Similar letters came from Chicago, Brooklyn, Philadelphia, Ottawa, and many other places. Most correspondents were careful to praise their own talents. For example on 25 August 1876 Mr Salisbury declared: 'I pitch both the in curve and out, also rising and falling balls.' Sleeman— who usually offered $100 per month plus board and transportation to and from Guelph—almost singlehandedly set in motion the commercial chain of events that compelled other communities and clubs to follow suit.

On 7 April 1876, at the Walker House Hotel in Toronto, the Canadian Base Ball Association (CBBA) was formed at a convention held for that purpose.[24] Sleeman was elected president of the five-team league. The London Tecumsehs, the Guelph Maple Leafs, the Toronto Clippers, the Hamilton Standards, and the Kingston St Lawrence each paid the required $10 fee to enter 'championship' play, to be composed of four games against every other team (each team would play 16 'championship' games). The team achieving the greatest number of victories would be declared the winner. The CBBA copied the constitution and by-laws verbatim from the National Base Ball Association of the United States.[25] A 'Judiciary Committee' of five members—the real power or functional executive of the CBBA—decided on all matters of dispute, awarded the 'championship stream' (pennant), and set the 25¢ admission to all championship games, with the visiting clubs to receive forty per cent of the game's cash receipts after expenses were deducted. Clearly the injection of commercialism into the CBBA was inspired by Sleeman's success with his semi-professional Guelph team.

As for Sleeman himself, he remained heavily involved with the Leafs until the end of the 1877 season. His final baseball hurrah was his direction and promotion of a barnstorming tour by the Maple Leafs in 1886—a 54-game journey through Canada and the United States (as far away as Wheeling, West Virginia). For Sleeman and for baseball, the tour was highly successful. The Leafs won 47 games. On game nights Guelph citizens swarmed around the telegraph offices to catch game reports.[26] When the Leafs returned, 3,000 people gathered at the train station to greet them. This was the final tribute to Sleeman, who in a few years had not only masterminded the rise to international success of the Leafs but made an imprint on baseball in general by helping to found the CBBA.

Between the mid-1850s and 1876 baseball's thread of development stretched from Hamilton to Woodstock to Guelph and then to London, which had a team as early as 1856. The London and Forest City clubs

A composite by Edy Bros. of a baseball game in Tecumseh Park, London, between the London Tecumsehs and Syracuse, 1871. The Middlesex County Court House can be seen in the background. (Courtesy the National Archives of Canada, PA 31482.)

amalgamated in 1868 to form the Tecumseh Club, which by 1876 was one of the best-known teams in North America, playing serious professional baseball by American rules and with American players.[27]

The real force behind the 1876 Tecumsehs was Jacob Lewis 'Angel' Englehart. Only 29 years of age, Englehart ran his own petroleum producing and refining company. By 1880 he was vice-president of the Imperial Oil Company, and his personal net worth was estimated at around $100,000.[28] With the formation of the CBBA in April 1876 London's oil baron set out to run the Tecumseh Club in a businesslike manner. Its executive body was a grade up the social hierarchy from the early organizers of Canadian baseball and bespoke an advancement in managerial sophistication beyond the one-man-rules and style of earlier times:

John Brown	Honorary President	City chamberlain
H.W. Birell	Vice President	John Birell and Company Wholesale Dry Goods
E.M. Moore	Treasurer	Tecumseh Hotel Proprietor
J.T. Lawrie	Secretary	Cutter
H. Gorman	Managing Director	Printer for London Advertiser
J. Plummer Jr.	Manager	Plummer and Sons Wagon and Carriage Makers.[29]

Forty per cent of the 129 officers of the CBBA itself were white-collar workers and another twenty-seven per cent were of the mercantile class (shopkeepers and hotel owners). Interestingly twelve of the 129 CBBA personnel were existing or future mayors.[30] Englehart, then, represented the movement towards baseball organizers who were small manufacturers and/or local businessmen—an entrepreneurial orientation comprising a more broadly based group than the established businessmen and professionals who controlled major amateur sport organizations during the last third of the nineteenth century.[31]

All 10 players of the Tecumsehs' 1876 roster—called the Redmen—were Americans. (Sleeman's barnstorming team was also composed entirely of Americans.) Prized among the Redmen was pitcher Fred Goldsmith, a master of the 'twister' or curveball from New Haven, Connecticut. He devastated batters; under his pitching prowess the Tecumsehs were a dynamo team. In the first 'championship' game of the CBBA series, played against Guelph in London at the Exhibition Grounds, 6,000 spectators were drawn to the field on 25 May 1876. The Tecumsehs beat the reigning Canadian champions, the Maple Leafs, 8 to 7 in an extra inning. The *London Free Press* (27 May 1876) captured the community's reaction:

> Our London contemporaries are nearly frantic over the results. For years the Londoners have in vain endeavoured to win a single game from the Guelph boys, but at last by the aid of half a dozen said professionals [an underestimate] they have succeeded in beating them by one run.

And more germane to inter-community baseball rivalry:

> There is woe, and weeping, and gnashing of teeth in Guelph upon the Speed. The citizens move about in funeral array, and the sound of sobbing comes from out every man's doorway . . . . What has broken the heart of every Guelph man able to sit on a fence and watch a game of ball, is the defeat of the 'boys' by the Tecumseh club of London.[32]

This CBBA championship series was entirely Guelph versus London; the Tecumsehs played only six games with the three other teams over the 1876 season. Scores were extremely lopsided in favour of the Tecumsehs; often the Redmen 'Chicagoed' (shut out) their opponents. There was just no drawing-power in the other teams, which were unable to match, or afford, or commit to the professional underpinnings of the two major teams. Mostly for this reason the CBBA collapsed after only one year.

Londoners were showered with top-notch baseball games in 1876. In addition to the series games, the Tecumsehs played 36 exhibition games against a variety of American teams and sustained a 31:5 win:loss record—strong evidence of their high calibre. Londoners attended games held locally in crowds ranging from 2,000 to 6,000, proof positive to Englehart and others of the potential market for high-quality professional baseball. When Ed Moore, treasurer of the Tecumseh organization, umpired the third game of the London:Guelph 1876 series, he apparently bet a box of cigars with a friend on the Tecumsehs. They were indeed victorious, but Sleeman protested the result to the CBBA Judiciary committee, who upheld the protest and declared the contest null and void.[33] The Toronto *Globe* was quick to forecast doom for baseball:

> There seems to be a good deal of feeling manifested on both sides, each club accusing the other of having professional players engaged, and neither of them giving the charge a direct denial. That there should be any foundation for such charges is having a disastrous effect upon the popularity of Base Ball; for when it begins to lose the character of a genuine amateur amusement . . . and partakes of the nature of a speculation in the engagement of mercenaries, and as a game for gamblers, its sordid side is sure to extinguish whatever favour it may have possessed, at least in the eyes of the Canadian public.[34]

The journalist was obviously influenced by the conservative British ideals of amateurism so well entrenched in most Canadian sports emerging during the 1870s. Baseball, however, was propelled by American forces, Canadian local entrepreneurs, and rural communities, not by British tradition or by large urban sporting configurations.

In February 1877 the Tecumseh and Guelph organizations decided to join the International Base Ball Association (IBBA), comprised of the two 'Canadian' entries and five strong American teams: the Alleghenys, Live Oaks, Ohio Buckeyes, Manchester, and Rochester. The Tecumseh executive raised subscriptions to build Tecumseh Park (now Labatt Park) on the outskirts of London and brought in five new American players, retaining five from the 1876 team. At the start of each Tecumseh season (from 1876 to 1878) the London papers printed the name, playing position, height, and weight of each of the Redmen. Since home runs were rare in an era of a dead or heavy ball (made with less India rubber then in the 1850s or 1860s), the intent was probably to introduce the hired 'meat-on-the-hoof' and, by extension, to imply athletic prowess by height and weight information. Numerous pictures of baseball teams of the 1870s reveal sturdy players, almost all of whom wore full moustaches. The most important ingredient of a successful baseball team, however, was not the players' size but the 'battery'; that is, the pitcher and the catcher. In Goldsmith, London had a real advantage in offensive play; coupled with catcher Phil Powers, the Tecumseh battery was formidable. Typical of descriptions of Powers' skill was the following tribute to a finesse play that was admired in the sport for decades:

> A man was on first [leading off first] when the striker made a foul tip. Powers grasped it [the ball] and in a twinkling sent it to Bradley [first baseman], catching the baserunner who was some ten feet from the bag. The ball was scarcely visible from the moment it left Goldsmith's hand till Bradley held it for a double play and the play was rewarded with well deserved applause.[35]

In 1877 crowds were drawn in great numbers and were rewarded by high drama and high-quality baseball. After 47 wins, 26 losses, and 7 ties the IBBA championship came down to the final game, a crowd-thrilling one, between the Tecumsehs and the Alleghenys in London on 3 October 1877. Englehart's team emerged victorious, giving rise to the notion that a 'Canadian' team had beaten the Americans at their own game.

Correspondence in the Sleeman Papers reveals that the Tecumseh executive, which remained virtually unchanged over the three-year period, administered the Club meticulously as a business whose product was high-quality baseball. Their aim was not to make a profit but to promote the sport, along with the London community. Their sophistication was reflected in their stationery, which carried the name Tecumseh Base Ball Club in script; flanking it in the top left corner was a finely sketched naked torso of a North American Indian (their idea of Tecumseh?) in hunting pose and surrounded by trees.

Eighteen teams were entered in the 1878 IBBA series: Guelph and London were the only Canadian ones. One of the earliest games of the season was in Buffalo. London won and the local press delighted in reprinting an excerpt from a Buffalo newspaper:

> There are several sorts of bereavement which may cast a gloom over the community, but few can so utterly strip the cloud of its silver lining as a defeat of local ball consocialton [sic] by nine unfeeling gladiators from H.B.M.'s [Her British Majesty's] dominion. Of all the disappointments in life, this is apparently the most harrowing, the amenable conmutation [sic]. It eclipses the gayety of nature and improvides [sic] the public stock of harmless pleasures.[36]

The irony, of course, was that the 'gladiators' were as American as the host team. However, London's inflated baseball bubble had burst by mid-July 1878. The Tecumsehs were not as dominant and the crowd size diminished. Moreover, there was a widespread belief that the Tecumsehs threw a game against the Syracuse Stars in early July.[37] Even the suspicion of fraud is unacceptable in both sport and business. Tecumseh game attendance waned and when in mid-August it was clear the Tecumsehs could not win the series, a fickle executive, led by Englehart, 'resolved that the nine be paid off on Saturday and released from their engagement'.[38] This was done and the team folded. Professional baseball in a small town or city, without the protection of an umbrella organization, was a fragile thing and remained so whenever high-calibre baseball was embarked upon.

From the late 1870s onward baseball's diffusion throughout Canada, at all levels—from spontaneous games and informal play to élite professionalism—was phenomenal. Top athletes in the sport, normally American imports, were called 'ballists'. Although Canadian newspapers focused on American major-league baseball between 1880 and 1884, baseball matches were prevalent in Victoria and New Westminster, often against clubs from the State of Washington, and inter-town matches were being played among Halifax, Saint John, Moncton, Truro, and Pictou. Unlike most Canadian team sports and forms of competition, Canadian baseball was structured on a north-south basis. That is, it continued to look to the United States for all levels of competition, and for players in semi-professional and professional leagues, until well into the twentieth century.[39] The American influence that pervaded the sport in Canada was therefore its most stabilizing influence. Although teams and leagues in the eighties and nineties may have appeared, disappeared, and (some) reappeared, this pattern was not baseball's 'malady', as one sport historian implies.[40] Rather it was how baseball survived. Its tide never ceased in Canada.[41]

In the mid-1870s there were six teams in the Saint John Baseball Association in New Brunswick for which most players practised at 5:30 a.m. in order to be at work by 7:00.[42] When the great fire of Saint John occurred in 1877, baseball died out for two years owing to both the destruction of the city and the fact that many of the ball-players moved west to look for jobs. In the early 1880s, however, the Saint John Cricket Club was active, and baseball bounced back in 1884. In that era children made their own baseballs, 'centred on the nose of a sturgeon and covered with yarn'.[43] A tremendous rivalry developed between the team of the Protestant Saint John Athletic Association and the Shamrocks, and high-calibre baseball resulted. Up to 2,000 fans attended games between the two teams, a demonstration of support that led to the formation and two-year existence of the professional New Brunswick Base Ball League, beginning in 1888. Moncton and Fredericton completed the four-team league.

Both Saint John Clubs recruited heavily in Maine and Massachusetts for American players. Normally American college students, especially good 'batteries', were financially induced to spend the summer in New Brunswick and play 'Canadian' baseball under aliases in order to protect their amateur status south of the border.[44] In 1890 Moncton had only three Canadians on its team.[45] With the professional treadmill set in motion, baseball became a fact of civic and spectator interest. 'Housewives, doctors, clerks, lumbermen, merchants, and fishermen could be seen sitting in the grandstand or standing along the sidelines.'[46] Moreover, the CPR Telegraph Company erected a scoreboard at the corner of King and Germain Streets in Saint John for the benefit of those who could not get into the game. During games the corner was a veritable hive of betting activity. Inevitably the question arose: which was the best baseball team in the Maritimes? To decide the issue the Saint Johns met the Halifax Atlantas in a three-game series that lasted only one game because it was determined that the umpire had been 'bought off' by the Atlantas. This 'scandal' created ill-feeling between the two municipalities for some time; but for baseball it was just part of the perpetually repeated evolutionary process. When the Shamrock fans got out of control in an 1890s contest against the Saint Johns, the latter team withdrew from the league because of ill-treatment and Moncton followed suit, owing to the same financial difficulties that plagued the weaker teams in Ontario's CBBA 1876 series.

Between 1890 and 1905 Saint John retreated to 'amateur' baseball—amateur in the sense that the inclusion of paid players was not declared, just known. The best intra-city teams were the Roses, Starlights, Gashouse, YMCA, Strawberries, and Alerts. The Alerts and the Roses were notorious throughout the 1890s for bringing in paid American batteries, but since there was no amateur affiliation or governance, the practice was regarded as part of baseball. A good local pitcher like Jim Whelly in the late-1890s Alerts often came home with his hat full of silver dollars. The contests between teams were usually played for $100 a side as well as 75 per cent of the gate receipts.[47] As elsewhere, money was a necessity in the Maritimes for the survival of good teams and leagues. The Halifax Orients even travelled with a theatrical group, using performance receipts to cover expenses. Several leagues folded in Halifax over lack of financing.

Although baseball on Prince Edward Island was insulated from intercity competition with other Maritime locales, it took root mainly in the rural communities of Pisquid, Tracadie, Peakes Station, Roseneath, Stanhope, and Baldwin's Road during the 1890s. In the same decade there was a strong network of intra-city contests in Charlottetown.[48]

In the western provinces and territories, baseball teams had a fledgling existence in the 1870s. By the early 1880s lacrosse was the favoured summer sport in Manitoba, and soccer and rugby had a greater following than baseball. In 1885 the three best baseball clubs in Winnipeg—the CPR, the Metropolitans, and the Hotelkeepers (financed by hotel proprietors)—actively recruited the best players in the province and gave them good jobs in return for baseball service. But each team inevitably began to import salaried players—usually batteries—from the United States in order to remain competitive and financially viable in the Winnipeg Base Ball League.[49]

Fuelled by the Winnipeg newspapers' extensive coverage of all North American professional leagues—one hotel even offered daily telegraphed reports of games on the continent—Winnipeggers were said to be 'suffering from baseball mania' in 1886. All kinds of groups in the city—printers, civil servants, lawyers—formed baseball teams for sheer enjoyment. The three-team Manitoba Baseball League of 1886 was at the top of the baseball echelon and enjoyed the status of being the first professional sport league on the Prairies. Games typically drew ten per cent of the city's population of 20,000. By the late summer of 1886, however, baseball began to fall into disrepute over betting. Open gambling on the final score, margin of victory, hits by various players, and total game score—of which the umpire might have pre-game knowledge—raised public concern, which increased when collusion by players to fix outcomes was suspected. Attendance declined, teams disbanded, and the league collapsed. A tournament style of baseball prevailed for the next sixteen years. In 1902 Winnipeg obtained a franchise in a North Dakota and Minnesota professional league and the city's baseball fans absorbed the quality games along with the misfortunes of financial difficulties, corruption, and on occasion rough play, until the First World War.[50]

From the late 1880s until the First World War many prairie cities and towns had baseball teams at all levels up to the tournament format (on weekends and holidays). Lethbridge, Wiste, Medicine Hat, Sturgeion, and Edmonton all generated the same civic pride in baseball prowess.[51] Consider the recollections of one prairies pioneer, *circa* 1910:

> Everything in them days you could say was baseball. Every town would have a pasture with a chicken wire backstop, and when you was gonna have a game you'd chase the town cows off it and scrape up the cow plops and that was about it. Town teams always played town teams. Like there would be a town down the line and they'd wire us they'd be up on a

An early baseball game on the Prairies—between Lethbridge and Calgary at Lethbridge, Alberta, 21 January 1905. (Courtesy the Glenbow Archives, Calgary, Alberta.)

> Saturday afternoon. It was baseball in them days too, good ball. There was none of this spares business and four or five pitchers. Not then. If your pitcher had a sore arm, well maybe he'd trade off with the shortstop and the shortstop would pitch that game and so it went.[52]

In Quebec's Eastern Townships, baseball flourished after the turn of the century[53] and French-Canadian rural communities promoted the game through schools, churches, and challenge tournaments.[54] Though Montreal was an early centre of amateur sport—notably lacrosse and rugby-football—baseball was for a time resisted there. This was perhaps logical, given the game's informal structure linked to commercial adventures in gambling and player imports, and its professional tendencies. Nevertheless, the Montreal Base Ball Club (affiliated with the prestigious MAAA) competed in an 1886 and 1887 league made up of the Beavers, the Gordons, and the Clippers until the Gordons resigned to try professional baseball (unsuccessfully).[55]

In Ontario, baseball blossomed in the 1880s and 1890s. At the grassroots level, village networks were thriving: Burnamthorpe, Caledon, Cheltenham, Churchville, Ebenezer, Forks of the Credit, Malton, Palgrave, Stanley Mills, Terra Cotta[56] and many other communities carried on the rural traditions of baseball with games on civic holidays, and with challenge and tournament formats. At the same time 'ringers' playing under aliases—top-flight players brought in from outside—and loaded baseball bats were common at the élite levels of the sport, but so was tremendous fan support. For example, the Alton Aetnas were one of the best teams in the province from 1893 to 1907. Formed in 1875 by Samuel Barber, a carriagemaker and blacksmith, and J.F. Holden, a druggist and station-master, the Aetnas attracted rural fans within a 30-kilometre radius:

> Wherever the team travelled, there, too, went its supporters. Farmers of the surrounding district forsook their ploughs, mechanics in the village laid down their tools, Alton men and women alike donned their Sunday best, and went out to cheer their Aetnas, at home or abroad.[57]

'Abroad' implied an invitation from Owen Sound to play at that centre's Railroad Conductors' Picnic in 1893. Public subscriptions from Alton residents were used to make up the $100 wagers on games, such as one with Orangeville for which local carriagemaker Sam Boggs in 1897 used his traction threshing engine to pull three farm wagons, covered with tarpaulins and decorated with humorous signs, to Erin.[58] It was a community-prompted promotion stunt and typified the ingrained popularity and festive atmosphere of late-nineteenth-century baseball.

The attractions of the game at holiday gatherings organized by churches, schools, local business entrepreneurs, and small civic-based institutions were just not strong enough to ensure the development of professional baseball throughout Canada. While most towns flirted with commercial or professional practices, only the largest urban centres—Toronto, Montreal, Winnipeg, Victoria, and Vancouver—had a large enough population to sustain a club during both winning and losing seasons.[59] In Toronto, and later in Montreal, pro baseball became viable and tremendously popular, beginning in 1885.

In that year five prominent Toronto citizens—Deputy Police Chief Stark, Peter Ryan, E. Strachan Cox, William Macpherson, and Thomas Hunter—met at the Rossin House to form the executive of the Toronto Base Ball Club.[60] They formed a joint stock company, paid out $4200 in salaries, grossed $8500 in receipts, and at the end of the season placed third behind Hamilton and London in the Canadian Baseball League, of which Guelph was a fourth member. (The league's name was a misnomer typical of central-Canadian sport organizers.) The following season (1886) the Torontos moved baseball into the realm of commercial entertainment by joining with the powerful International League of the United States. With this it remained—in spite of some name changes and one five-year absence in the 1890s—until 1967. Sunlight Park, Toronto's first baseball-specific facility, was completed in 1886 for $7000 on eight acres of land south of Queen Street East, adjacent to the Don River. All 2,000 seats were cushioned, armed, and backed, and the grandstand was covered.[61] Over the next few years the Toronto press gilded the pro-team athletes with nicknames. W.W. 'Peekaboo' Veach, 'Daisy' Davis, Bob 'The Wig' Emslie, and Ned 'Cannonball' Crane (arguably one of the fastest pitchers in baseball at the time) became household names in the late 1880s, strengthening the popularity of baseball in the process. Toronto won the 1887 International League championships.

When city teams in the International League began jumping from one league to another, the Torontos retreated to quasi-amateur baseball from 1890 to 1895. (Meanwhile strictly amateur baseball in Ontario at the senior, intermediate, and junior levels was prospering.)[62] In 1896 Toronto joined seven American teams in the Eastern League. The next year the team moved into the new Hanlan's Point Stadium on Toronto Island. Lol Soloman owned a restaurant on the Island, as well as the Toronto Ferry Company, which purchased the Toronto franchise to lure the people over. In the same year Montreal was able to buy the Rochester franchise in the Eastern League. A Canadian baseball great, 'Tip' (James Edward) O'Neill (1858–1915)—who played with Woodstock before beginning a memorable ten-year career in St Louis that included nearly 1,400 hits and 52 home-runs—was president of the League. In 1898 the popular Montreal Royals were organized. Playing in the newly built stadium in Atwater Park, they won the pennant the first year. (They lasted, in this incarnation, until the Great War.) Thus by the turn of the century viable professional baseball had arrived in Canada's two principal metropolitan centres, in spite of conservative amateur ideas, such as those expressed in *Saturday Night* in 1895:

> The true nature of professional baseball is well shown in the present relation held by Toronto to the Eastern League. There is not a Toronto man, or even a Canadian, in the whole aggregation of game-losers wearing the Toronto colours; the manager of the club is Mr. Chapman of Rochester, and the money that floats the venture is Buffalo money.[63]

This observation, deriding the by-now accepted high American component of Canadian teams—clearly a characteristic of the Toronto club—was rooted in out-dated amateur ideals. Professional baseball was becoming permanently established in Toronto. The Canadian delirium for the game in general, and for professional baseball in particular, was looming.

Between 1900 and 1920 baseball was Canada's most popular sport.[64] Even in Quebec the game spread via the league system of competition among Anglophones in urban areas. French Canadians, who were playing in small colleges in Montreal and Trois-Rivières in the 1870s and 1880s, adopted the challenge and tournament format of the game.

Newfoundlanders took up the game some time around 1913 when the St John's Amateur Base Ball League was formed at the instigation of the employees of the Imperial Tobacco Company, the Bank of Montreal, and the Reid-Newfoundland Railway. When Imperial Tobacco's vice-president, G.G. Allen, donated a silver cup for championship play that year, baseball games were a natural activity for the Wednesday-afternoon commercial half-holidays.[65] Such leagues featuring industrial sponsorship were a major component of baseball across Canada during its golden years, but in Newfoundland the First World War stymied it, and it never really took root there again.

In the Maritimes and the West semi-professional leagues continued to flourish and abate. On Prince Edward Island strong junior, intermediate, and senior city leagues were in full swing in Charlottetown and Summerside. These tiers eventually enabled the organization of an Island Championship Series and Maritime playdowns between 1925 and 1935, although PEI teams seldom performed well in the regional championship.[66] The New Brunswick-Maine League of pro ball enjoyed two years of financial success, beginning in 1911, but fan support, the league, and the sport itself dwindled during the First World War. Revived in the 1920s, New Brunswick baseball went through the inter-city, semi-professional, professional, amateur cycle repeatedly in the twenties and thirties.[67] Nova Scotia teams, by contrast—at least those from Halifax, Yarmouth, and Springhill (the renowned 'Fencebusters')—were very strong and attracted 5,000 fans at Halifax for games against New England teams in the hope that the Bluenosers could 'lay a whuppin' on American teams.[68] In Cape Breton—where baseball had been avidly played in the coal-mining towns of Sydney, Sydney Mines, Glace Bay, and New Waterford, among other places, since the early years of the century—the all-Canadian Colliery League had a short but remarkable existence in the 1930s. When the League turned professional in 1937 the games, players, and feats of the Glace Bay Miners, the Steel City team of Sydney, and the New Waterford Dodgers became famous throughout the Maritimes and in New England. The Second World War unfortunately brought it to an end.[69]

The Western Canada League was formed in Alberta in 1906, and in Saskatchewan high-calibre teams with intriguing names like the Saskatoon Quakers and the Regina Bonepilers were popular.[70] Between 1910 and 1915 railway travel expenses in the western provinces—even in the north-south direction of competitions—plagued commercial baseball development. Curtailed even further by war, western baseball was promoted by countless tournaments at the grass-roots level and by barnstorming tours of good American and Canadian teams. Westerners even tried to formalize gambling pools, but they were closed down in 1923 by the Manitoba Court of Appeal. During the 1920s tournaments in the West were sponsored by rummage sales and merchants in order to offer $1000 prizes.[71]

From Manitoba to British Columbia—where baseball was at a feverish pitch with 60 teams in Vancouver's Sunday School baseball league—strictly amateur baseball was very popular in the first twenty years of the century. Twilight leagues were formed in several centres as early as 1908, while the Sunday School leagues were strongly supported and well organized in Edmonton, Calgary, and New Westminster, as well as in Vancouver.[72] YMCAs also provided baseball leadership and facilities across the West (and across Canada). At senior and other levels the sport was greatly curtailed by the war, although many exhibition matches raised money for the Red Cross. Military baseball leagues served to carry competitions, while professional leagues like the International League carried on with business-as-usual.[73] Professional franchises, however, like the Toronto Maple Leafs (formerly the Toronto Baseball Club) were shrewd in portraying the patriotism revered during the war years. The Toronto *Globe* carried a large photograph of the Maple Leafs taking rifle practice in their baseball uniforms.[74]

Such propaganda as the foregoing example was only the tip of the media iceberg during baseball's 'golden era' in Canada. The country was literally saturated with game coverage. With nation-wide baseball activities being stimulated by more and more American college imports, barnstorming teams, and international leagues, Canada's other summer sport, lacrosse, was deprived of playing and spectator interest as baseball skyrocketed. This situation, however, was in no way a case of the rape of Canadian sport; it happened by mutual consent and Canadian solicitation.

The massive expansion of baseball at all levels, and the involvement of so many commercial and social institutions, can only be understood against the backdrop of the media's influence. The major newspapers in Canada from Halifax to Vancouver show that baseball in 1915 ranked first in percentage coverage of all other sports. Furthermore, fifty per cent of the baseball coverage in the same papers between 1885 and 1915 was concerned specifically with American leagues, especially major leagues.[75] The frequency and prominence of newspaper coverage of predominantly American-league baseball in the Canadian press out-

A baseball game at Cobden, Ontario, 27 July 1909. (Courtesy the National Archives of Canada, PA 55947.)

ranked even that of hockey in Halifax, Montreal, Toronto, Winnipeg, and Vancouver between 1927 and 1935. Even though the National Hockey League was booming in these years, and in 1928 and 1932 Canadian teams won Olympic gold medals, press coverage still favoured American-league baseball.[76]

At the hub of Canadian sport in general, and Canadian baseball in particular, was the City of Toronto and its vaunted professional baseball team. Between 1900 and 1910 it played in three different parks and changed ownership twice. In 1900 fifty-two Toronto businessmen—spearheaded by Ed Mack, a tailor, Jes Applegath, a hatter, and Thomas Soole, a printer—paid $8,000 to the Toronto Ferry Company to buy the Toronto franchise and move from the Island Park to another park, given the name Diamond Park, on Fraser Avenue, east of Dufferin and south of King Street West.[77] As well as continuing the importation of American players, the executive brought from the U.S. Edward Grant Barrow as manager for a salary of $1500, plus $300 if the team finished second or first.[78] Barrow was the creative genius behind the building of the New York Yankee dynasty of the twenties, thirties, and forties.

Torontonians flocked to games motivated by publicity extravaganzas and lured by the aura of baseball culture. On the opening day of the 1901 season, thirteen tallyhos (horse-drawn carriages) formed a parade to transport players in uniform, sportswriters, and equipment led by the Queen's Own Rifles along Simcoe, King, Yonge and Queen Streets before thousands of spectators, until the entourage stopped in front of the then-new City Hall for speeches and introductions.[79]

A baseball game in the new Hanlan's Point Stadium, Toronto Island, c. 1904. (Courtesy Metropolitan Toronto Library, T 11743.)

By 1906 the Toronto franchise was worth $25,000. The team returned to the Island in 1908, but a fire destroyed the stadium in 1909 and it was back to Diamond Park until a new 18,000-seat stadium, Maple Leaf Park, was built on Hanlan's Point. (This is where nineteen-year-old Babe Ruth, a pitcher for the minor-league Providence Grays against the Torontos, on Labour Day, 5 September 1914, batted his first home run.) Bags of peanuts by the thousands were sold at the games in pre-hot-dog days. This was a time when players were not above physically attacking umpires (for which appropriate fines were levied), incidents that could not help but excite spectators. A rowdy atmosphere infested the games, which on 4 August 1906 was deplored in *Saturday Night*:

> In the first instance the visiting Rochester players made their exit from the grounds in the most approved theatrical style, that is, amid a shower of mud, stones and other more malodorous missiles [rotten cabbages], hurled by the riff raff of hoodlums who, somehow or other, form the entourage of baseball and baseball players.

Nevertheless in 1908 *Saturday Night* reported in its issue of 16 May that the 'true fan' goes to the game every afternoon during the season, 'his mind quite controlled by sheer adoration of baseball' and the 'mere finance and travail of toil may go hang for all of him while the season lasts.'

Fans in Toronto (and Canada) became riveted on the game when the first news of major-league baseball was leaked in one small corner of the sports page in the dead of winter, and reports gradually included rumours of trades, player injuries, pennant hopes, and grew into larger articles on training camps in the southern United States; and then full pages were devoted to major-league coverage. Press reports were not banal items but were rather written in a lingo that satisfyingly cocooned baseball fans in their own cotton-wool world of the sport: 'So the Cincy [Cincinnati] push dodged the hook and went away from that place with two notches in their tally stick'.[80] In Toronto a simple 'Out at first!' in 1909 could engender more discussion, it was said, than the election of an Anglican bishop or a dispute over the earlier chapters of Genesis.[81] Even W.A Hewitt of the Ontario Hockey Association, and a guardian of the amateur principle, travelled with the Torontos. He once purchased with Tommy Ryan (the Canadian inventor of five-pin bowling and founder of the Miss Toronto Beauty Contest) the 'Paragon Score Board', which was operated at Shea's Theatre, the Star Theatre, and Massey Music Hall during the World Series games. A telegraph agent and announcer received the reports and dramatized the games on an electric board whose lights indicated balls and strikes, runners on base, and when balls were hit and where they landed. Capacity crowds filled these theatres until rental costs became prohibitive.[82]

The combination of commercialism, pastoral afternoons at the park, and rabid fans enhanced the excitement of the game itself. Torontonians left work early on Wednesday afternoons or ventured out early on Saturday mornings, eventually to fight their way out of the streetcars and across the railway tracks to the docks in order to board the ferries to Toronto Island. Waves of spectators, laden with hampers of food, were unloaded at Hanlan's Point to line up for tickets, tour the sideshows, ride the merry-go-round or roller-coaster, or to boat through the 'Tunnel of Love', and maybe even take in the outdoor-theatre vaudeville acts before going to see the game. Once inside the stadium, the hypnotized fan yielded to the environment of baseball, in a way that people not interested in the sport find difficult to understand:

> Once you are there you are caught in the maelstrom of baseball emotion. You enter into the mob-spirit of yourself. You act like one of your antediluvian ancestors. It is all you can do to keep from climbing up into the rafters, hanging by one foot, and spitting at the umpire. Your manner of eating peanuts isn't entirely human. And the things you shriek at the respectable middle-aged official who prevails over the plate. And all because of what a number of American gentlemen do to a horsehide American ball with bats made in Chicago or Philadelphia.[83]

This is *Saturday Night* again, venting its sarcasm against the American-ization of Canadian baseball in 1912. But of course no one cared. Baseball was public theatre in Toronto, as elsewhere, and the involvement was total. The following invented exchange of 1908 pretty well stands for what might be heard, or imagined, today:

'Here's an *easy* one, Bill. Get this guy. He can't hit a box-car with a buggy-whip. It's a cinch, Bill—'

The Umpire—'Baw-aww-H WUN.'

The Fan—Aw thass aw right. Thass AW right. 'S only one, Bill. Poor old Umps is dizzy watching yuh, kiddo. Take y'time now. *Take* your time. Slant it over—sul—lanttit—'

The Umpire—'Sss-turrr-IKE.'

The Fan—'T-H-A-T-'S the way. ThataBOY, Bill. He can't see'em. He don't know where you're standing kid. Twist it round his face, Bill—'

The Umpire—'Baw-WULL, tuu-u-hh.'

The Fan—'Why hello, Ump! When did you get here?

Too bad about your poor eyes! *Never* mind, Bill, that's just merely two. Two and one. Two and one. Take y'time. *Take* y'time. Slow him down, Jerry—WORK hard. All a' time a-working hard. ALLatime. GET this boob—'

The Umpire—'Sturr-rr-ike TUH.'

The Fan—'Oh, kina'bad, hey? Kinda' wretched, what?

That was a slow one, too. Just lob'em up, kid—he wouldn't be here if he didn't need the money. Let him hit it just to show your heart's in the right place—'

The Umpire—'Sssssss-turr-ike thr-rrr-eeeeeeeee.'

The Fan—'WOW-wow-wow-wow, Bill. THAT'S flingin' em some. That's gettin'em' over. There's one death in the family. Here's another cripple. Work hard. Get this dopechewer.[84]

MODERN TIMES

The Montreal Royals were revived in 1928 when the Syracuse franchise in the International League was acquired by Althanase David and Ernest Savard. They played in the new 22,000-seat Delormier Downs stadium. A few years later, in 1931, the Royals, and the stadium, ran into financial trouble. They were saved by three investors—one of them Pierre Elliott Trudeau's father, Charles-Émile Trudeau—and went on to many successes. Until they were dissolved in 1961, the Royals won seven International League pennants, and in 1946 and 1948 they won both the pennant and the Little World Series. In 1945 there occurred an event that put the Royals into the history books. This was the hiring of Jackie Robinson.[85] The Royals had been bought by the Brooklyn Dodgers in 1944 and was the top farm team of the Dodgers when its general manager, Branch Rickey, assigned Robinson to the Royals in 1945 as part of a scheme to launch him into the big-time as the first black player in the major leagues.[86]

Many of the best ballplayers have been blacks. Black players of exceptional skill played baseball in Canada in the last decades of the nineteenth century, but sadly met with immediate hostility.[87] (In the United States, where the hostility was greater, all-black teams were formed.) Bud Fowler (b. 1854), an American, played briefly for Guelph in 1881, but in spite of his obvious ability he was soon released. The *Guelph Herald* reported:

> We regret that some members of the Maple Leafs are ill-natured enough to object to the colored pitcher Fowler. He is one of the best pitchers on the continent of America and it would be greatly to the interest of the Maple Leaf team if he were re-instated . . . . He has forgotten more about baseball than the present team ever knew and he could teach them many points in the game. We are glad, however, to find that it is only a few in the team who have done so.[88]

Canadian-born Jimmy Claxton (b. 1892) left Canada as a child and achieved prominence with the Oakland Oaks, of the Pacific Coast League, and never returned. Ollie Johnson, born in Oakville, Ontario, played with the Cuban Giants, a black team based in Buffalo; though he returned to Oakville and died there in 1977, he never played baseball there. Hamilton-born Bill 'Hippo' Galloway joined the Woodstock team in 1899 but prejudice eventually led him to leave the country and join the Cuban Giants. For many years black players were seen in Canada only on all-black teams playing against all-white teams. A break-through in integration occurred in Montreal with the Quebec Provincial League, which began in 1935, with Alfred Wilson, who played for one season as pitcher and outfielder. For two years, 1936 and 1937, an all-black team, the Black Panthers, made up mostly of American southerners, played in Montreal. The atmosphere there of semi-tolerance—players could live wherever they liked—probably influenced Robinson's placement with the Royals. When he arrived in Montreal he felt he was accepted. But when the Royals played in Louisville in the Little World Series, he heard 'Go back to Canada, black boy!' shouted at him. On his return to Montreal:

> We discovered that the Canadians were up in arms over the way I had been treated. Greeting us warmly, they let us know how they felt . . . . All through that first game, they booed every time a Louisville player came out of the dugout. I didn't approve of this kind of retaliation, but I felt a jubilant sense of gratitude for the way the Canadians expressed their feelings.[89]

Ferguson ('Fergie') Jenkins.
(Courtesy the Baseball
Hall of Fame, Toronto.)

When the Royals won the Little World Series, Robinson was mobbed as a hero. The adulation prompted an American reporter to make the following often-quoted observation: 'It was probably the only day in history that a black man ran from a white mob with love, instead of lynching, on its mind' Robinson played his first game for the Dodgers, as first baseman, on 15 April 1947. (Roy Campanella followed Robinson with the Royals in 1947 before he too joined the Dodgers.) Some twenty years later a Canadian-born black player, **Ferguson ('Fergie') Jenkins** (b. 1943), began his spectacular climb to the top. From the late sixties to 1983 he was pitcher for the Texas Rangers, the Boston Red Sox, and the Chicago Cubs, pitching 284 wins, 3,192 strike-outs, and attaining a major-league record by a pitcher of 363 putouts. He won the Lou Marsh Trophy in 1974, was Canadian male athlete of the year four times, and was elected to the Canadian Baseball Hall of Fame in 1987.

In the early 1920s the Toronto Baseball Club wanted a new stadium on the mainland for the Maple Leafs, who were playing in the International League, and plans for a War Memorial Stadium on Fleet Street were drawn up in March 1922.[90] It was to be paid for by the city and the cost was estimated at $400,000, which was cut back to $150,000. It was an issue in the civic elections of 1 January 1923 and was voted down as being too expensive (the estimated cost had risen to $263,000). In 1924 the Toronto Harbour Commission, an agency of the federal government formed to develop harbour lands, asked for a grant of land on the same site—responding to renewed pressure from the Club for a stadium and considering that it would be a money-making proposition. Plans for a poured-concrete building were drawn up by Chapman, Oxley, and Bishop—the architects of several important Toronto buildings (including that of the Harbour Commission)—and the Maple Leaf Stadium opened on Fleet Street in 1926. Costing $300,000 and seating 17,500, it was the most up-to-date stadium in the minor leagues. In that first year 220,000 fans watched the Leafs play.

In the 1930s, however, baseball had a rocky history in Toronto.[91] The Stadium was not near public transport, and while the opening games were well attended, spectator interest declined in the summer. In 1931 the Club, which was responsible for taxes and rent, fell behind in payments and lost control of the Stadium to the Harbour Commission. The first night game, against Rochester, was on 28 June 1934, and did not begin until it was dark, which meant 10 o'clock, and because the floodlights seemed to slow the play down, it did not end until 1 a.m. The crowd was not pleased—though there was jubilation over Ike Boon's hitting a homer for the Leafs. The dismal record of the Leafs in the thirties ended with their taking last place. (Seven of its players and managers, however, were elected to the International League Hall of Fame.) But games continued during the war, in spite of the fact that most of the younger players were in the services.

The Leafs won their eighth League pennant in 1943 and there were many notable players in the forties: pitchers Luke 'Hot Potato' Hamlin, who retired at the end of the 1948 season with a 91–58 won-lost record, Burleigh Grimes, Nick 'Jumbo' Strincevich, Dick Conger, and Tom Ananicz; hitters Ed Sanicki and Bill Glynn; catchers Gene Desautels and Stan Lopata—and a great many more, some of whom graduated to the majors. During the war over a quarter of a million troops were allowed into the Stadium free, 'as guests of the Maple Leaf Baseball Club.'

The next decade has been called the Leafs' Fabulous Fifties because Jack Kent Cooke assumed ownership, and not only bought top-flight players but introduced innovations that grabbed the attention of post-

Maple Leaf Stadium, Toronto, 1922. (Courtesy the City of Toronto Archives.)

war Torontonians who wanted to be entertained. Sunday baseball was introduced. Fireworks, music, stunts, and entertainers drew huge crowds and the Leafs soared—in 1954 they won 97 games. The most valuable player that year was Elston Howard, whom Cooke had borrowed from the New York Yankees; he hit a homer in his first game. Among the large array of star players Cooke acquired were hitters Mike Goliat, Lew Morton, Rocky Nelson; pitchers Lynn Lovenguth, Don Johnson, and Eddie Blake; and catcher Andy Anderson. The Leafs won the pennant again in 1956 (8–7 against Rochester) when Ed Stevens scored the winning run and Hector Rodriguez made the winning hit.

The Leafs entered their final decade in the sixties. Cooke left Canada in 1961 and oversaw the team's activities, and the Club's losses, from California. No player captured public interest—players seemed to come and go without making names for themselves—and attendance at games decreased. In 1964 Cooke sold his interest in the Leafs to a group headed by Robert Lawson Hunter and Sam Starr, and a new organization, Toronto (Community) Baseball Ltd, evolved. This lasted only until 1967. On 4 September, when the Leafs played their final game, only 802 spectators watched them lose, 7–2, to Rochester. The end came at a meeting of the International League in Cleveland on 17 October 1967. The Club was sold and the Stadium was demolished the next February.

Cooke had longed to enter the major leagues but was discouraged by the high cost of doing so. A Canadian team did not accomplish this until 1969, and it happened not in Toronto but in Montreal, when a new team, the Montreal Expos, partly owned by Charles Bronfman, was admitted to the National League. The Expos played their first game on 9 April 1969 at New York's Shea Stadium, beating the Mets 11–10. On 14 April they played their first Montreal game in Parc Jarry, where Mack

Jones hit the first homer and they beat the St Louis Cardinals 8–7. They remained in Parc Jarry until 1977, the year they moved to the new 60,000 seat Olympic Stadium and achieved their first winning season. (The unpopular stadium—the Big O—made headlines because its cost hit the stratosphere: $1.2 billion.) The Expos quickly earned a huge following and sparked a revival of national interest in baseball. Between 1979 and 1983 they had the best overall winning percentages in the National League (.548) and in 1987 they finished only four games out of first place.

It took a while for Toronto to catch up with Montreal by acquiring a major-league team of its own. The Toronto Blue Jays—formed by Imperial Trust Ltd, Labatt's Breweries, and the Canadian Imperial Bank of Commerce—were admitted to the American League and began to play in Toronto's CNE Stadium, which was renovated for them, on a snowy day in April 1977. After a very slow start they had their first winning season in 1983, for a fourth-place finish, and have never looked back. The Blue Jays have boasted many winning players, including Dave Stieb, Alfredo Griffin, Lloyd Moseby, Willie Upshaw, and George Bell, who was named the League's most valuable player in 1987.

They played their first game in Toronto's new SkyDome on 5 June 1989 against Milwaukee, two days after the official opening of the stadium. Financed by private investors, the Province of Ontario, and Metropolitan Toronto, and costing more than $560 million ($319 million over the estimate of 1986), including $30.6 million for the giant video-screen scoreboard, the SkyDome has catapulted Toronto, and Canada—which had entered the major leagues of baseball so recently—into world-wide prominence as a provider of space-age facilities for the mass enjoyment of sport. The stadium—seating 52,000 for baseball, 54,000 for football, and up to 65,000 for concerts—is part of a huge complex that includes restaurants, a health club, a hotel, and a broadcast network. But above all its innovations—and, visibly, above the stadium itself—is its retractable roof, which almost miraculously realizes the sportslover's dream of being able to enjoy baseball and football out of doors while still receiving fairly speedy protection from inclement weather. (The plan for the retractable roof began to germinate on a cold fall day in 1982 at the CNE Stadium when Ontario Premier Bill Davis and Metro-Toronto Chairman Paul Godfrey—who had wanted a domed stadium in Toronto since 1969—were among the fans whose enthusiasm for the Grey Cup game was almost snuffed out by the freezing, drizzling weather.) Whatever its impact on Toronto will be—and it is thought that it will be immense— the SkyDome, considered in the context of Canadian sport history, surely stands as a monumental symbol of the end of one era and the beginning of another.

More than any other sport, baseball—which has been called America's national pastime—is firmly entrenched in the popular culture of both the United States and Canada. Examples are endless. The phrases 'striking out', 'dig in, 'home run', 'touching base', 'out in left field', 'two strikes against you', 'lead-off man', 'take a rain check', and 'throwing a curve' are among our everyday expressions. The song 'Take Me Out to the Ball Game', the mock-heroic poem *Casey at the Bat* (written in 1888 by Ernest Lawrence Thayer), and Abbott and Costello's skit 'Who's on First?' are known to almost everyone, at least by their titles. In theatre *The Umpire* of 1905 enjoyed a long run in Chicago, and *Damn Yankees* (1955)—based on the novel by Douglass Wallop, *The Year the Yankees Stole the Pennant*—is a classic American musical, and was filmed. Hollywood has apotheosized Lou Gehrig and Babe Ruth, and has recently produced *The Bingo Long Traveling All-Stars and Motor Kings*, about the black leagues of the 1930s, *Eight Men Out*, and *Bull Durham*. In literature the distinguished American novelist Bernard Malamud wrote *The Natural* (1952), which treats comically the mythic view of the American hero in terms of baseball. More recently a Canadian, William Kinsella, has celebrated baseball in his 1982 novel *Shoeless Joe* (on which the film *Field of Dreams* was based) and in collections of memorable short stories. In 'The Thrill of the Grass' he describes a community effort to replace artificial turf with sods of real grass during a baseball strike. 'What do you think about artificial turf?' the narrator asks a new acquaintance. 'Hmmmmf,' he snorts, 'that's what the strike should be about. Baseball is meant to be played on summer evenings and Sunday afternoons, on grass just cut by a horse-drawn mower.'

Nostalgia for the past seems to be part of baseball's mythology. Yesterday it was two teams with a ball and a bat playing on a wide stretch of grass in a village, on the sandlot of a town, or in a city park, half surrounded by spectators standing or sitting in bleachers.(Max Braithewaite's 'Why Girls Should Not Play Baseball' in *The Night We Stole the Mountie's Car* is a classic tribute to country baseball.) Today we have Montreal's Olympic Stadium, and Toronto's gigantic outdoor/indoor SkyDome—or our own livingroom, where we see virtually nothing but an electronic image of the plays themselves, as far removed as possible from the game played on grass, passionately observed by townsfolk on a summer evening.

In the long history of baseball in Canada, teams have formed and folded; leagues have been created and disbanded; American 'imports' (known at various times as 'baseball's foreign legions') have been lured to teams from Halifax to Victoria; local entrepreneurs have sponsored high-calibre teams; competitions have been played out in tournaments, challenges, and barnstorming tours; one intra-city competition has led to another and then another; the cycle of amateur teams leading to semi-professional teams leading to professional teams leading to the demise of professional teams and the resurgence of amateur teams—this un-ceasing ebb and flow has been at the core of the Canadian baseball experience and has simply proved that the game has an invincible hold on the public's affection. In 1989, when the games of the Expos and the Blue Jays reach millions on television, the popular interest in Canadian baseball has attained a height that could not have been imagined a hundred years ago—or even twenty years ago. This might raise the question: Will baseball maintain its strength and popularity, or will in-terest decline through over-exposure? Thinking of its unbroken though chequered nation-wide history, of Canada's two major-league teams, and of what has been called 'the perfect game'—with its potential for excitement and suspense, for the glorification of teams and of individual players in their demonstrations of power, precision, and speed—and even of the game's unlimited generation of statistics, which a true fan delights in memorizing, one cannot foresee any decline in interest. The setting may have changed in scale, but the game is the same, the skill simply increases.

But there is another ingredient that should not be overlooked. Baseball feats, and memories of games, lend themselves to fantasizing, as in Hugh Hood's story 'Ghosts at Jarry', and in many stories by Kinsella. In the introduction to his collection *The Thrill of the Grass*, Kinsella writes: 'I am often asked about the relationship of baseball and magic. I feel it is the timelessness of baseball which makes it more conducive to magical happenings than any other sport.' Baseball is unique among sports in its capacity to seize the imagination. This, above all else, ensures its longevity.

7
Football

Some form of a game in which two teams strive to move a round object past a goal line or into the opponent's goal area has been played since the days of ancient Greece. In the Middle Ages a kind of football game became popular in England. The modern history of the game begins in the early nineteenth century when it was played in English public schools such as Eton, Harrow, and Rugby. Two forms of football developed there. One was mainly a kicking game, later called association football (soccer), and the other was the game as it was played at Rugby, called rugby-football after the school. In 1823, according to legend, a Rugby student named William Webb Ellis picked up the ball and ran with it, contrary to the accepted rules. This style of play, and tackling the ball-carrier, changed the game forever. Later an oval ball was introduced because it was easier to carry than a round one. On 28 August 1845 the school codified thirty-seven 'Laws of Football played at Rugby School',[1] beginning:

> i. FAIR CATCH, is a catch direct from the foot.
> ii. OFF SIDE. A player is off his side if the ball has touched one of his own side behind him, until the other side touch it.

Rugby School is the setting of the famous boy's book *Tom Brown's School Days* (1857) by Thomas Hughes, 'An Old Boy'. Tom first heard about the game of football as played at Rugby from his new friend East:

> '. . . I love football so, and have played all my life. Won't Brooke let me play?'
> 'Not he,' said East, with some indignation; 'why, you don't know the rules—you'll be a month learning them. And then it's no joke playing up in a match, I can tell you. Quite another thing from your private school games. Why, there's been two collar-bones broken this half, and a dozen fellows lamed. And last year a fellow had his leg broken.'
> Tom listened with the profoundest respect to this chapter of accidents, and followed East across the level ground till they came to a sort of gigantic gallows of two poles eighteen feet high, fixed upright in the ground some fourteen feet apart, with a cross bar running from one to the other at the height of ten feet or thereabouts.

'This is one of the goals,' said East, 'and you see the other, across there, right opposite, under the Doctor's wall. Well, the match is for the best of three goals; whichever side kicks two goals wins: and it won't do, you see, just to kick the ball through these posts, it must go over the cross bar; any height'll do, so long as it's between the posts. You'll have to stay in goal to touch the ball when it rolls behind the posts, because if the other side touch it they have a try at goal. Then we fellows in quarters, we play just about in front of goal here, and have to turn the ball and kick it back, before the big fellows on the other side can follow it up. And in front of us all the big fellows play, and that's where the scrummages are mostly.'

Tom's respect increased as he struggled to make out his friend's technicalities, and the other set to work to explain the mysteries of 'off your side,' 'drop-kicks,' 'punts,' 'places,' and the other intricacies of the great science of football.'[2]

The boys played rough. The game of rugby-football was described as a hooligan's game played by gentlemen (while soccer was described as a gentlemen's game played by hooligans). Still, they never forgot that they were gentlemen by wearing white trousers, even in November—to Tom's amazement. (The snobbish East explained that this was 'to show 'em we don't care for hacks [non-gentlemen]'.) The Rugby sweater had a collar to shade the neck from the sun, and the trousers had pockets, for a gentleman would never be without a handkerchief!

Graduates of the school—who became civil servants, military officers, and teachers—spread the game to the colonies. By the 1860s it was being played in Canada, particularly in Montreal—by the Montreal Football Club, founded in 1868, by members of the garrison, and at McGill University. McGill developed its own rules and codified them in 1874. They were a hybrid form of those that had been codified and standardized by the newly formed Rugby-Football Union in England in 1871:

1. Each goal shall consist of two upright posts, sixteen feet high and fifteen feet apart, with a cross bar at a distance of ten feet from the ground. The maximum length of the ground shall be 180 yards, the maximum breadth shall be 75 yards.
2. The number of players on each side shall be not more than twenty or not less than ten. The definite number to be settled by the captains before each match.
3. The winner of the toss shall have the option of kick off or choice of goals. The game shall be commenced by a place kick from the center of the ground and the opposite side shall not come within ten yards of the ball.
4. The ball shall be kicked off

  (i) at the commencement of the game;
  (ii) after a goal has been obtained; or
  (iii) at the end of each half hour.

5. After a goal is won, ends shall be changed, and the losing side shall kick off. In the event, however, of no goal having fallen to either side at the lapse of half an hour, ends shall then be changed.

6. The ball may be caught on the bounce and carried; the player so carrying the ball may be 'tackled' or 'shouldered', but not hacked, throttled or pummelled. No player may be held unless in actual possession of the ball.

7. In the event of any player holding or running with the ball being tackled, and the ball fairly held, he may at once cry 'have it down'; he shall be allowed to place it on the ground unmolested: but he need not do so until his own side comes up.

8. A goal can only be obtained by kicking the ball from the field of play direct (i.e, without touching the dress or person of any player of either side) over the cross-bar of the opponents' goal, whether it touches such cross-bar or the posts or not; but if the ball goes directly over either of the goal posts, it is called a 'poster' and is not a goal. A goal may be obtained by any kind of kick except a 'punt'.

9. A match shall last for three half-hours. It shall be decided by the majority of goals, or in the event of no goals being obtained, by the majority of touch-downs; three touch-downs counting as one goal.

10. Every player is on side, but is put off-side if he enters a scrummage from his opponents' side, or being in a scrummage, gets in front of the ball, or when the ball has been kicked, touched, or is being run with by any of his own side behind him (i.e., between him and his goal line). Every player, when off-side, is out of the game and shall not touch the ball in any case whatever, or any way interrupt or obstruct any player, until he is again on side.

11. A player being off-side is put on-side when the ball has been kicked or touched the dress or person of any player of the opposite side, or when one of his own side has run in front of him either with the ball or having kicked it when behind him.

12. It is lawful for any player who has the ball to throw it back towards his own goal, or to pass it back to any player of his own side who is at the time behind him, in accordance with the rules of on-side.

13. If a ball goes into touch, the first player, on his side, who touches it down must bring it to the spot where it crossed the touch line; or if a player, when running with the ball, cross or put any part of his foot across the touch line, he must return the ball to the spot where the line was so crossed, and then either:
  (i) bound the ball in the field of play, and then run with it, kick it or throw it back to his own side;
   or

(ii) throw it out at right angles to the touch line.

14. The goal line is in goal, and the touch line is in touch.
15. If the ball be sent beyond the side-bounds and yet behind the goal line, it shall be touched down and thrown in from the corner in a diagonal direction by whoever touches it down.
16. It is not lawful to take the ball from off the ground for any purpose whatever, unless it be in touch.
17. No hacking, or hacking over, or tripping up shall be allowed under any circumstances. No one wearing projecting nails, iron plantes, or gutta percha on any part of his boots or shoes, shall be allowed to play in a match.
18. In any case of distinct and wilful violation of these Rules of Play, a free kick shall be forfeited to the opposite side from the spot where the infringment took place, but in no case shall a goal be scored from such a free kick.
19. Continued transgression of rules by any player, the side to which he belongs shall loose him.
20. All disputes to be settled by the Umpires, whose decision shall be final.

Definition of terms
1. A drop kick is made by letting the ball fall from the hands and kicking it the very instant it rises.
2. A place kick is made by kicking the ball after it has been placed in a nick made in the ground for the purpose of keeping it at rest.
3. A punt is made by letting the ball from the hands and kicking it before it touches the ground.[3]

In 1874 the captain of the McGill team, David Rodgers, challenged Harvard University to two games—one to be in Cambridge, Mass., the other in Montreal—and Harvard accepted. The game played at Harvard in May turned out to be two games. When the McGill team arrived in Cambridge and began to practise, the bewildered Harvard hosts asked what game they were playing. Harvard's was the kicking, or soccer, variety. The two sides compromised, agreeing to play each of the two games under the other's rules. The game of 14 May, played under American rules, ended in a 3–0 victory for Harvard; the contest of 15 May, played under McGill rules, but with a round ball, was a 0–0 tie. The Canadians' oval ball was lost and never used, but their game made a good impression. The editor of the Harvard *Magenta* thought it much better 'than the somewhat sleepy game now played by our men.'[4] In October Harvard returned the visit—and won again, playing by the McGill rules. After sending to Rugby School for a copy of the approved

A Notman composite of the McGill-Harvard football match, 12 November 1875. (Notman Photographic Archives, 21493-II, courtesy the McCord Museum of McGill University.)

rules, Harvard began playing this game and introduced it to other universities in the northeastern states. There it soon displaced the old version and evolved into the American football of today.

The sport quickly spread in Canada. The Toronto Argonauts formed in 1874, followed by the Winnipeg Rugby Football Club in 1880, and the Ottawa Rough Riders and the Hamilton Tigers in 1883. Leagues came into being to oversee the teams' activities: the Quebec Rugby Football Union and the Canadian Rugby Football Union in 1882, and in 1883 the Ontario Rugby Football Union, made up of the Toronto Rugby Club, the Toronto Argonauts, and the clubs of the University of Toronto, Upper Canada College, and Trinity College (Port Hope).

It soon became apparent that two opposing views were in a conflict that would continue for some years. How close should the game remain to its British roots? How much should it reflect the innovative developments of the American game? By 1882 the traditional English scrummage (the unpredictable method of putting the ball into play) was removed. The Americans had adopted the 'snapback' system, where the centre handed back the ball through his legs to a team-mate directly behind him. They wanted more control over the flow of play; there was too much uncertainty in the scrum and not enough opportunity for 'scientific' tactics. The Canadian Rugby Union wasn't prepared to go so far.

Theirs was a compromise rule that allowed for more strategy, but also some unpredictability because of the 'heeling out' of the oval ball.

> Our system of scrimmaging then, consists in a centre man with a man on either side of him. When one side has possession of the ball, it is given to the centre who, putting the ball down in front of him, together with his confreres, endeavors to keep the opposing scrimmage in check and at the same time, heel the ball back to the quarter; the object of the other scrimmage being to prevent this by either kicking the ball through and following it up or pushing their opponents to their knees.[5]

This revision of the rules, which guaranteed that one side would keep possession of the ball, was by far the most radical change ever introduced into Canadian football. As a team could retain possession indefinitely, much of the spontaneity of the game was removed.

The set-up for a snap (Edmonton Eskimos, c. 1919), showing the two scrim supports for the centre with the quarterback. (Courtesy Frank Cosentino.)

Some teams, particularly in Ontario, approached the new style with enthusiasm; others, mainly those of Quebec, refused to change. It soon became impossible for teams from Quebec to meet with teams from Ontario. With the rugby-football scene in turmoil, the Canadian Rugby Football Union disbanded and re-organized under the same name on 19 December 1891 in an effort to ensure competition between the two provincial unions. The new rules were basically those of the Ontario Union: there were fifteen to a side; a game consisted of two 45-minute halves, a foul was called when a player threw or knocked the ball forward—it could only be passed to a player behind the ball. It was also illegal to tackle a player below the knees, which removed the spontaneity of the game by stopping the play to allow a scrummage to occur. There was no specification about the size of the ball. This did not come until 1906 when a 'legal' football was described to be '11 inches in length, 23 inches in circumference of width and 13 3/4 oz. in weight (Spalding or Wilson make).'[6]

The English system of awarding the game on the basis of goals and tries was put aside in favour of a point system previously adopted by the ORFU in 1891:

> A match shall be decided by a majority of points. A goal kicked from a try shall be 6 points; from a drop kick 5 points; from a flying or free kick, 4; a try shall score 4, a safety touch 2 and a rouge 1.[7]

It is interesting to note that the only point values that are still the same in Canadian football are the safety touch (2 points) and the rouge (1 point). The safety touch was included to penalize the conceding team for taking the ball from the playing field into its own end zone or goal area under its own momentum, in order to maintain possession. The origin of the term rouge (French for 'red') is unknown, but it could mean that a team was embarrassed at having been caught in its own goal area, unable to advance the ball before being downed. (The word seems to have been used in English rugby to describe that same situation.) In a scoreless or tie game, the number of times a team was caught in its own goal area was recorded and the side having been caught the fewest times was declared the winner (e.g., if it was necessary to declare a winner in a championship game). The Canadian Union decided to award one point to the opposing team each time it downed the other team in its goal area.

In addition to the safety touch as a means of providing scoring opportunities to both sides, the first attempt to ensure a turnover of the ball came in 1897. 'If in three consecutive downs, unless the ball crosses the goal line, a team shall not have advanced the ball 5 yards or taken it back 20 yards, it [the ball] shall go to the opponents on the spot of the fourth down.'[8]

In 1898 universities in Ontario and Quebec—which had previously belonged to their provincial union—formed their own league, the Canadian Intercollegiate Rugby Football Union, to compete for the Yates Cup, a trophy that is still awarded to the Ontario/Quebec champion. While it signified the further spread of football, it also meant that still more variations of the rules were introduced. 'National' championships were becoming more difficult since the CRU tended to alternate rules from year to year according to those of one of the Unions. This would usually mean that one of the two competing teams for a Canadian title would be handicapped by having to observe relatively unfamiliar rules. When yet another Union, the Interprovincial Rugby Football Union, came into existence in 1907, the problem was now compounded. Known colloquially as the 'Big Four', the IRFU included the two best teams from the Quebec Union, Montreal and Ottawa, and the two best from Ontario, the Toronto Argonuts and the Hamilton Tigers. These losses virtually destroyed the Quebec Union and severely weakened the Ontario Union, but strengthened the power of the CRU, since the new league agreed to abide by CRU rules. The Intercollegiate, however, decided to continue with its own variations, much as it does even today.

Generally speaking, then, by 1909 the game of Canadian rugby-football was neither rugby in the traditional sense nor football in the modern.[9] There were 14 players; the ball was heeled out; no interference was allowed. There was no forward passing. It was a sport developing its own approach, somewhat removed from its British roots but consistently emulating the American—the typical Canadian compromise.

There were two main proponents of football: the city teams and the universities, which viewed sport as a function of education. This concept was endorsed in 1909 in the Toronto *Globe*:

> Rugby is too tough a game. How often the followers of the gridiron hear comments like this about the game—'it's too rough', and 'it isn't good for them.' Of course if fond mommas want their youthful pride and hope to grow like a banana plant in a green house, there is little sense in arguing the point. The game is too rough for molley coddles. On the contrary, if the boy is to be taught to fight his way in the great battle of life, there is no game that will teach him how in a better way. He'll get plenty of knocks and raise many a crop of healthy bruises but he gains stamina and the knocks he gets, if he is an ordinary cuss, in later life, will be equally as hard.[10]

One reason the university union was formed 'was to influence more effectively the spirit and practice of the game and to check a seeming tendency towards professionalism.'[11] The city teams were constantly being accused of offering gifts of money or other inducements. Amateurism, although weakening, was still the officially approved *raison d'être* of sport. Nevertheless the university teams of Toronto, McGill, and Queen's challenged city teams for the Grey Cup. Indeed, from 1909 to 1924 they established their pre-eminence as the superior football league in the country.

Whether because of their love of sport, acquired in English public schools, or their belief that it could help to unify a young nation—or a combination of both—Governors General of Canada have sponsored various trophies to mark supremacy in sport: the Connaught Cup for soccer, the Minto Cup for lacrosse, the Stanley Cup for hockey. Canadian football has two such trophies: the Earl Grey Cup, donated by Lord Grey in 1909 for the Dominion championship, and the Vanier Cup, donated by Georges Vanier for inter-university supremacy. Three trustees were appointed to draw up rules for the Grey Cup: H.B. McGiverin, MP for Ottawa; Percival Molson of the National Trust Company of Montreal; and the Rev. D.M. Macdonald, rector of St Andrew's College, Toronto. In the beginning it was clearly understood that 'the Cup must *remain always* under purely amateur conditions.'[12] This objective was maintained, however, only until 1921, when the trustees turned the trophy over to the Canadian Rugby Union. In 1966 the CRU gave its administration over to the Canadian Football League, at which time the Cup was competed for only by professional teams—members of the CFL. The CRU then became the Canadian Amateur Football Association.

The University of Toronto won the Grey Cup in three consecutive years, from 1909 to 1911. Under 'honorary coach' Harry Griffiths, who taught French at Trinity College (professional coaches, those hired specifically for that purpose, were frowned upon at the time), the U of T team defeated representatives of both other leagues and were led by their outstanding runner, Smirle Lawson, the first to be known to the Canadian public as 'the Big Train'. (Later the sobriquet would be given to Lionel Conacher, a leading football player in the early 1920s, when he became even more famous in hockey.) 'Lawson's equal has never been seen,' the *Globe* enthused. 'Stick him with Yale or Harvard and Americans would never cease talking of the great plunging back.'[13]

Even in those early years the Grey Cup competition aroused enormous interest. For the 1910 game, played in Hamilton between the Tigers and the University of Toronto,

Varsity's 'Big Train', Smirle Lawson, hurdling McGill tacklers in 1909.

. . . as early as six p.m. Monday, boys and old men began to gather in front of Stanley Mills' store and before midnight the line extended down Hughson St. Camp stools, biscuit boxes and orange crates were used as seats and the big gathering passed the cold dreary night as best they could, cracking jokes and comforted by the hope that when morning came, they would be well rewarded. Some late arrivals paid as much as $2.00 for a place in line to secure a 50 cent bleacher seat. Grandstand tickets brought $5.00 during the morning and some who were very anxious to witness the game paid as much as $15.00 a pair.[14]

Twelve thousand is listed as the official attendance at the game, won by Toronto 16–7, but

. . . other thousands were outside the enclosure trying to get in. They rushed the fences only to be driven back by mounted police until by sheer force of numbers they overcame the officers and joined the cheering throng inside.[15]

Again in 1911 the University of Toronto repeated as Grey Cup champions, this time defeating the Toronto Argonauts by a 14–7 score before some 15,000 spectators—4,000 over the capacity of the newly built Varsity Stadium. McGill, however, began to take centre-stage as a football power with the arrival of Frank 'Shag' Shaughnessy as their coach. A native of Amboy, Illinois, he attended Notre Dame University, earning a degree in pharmacy and later a law degree. He coached at Clemson University, South Carolina, and made his way north to Canada to coach the Ottawa entry in the Canadian Baseball League. In 1912 he agreed to coach the McGill football team, but only if he was given complete control—university faculty and alumnae could not interfere in team operations as they had done formerly.

One of Shaughnessy's first acts as coach seemed designed to show everybody associated with the team that he did indeed have complete control. Eric Billington, the star kicker of the McGill team, had gone to Brighton, England, for a visit, and was due to return to Montreal on 5 October, the same day that McGill was to play the University of Toronto in the first game of the season. Shaughnessy sent him a blunt ultimatum by cable, saying that only those who were fit and had practised with the team could play.[16] Billington returned early.

Knowledgeable, thorough, and well prepared for eventualities, Shaughnessy can be considered the first truly 'professional' coach in Canadian football history. He established a 'training table'—providing free meals after every practice—for his players, left for 'away' games up to two days early so the team would be rested after the long train ride, and mastered the rules so as to design a system that would exploit all the options available. McGill dethroned Varsity (University of Toronto) in a play-off game in November 1912. But surprisingly they declined to proceed further towards the Grey Cup. The overwhelming favourites, the best team in the country, proceeded to draft a resolution, which they presented to the 'faculty, governors, graduates, undergraduates and supporters of Old McGill':

> In view of the fact that our examinations are fast approaching, we do not deem it advisable to prolong further an already lengthened football season, which has cost us considerable sacrifice in respect to our academic work. We trust that our position is appreciated by all.[17]

The next year, 1913, McGill were intercollegiate champions and once again they declined to proceed to the Grey Cup, this time citing the 'professionalism' in the Interprovincial Union. The Toronto Argonauts won their first Grey Cup in 1914. They were able to keep it through the war years because there were no games, but they lost it to the University of Toronto in 1920 when the Great War was over.

With the end of the war a number of changes occurred in football. There was no question that there was still great enthusiasm for the game. Nearly 15,000 witnessed the 1920 renewal of the Grey Cup at Varsity

Stadium—between Varsity and the Argonauts (Varsity won). There were several exciting developments: a new rules committee of the CRU had been struck, its composition bypassing traditional 'nabobs' of sport such as Harry Griffiths and W.A. Hewitt, sports editor of the *Toronto Daily Star*. Younger men, all of whom had been active as players in recent years, were selected in their stead. As well, in March 1921 the West served notice that it 'would send its champion east to play for the Grey Cup.'[18]

East Meets West. Football had been organized in central Canada, the most populous area of the country—referred to vaguely and sometimes resentfully by westerners as 'the East'—and Manitoba had only an honorary membership in the CRU, which was given in 1892. It was not until 1911, six years after the provinces of Saskatchewan and Alberta were created, that the Western Canada Rugby Football Union was formed, composed of unions from the three Prairie Provinces. The Hugo Ross Trophy was donated as the award to be competed for in the West, and the first winners were the Calgary Tigers. When the WCRU, full of confidence, applied to compete for the Grey Cup in 1912, they were told that only those who joined the CRU at an Annual Meeting could challenge. When the West duly made a second application after joining the CRU at the General Meeting in January 1912, the CRU minutes discouragingly stated:

> . . . that in view of the many difficulties in playing final games owing to the great distances that intervene, the application of the WCRU for admission to the CRU be not entertained, but that the WCRU be admitted to honorary membership in the CRU—carried unanimously.[19]

By 1921 distances did not seem so great and all obstacles had disappeared: the West would compete for the Cup and play by the revised rules. The new rules committee of the CRU moved farther from the British game and closer to the American. The main features were:

1. Twelve men to a side.
2. Snap back instead of scrimmage.
3. Quarterback may carry ball beyond the line of scrimmage.
4. At least five men of the attacking team on line of scrimmage when ball is put into play.
5. Substitutes allowed at any time, and no more than 18 players of one team shall take part in any one game.
6. Only ten men allowed on a 'buck' until play is through line of scrimmage.
7. Unearned try abolished. A scoring as before: 5 for a try, 1 for a convert, rouge or a touch in goal, and 2 for a safety touch.[20]

As if to ensure some measure of uniformity of interpretation of the rules, the CRU issued five separate bulletins to each Union, outlining approved rulings and interpretations. In addition, the Hamilton Tigers in September 1921 were sent on a western tour to acquaint the Westerners with the Eastern style of play. It was a resounding success. In Edmonton the prospect of their visit filled one writer with pride:

> The fact that they are coming shows that Edmonton is getting to be a centre of importance. Big enough to attract the best in anything. Four thousand people should be at the game on Thursday. Think of it, a game of Rugby against the best team in Canada, that has travelled three thousand miles! Rugby is the great game in the east and in the United States in the fall. It draws bigger crowds than any other game played. It is a game that cannot be played every day—too strenuous. It compares favorably with the old gladiatorial combats in the Flavian Amphitheatre in Rome. A rugby fan in a rugby country is lucky if he sees four or five big contests in one season. The best that one can see in Edmonton will be three more games after the Hamilton one.[21]

The first Grey Cup meeting between East and West took place in Toronto a few months later, on 3 December 1921, before more than 9,000 spectators. The Edmonton Eskimos, undefeated that year, represented the West; the Toronto Argonauts the East. The game was an interesting contrast in styles. The Argonauts played the traditional 'single-wing' alignment, featuring extension plays and end-runs; the westerners, with their 'American tactics', played an early version of the T-formation, the quarterback handing the ball to one of his running backs who was plunging directly into the line of scrimmage in an effort to gain yardage or a touchdown.

It was the Argonauts who prevailed, as much because of Harry 'Red' Batstone and Lionel Conacher as their style of play. Deacon White, the American coach of the Edmonton team, was generous in his praise of Batstone and Conacher, who were a joy to watch:

> We could not successfully stop their end runs which were a spectacular and marvelous exhibition of skillful passing and handling the ball. It was the acme of perfection in this art, each man getting rid of the ball at the psychological moment almost uncannily. It is a beautiful style of play to watch and one can well understand the public's interest in rugby here when it is treated to such displays.[22]

Conacher, the new 'big train', scored fifteen points on two touchdowns, a drop-kick field goal, and two single points. As far as White was concerned,

the teams would have been evenly matched had Conacher not been playing with the Argos. Say, he is a running fool—not tricky but just runs like
hell. He weighs about ten off two hundred and is six feet two inches-legs
on him like an ox. If he can't get past a man he charges him. He made
several forty and fifty yard runs, and booted the ball on a similar average.[23]

All Conacher's points came during the first three quarters of the game.
In what seems an incredible display of virtuosity, Conacher actually left
the Grey Cup match before it was over in order to play an important
hockey game with his Aura Lee teammates against the Toronto Granites!

While Conacher moved into hockey and a variety of other sports—in
1950 he was selected as Canada's outstanding athlete of the first half-
century—Batstone enrolled at Queen's University, where, along with
Frank 'Pep' Leadley, he led its team to the Grey Cup championship in
three successive years. Indeed, the feeling was prevalent that the best
football in the country was being played in the East. In 1922 a playoff
game between the Argonauts and Queen's attracted more than 16,000
spectators; the Grey Cup game that same year between Queen's and
Edmonton, in 1922 known as the Elks, drew fewer than 5,000. Queen's
won in 1923 against a new representative from the West, the Regina
Roughriders (the score was 54–0!), and in 1924 against the Toronto Balmy
Beach Club.

It was not until 1935 that the West won a Grey Cup championship,
the Winnipeg Blue Bombers defeating the Hamilton Tigers 18–12. Much
of the credit for the victory was given to a fleet North Dakotan, Fritzie
Hanson, one of nine Americans with the Winnipeg team. Unfortunately,
it was the East the next year (Sarnia), though the Blue Bombers reclaimed
the Cup in 1939 and many times later. 'Out where the Grey Cup is come
to stay,/ That's where the West begins,'[24] ran some doggerel.

American Influences

. . .the West is moving ahead rapidly with its football. We're swinging
more to the American code each year and the customers are with us. Our
season is much shorter than in the East and we're just about fed up with
efforts to keep pace with the authority flaunted over us by the Canadian
Rugby Union.[25]

Little by little western teams were giving in to American influences.
Many of them used American players, who disdained the English name
rugby for their game of football. They also introduced the forward pass,
the American play that greatly opened up the game. It had been used
in the Grey Cup game of 1929 but not in 1930, since the governing body

of the CRU decided that it could be used only if it had been part of the playing rules in both East and West that year; since it had not been used in the East, it was not allowed. In 1931, however, the CRU declared that the forward pass would be incorporated into its playing schedule—and the traditional Canadian game was changed forever. The general feeling was that all teams would start off and improve at the same level as teams become more proficient in the change in tactics. Frank Shaughnessy felt that as Canadians were not familiar with the forward pass it would only be a matter of time before they became adept at it through trial and error.

He was fortunate in having access to an American player, Warren Stevens, who knew the value of the pass as an offensive weapon. A graduate in science of Syracuse University, where he was an all-round athlete, Stevens was attending McGill as a graduate student. He chose McGill because he wanted to have a better grasp of the game of hockey, which he considered to be the sport of the future. While there, however, he was asked to instruct the McGill players in the forward pass; Shaughnessy also introduced him to Clary Foran, coach of the Montreal Amateur Athletic Association team known as the 'Winged Wheelers'. Stevens was offered 'a job with an oil company and a Christmas present of $100' to quarterback the MAAA.[26] He accepted and proceeded to lead them to an undefeated season and the Grey Cup of 1931.

The forward pass affected Canadian football at its very roots. To some of the players, 'the way football was played that year, it seemed like you needed roller skates to play the game.'[27] Morale was broken. After ten or fifteen plays of marching the ball downfield, a team felt immense satisfaction in the resulting 1, 3, or 5 points—only to have Stevens gain the same yardage in one pass! Journalists were upset with Montreal and the CRU. In Winnipeg a fourth A was added to the MAAA abbreviation when it was called the Montreal Almost Amateur Athletic Association.[28]

In Hamilton, where the forward pass was nullifying the specialty of the Tigers—the powerful running advances made by 'the old man of the mountain', Brian Timmis, and by Dave Sprague—the *Herald* referred angrily in 1931 to the time when 'the Canadian Rugby Football Union turned yankee and accepted the forward pass into the Canadian game . . . .'[29] Harry Griffiths, the former University of Toronto coach and a conservative, was in favour of the *status quo*, fearing that amateurism would lose its hold on football with the introduction of the forward pass and the changes that would follow. He foresaw interference of 10 and 15 yards being added, and the need for tactical training that amateur teams did not have the time to learn or the resources to supply. 'Keep this a Canadian game,' he was quoted as saying. 'Let us call a moratorium on rule changes for ten years.'[30] But out west there was no such lament. Al Ritchie, a coach of the Roughriders, was quite happy with the rule and was convinced that the CRU had acted logically:

> We are living in an age of speed. There is a wave passing over the world demanding speed and action. The inclusion of the forward pass in Canadian football is not only a progressive step in keeping with this development, but it will provide a more fascinating game for spectators and players alike.[31]

This approach to Canadian football could not resist change—not only because of the forward pass, but also because of the Depression, and the attraction of the Grey Cup. The American seed had been planted and was seen by some as bearing valuable fruit, such as an American quarterback. And if he could make such a difference, what could a team not do with Americans at other key positions?

In the East, Sarnia, an oil centre, suddenly became a football power by virtue of its being able to attract football talent—especially Americans—with jobs. Sarnia won the Grey Cup in 1934 and 1936. Teams in Regina and Winnipeg were also hiring Americans. In 1932, 4,000 spectators paid a dollar for reserved seats and fifty cents for standing-room to watch the Regina Roughriders play the Winnipeg St John's. Regina won by a 9–1 score, but post-game discussion was heard 'that the Regina amateurs [i.e. Canadians] were better than the Winnipeg amateurs, and the Regina Americans were better than the Winnipeg Americans.'[32]

On the whole, the West took the initiative in becoming 'Americanized', and there were some good reasons. For example, in Winnipeg there was no league in which to play, and a schedule of exhibition games was drawn up with American colleges in Minnesota and the Dakotas. These games prepared Winnipeg for playoffs with Saskatchewan and Alberta in which they invariably earned the right to represent the West in the Grey Cup. Just as important, the games decreased resistance to rule changes, while incidentally providing valuable information on prospective American players. In 1935 the general manager of the Winnipeg team, Joe Ryan, journeyed into the 'Swede Belt' of the northern states and returned with seven American players. Added to the two Winnipeg already had on its roster of twenty, the nine were paid a total of $7400 and were much responsible for the West's first Grey Cup victory in 1935.[33] They won again in 1939 under the name Blue Bombers, given to them by sports writers at a time when Joe Louis was celebrated as the 'brown bomber'.

While such successes made for great joy in Winnipeg and the West, there was consternation elsewhere. It was alleged that Canadian players were being overlooked because of the 'trafficking of US stars'.[34] A movement to restrict the number of Americans first manifested itself through residence rules imposed by the CRU (players were to have lived in the community where they played from a certain date), and later through specific limiting legislation. As the game was still considered 'amateur', authorities steeped in that tradition saw Americanization as an 'imported' movement brought in from outside, rather than emerging from within. Feelings ran high, with western leagues either being barred or resigning from the Canadian governing body. At the time of the Second World War, the future of football and its traditional role in the country was in jeopardy.

Post-war Transition. Football clubs did not immediately renounce their amateur status; they simply chose to ignore it. Nor did they openly embrace professionalism in the years directly following the war. At the annual meeting of the CRU, on 23 February 1946, the residence rule that had been in effect since 1936 was abolished. Interference of ten yards was permitted for all linemen and five Americans would be allowed on each team. The changes were largely due to the initiative of Joe Ryan, who had moved from Winnipeg to become a shareholder and part-owner of the new Montreal team, the Alouettes. The irony of the situation did not escape all observers. Jim Coleman, writing in the *Globe and Mail*, satirized the situation:

> Ryan cleared his voice and said: 'Gentlemen! I move that we permit linemen to block 10 yards past the line of scrimmage.'
> 'Agreed! Capital! Splendid! Sensational!' yelped the members of the Old Guard, passing the resolution without a dissenting whinny. 'Didn't those dastards from the West propose such a course 10 years ago?' asked Phineas, uncomfortably. 'Oh yes, but they were just trying to cause trouble,' replied Doc Cascara. 'This proposal comes from Montreal and obviously it is the result of mature consideration and will be of inestimable benefit to the game.'
> Holding his old school tie right out in front of him, Ryan said: 'And now I propose that we should permit any team to import five United States players. I propose that this rule should remain in effect for two years.'
> 'Agreed! Agreed! Splendid! Sensational! Epochal!' thundered the delegates. 'Didn't those dastards from the West want to import players from the United States a few years ago and didn't we find it necessary to clamp down on them?' asked Phineas. 'Yas, Yas,' replied the Doc, 'but this proposal comes from Montreal, which after all is ALMOST in Eastern Canada—after all it's only a few miles from the Ontario boundary'.[35]

Not all clubs rushed to import players. The Toronto Argonauts stead-fastly refused to do so—and won three consecutive Grey Cups in 1945–7. Once again, however, a team from the West provided the pattern for success. The Calgary Stampeders of 1948, under its American coach Les Lear, sought *former* American professionals, while other teams were still hiring younger players from small American colleges. Not only did the Stampeders win twelve games consecutively; they won the two-game total-point series with Regina, and the Grey Cup, with a 12–7 victory over Ottawa. If Calgary's Alberta neighbours in Edmonton had made the Grey Cup 'national' in 1921, Calgary had turned it into a 'celebration'. The Grey Cup would never be the same again. In the words of Douglas MacFarlane of the *Globe and Mail*:

> As a spectacle, this Canadian football championship affair had all the colors of the spectrum. It had the gaudiest build-up cowboys and Indians, cops and robbers, the football teams could produce. The Stampeders with their ponies, their chuck wagons,their Indian chief cheerleader, their flapjacks and their western brand of enthusiasm, had taken over the town long before game time. . . All Saturday morning, the cowboys paraded at the drop of a tuba note. They finally wound up at City Hall, fried some flaps for some Jacks, gave a guy by the name of Hiram (Toronto Mayor Hiram McCallum) a ride on their ponies and headed for the stadium. It was quite a piece of mobile vaudeville by the time it hit Bloor Street. One prairie schooner even had a little prairie schooner tagging along behind. There were wagons and trucks and cars and dogies and on them all were people, most of them peculiarly dressed in great big hats and great big boots and all of them shouting great big boasts. [36]

By 1956, while teams officially considered themselves amateur, most—indeed all the best ones—paid their players generously. Those that could not match these payments withdrew from Grey Cup competition or disappeared. On the other hand a new team, the Vancouver Lions, was formed in 1954 and joined the Western Inerprovincial Football League. At least three Canadian teams—the Argonauts, the Ottawa Rough Riders, and the Lions—were so aggressive in their search for players, stealing them away from American teams with better contracts, that relations between Canadian football and the National Football League in the U.S. were strained, to say the least.

Television entered the world of football at the Grey Cup game of 1952. Images of fiercely fought games thereafter became ingrained in the public consciousness. Anyone with access to a TV set could see such games as the 1953 Grey Cup, which Ted Reeve called 'one of the greatest games in Grey Cup history'. This was the game in which Winnipeg quarterback

Jack Jacobs, in the dying moments of the game, passed the ball to Tom Casey (to tie the game), but Hamilton's Lou Kusserrow and the ball arrived simultaneously. Kusserow hit Casey from behind, he lost the ball, and Hamilton's win was preserved. (Followers of Winnipeg were convinced that Kusserow arrived too early and should have been penalized for interference; Hamilton supporters lauded 'Columbia Lou' for his great play.) In his column 'Sporting Extras' in the *Toronto Telegram*, Reeve went on to describe other moments in the game:

> Etched in the memory, though, of this strife will be three clearly defined pictures . . . .
> Firstly, that number 62 jersey [Dick] Huffman, moving around in the manner usually reserved for kodiak bears. Piling up interference, leading his ball carriers knocking down the plays that were coming his way and then sliding to the other side to overtake the traffic that was going that direction.
> Two . . . that last march of the Bombers . . . as the roar started to roll down from the crowd and the cold wind cut across the waning sunshine. The huddle, the quick precision march step of those huge men in the deep navy blue, up to the formation . . . the tall Indian [Jack Jacobs] just back of them and his fast four movers crouched for action. Another first down and the clash doming to a crescendo
> Finally . . . a gladiator . . . a man named [Vince] Mazza . . . picking himself from the end of the bench . . . shaking off a season of bruises and aches . . . they point him in the right direction, the wonderful big stiff trundles into position and a tattered battalion came up to give us a finish that the Iron Duke would have cherished.[37]

Another memorable image on countless television screens across the country was the sight of Jackie Parker, of the underdog Edmonton Eskimos, scooping up a loose 'fumble' from Montreal's Chuck Hunsinger and racing 95 yards, out-running the last man in a position to tackle him, Sam Etcheverry, to score the tying points. That overshadowed a courageous and dramatic point after touchdown. Eagle Keys, the Edmonton centre, limped onto the playing field with a hairline fracture of the tibia to snap the ball for the all-important convert kicked by Bob Dean. It was the first of three consecutive Grey Cup victories (1954, 1955, 1956) by Edmonton over the Alouettes.

Towards a CFL. Buoyed by a record attendance of 30,417 and receipts of $315,000 at the 1955 Grey Cup game, the two dominant leagues, the 'Big Four' and the WIFL, assumed a measure of unity in 1956 with the formation of the Canadian Football Council, which was renamed the

Canadian Football League (CFL) in 1958. It was like a governing body for the two leagues, a loose federation made necessary because of common interests. Ralph Cooper of Hamilton was named Chairman, Ralph Misener of Winnipeg the Vice-Chairman, and G. Sydney Halter the Registrar. Halter was also the Commissioner of the Western League, an office he had held since 1953. The East decided in 1956 to name Judge Allan Fraser Commissioner of the CFC.

The first priority of the new enterprise was 'to make a peaceful living arrangement with the National Football League through its Commissioner Bert Bell' because of the 'raiding' of NFL rosters by various Canadian clubs.[38] As well, a more business-like approach was taken. Negotiation lists for all teams were approved; the visiting team's share of the gate was raised from fifteen to twenty-five per cent, and a waiver price of $750 was set for an American, $500 for a Canadian. A draft of Canadian college players was instituted for all nine teams; previously only the eastern clubs had participated in the annual draft and this allowed the college athlete to negotiate with a western team if the first drafting team's contract tendered was not acceptable, or if the athlete wanted to play one team off against another in the hope of a larger contract. The new arrangment did away with competition among teams.

The NFL became a model to be followed by the CFC. The president of the Edmonton Eskimos, Ken Montgomery, insisted that 'a player couldn't look neat unless he wore stockings' because the National Football League required that players wear stockings. 'Ergo, if they do it in the NFL, it must be good for the Grey Cup.'[39] There were other changes: the last Canadian coach in either of the two divisions of the CFC, Annis Stukus, was replaced by the American Clem Crowe in British Columbia; twelve imports were to be allowed in the 1956 Grey Cup game; and two backfielders were allowed to block ten yards on running plays. Perhaps the most contentious 'American' change came when the value of the touchdown was increased from five to six points.

In 1957 the names of positions were made to correspond with those in the American game: snaps became centres; inside wings, guards; middle wings, tackles; outside wings, ends; flying wings, wingbacks. This was also the first year that the Grey Cup game was telecast coast to coast, the CBC making arrangements with the American Broadcasting Company and the Atlantic Cable and Telegraph Company to supplement its facilities. In 1958 the Canadian Football League replaced the Council and G. Sydney Halter was named Commissioner. League contracts were now filed in the Commissioner's office, without reference to the CRU. There were more 'housekeeping' matters: the Interprovincial Rugby

Football Union, better known as the Big Four, changed its name to the Eastern Football Conference for the 1960 season. One of the reasons for the change in name was that the use of the term 'rugby' was confusing to Americans who were being recruited. The WIFL changed its name to the Western Football Conference the following year, when a partial interlocking schedule was approved. Each team in the East would play each western team once within its fourteen-game schedule (sixteen in the West).

With the emergence of a new television network, CTV, the Grey Cup game was open to bids. The CBC, perhaps because of its past service and ability to serve the greater part of Canada, was too low in its offer and the game was awarded to CTV. There was a huge outcry from the public—some 5,000,000 viewers—in those areas not served by the new carriers. CTV 'offered to let CBC carry the game complete with commercials (in return for $41,000 in sponsors fees)'.[40] The CBC, suspecting that it had been used to help the CTV sell its shows to sponsors, declined, offering instead to carry the game free 'using plugs for the Red Cross instead of sponsors' commercials.'[41]

When the Board of Broadcast Governors proposed that the CBC carry the game 'in the national interest', with CTV's advertising if necessary,[42] the CBC secured a legal opinion that the BBG edict was beyond its powers. As *Time* reported:

> In the Commons, Liberal Lionel Chevrier last week rose to move an emergency debate on the telecast as 'a definite matter of urgent public importance'. The Speaker turned him down, but across the country thousands of others saw the emergency. A Prince Albert housewife tearfully asked if she would be 'deprived of watching the game simply because these two giants are locked in a struggle'. Publisher Fred McGuinness of the Medicine Hat News backed the CBC: 'I'm not interested in watching US citizens play football, and if the CBC suffers Canada will suffer.' CTV's late-evening star Pierre Berton independently proclaimed: 'I've never been prouder of the CBC.' In Calgary, Board Chairman Gordon Love, of CTV affiliate CFCN-TV, declared that the affair showed the CBC to be a 'monster riddled with communist-type thinking.'[43]

The CBC relented and millions of viewers saw the 1962 Grey Cup— a game that has come to be known as the 'Fog Bowl'. On the first day, in Exhibition Stadium, a heat inversion caused fog to roll in from Lake Ontario, making viewing conditions gradually impossible. To television viewers the players looked like phantoms in a mist. The game was called in the fourth quarter with nine minutes and twenty-nine seconds to play and Winnipeg leading Hamilton by a 28–27 score. (It had created much interest also in the United States, since it was being televised live by ABC's Wide World of Sports.) The remaining time was played on Sunday with no change in the score. This was typical of games played between Winnipeg and Hamilton. From 1957 to 1965 the two teams met in the Grey Cup six times, Winnipeg winning four Cups!

The Non-Important Years. By 1965 the CFL decided to allow, in the roster of 32 players, fourteen Americans per team, and rather than permitting an unlimited number of naturalized Candians on a team (there were American-born players who, after playing and living in Canada for five years, became Canadian citizens), limited them to three. Not only would they improve the calibre of play, but all clubs—whether or not they were in areas of business opportunity—now had an equal chance to persuade Americans to stay and perhaps even to change their nationality. Also, the limitation of three naturalized players meant that there would be more opportunity for 'homebrew' team members.

Because of this manoeuvre there were now four basic categories of 'Canadian': the naturalized Canadian (John Barrow of the Hamilton Tiger-Cats); the university-trained Canadian (Don Getty, Edmonton); the non-university-trained Canadian (Tommy Grant, Hamilton); and the Canadian American—that is, the player who was born in Canada but whose family left at an early age, or whose parents were Canadians and as a result left him with dual citizenship, leaving him to exercise the Canadian option (Bronko Nagurski Jr., Hamilton)—an area that was often a bone of contention since proof was not always forthcoming. For example, in 1965 Tom Cloutier, an end with the Montreal Alouettes, born in the United States but classified as a Canadian under this category, was 'waived' by the Alouettes and claimed by the Argonauts. 'It was revealed by Cloutier himself that he played for the Als under falsified citizenship conditions, that at the behest of a former Alouette official, he had claimed Canadian citizenship.'[44] Each of the five categories (one American plus four Canadian) had its own salary range.

When the League decided to put a limit on the number of naturalized Canadians that a team could carry, a chain of events was set in motion. Three players—Milt Campbell, Angelo Mosca, and Kaye Vaughan, naturalized Canadians all—served notice that they were filing a grievance with the Ontario Human Rights Commission. It was later withdrawn. The CFL Players' Association was formed, in some respects because of the issue and the high-profile players who would be supportive of the fledgling organization. In the light of the adverse publicity the League reviewed the legislation and took a different approach; it eliminated the categories of American and Canadian, replacing them with 'imports' and 'non imports'.

An 'import' was a player who received training in football outside Canada by having participated in a game outside Canada prior to his seventeenth birthday, or a player who had received training in football outside Canada after his seventeenth birthday but who had received none in football in Canada prior to his seventeenth birthday.[45] The new regulation was to affect only those who came into the League after 20 July 1965.

Two other changes in the League's approach to 'imports' were effected shortly after. In 1968 the League allowed each team to 'designate' an import: this man, the fourteenth member of the team, could substitute for another team-member, who in this case would not be able to return to the game. The 'B option' was attached to the rule in 1970. If the 'designated import' were a quarterback, he and the quarterback he replaced could alternate freely at that position at any time during the game. This rule was in effect until 1986. The assumption that the quarterback position had to be taken by an American—which began to take hold with the arrival in Canada of Warren Stevens in 1931 and his exploitation of the forward pass—was now firmly entrenched.

Supplementing the rule was the overwhelming preponderance of Americans who occupied coaching and managerial positions in the CFL. The situation was the reverse of that which Mike Milbury, an American hockey player (later coach) with the Boston Bruins, described in the National Hockey League in 1973:

> It's been there all right—prejudice, or at best, skepticism . . . In general, I think Canadians have had an automatic edge, just because they were Canadians. And Americans have been at a disadvantage, just because they were Americans. It was inevitable. Almost all the executives, coaches and scouts in pro hockey are Canadians. It's only natural for them to lean towards what they're familiar with. All their experience tells them that young hockey players are found in the minor leagues at home. Why waste time on some American freak playing a funny style of hockey at a school they never heard of?[46]

It soon became obvious that the quarterback position would no longer see the likes of another Joe Krol (Argonauts), a Don Getty (Eskimos), or a Russ Jackson (Rough Riders)—Canadians all who had played starring roles at the national level.

But the close of the sixties seemed to provide for optimism: J.G. 'Jake' Gaudaur became the new Commissioner on 1 April 1968—giving the

Don Getty (who became Premier of Alberta in 1985) as quarter-back for the Edmonton Eskimos, c. 1956. (Frank Cosentino.)

CFL his twenty-three years of experience as a player, director, and general manager, improving its relations with the NFL, and creating harmony among the CFL's member teams. The 1968 Grey Cup game, which the Ottawa Rough Riders won against the Calgary Stampeders, was the first to be carried in colour by the CBC; Prime Minister Pierre Elliott Trudeau performed the ceremonial kickoff before 32,655 spectators at Toronto's CNE stadium. The euphoria in Ottawa carried through the 1969 season. Quarterback Russ Jackson, playing in his last season, not only led his team to yet another Grey Cup but was also selected the Schenley winner as the Most Outstanding Player as well as the Most Outstanding Canadian Player of the Year!

Perhaps because of television, an increasingly buoyant economy and greater amounts of leisure time, as the seventies unfolded football attained new levels of popularity, both in Canada and the United States—

where the rival American and National Football Leagues had merged into a reconstituted NFL. The overabundance of available players caused promoters to develop a new league, the World Football League, involving cities that did not have franchises in the NFL. In Toronto, the only Canadian city in the new league, a franchise was awarded to Johnny F. Bassett, son of the owner of the Argonauts, for his team the Toronto Northmen.

Two years earlier, in 1972, the Minister responsible for sport, John Munro, 'publicly warned the CFL that the Federal government would impose sanctions to prevent CFL expansion south of the border, or expansion of the US leagues into Canada and would even prevent the formation of new leagues with Canadian entries.'[47] The federal government seemed to be saying that the Canadian Football League was an important nation-building instrument, an equivalent to the building of the railroad after Confederation, linking East with West, and should be protected from competition. In 1974 Health Minister Marc Lalonde carried out the threat, first in a speech in Regina, then with numerous public announcements and 'open-line' radio appearances, and finally with the introduction of Bill C-22, 'An Act Respecting Canadian Professional Football', into the second session of the twenty-ninth Parliament. The Bill served its purpose by forcing the Northmen to leave the country. Bassett moved them—with their highly paid American trio of Paul Warfield, Larry Csonka, and Jim Kiick—to Memphis, where they became the 'Southmen'.

Some, particularly conservative critics such as Dalton Camp, felt that the Liberal government should not be protective of 'inferior' football; that the market—that is, the public—should determine what was made available. For these people, Americans dominated Canadian football now; they were surrogates for the League's cities, and

> the spectators know they are watching a swarm of Americans with work permits playing a game that is not really a game they would rather play, nor the turf they would rather play it on. . . . If he [Lalonde] is saying that the grand old game of Canadian football cannot withstand the presence of another team of Americans playing with a different ball on a narrower field, then he only confirmed what the Canadian citizen suspects—that the game is over. The dilemma is typically Canadian, I fear, and so, I fear, will be the denouement.[48]

Indeed, as Camp perceived, a dénouement that saw the CFL gradually decline did seem to be set in motion with that confrontation. The Bassett family, Conservatives and staunch supporters of the CFL, withdrew their active support. John Bassett's CTV flagship station, CFTO in Toronto, was actively critical of the CFL. The media, print as well as electronic, took sides according to which political party they supported. The irony, however, was that while the perceived American threat from the outside was being rebuffed by the leadership of the federal government, within the CFL itself the effects of the designated import rule and the role of imports versus non-imports was hardening.

With the retirement of Russ Jackson after the 1969 season and the passage of the 'B' section of the designated import rule in 1970, it became increasingly difficult for a non-import, i.e. a Canadian, to win a spot at the quarterback position. In 1975 the Rough Riders were in need of quarterbacks and signed two imports, Condredge Holloway and Tom Clements, and one non-import, Bill Robinson, who in 1974 was judged to be the best university quarterback in Canada. He had led his university team, Western Ontario, to a Vanier Cup victory in 1974 and the previous year had quarterbacked St Mary's to a similar title. The Ottawa coaches, however, seemed to have made up their minds that the quarterback position would be filled by the two imports. Robinson was ignored on the practice field and rarely played in the exhibition games; yet when he did, he played on a par with, if not better than, his team-mates. Nevertheless, this non-import was generally treated as non-important.

But in Ottawa—the city where Russ Jackson's successes were still fresh in the minds of the public—the fans took notice. Open-line shows bristled with comments about the situation, letters-to-the-editor appeared with regularity in the city's newspapers, and sports journalists wrote probing articles. All this attention served to put pressure on the Riders, already leery about declining attendance and its public image. But their perverse solution was to put Robinson on the twenty-one-day disabled list, giving the problem as tonsils. (It was obvious that the team was attempting to buy time until fan interest in the player had cooled, because Robinson had no tonsils!) Eventually the All-Canadian came back from the disabled list, was activated, played minimally at quarterback, ran downfield to cover kick-offs, substituted occasionally at defensive back—and was subsequently released. A dejected and disbelieving Robinson, crushed by this treatment, reflected: 'I never thought being a Canadian would be a bad thing.'[49]

The case of Jamie Bone, a quarterback who had led Western to consecutive Vanier Cups in 1976 and 1977, was even more dramatic. In 1977 he was drafted by Winnipeg and in the following spring was traded to Hamilton, where he was offered a $14,000 contract on a 'take-it-or-leave it' basis. The Hamilton club's attitude to Bone was one of indifference, even neglect. He was not notified about the beginning of training-camp, he was ignored during practices, was given no playbook, did not play in the club's first exhibition game, and was released after twelve days. Bone appealed to the Ontario Human Rights Commission, which ruled that he hadn't been given a full opportunity to display his talents because the club was set on having Americans at quarterback. He was awarded $10,000—$7,000 for lack of fair opportunity, and $3,000 for injuries to feelings and loss of reputation—in addition to a five-day trial wherein the Tiger Cats had to give him a fair chance to compete for another place on the team.[50]

Bone chose to reject the tryout, feeling that he had prejudiced his chances. Instead he accepted an offer from the Dallas Cowboys of the NFL. After being given every opportunity to display his talents, he was released—he was not considered good enough. Nevertheless, Dallas and the NFL were praised as at least giving a Canadian the opportunity to make the team on his own merits as a player.

The designated import rule and the Jamie Bone victory in the courts combined to dissuade CFL clubs from even drafting Canadian quarterbacks. A succession of winners of the Hec Crichton Trophy for the most outstanding university player in Canada, who also happened to be quarterbacks, was virtually ignored by the CFL: Dan Feraday, Paul Paddon, Andy Parichi, Dave Pickett, Bob Cameron, Jamie Bone, Scott Mallender, Rich Zmich, Greg Vavra, Phil Scarfone, Jordan Gagner. They read like an honour roll of players the CFL apparently thought non-important.

Coincidental with these happenings was another development in the CFL's style of play. In 1977 Hugh Campbell took over as coach of the Edmonton Eskimos. A former outstanding receiver himself, he decided to implement a short, high-percentage passing game, predominantly with 'three step drops', occasionally 'five step drops', and only rarely 'eight-step' or deep passes. The amount of time needed to protect the passer under such a scheme was minimized because of the shortened 'drop' and the quarterback's quicker release. Runs were minimized, and protection for the quarterback was emphasized.

Among the various teams in the league, there had previously been a mixture of imports and non-imports on the offensive line and few, if any, in the backfield; these were important positions. Under Campbell's scheme the non-imports were used as a supporting cast for the quarterback; the offensive line plus the backs were assigned to the non-imports, who were given one task: protect the quarterback. He, however, didn't need as much protection as former schemes demanded, and the task became a non-important one. It was hard to believe that CFL coaches had not so long ago let it be known to the public that the Canadian university system was unable to supply enough talent for these positions. It was now obvious that it could! As each of the CFL teams sought to copy the pattern and formula initiated by the Eskimos and Campbell, non-imports demonstrated that they could perform these tasks. What's more, as teams began to move to a more balanced offensive approach, they acquitted themselves similarly with running and related blocking assignments. Though they laboured well, however, the non-imports did so in virtual anonymity. The were still non-important.

Other influences contributed to the decline of popular support for the CFL. In the early eighties football began to feel the effects of a great increase in competition for the entertainment dollar. Stage shows, films, rock concerts, sporting exhibitions, tournaments, VCRs, symphonies, travelling, and a host of other areas where disposable income could be spent all drew the crowds away from football. At the same time baseball, which was seen to be associated with the 'big time' and the 'big leagues', was becoming firmly established in Canada, with the Montreal Expos in the National League and the Toronto Blue Jays in the American. Canadian media attention began to tune in on the great American pastime. As the baseball teams' successes grew, so too did coverage. Reporters and columnists concentrated on the team, the league, the personalities involved. Conversely, coverage for football declined, relegated to junior reporters or on the back pages, and given scant time on the electronic media. The old concentration on pre-game and post-game analyses, opinion, and hype was a thing of the past. Baseball reigned supreme. Even in the off-season, coverage of rumours, free agents, trades, spring training, baseball caravans, and any incident drummed out by public-relations' personnel, continued unabated.

In other areas the CFL seemed insensitive. It was somewhat paradoxical that during a time of when women insisted that they not be treated as objects, clubs persisted in 'entertaining' their fans with scantily clad young ladies bumping, grinding, and gyrating. There were complaints that spectators were too rowdy and ill-behaved, that no longer were the stands an area where a 'family atmosphere' prevailed. Certainly youth seemed disaffected. A group with a large amount of disposable income, young people were conspicuous by their absence at most games.

By 1987 interest in the CFL seemed to be restricted mainly to the Grey Cup game—the league had become non-important. In 1977 the Montreal Alouettes defeated Edmonton 41–6 before the largest crowd in Grey Cup history, 68,318, at Montreal's Olympic Stadium. Revenue was $1,401,930. In 1987 Edmonton defeated Toronto 38–36 before 59,498 spectators in

Vancouver's domed stadium, and with a gate of $3,404,740. During that year, however, there were many serious signs of the general decline of public interest in football. The CFL's television contract—worth $33,000,000 for three years—was not renewed; the Montreal Alouette franchise ceased operations on the eve of the beginning of the season; play-off games featuring traditional rivals, Calgary and Toronto, in Edmonton and Hamilton respectively, attracted poor crowds; franchises in Calgary, Saskatchewan, British Columbia, and Ottawa were in serious trouble. Commissioner Doug Mitchell, who had replaced Gaudaur in 1984, was put on the defensive when his large salary was publicized at a time when players were being asked to take salary 'adjustments'—that is, cuts. Finally, the media were relentless in their reports on the 'demise' of the League.

Yet the League has appeared to rebound. Under Mitchell it began its own television network in order to generate funds and favourable publicity; Winnipeg was moved to the Eastern division; a salary cap of $3 million per team was put into effect; community groups rallied to the support of franchises in Calgary, Saskatchewan, and Ottawa; the designated import rule was dropped; team marketing schemes improved; the League's first female General Manager, Jo-Anne Polak, was hired by Ottawa for the 1989 season; the CFL Players' Association was asked for and authorized concessions from the players of a twenty-five per cent hold-back of salaries, more games, less money in training camps, and an 80-20 change in the medical plan from the one hundred per cent previously paid by the League.[51] The Commissioner's position was redefined and the retiring Mitchell was replaced as Commissioner by two people, Roy McMurtry and Bill Baker, the latter a Saskatchewan player and general manager of the Roughriders who was given much credit for the revival of the Saskatchewan franchise. Baker's responsibilities included the day-to-day aspects of the Commissioner's tasks. There was enough confidence in the League that entrepreneur Harry Ornest could pay $5,000,000 to Carling O'Keefe for the Toronto Argonaut franchise, which was due to play its 1989 home games in the newly completed SkyDome.

At the turn of the century Canadian football was a hybrid form of the English game; today many would say it is a hybrid form of the American game. Nevertheless, for eighty years its coveted trophy—one that continues to yield more and more excitement each year—has been an Englishman's Cup.

8

Hockey

The origin of the modern game of ice hockey is shrouded in mystery and sketchy facts. It is thought in the beginning to have combined variations of several archaic games—including bandy, shinty, hurley, and field hockey. Bandy has been described as a kind of field hockey 'played with sticks called "bandies", bent and round at one end, and a small wooden ball, which each party endeavours to drive to opposite fixed points.'[1] (The stick used in all these games was not unlike that used today in field hockey.) According to Henry Roxborough, it was played in England in the 1830s to a definite set of rules, some of which are similar to those used in contemporary hockey:

1. No bandy stick shall be more than two inches wide in any part.
2. No one is allowed to raise the bandy above his shoulder. Only the goalkeeper may hit the ball while it is in the air.
3. No player is to be considered offside when within his own half of the playing ice.
4. The game begins by the referee throwing up the ball in the centre of the ice.
5. The team consists of eleven players.[2]

As Peter Lindsay has pointed out, shinty and field hockey did not differ all that much from bandy.[3] In shinty the object was to drive the ball *beyond* the opposing team's goal, rather than *through* a marked area, as in field hockey or bandy.[4] Hurley, or hurling, an Irish variation of hockey, may be the oldest form of a hockey-like game. Named for the broad stick used, hurling dates back to the second century.[5] The first known report of hockey, or hurley, in British North America was in 1833 when the *Novascotian* described women skaters on Lake Lily near Saint John, New Brunswick, playing hurley,[6] though Thomas H. Raddall, in *Halifax, Warden of the North* (1948), says that the first hockey in Canada was played in the region of Dartmouth, Nova Scotia:

Ice hockey, Canada's national game, began on the Dartmouth Lakes in the eighteenth century. Here, the garrison teams found the Indians playing a primitive form of hurley on the ice, adapted it, and later put the game on skates. When the soldiers were transferred to military posts along the St. Lawrence and the Great Lakes, they took the game with them, and for some time afterwards continued to send to the Dartmouth Indians for the necessary sticks.[7]

The first recorded game of ice hockey in Montreal was in 1837. Describing Canada's first 'ice-hurtling game', the *Montreal Gazette* reported:

> In the first game between the Dorchesters and the Uptowns on the last Saturday in February, 1837, the Dorchesters claimed the championship of Montreal when the crowd flocked onto the ice after Dorchester had scored the only goal of the game and the teams were unable to continue.[8]

Owing to the abrupt ending of this contest a rematch was played two weeks later, with the winner to be the first team to score three goals.[9]

In the Canadian Amateur Hockey Association's Report of 1942, *The Origins of Hockey in Canada*, Kingston enters the field as an early venue:

> The first hockey was played by the Royal Canadian Rifles, an Imperial unit, stationed in Halifax and Kingston in 1855; it is quite possible that English troops stationed in Kingston from 1783 to 1855 played hockey, as there is evidence in old papers, letters, and legends that the men and officers located with the Imperial troops as early as the year 1783, were proficient skaters and participated in field hockey. It is more than likely that the pioneers played their field hockey in those early days on skates but it is not an established fact. The playing of hockey games as early as 1855 in Kingston is certain.[10]

Shinny—different from shinty in that a player had to 'shinny' to the side on his skates in order to avoid a sharp blow from a stick on the legs or feet—was played in Kingston in 1846 and 1847. Henry Roxborough, drawing from the records of soldiers' activities in these years, says:

> Shinny was their great delight. Groups would be placed at the Shoal Tower (opposite City Buildings in the harbour) and Point Frederick (the point of land where the Royal Military College stands); and fifty or more players on each side would be in the game.[11]

Yet shinty was played informally on the harbour ice at Kingston as early as 1839.[12] These games were evidently mass affairs, witnessed by 'gentlemen and ladies'. For a New Year's match in 1841 there were upwards of 200 people on the ice, both old and young.[13] Players merely had to supply their own sticks, and competitive rules were hardly observed. In a similar match in 1843, the number of spectators was so great that their presence impeded play and annoyed the players.[14]

In Toronto in October 1863 the *Globe* reported that the mayor, John George Bowes, himself an active sportsman, ordered the arrest of a group of boys, aged thirteen to sixteen, whom he had observed playing shinty on the harbour ice on a Sunday,[15] because the Lord's Day Act forbade sport of any kind on the Sabbath.[16] Only one of the boys was caught, but he was released on the orders of Alderman John Ewart, who had seen him being escorted to jail. George Brown, the *Globe*'s editor, was unsympathetic; he editorialized a few weeks later that 'twenty-four hours in the cells would be a good means of stopping boys from practices of this kind on the Sabbath.'[17] The playful, or sometimes not so playful, use of the stick by youngsters when not playing a game (a practice that has continued to this day) was noted in Kingston in 1867, when some 'unruly boys' were reported to have found amusement through using their 'shinties' to trip young ladies on the public skating rink.[18] But in the nineteenth century hockey—like virtually all other sports—was mainly played by adults, and by the few, not the many—by soldiers, legislators, and businessmen who had the time and money to spend on such leisure pursuits.[19]

By Confederation ice hockey existed only through its variant forms of localized play. Little if any inter-city or inter-town play had yet materialized. Poor travel and communication links restricted the arrangement of matches. (The Grand Trunk Railroad between Montreal and Toronto did not open until 1856.) Telegraph communication would not play a role in match arrangements until the late 1870s.[20]

The first game of ice hockey more or less as we know it today—played under formalized rules and with a puck rather than a ball—was in Montreal.[21] Unlike the games of hurley and shinty, which were played out of doors and were subject to the vagaries of winter weather, ice hockey almost from its formal beginning was played indoors, where the facilities helped to impose uniformity on the method of play. The first 'public exhibition' was held on 3 March 1875 in the Victoria Skating Rink, whose ice surface measured 200 feet by 85 feet (the present dimensions of hockey rinks).[22] The *Montreal Gazette* previewed this game:

A game of hockey will be played at the Victoria Skating Rink this evening between two nines from among the members. Good fun may be expected, as some of the players are reputed to be exceedingly expert at the game. Some fears have been expressed on the part of the intending spectators that accidents were likely to occur through the ball flying about in a too lively manner, to the imminent danger of on-lookers, but we understand that the game will be played with a flat, circular piece of wood, thus preventing all danger of its leaving the surface of the ice.[23]

One of the men who played in this first match was J.G.A. Creighton. A McGill University student, and later a prominent engineer and lawyer, he was credited with devising the McGill Rules for ice hockey, which were first published in the *Montreal Gazette*. Much the same as those for rugby-football and lacrosse[24]—the McGill rules for rugby-football were employed in the first intercollegiate game between McGill and Harvard in 1874—they were the building blocks upon which today's hockey rules evolved.[25] The number of players totalled eighteen, nine to a side (as in both rugby and lacrosse). Further, ice hockey had accepted lacrosse's method of making the length of the game dependent on the scoring of three goals. After 1875, hockey adopted rugby's rule of dividing the game into two 45-minute halves. The positions of the nine players on an ice-hockey team were like those in rugby: the terms rover, wing, and forward became part of the established vocabulary for both games. Additionally, a referee was added to the rules of hockey so as to adjudicate the process of play and to police 'bullying' or aggressive physical contact, particularly in a 'face-off', which had just been introduced into the game. An adaptation of the 'line-out' or 'scrum' in rugby, the face-off was not only a reasonable way of commencing or restarting play but was also an exciting way of creating the possibility of rough body contact between opponents. This, along with the speed and fluid style of play, quickly made ice hockey the darling of all organized spectator sports in Canada.

The rules for ice hockey were also influenced by those for field hockey. A game with a long tradition in England, field hockey was not formalized in Canada until 1875, when the Field Hockey Association of Canada was organized. It soon influenced ice hockey by making it an 'on-side' game: players of an attacking side were not allowed to be in advance of an opposing player, or the ball or puck.[26] Further, players were now penalized for certain infractions of the rules (though there is no record of the duration of the penalties). One of the infractions, taken over from field hockey, was carrying the stick above shoulder height, a practice that was so prevalent in hurling. Other infractions were attempting to carry the puck forward by catching it within a part of the body other than the hands, which controlled the stick, and charging from behind, tripping, collaring or 'holding', and kicking.[27] Many of these tactics are still considered illegal, and penalized, in today's hockey. Field hockey also reinforced the idea of a face-off to restart play, predating rugby and lacrosse in using this technique for game resumption.[28] By the time the Montreal Hockey Club and the McGill University Hockey Club were

The McGill University Hockey Club in 1881. Hats, sweaters, pants, sticks, and skates were not standardized until the early 1900s. The American flag can be seen in the background. (McGill University Archives photograph loaned to the National Archives of Canada, C 81739.)

established in 1876 and 1877 respectively, ice hockey had acquired some definite form and structure and was developing into a unique activity.[29] Even athletic clubs dedicated to other sports—such as two lacrosse clubs in Montreal (the Montreal Lacrosse Club and the Shamrocks) and one in Toronto—decided to organize their own hockey teams.

Once the McGill Rules became standardized and widely accepted, the game of ice hockey spread and became popular. In 1879 McGill introduced an important change in the Rules: each team was reduced to seven, so as to speed up the game. Also, a vulcanized rubber puck replaced its wooden predecessor—it was heavier and less likely to break or fly off in the direction of spectators.[30] The McGill Rules were endowed with more than local significance when they were employed in the first unofficial 'world championship' ice-hockey match held at the Montreal Winter Carnival in 1883.[31] Won by McGill, this match was widely reported and raised public interest in the sport. It also led to the development of leagues, made up first of teams within a city, and then of teams in two competing cities. Teams acquired their own uniforms, which were anything but protective. In one of the earliest-known photographs, dated 1881, the McGill University team is shown wearing striped sweaters, 'knickers' or long trousers, a variety of tams, tuques, and skull caps, an assortment of single-blade figure skates, and sticks that resemble crudely made hurley 'bats'.[32] Gloves were either not worn or were nondescript.

The first league in Canada—the Montreal City Hockey League—was organized in 1885 and included the Montreal Victorias, the Montreal Crystals, the Montreal Amateur Athletic Association, and the McGill University Hockey Club. (Each team was usually named for its major sponsor or its home rink.) The organization of the Amateur Hockey Association of Canada followed in 1886.[33] It intended to regulate and convene hockey contests throughout Ontario, Quebec, and the Maritimes, but this did not occur because the Association was criticized for representing only the interests of the Quebec teams. An 1898 editorial in the Toronto *Globe* complained that the Amateur Hockey Association of Canada was not what it was called, 'but simply the Quebec Association.'[34]

Toronto, while informally interested in ice hockey, did not readily accept the game in its structured, codified form until 1888. The first exhibition matches to be played under the McGill Rules were between the Toronto Lacrosse Club and the Toronto Caledonia Club at the Caledonian Ice Skating Rink.[35] Later in the year, when a league had been formed, the Caledonians played the first regular league match in Toronto by taking on the Toronto Granites, of the Granite Club.[36] Both these teams were offshoots of curling clubs and used their own club's well-groomed rink. League games then became more frequent in Toronto. In the fall of 1890 Ontario hockey promoters formed their own regulatory body, the Ontario Hockey Association, to watch over the development of leagues within the province.[37] One of its founders was Arthur Stanley, son of Lord Stanley, the Governor General, who in 1893 donated a cup as a trophy for Dominion amateur-hockey championships (later named the Stanley Cup). Young Stanley was an active player at Rideau Hall and was instrumental in organizing the Rideau Rebels Hockey Club of Ottawa.[38] The teams that made up the original nucleus of the Ontario Hockey Association were those of Queen's University, the Royal Military College, 'C' Company of the Royal School of Infantry, the Toronto Athletic Club, the Toronto Lacrosse Club, Osgoode Hall, the Toronto Granites, St George's (a fraternal society), the Victoria Skating Rink in Toronto, the Rideau Rebels, and a team from Bowmanville, Ontario.[39]

The Ontario Hockey Association had a phenomenal effect on the evolution of ice hockey in the province. Under its direction the growth of the game far outdistanced that sponsored by the Amateur Hockey Association of Canada. Within a year of its formation the Ontario Hockey Association included teams representing schools, fire brigades, lawyers, bankers, bachelors, and politicians, as well as universities.[40]

In the Maritimes ice hockey—in a formal, rule-bound context—was slow to evolve, mainly because of the relatively mild weather. Ice was difficult to maintain and play was relegated to sporadic bouts of indeterminate lengths. As a result, spectator interest was never sizeable. Halifax's first hockey league was not formed until 1896.[41] The Maritimes' first inter-provincial contest with central-Canadian teams took place in 1897, when the Halifax Wanderers surprised many hockey enthusiasts by defeating Montreal 4 to 3.[42] That same year the Wanderers defeated the Chebuctos of Dartmouth for the Championship of the Halifax-Dartmouth region and won the Star Manufacturing Trophy, becoming the first team to defeat the Chebuctos. Fredericton, New Brunswick, did not organize a club until 1896,[43] but by 1900 leagues were well established in most regions of Maritime Canada.

THE DEVELOPMENT OF HOCKEY IN THE MIDDLE-WEST

Ice hockey naturally developed later in western Canada than in the East because settlement occurred much later there. In the eighties and nineties, when hockey was becoming highly organized in eastern Canada, the West was barely past its frontier stages and much of the territory was known only to natives. Manitoba became a province in 1870 and Winnipeg was incorporated as a city in 1873. The first transcontinental railway, the Canadian Pacific, was completed in November 1885 and provided not only relatively fast and efficient transportation for settlers but also important communication links between growing settlements. The railroad was closely followed by the telegraph, which served to connect the most isolated regions of the Prairies. Telegraph offices and their respective 'message boards' at railway stations were the settlers' 'windows-on-the-world'—eventually the world of sport. Calgary, Regina, Edmonton, and Saskatoon were incorporated in 1893, 1903, 1904, and 1906 respectively, and the provinces of Saskatchewan and Alberta were created in 1905.

Large groups of Germanic, Icelandic, and Scandinavian settlers had little or no knowledge of hockey, with the result that the game was played very tentatively at first. But by the 1890s the hockey population, in Manitoba particularly, had increased substantially and included all ethnic groups. In 1892 both the Manitoba and Northwestern Amateur

Hockey Associations were established, the latter being responsible for the administration of hockey in Saskatchewan, Alberta, the Yukon, and the Northwest Territories.

The Winnipeg Victorias—named for the rink they played on—and the Winnipeg Hockey Club were both formed in 1890. Two years later there were no less than thirty teams in Winnipeg, some of which played on open stretches of marsh or river in the environs. Arenas would not be built in the West until the early years of this century, but outdoor ice hockey was popular. To westerners, playing hockey in the bitter cold made the game not only more fun but also more challenging, with the result that when they came to play indoors they were well trained to pass the puck, turn sharply, and skate faster.[44]

'The winter of 1892–93 was marked by a wave of hockey that rolled over the North West like a flood,' wrote one contemporary in 1896.[45] In these years a group of Winnipeg hockey promoters felt they should get a team together to travel to central Canada and show the East what hockey was about in the West. This they did in February 1893. Composed of players from the Winnipeg Victorias, the Winnipeg Dragoons, and the Winnipeg Hockey Club, the team toured Ontario and Quebec and won every match but two.[46] It played teams from Kingston, Rideau Hall, Peterborough, Southwestern Ontario, and Niagara Falls—losing only to Ottawa and Montreal—and gave notice that eastern teams could no longer be considered supreme.

Early in January 1893 Calgary sprang to the fore with several teams representing various segments of its population. Policemen, firemen, bankers, railroadmen, and ranchers all contributed teams to the new city's hockey environment.[47] In Edmonton, traders and trappers from the Hudson's Bay Company's post challenged several local merchants to a match in November 1894, one that was replayed often in the years following.[48] Hockey was slower to evolve in the rural West, but once rail and telegraph communications were installed, each village or hamlet founded its own team and challenged some other place for a game, rallying local loyalties.[49] Hockey was a wonderful diversion during the long and arduous winter months prairie settlers had to endure. And in the West it was not played by men only. In 1897 Calgary saw the first women's match, which no spectators were allowed to watch in case one of the ladies met with the indignity of falling ungracefully to the ice or of colliding with one of her opponents. Most people, however, felt that this activity was unladylike and highly injurious to a woman's sensitive constitution.[50]

By 1905 Saskatchewan boasted many rural teams, but the first reported hockey game in the province was in 1894 in Regina.[51] In a match that pitted the Regina team against the Moose Jaw Hockey Club, which was only a few months younger, Regina defeated Moose Jaw. Inter-city rivalries in both Saskatchewan and Alberta spurred small towns to adopt the game and organize teams in the hope of playing against more populous neighbours. By 1905 Oxbow, Estevan, Almeda, Glen Ewan, Gainsboro, Carvale, Camrose, Wetaskewin, Red Deer, and Spruce Grove all had ice-hockey teams.[52]

THE STANLEY CUP AND THE EVOLUTION OF THE NATIONAL GAME

Ice hockey had a firm grip on most of the country by the 1890s. (Hockey was slow to get started in British Columbia, however, owing to its mild climate. Its first indoor hockey rink was built in Vancouver in 1911.) Leagues were well developed and active, better travel conditions allowed for matches between distant cities and towns, and hockey minds were beginning to think of how to nationalize the game. The most enthusiastic proponent of ice hockey was none other than the Governor General of Canada, Sir Frederick Arthur Stanley, Baron Stanley of Preston. He, like other Governors General before him, had a pronounced interest in sport and in how it influenced Canada's life-style. But his interest in ice hockey went much deeper than mere patronage—like that of the Marquis of Lansdowne in rifle-shooting or the Earl of Minto in donating a cup to honour the nation's lacrosse champions. It even surpassed Earl Grey's and Lady Byng's charitable patronage of football and hockey. The key to Lord Stanley's unflagging support of the game was the fact that his two sons, Algernon and Arthur, were enthusiastic players in the Rideau Rebels Hockey Club. As a loyal father of two hockey-crazed sons, Lord Stanley not only sponsored the erection of a large outdoor rink at Rideau Hall, the Governor General's residence, and the formation of a Government House team in 1891–2, but he also saw it as part of his duty to suggest an award for the hockey championship of Canada. At a banquet given in his honour at the Ottawa Club on 18 March 1892, his aide-de-camp, Lord Kilcoursie, read a letter from the Governor General:

> I have for some time been thinking it would be a good thing if there were a challenge cup, which could be held from year to year by the leading hockey club in Canada [the Amateur Hockey Association of Canada]. There does not appear to be any outward or visible sign of the championship at present, and considering the interest that hockey matches now elicit, and the importance of having the games fairly played under generally recognized rules, I am willing to give a cup that shall be annually held by the winning club.

> I am not quite certain that the present regulations governing the arrangement of matches give entire satisfaction. It would be worth considering whether they could not be arranged so that each team would play once at home and once at the place where their opponents hail from.[53]

In order to appear fair in all decisions relating to the championship, Lord Stanley removed himself from the adjudication process and appointed a small board of trustees, the initial members being two prominent Ottawa sportsmen, Sheriff John Sweetland and P.D. Ross.[54] Through Lord Stanley's aide in Britain, Captain Colville, they purchased for about ten guineas a gold-lined silver bowl that stood on an ebony base. Before leaving Canada in the fall of 1893 Lord Stanley was able to witness the first competition for the 'Lord Stanley Cup'. It had been his fond hope that the first winner would be his favourite Ottawa team, the Ottawa Senators. But instead the Montreal Hockey Club, playing under the name of the Montreal Amateur Athletic Association, came out on top by virtue of winning the championship series. The Montreal Amateur Athletic Association, however, refused the Cup because the Montreal Hockey Club had no right to adopt the Association's name—it was not affiliated.[55] But in 1894, the first 'official' year of presentation, a team made up of members of the Montreal Amateur Athletic Association won the series for that year and the Association took possession of the Cup.

Lord Stanley suggested that some conditions should be attached to the use of the Cup as a trophy:

1. The winners shall give bond for the return of the cup in good order, when required by the trustees, for the purpose of being handed over to any other team that may in turn win.
2. Each winning team shall have at their own charge, engraved on a silver ring fitted on the cup for that purpose, the name of the team and the year won.
3. The cup shall remain a challenge cup, and should not become the property of any team, even if won more than once.
4. In case of any doubt as to the title of any club to claim the position of champions, the cup shall be held or awarded by the trustees as they may think right, their decision being absolute.[56]

Lord Stanley's ultimate wish was that the Cup competitions would be open to all, rather than competed for by teams affiliated with any one organization or association. His intent was to have each sports body, from all regions of Canada, nominate a team that it thought had the best chance of competing for and winning the Stanley Cup, the nominee usually being the winner of each local championship. The implementation of this format proved both workable and successful in enlisting the participation of teams from much of the country. As a result, hockey began to earn its reputation as Canada's 'national game'.[57]

Because no forward-passing was allowed between the two blue lines before the turn of the century, players had to advance the puck by stick-handling and skating their way towards the opponent's zone—stick-handling was the chief skill of the best players. Periodic 'back' passes were necessary if the checking became too close, and frequent changes in puck possession were customary. During this period the primary responsibility of the half-back—the current name, borrowed from rugby, for today's defenseman—was to shoot the puck into the rafters of the arena and hope that its unobstructed path would take it down the length of the ice and into the opponent's end, whereupon the attacking team would rush in and scramble for it. Then, passing in any direction was considered legal so long as it was in the opponent's defensive zone; the 'shoot-the-puck-in-and-chase' play therefore became a feature of the early game.[58]

Also before 1900 some important advancements in the game changed forever the format of play. Artificial ice as a playing surface was introduced in 1895 by way of the United States. The first Canadians to play on an artificial rink were a group from Quebec who played a match at Johns Hopkins University, Baltimore, in April 1895.[59] That same year artificial rinks were constructed specifically for ice hockey in Kingston and Ottawa. Canadians improved on the American innovation by adding 'boards' to the circumference of the rink. Though only 12 inches high, they stopped the puck and became almost an 'extra player' in the game by deflecting puck direction; however, they did not keep a player who had been body-checked from being pushed unceremoniously into the arms of spectators, or into the nearby wall of the arena.[60] The goal consisted of only two vertical sticks, giving rise to many disputes about whether or not a goal had been scored—a prime source of contention in the early days. Netting was added to the goal posts to trap pucks, and the first use of goal nets was at Montreal's Victoria Rink on 30 December 1899. Goal pads for goaltenders were introduced in 1896. This was after George H. Merritt—the goaltender for the Winnipeg Victorias when they became the first western team to win the Stanley Cup—wore white cricket pads, which immediately caught the attention of fans and players alike.[61] The effective way he blocked shots with the pads, all the while avoiding injury, secured in perpetuity a significant British influence on ice hockey. 'Tube' skates were introduced in 1899–1900. Developed and first used in Winnipeg, the tube skate was considered lighter and more durable than the single figure-skate blade, which was subject to cracking or breaking from the impact of a hard shot. It was not accepted and widely used in the East until after 1901, the year the Winnipeg Victorias once again won the Stanley Cup, defeating the Montreal Shamrocks, who had won in the two succeeding years.[62] Eastern teams thereafter wore tube skates.

Before 1900 ice hockey was for the most part not bedevilled by the amateur-versus-professional conflicts that beset such sports as track and field, rowing, and cycling. Because arenas and spectator crowds were both small, the game had little commercial potential and gate receipts had no attraction for greedy promoters. But after 1900 things began to change. Teams in the United States began to offer financial incentives to players who were willing to play a specified number of games for them. The first team to do this was the Pittsburgh Hornets. A city that proudly maintained artificial ice for six months of the year, an unprecedented length of time, Pittsburgh in 1902 offered players thirty dollars a week to join its team. The knowledge that good money could be made from playing a game that provided both satisfaction and enjoyment spurred players to seek professional employment. Nevertheless the Canadian Amateur Athletic Union and the Ontario Hockey Association were adamant in decreeing that if a player wished to be eligible for Stanley Cup competition, he would have to remain an amateur.

The enticement from Pittsburgh to 'play-for-pay' had two significant effects on hockey. First, it breached the code of amateurism; and second, it created in some circles a hidebound prejudice against the very idea of professionalism.[63] When players jumped at the chance to make money from their hockey skills, amateur-sport governing bodies widely publicized the impression that professionalism denoted a kind of moral laxity: in being tied to commercialism, it lowered the athlete's status.[64] An editorial on the subject of professionalism that appeared in the *Toronto Star* on 16 December 1902 quoted an official of the Ontario Hockey Association as saying: 'Keep away from Pittsburgh or out you go into the darkness of professionalism.' When other teams—such as the Rat Portage Thistles (of present-day Kenora, Ontario) and the Houghton Monarchs from Michigan—also offered salaries, and players skipped from one team to another in quest of the highest offer, professionals were seen to be disloyal and interested only in their share of the gate receipts. From this point on ice hockey, and the perceptions of its future development, changed significantly.

Before and after 1900, when sport was very much the preserve of the élite, the concept and definition of professionalism underwent several changes. Initially, any man who competed in sport for financial reward—virtually always a member of the working class—was considered a professional. This view was codified in 1880 when the Canadian Association of Amateur Oarsmen defined an amateur or a non-professional as one 'who has never assisted in the pursuit of athletic exercises as means of livelihood.' Here the idea of a sport as a money-earning occupation officially entered the definition of professionalism. Then in 1884 the Canadian Amateur Athletic Association further refined the definition of a non-professional by stating that an amateur was someone who had '. . . never competed for a money prize, or staked a bet, or with or against any professional for any prize, or who has never taught, pursued or assisted in the practice of athletic exercises as a means of obtaining a livelihood.' This concept of amateurism banned competition with or against anyone who earned a living from sport; but the prohibitions did not stop there. In 1896 the Canadian Amateur Athletic Association added to its 1884 definition, '. . . or who has never entered any competition under a name other than his own.' To avoid censure, many athletes had been assuming aliases to compete for financial reward or to play against professionals. But the ultimate definition of an amateur materialized in 1902, when the Canadian Amateur Athletic Union stated:

> An amateur is a person who has not competed in any competition for a staked bet, monies private or public or gate receipts, or competed with or against a professional for a prize; who has never taught or assisted in the pursuit of any athletic exercise or sport as a means of livelihood; who has never directly or indirectly, received any bonus or payment in lieu of loss of time while playing as a member of any club, or any money considerations whatever for any services as an athlete except his actual travelling and hotel expenses, or who has never entered into any competition under a name other than his own, or who has never been guilty of selling or pledging his prizes.[65]

Between 1902 and 1907—known as the 'Athletic Wars' period—debates and controversy raged about who was and who was not an amateur, whether amateurs could compete with professionals and maintain amateur status, and whether professionals could be reinstated as amateurs after a career of financial gain. A truce of sorts was declared in 1908–9 when the Amateur Athletic Union of Canada was established to adjudicate all amateur-professional disputes, many involving hockey players. It was a middle-of-the-road organization that in most cases acted fairly towards amateurs and professionals alike and did much to raise the image of professionals and close the gap between opponents of professionalism.[66] In this context professional hockey grew steadily, with opposing factions resorting to their own leagues and associations.

The advent of professional leagues in Canadian hockey in the early 1900s, after Pittsburgh's unexpected move to 'full professionalism' in 1902, led to disputes about whether amateurs and professionals could play together and co-exist. In 1899 this conundrum had been put to a vote, and there was a resulting split in the ranks of the Amateur Hockey Association of Canada, which had traditionally held a strict line in disallowing paid players to compete in its league. A rival league was therefore formed in the spring of 1899 that was softer on the point of allowing paid and non-paid players to compete with one another. This was the Canadian Amateur Hockey Association, which was born with a five-team league, including the Ottawa Capitals, the Montreal Hockey Club, the Montreal Victorias, the Montreal Shamrocks, and the Quebec Bulldogs.[67] This league eventually represented the cream of both amateur and professional hockey in Eastern Canada and went on to win the Stanley Cup six times in the next eight years.

From 1902 to 1908 hockey languished in the uncertainty of the amateur-professional conflict. The Canadian Amateur Athletic Union re-examined its amateur code and decreed that payments to hockey players for travelling and hotel expenses were considered part of the amateur game, and that any professionals who competed with amateurs should be publicly identified so as not to jeopardize the amateur standing of any unannounced player.[68] As well, 'open competitions' became the norm to determine championship teams. It was an unhindered format that allowed professionals and non-professionals to compete together. This somewhat removed the black cloud from the declared professionals and modified the harsh opinion of those who thought of professionals as sneaky and money-hungry.[69] More strikingly, the open competitions allowed an ever-increasing number of spectators to witness an improved brand of ice hockey, introduced by professionals who did little else except practise and compete. As a result, the professional game began to exceed in public interest the amateur game, which in the estimation of the public was becoming somewhat downgraded because it was essentially the domain of men who worked full-time at day-jobs and played sporadically throughout the season. By 1906 the idea that professional hockey players were paid money to play a superior and faster game was easily accepted as spectators saw in the professional hockey game the highest calibre of hockey skills. No longer were mixed amateur-professional open matches the epitome of ice-hockey. Rather, hockey fans discovered that it was more exciting to watch skilled professionals play, and they were prepared to pay high prices in order to do this. Up to

1908 there were fewer mixed matches and greater emphasis on, and attention paid to, the professional aspects of ice hockey. The first official professional hockey league in North America was started in the United States in 1904.[70] The International Hockey League, which is still in existence, featured teams from Pittsburgh; Houghton, Calumet, and Sault St Marie, all in Michigan; and Sault Ste Marie, Ontario. The players were paid anywhere between 25 and 75 dollars a week and the twelve-game schedule lasted for approximately three months.

In 1903 a major change came about in the method of how the Stanley Cup was awarded. Until then it had been won on a challenge basis, but in 1903 it was determined by the trustees that the champions of the Canadian Amateur Hockey Association would assume the distinction of defending Lord Stanley's trophy.[71] In that year the Ottawa Senators (affectionately called the 'Silver Seven') won the Stanley Cup and fulfilled Lord Stanley's wish to have the name of his favourite Ottawa team on the Cup. The roster included 'Bouse' Hutton, goal; Harvey Pulford, point; Art Moore, cover-point; Frank McGee, centre; and the three Gilmour brothers—Bill, Dave, and 'Sudie'—at rover, left wing, and right wing respectively. All were local boys and all were versatile athletes. For example, Harvey Pulford—who was a solid, hard-hitting defenseman in hockey—was also nationally famed in rugby-football, rowing, paddling, squash, and boxing.[72] All of Ottawa's 'Silver Seven' were strong skaters, good scorers, and rugged checkers, and all had the ability to play more than one position. They were capable of playing clean or rough, depending on the intentions of their opponents, and they were also capable of altering their performance according to the ice surface and the passing style of the game. These were the ingredients that won them the Stanley Cup in 1903, 1904, 1905, 1909, 1911, and later in 1920, 1921, and 1923.[73]

Evidence for the wide acceptance of hockey as Canada's 'national game' came in the 1903 contest for the Stanley Cup. A team from Rat Portage (now Kenora, Ontario) won the right to compete for the cup by virtue of its league win in the Manitoba Hockey Association. In quest of a Stanley Cup championship, Rat Portage hired an outstanding professional named Tom Phillips to play centre for them. Phillips was a standout in the three-game series, scoring four of Rat Portage's nine goals in the first game. Rat Portage outdistanced Ottawa by six goals. The rage of Ottawa fans at this defeat had the potential for a national calamity: thousands of spectators jammed the Ottawa arena for the second game. Tickets sold for three times their original value and the doors to the arena were closed at seven-thirty, half an hour before game time, to prevent the building from collapsing, while hundreds of disappointed fans milled about on the street. Frank McGee and Bill Gilmour, who had sat out the first game because of injuries, strengthened the Ottawa side in the second game.[74] The Silver Seven prevailed by a score of 4 to 2, and this set the stage for the all-important final game. The arena was once again sold out. As was typical of later east-west challenges, disputes arose over what rules to use. In this final game it was decided to have two referees—one from the East and one from the West, each employing the differing rules of their respective leagues. The western referee worked the first half of the contest, with the eastern official, Mike Grant, working the second half. Like so many games in this era, the start was delayed by about an hour, but once the game commenced this final match was touted as the 'most scientific' ever. The skating and body-checking were furious and took their toll on both sides. One Rat Portage player was so exhausted that he had difficulty rising from the horizontal to the vertical after he had tumbled in front of his own team's net. The referee cruelly handed him a five-minute penalty for obstructing the goal! At half-time Rat Portage led by two goals to one. During most of the second half the teams were never separated by more than one goal. With less than two minutes remaining, the score was tied. Then, with less than a minute remaining, Frank McGee, Ottawa's outstanding centre, scored the winning goal for the Silver Seven. When the final bell sounded, 'Old fans and young, wild with the joys of victory, leaped from bleachers, boxes and beams, and jammed the ice surface.'[75]

A Cup story that captured the imagination of Canadian hockey fans in 1905 was about a challenge match that pitted a team from Dawson City, Yukon, against the Silver Seven. Introduced in 1900 by prospectors from the south who were familiar with the game, hockey was the greatest recreational attraction in the Gold Rush region of the Yukon.[76] In early January 1905 eight members of the Dawson City team set out for the nation's capital, a journey of some 4,400 miles. They travelled by dog-sled until they reached the rushing Athabasca River, where they climbed aboard a Durham boat that took them close to Edmonton. There they boarded a train that delivered them to Ottawa a few days later. The entire trip took 23 days.[77] Understandably, the weary Dawson players were easily defeated by the Silver Seven. Ottawa won the best of three matches in two games by outscoring the so-called 'gold diggers' 9–2 and 23–2 respectively. Frank McGee, a future Hall of Famer, scored 14 goals for Ottawa in the second game.

In many small towns—where the citizens quite rightly saw themselves as contributing vitally to the nation's economy by harvesting the natural resources of the region—hockey became an important institution. This was particularly true in towns of northern Ontario where iron ore, silver, and copper were being mined successfully and civic pride was developing accordingly. A hockey team became the symbol of a town's prosperity. New Liskeard, Cobalt, and Haileybury all boasted professional hockey teams. As aggressively as they mined ore, the managers were equally dogged in 'prospecting' for the best professional players. Haileybury, for instance, was so intent on winning a Stanley Cup that it hired star players like 'Paddy' Moran and Art Ross, later the coach and manager respectively of the Boston Bruins. While Haileybury never won a Stanley Cup, other small towns did, or came close. Kenora (Rat Portage), unsuccessful in 1902, beat the Montreal Wanderers in 1907, thanks in part to players like Fred 'Cyclone' Taylor, Didier Pitre, 'Newsy' Lalonde, and Tom Phillips.[78] When the Ottawa Valley Hockey League was established in 1908, teams from Renfrew, Cornwall, Smith's Falls, and Ottawa (the Senators) bid for the best professional players. By this time hockey had become a 'player's market', meaning players could demand almost any price for their services. Often different towns would openly compete in the press, in a bidding war, for the services of a special player. There was the famous case of **'Cyclone' Taylor** (1883-1979), one of the outstanding players of the day. Prior to his moving from Kenora to Ottawa in 1907 and from Ottawa to Renfrew in 1908, the open bartering made him North America's highest-paid professional athlete, notwithstanding baseball, rugby-football, or basketball.[79] His salary disputes were so well publicized that he even rivalled the popularity of the American baseball player Ty Cobb as the best-known professional of the era. But Taylor's bouncing from one team to another had an alternative effect on the professional game. It served to reinforce the point that professionals needed to sign a contract in order to restrict the frequency of their moving from team to team. In effect the 'reserve clause' (a hotly contested issue in the early 1970s in the Curt Flood versus Major League Baseball suit) was introduced into professional sport via hockey in 1906—later altered in 1909—to restrict excessive player movement and to protect the image of the game and keep the financial outlay of the sport within reasonable bounds.[80] By 1909 every team that competed for the Stanley Cup had a complement of exceptional players.

The result of the bitter salary wars and the push for dominance in the lucrative professional game was the formation of professional leagues, each publicizing itself to be *the* league where the best players were resident. In 1909 a rival to the Ottawa Valley Hockey League materialized, called the Eastern Canada Hockey League, which was an outgrowth of the earlier Eastern Canada Amateur Hockey League, founded in 1906. It was composed of the Montreal Shamrocks, the Montreal Nationals, the Montreal Wanderers, the Quebec Bulldogs, and the Ottawa Capitals. The Ottawa league had tremendous difficulty signing players during the 1908 season because of high salary expectations. Furthermore those it did recruit were criticized for their violent play— they were called the 'Goon League' and the 'Professional Butcher's Association'.[81] In response to this situation, the Canadian Hockey Association was organized late in 1909, and it set out to regulate salary expectations and made an attempt to 'clean-up' the professional game. The CHA began with franchises granted to Ottawa (the Capitals), Quebec, the Montreal Shamrocks, the Montreal Nationals, and the All-Montreals.[82] By forming this new league, the officials of the Canadian Hockey Association 'froze-out' those teams they felt were disruptive forces, these being the Montreal Wanderers and the Renfrew Creamery Kings or Millionaires.[83] Both had been accused of money violations to professional players and excessively violent play. It was also believed that ridding the league of the Montreal Wanderers—who had won the Stanley Cup in 1906, 1907, and 1908—would increase the chances of other less-aggressive clubs for winning the coveted national championship trophy. The only league to rival the new association in eastern Canada was the Ontario Professional Hockey League, founded in 1907.[84] The 'Trolley League', as it was otherwise known, was composed of teams from Waterloo, Berlin (Kitchener), Guelph, Brantford, Galt, and Toronto. Waterloo and Galt, owing to financial and organizational difficulties, were quickly dropped, but the remaining four teams played full schedules between January and March in 1907 and 1908. For all intents and purposes the presence of these two professional leagues in the East drove a nail into the coffin of amateur ice hockey.

One of the individuals frozen out of the Canadian Hockey Association was Ambrose O'Brien, the multi-million-dollar proprietor of the Renfrew Creamery Kings and the owner of the Cobalt and Haileybury teams of the Ottawa Valley Hockey League.[85] An abrasive and outspoken character, who enjoyed seeing rough-and-tough hockey, he was also dedicated to raising the standard of the professional game. To ensure that his brand of hard-nosed ice hockey continued, and to construct a vendetta league against the Canadian Hockey Association, O'Brien organized in 1909 another rival league, the National Hockey Association.[86] The teams—wholly financed by the O'Brien family—were from Cobalt, Renfrew, Haileybury, and Montreal. In Montreal he organized two teams in order to undermine the success of the Canadian Hockey Association in the city and make a grab for the spectator dollar. Being a shrewd businessman, O'Brien rationalized that in order to draw fans to the arena in Montreal and away from the Nationals, Shamrocks, and All-Montreals, what better way was there than to develop a squad of players who were solely French Canadian? Hence Les Canadiens was born.[87] The other team was created from the now-defunct Wanderers and retained the name. The league prospered as a result of O'Brien's outbidding the CHA teams for players and offering those recruited high-paying jobs in the off-season. O'Brien staked his fortune on the success of his league. By spending large sums of money he was able to attract players like 'Cyclone' Taylor, 'Newsy' Lalonde, Didier Pitre, Bert Lindsay, and Frank and Lester Patrick.

So successful were O'Brien's plans to quash the rival league that late in 1909 the CHA, suffering badly from gate receipts and declining quality of play, asked O'Brien to merge with it. O'Brien refused, yet was open to accept any team that wished to move from the CHA. While all wanted to move to his league, he accepted only Ottawa and the Montreal Shamrocks—enough, he figured, to ensure the demise of both the Ontario Professional Hockey League and the Canadian Hockey Association. By the end of 1909 only one professional league in Canada stood preeminent, the National Hockey Association.[88] Leagues in Saskatchewan, Manitoba, and Ontario continued to function, but all were subservient to the stronger NHA.

Ice hockey in Canada had now passed into the era of 'big-business'. O'Brien realized that in order to retain loyal fans and to keep his league viable, certain conditions would have to be met. One condition was a professional player's contract, which explicitly stipulated salary and length of employment time. This discouraged public bartering in the press (though it did not rule out heavy contract-renewal negotiations). It also stated that the players would 'conduct themselves with gentlemanly, respectable manners.'[89] The condition that after 1911 payrolls would be frozen at under $5,000 per team pleased the fans, who were critical of what they thought of as players' unreasonably high salary expectations. Fans now believed that the administrative control of the players was well in hand and that the stars of the game, whom they had come to love and admire, would no longer be seeking to jump from one team to the next to gain greater financial rewards. O'Brien felt the salaries were too high, so in order to maximize profits he dropped his teams to a six-man roster instead of seven—the game would be speeded-up and less expensive if fewer men were on the ice. And with fewer men playing, it was decided to change to three periods, with two ten-minute rest periods, so as to give the players adequate revitalization time to keep the quality of play at a high level. (Until 1909 the game had been played with two thirty-minute halves and one fifteen-minute rest period.)[90] Thus the NHA made several changes that would affect the game permanently. The professional game was here to stay and it was actively seeking to market itself as a respectable, serious business. The only thing the NHA lacked was a competitive league with which it could compete for the now 'professional only' Stanley Cup championship.

The problem of equitable competition was solved in 1911–12 with the formation of the Pacific Coast Hockey League, financed and administratively backed by **Frank** (1885–1960) and **Lester** (1883–1960) **Patrick**.[91] The Patrick brothers had previously been star players with McGill University, and in Brandon, Manitoba, with the Montreal Wanderers, the Renfrew Creamery Kings, and the Edmonton Eskimos. Their early lives in the West had been very happy and it was always their intention to return some day to begin a professional hockey league. Frank, the younger, who had always dreamed of artificial-ice arenas and a professional league on the Pacific Coast, was the brains behind the construction of artificial-ice arenas in Victoria and Vancouver in 1911, with Lester's support. The Vancouver arena was a state-of-the-art facility unrivalled anywhere in Canada. It seated 10,000 and cost approximately $350,000.[92] Frank and Lester had financed the construction of both arenas by selling off the assets of their family's saw-mill and lumber business in Nelson, B.C.

For their Pacific Coast Hockey League the Patricks raided the NHA for players in 1912 and were able to come away with many of the stars. Of the sixteen recruited from the eastern association, four were Montreal Wanderers: Ernie Johnson, Jimmy Gardner, Harry Highland, and Walter Smaill. Others included 'Newsy' Lalonde, Tom Phillips—regarded as the game's finest winger—Tom Dunderdale, Bobby Rowe, Fred Harris, Bert Lindsay, and Hughie Lehman.[93] Many others, like Si Griffis, either came out of retirement or were transfers from the Ontario and prairie leagues. Few players, including 'Cyclone' Taylor, could refuse the temptation of $22,200 for a 14-game season. No man had ever earned this much in the NHA. The League consisted of the Victoria Aristocrats, the Vancouver Millionaires, and the New Westminster Royals.[94] (While it was planned to have teams from Edmonton and Calgary included in the original Pacific Coast Hockey League, financing for these teams became too exorbitant, and therefore the idea was dropped.) Frank Patrick, the president, was the owner-coach-captain-player of the Aristocrats. The New Westminster entry was owned jointly, with friend Jimmy Gardner acting as coach and player. The distribution of the 28 'signed' players among the three teams was carefully handled, and surprisingly the parity between all three was relatively close. Although the Victoria Aristocrats won the first championship of the League, they did so only by the smallest margins over Vancouver and New Westminster.[95] It appeared that the Patricks' dream of having a successful hockey league on the West Coast was well underway. Fan support exceeded expectations and the teams were able to break even in their initial year.

This success could not have been more discouraging to eastern hockey promoters. They were not only forced into a position of accepting the fact that they had market competition for the best players in the country, but they were also shaken to realize that if the general good of hockey was to be served, a more co-operative spirit between the two premier leagues would be necessary. Consequently after the 1913–14 season of both the Pacific Coast Hockey League and the National Hockey Association, it was agreed to hold an inaugural non-Stanley-Cup-oriented 'world championship'. The East believed this would be a good way to show the maverick westerners where the best hockey was being played in Canada. Unfortunatley for the East and its representative, the Quebec Bulldogs, the first 'world championship' went to the Patricks' Pacific Coast Hockey League and their representative, the Victoria Aristocrats.[96] In eating the proverbial crow, NHA officials were coerced into accepting a format for the contesting of future Stanley Cups competitions. Beginning in 1914–15 it was decided that the Stanley Cup would be competed for not on a challenge basis—which had been the tradition up until then—but rather on an inter-league arrangement between champions of the Pacific Coast Hockey League and the NHA. To this end, and again to the disheartening amazement of eastern promoters, the Patricks and the Vancouver Millionaires defeated the Ottawa Senators in 1915 for the first inter-league championship. For the first time the Stanley Cup rested on the west coast. Although this win was a traumatic blow to eastern hockey interests, the rivalry between the two leagues served to bring high national focus and interest to the game, and cemented the idea of professional hockey in the minds and hearts of all Canadians.

In 1917 the National Hockey League evolved from the National Hockey Association because the example of the Pacific Coast Hockey League showed that a small league could survive and effectively exploit metropolitan markets only so long as it was in a rather confined geographical region. The new league would not even pretend to represent hockey throughout the country. It focused attention on the qualitative aspects of hockey organization in the East and its ability to maximize profits, features of the Patricks' cartel on the west coast. A stimulus to producing an effective organization came in the spring of 1917 when the Stanley Cup went to a Pacific Coast Hockey League team, the Seattle Metropolitans (the first American team to win the Stanley Cup), for the second time in three years.[97]

In 1917 the new NHL, in its attempt to become leaner administratively, dropped the Montreal Wanderers, the Quebec Bulldogs, and the Ottawa Senators, adding a new franchise from Toronto (the St Pats).[98] The former secretary of the National Hockey Association, Frank Calder, became the new president and secretary of the NHL. One of his first initiatives as League president was to reduce the ten-man roster of NHA teams to eight, and to suggest that perhaps expansion into the United States— by way of New York, Chicago, and Boston—would be the path to follow in the light of Seattle's success on the west coast. Thus from this point on the nature of future professional hockey growth had been sculpted and the popular appeal of the game had been captured. The NHL and the Pacific Coast Hockey League would prosper for another decade before a major shift in hockey emphasis came to the game Canada jealously regarded as its own.

THE NATIONAL HOCKEY LEAGUE

In the late teens and early 1920s hockey had taken on a central-Canadian and west-coast complexion, but the development of a rival league in the prairie region drew attention to the high calibre of hockey played there. In 1922 the four-team Western Canada Hockey League was established— consisting of teams from Calgary, Edmonton, Regina, and Saskatoon— and it hoped to compete equally with both the Pacific Coast Hockey League and the National Hockey League.[99] Of the fifty players signed, only eight had previous experience in the other two leagues. Nevertheless the new league showed from the start that it was capable of rivalling the longer-established associations. In a Stanley Cup playoff between the Pacific Coast champions and the Western Canada champions in 1922, the older league got quite a scare. Regina beat Vancouver by a score of 2-to-1 in the first game of a best-of-two-games total-points series. Vancouver was able to recover and outdistance Regina 4-to-0 in the second game to win the series on aggregate and the right to travel east and contest for the Stanley Cup. But the Western Canada Hockey League had established itself as a force to be reckoned with.

This format for the western semi-final playdown to decide which team should compete for the Stanley Cup lasted until 1925. In that year two significant changes occurred that greatly affected the growth of professional hockey in both Canada and the United States. First, the Pacific

Coast Hockey League folded after thirteen years of tumultuous yet popular operation.[100] Always teetering on the edge of financial ruin, the Patricks' league could not survive the financial collapse of the Seattle Metropolitans in the fall of 1925. To recover some monetary stability the Patricks applied for, and were granted, two franchise leases allowing their Vancouver and Victoria teams to play in the Western Canada Hockey League. This, the only league in the West, now consisted of six teams playing a 30-game schedule that lasted from 1 December to the end of March. The second major change came in 1925 as a result of the NHL's granting a franchise lease to Charles Adams of Boston, the first in the United States. The NHL was now the premier professional hockey league in North America, embracing teams in Hamilton (the Tigers, established in 1921 on the transfer of the Quebec franchise), Ottawa (the Senators, 1917), Toronto (the St Pats, 1917), two in Montreal (the Canadiens, 1909, and the Wanderers, re-established in 1925), and Boston (the Bruins). The League was truly international in scope with the addition of Boston. The growing interest in the fast-paced, hard-checking game was indicated when New York, Pittsburgh, and Philadelphia all applied for NHL franchises in 1925. Their requests were shelved, however, until such time as rising interest in hockey south of the Canadian border made League expansion a guaranteed option.

The expansion came sooner than expected. The New York Rangers were granted a franchise in April 1925, with the well-known Ottawa player Tommy Gorman elected as governor to serve their interests.[101] At the beginning of the 1926 season further expansion occurred when Hamilton was dropped and the Pittsburgh Pirates were added to the list of clubs. The League now held seven franchises. Hamilton's fall from grace was largely attributable to a player's strike in the previous playoff season.[102] The Tigers had finished atop the NHL standings in 1925 and were to await the winner of the Toronto and Canadiens play-off match— these clubs having finished second and third in the standings respectively. But under this new playoff arrangement, the Hamilton players felt they should receive additional compensation for the post-season matches because they would be required to prolong their season beyond the designated thirty games. Until this time, the team that had won most points in the thirty games was considered the seasonal winner of the NHL and usually met the western challenger for the Stanley Cup championship. But Hamilton's refusal to play post-season contests led to its suspension from further play-offs for the year and each member of the team was fined $200. League authorities decided that the winner of the Toronto-Montreal matchup would go on to compete for the Stanley

Cup. The incident showed that players' demands for equitable compensation for post-season play were being met head-on by a management team headed by Frank Calder, who had a bottom-line to recognize if League viability was to be a priority. Thus the hard-line management style of the National Hockey League had been established, with the teams' governors and owners in full control. This determined stance reinforced in the players' minds the fact that, if they wished to play in the NHL, they would have to abide by the rules and regulations set out by the administrative minority. No longer were players' whims and wishes sufficient to change League protocol—a practice that was rampant during the early years of professional hockey. Yet in the Western Canada Hockey League, players were still able to switch from one team to another, ultimately undermining the popularity of individual teams and shaking the financial stability of the League.[103] Luckily for most Hamilton Tiger players, the newly established New York franchise absorbed most of their playing contracts, so that the New York Rangers to a great extent duplicated in the make-up of its team the now-defunct Hamilton organization.[104]

In 1927 the NHL continued its expansion into the profitable American market. At the annual meeting of the board of governors—made up of one governor for each club in the League—it was determined that franchises in Chicago and Detroit would definitely meet with instant fan approval and that these cities were excellent sites through which to maximize NHL profits.[105] From the very beginning, one of the League's primary considerations had been ensuring that franchise locations would make money.For all intents and purposes this objective caused the dropping away of all smaller urban centres as well as the cities of the Western Canada Hockey League, which were incapable of consistently attracting crowds large enough to garner a profitable gate return. Further weakened by inconsistent fan support and the ability of players to jump from one team to another, the Western Canada Hockey League collapsed in 1927. Its players sought employment in the NHL, which commanded ever-increasing respect and offered larger salaries.

Both Chicago and Detroit were awarded full NHL franchises in 1927, but this was conditional upon adequate arena facilities. Chicago—which had a stadium that seated over 15,000—was immediately allowed to commence play, but Detroit needed to build a comparatively large arena in order to begin League matches and did not do this until 1928, when it then started competition.[106] Chicago was represented on the NHL board of governors by Major Fred McLaughlin and Detroit was represented by Charles A. Hughes.[107] Each gentleman was responsible for purchasing the rights to players of the defunct Western Canada Hockey League. Chicago took possession of most of the contracts of the Portland Rosebuds (the last team to be added to the WCHL in 1926), while Detroit took control of the playing rights of former Victoria players.[108] Frank and Lester Patrick reportedly sold their franchise rights to Detroit interests for $100,000. This was a considerable sum for any hockey entrepreneur to invest at the time and was doubly remarkable when one considers how little the Patricks spent in attracting star players to their league fifteen years earlier.

NHL clubs scrambled for the services of players who had been connected with the Western Canada Hockey League. The New York Rangers claimed Bill Cook and Fred Cook, two outstanding stars with Saskatoon; Chicago claimed Dick Irvin, runner-up to Bill Cook in the scoring race of the WCHL in 1926; Toronto claimed goal-tending great George Hainsworth of Saskatoon, although Montreal disputed this and won the right to sign him; and Boston, in an unprecented manoeuvre, signed four of the western association's most highly skilled players: Eddie Shore, Gordon 'Duke' Keats, Frank Frederickson, and Frank Boucher.[109] In dealing with the Patricks, however, Boston's owner Charles Adams had to spend approximately $50,000 to acquire these players and $15,000—an unheard of sum to pay for any player in the mid-twenties—to acquire the rising star of the Western Canada Hockey League, **Eddie Shore** (1902–85).[110] But Adams got an excellent deal. As a defenseman, Shore scored almost one point for every two games he played, an unheard-of phenomenon at a time when the professional game for rear-guard players was a very non-offense oriented one in the late 1920s and early 1930s. Shore was selected as the NHL's most valuable player and recipient of the Hart Trophy four times—another unprecedented accomplishment yet to be duplicated by a defenseman. Moreover, he was selected as an all-star no less than seven times in a career that spanned fourteen NHL seasons, and he played on two Stanley Cup championship teams with Boston in 1928–9 and 1938–9.[111]

The NHL did not have to rely entirely on western all-stars to draw fans to the arenas. Homegrown eastern players were also making their mark. In English Canada 'King' Clancy (1903–86), who broke into the League with the Ottawa Senators, and Lionel Conacher (1900–54)—who started his career with Pittsburgh, but later went to the New York Americans (an NHL franchise from 1927 to 1940), the Montreal Maroons, and the Toronto Maple Leafs—were star players. In Montreal Howie Morenz (1902–37) and Auriel Joliat (1908–86) were the toast of Quebec. In the late 1920s and early 1930s the 'star' qualities of players began to take hold in earnest when it became apparent that the NHL would be the premier hockey organization in North America. Fan support became very loyal, and players committed themselves to longer-term contracts with teams in order to increase their personal popularity and their subsequent monetary worth to their teams. The media, particularly newspapers, were rapidly expanding their coverage of sport at this time and would often attempt to equate a player's popular appeal with how much money he was making. This fact spurred players on to become spectator favourites so as to draw larger salaries from their hockey employers.

In the period leading up to the start of the Second World War the NHL experienced tremendous growth and consolidation. Many clubs were added, dropped, and readmitted, but the number of franchises remained relatively the same. During this era (1930–40), the NHL vacillated between seven and ten clubs and was composed of two divisions—a Canadian and an American. In 1930 the Canadian division included the Montreal Maroons, the Montreal Canadiens, the Toronto Maple Leafs (the name of the St Pats was changed in 1928), the Ottawa Senators, and the New York Americans (added to the Canadian division to equalize the number of teams in each division). The American division was composed of the Boston Bruins, the Chicago Black Hawks, the New York Rangers, the Detroit Falcons (called the Cougars in 1928 and 1929), and the Pittsburgh Pirates.[112] In 1931 the Pittsburgh franchise experienced financial troubles owing to poor fan support and as a result moved its home games temporarily to Philadelphia. The Quakers, as they were known there, had more financial hardship in 1931, finishing at the bottom of the League with a record of 2 wins and 20 losses. Ottawa was not far behind, as it posted a record of 5 wins and 14 losses. Unfortunately for both clubs their lack of fan appeal and profitability forced them to suspend operations after the season ended. This left four teams each in the respective Canadian and American divisions. Although the NHL had passed a policy of subsidizing some of the operating losses of the weaker teams, for the most part it was unwilling to absorb perpetual losses by clubs that were doing little to improve their situations. The players from both Philadelphia and Ottawa were distributed among the remaining teams, based upon need. This effort by the NHL to add parity among competing teams was the first incidence of what is now termed a dispersal draft: weaker teams drawing the best players.[113]

While Ottawa had suspended operations in 1932, it returned in 1933 with many of the same players it had in 1931, but bad fortune still plagued the team. In 1935 it had to suspend operations once again owing to the financial impossibility of running a franchise in Ottawa. Detroit, too, faltered in 1934 and was forced to reorganize with new investment capital. James Norris became the new owner of Detroit and changed the name of the team from the Falcons to the Red Wings.[114] The defunct Ottawa franchise was moved to St Louis in 1935, but once again it met with only marginal success. The St Louis Eagles lasted only one season and was forced to disband at the beginning of the 1936 hockey season. For the second time in NHL history a dispersal draft was necessary to distribute equitably the St Louis players among the remaining eight teams. Once more the draft was based upon need as the NHL sought to add parity in play to its interlocking divisional schedule. This would essentially guarantee the NHL closer competitive matches and, it was hoped, larger gate receipts resulting from increased spectator interest.

The eight-team League of 1938 was reduced to seven teams in 1939 when the Montreal Maroons succumbed to the effects of the greater popularity of the Montreal Canadiens and folded.[115] Because there was an unequal number of teams in each division they were unable to play an even number of division games. Therefore the divisions were abolished and the NHL became a single entity, with the first six teams competing in the playoffs for the Stanley Cup. The following year, 1940, the NHL was reduced by one more team when the New York Americans went into receivership and dropped from League play.[116] Attention to the rising troubles in Europe and the conscription of Canadian star players away from New York were the reported catalysts for the Americans' downfall. But like the Maroons, the Americans were forced to compete with a more highly successful cross-town rival team, the Rangers. By the time of the onset of the Second World War, the NHL had achieved a status and structure that would last until 1967, when a great increase in the number of teams enabled the League to restore its divisonal structure. From 1940 to 1967 the 'original six'—Toronto, Montreal, Detroit, Boston, New York, and Chicago—would enjoy a time of unprecedented success and stability, and would see the development of longstanding rivalries that cemented, in the minds of Canadians, the close relationship of hockey to the sense of Canadian identity.

TROPHIES AND AWARDS

During the development and consolidation of the National Hockey League and other professional hockey associations in the first four decades of the 1900s, certain trophies and awards materialized that recognized not only their presenters but also individual players, and teams that had won some distinction. The O'Brien Trophy was originally given in trust, in 1910, to the National Hockey Association, but after 1927 it was taken over by the NHL.[117] Donated by M.J. O'Brien, the father of Ambrose O'Brien, the cup originally was emblematic of the National Hockey Association championship. Shelved until 1928, the O'Brien Trophy honoured the winner in the Canadian section of the NHL through to 1939. From this year until 1967 the trophy was awarded to the runner-up in League play. After 1967 the O'Brien Trophy ceased to be used and was retired to the Hockey Hall of Fame.

Contemporary with the O'Brien Trophy was the Prince of Wales Trophy.[118]Presented by Edward, Prince of Wales, to the National Hockey League in 1924, the award initially honoured the League champion up to and including the 1927 season.[119] After 1927 it was awarded until 1939 to the leader of the American section of the League. In 1939, when the League was once again unified into one division, it was decided that the trophy should be awarded to the first-place team that was declared League champion. Consequently the O'Brien and Prince of Wales Trophies were the first cups to complement each other as divisional awards. It should be pointed out that competition for the Stanley Cup changed significantly after the 1927–8 season. The downfall of both the Pacific Coast Hockey League and the Western Canada Hockey League resulted in the Stanley Cup's being competed for exclusively by NHL clubs—the first time this had happened in the professional game.[120] After 1929 the Stanley Cup championship was decided by having the League champion play the winner of a semi-final series between the second- and third-place clubs. This traditional playoff protocol was followed until 1967, when further NHL expansion necessitated certain changes.

One of the earliest donated trophies to recognize outstanding individual achievement in hockey skill was the Hart Trophy. Donated in 1923 by Dr David A. Hart, the father of the long-time coach (1925–32; 1936–39) of the Montreal Canadiens, Cecil M. Hart, the cup was awarded to the player adjudged the most valuable to his club.[121] The first winner of the Hart Trophy in 1923 was **Frank Nighbor** (1893–1966), who was often called the 'Flying Dutchman' owing to his great speed on the ice. Nighbor, a discovery of the Patrick brothers, was a standout with the Ottawa Senators between 1915 and 1929.[122] One of the most talented players of the era, he led the Senators to Stanley Cup victories in 1920, 1921, 1923, and 1927. Before moving to Ottawa he assisted the Pacific Coast Hockey League's Vancouver Millionaires to a Stanley Cup victory against Ottawa in 1915, the first victory for the West Coast league.[123] Nighbor was also the first winner of the Lady Byng Trophy.

In 1925 Lady Byng, wife of the Governor General, presented a trophy to the National Hockey League that was given annually to the player who exhibited the best standard of sportsmanship and gentlemanly conduct, combined with a high level of playing ability.[124] Although Ottawa did not win the Stanley Cup in 1925, Nighbor's dominance as a goalscorer and as a 'clean player' secured him this coveted prize. The next player to distinguish himself as both talented and gentlemanly was **Frank Boucher** (1901-77), a Canadian star of the New York Rangers. Between 1927 and 1935 Boucher won the Lady Byng Trophy seven times (he was awarded permanent possession in 1935),[125] being beaten for the award only once in 1932 by Joe Primeau of the Toronto Maple Leafs. Lady Byng awarded another trophy in her name in 1936, and after her death in 1950 it was renamed the Lady Byng Memorial Trophy.

A third trophy that recognized individual achievement in the period leading up to 1940 was the Georges Vézina Memorial Trophy.[126] Given to the National Hockey League in 1925, it was awarded to the goaltender who had played a minimum of 25 games for one club and who had the lowest goals against average. The award—donated by Joseph Catarinch, Joseph Viateur, 'Leo' Dandurand, and Louis Letourneau, all former owners of the Montreal Canadiens—was presented to the National Hockey League in memory of **Georges Vézina** (1887–1926), a goaltender of the Montreal Canadiens who collapsed at the end of the first period in the Canadiens' first game of the season on 28 November 1925 and died four months later from tuberculosis. Vézina had led the Canadiens to five League championships between 1910 and 1925 and had been their stalwart goaltender in Stanley Cup victories in 1916 and 1924. His style of goaltending was such that his cool appearance under pressure earned him the nickname the 'Chicoutimi Cucumber'. It seemed appropriate that the inaugural Vézina Trophy winner in 1926 was another Canadien, George Hainsworth (1895–1950), who had been hired as a replacement for Vézina.

The last significant trophy to be given to the NHL League before 1940 was the Calder Trophy, first presented in 1937. It was donated by the then president of the NHL, Frank Calder (his tenure extended from 1917 to 1943).[127] Calder (1866–1943) recognized the large effort needed to become a quality player in a highly professional sport and believed that an award should be established for the NHL's outstanding rookie. Following his death, and Mervyn 'Red' Dutton's ascendance to the presidency of the NHL (1943–6), the award for the outstanding rookie became known as the Frank Calder Memorial Trophy.

While the professional game had enjoyed considerable patronage since 1910 in the form of trophies and cups, other forms of philanthropy had recognized the importance of the amateur and junior aspects of hockey.

In 1908 an award honouring the senior amateur hockey championship of Canada was presented by Montreal industrialist Sir Hugh Montague Allan, son of Hugh Allan, who founded Canada Steamship Lines.[128] The Allan Cup became an important trophy for those hockey clubs that wished to remain truly amateur. Amateur athletic associations, universities, colleges, military detachments, fraternal orders, and occupational teams all vied for the prestige of temporarily owning this Cup. Since its inception it has been a measuring-stick for selecting teams to represent Canada at international competitive tournaments. Allan Cup champions—such as the Winnipeg Falcons (1920), the Toronto Granites (1924), the Toronto Varsity Grads (1928), and the Trail Smoke Eaters (1962)—have all won either an Olympic or a world-hockey championship.[129]

A second amateur trophy, which recognized Canada's junior hockey champions, was the Memorial Cup. Donated by the Ontario Hockey Association in 1919 to commemorate the valour of Canada's war dead in the Great War, it served to remind young athletes that courage and strength in sport was a testing ground for courage and strength in life.[130] The University of Toronto Schools (1919), the Regina Pats (1925), St Michael's College, Toronto (1934), and the Winnipeg Monarchs (1937) were all early winners.

FROM EDDIE SHORE TO BOBBY ORR

The period between 1926 and 1940 had been one of tremendous change for professional hockey. Leagues consolidated, hockey captured the interest of large urban populations, the National Hockey League stabilized the number of franchises, a disciplined management of the professional game materialized, players' actions during the game were more regulated, with infractions penalized, salaries were kept in perspective, hero-worship of hockey's big names began, major awards became the focus of seasonal play, and the amateur game took on a unique and clear characterization, separating it from the 'big business' aspects of professional hockey. In no other era in the development of hockey had the game witnessed such a rapid and decisive growth. Along with these changes were alterations in the way the game was played. Two changes particularly affected play on a permanent basis. When the NHL introduced the blue lines in the 1929–30 season, forward-passing was allowed in all three zones of play: the defending zone (between the blue lines), the neutral zone, and the attacking zone. But no passing was permitted across the blue lines, and this made the game quite slow and tedious owing to frequent interruptions for off-side passing. To correct the situation the NHL added in 1943 a red line at the centre of the rink, allowing teams to pass the puck across the blue lines towards the middle of the rink. The longer passes that resulted from this rule change speeded up the method of play, cutting down on the number of play stoppages, and gave fans a faster and more exciting brand of hockey. Hockey was called by the *New York Times* (in 1929 and 1930) 'the fastest game in the world'.[131] At a time when gate receipts were vital to the survival of the fledgling NHL, fan appeal was all-important.

Besides producing rule changes to speed up the game and make it more exciting, the NHL saw the need to market its most valuable re-source—its players. They did this by encouraging newspapers to pub-licize the antics of certain players in the expectation that fans would be drawn to return again and again to see them perform, as well as the games themselves. **Eddie Shore**, who played for the Boston Bruins from 1926 to 1940, was the NHL's first major marketing phenomenon. Since his early playing days in Melville, Saskatchewan, he had a reputation for being tough but also skilled. He could skate, stick-handle, and score with the best players of the period; he could also punch, kick, and scrap with the best. He was a natural gate attraction to spectators who wanted to see a well-played game but also some rough-and-tumble excitement. Shore's flair for the unusual, and his ability to give the fans exactly what they wanted, particularly in Boston, made him one of the most-loved, yet by his opponents one of the least-liked, players in the NHL. It has been said that he did for hockey what Babe Ruth did for baseball.[132]

The Bruins knew Shore's value and gave him star treatment in the late twenties, while also allowing him to indulge himself. After the opposing team and the majority of the Bruins had skated onto the ice and had warmed up, the Boston Gardens would be darkened and the crowd silenced. Then a spotlight would hit a corner of the arena and 'Hail to the Chief' would be blasted out over the loudspeakers. Imme-diately Eddie Shore, adorned in a black-and-gold cape and followed by a young valet, would glide swiftly onto the ice blowing kisses in every direction. The Boston fans would go wild and the oppostion would cringe in disgust as Shore circled the ice.[133] In 1928, in an attempt to outdo Shore, the New York Americans plotted their own grand entrance for one of their players in Madison Square Gardens. Following Shore's entrance, some of the Americans grabbed a rolled carpet off the players' bench, carried it to centre ice, then quickly unrolled it to expose Rabbit McVeigh, who then pranced around the rink waving palm branches.[134] This was too much for the board of governors, who ordered NHL presi-dent Frank Calder to restrict Shore and others from making a mockery of the sport. At the same time they were not unaware of the effect on fans of Shore's behaviour, and this episode introduced permanently into hockey a certain degree of cavorting, shouting, and even fighting from the players in the interests of entertaining the fans.

Shore then became better known for his courageous and brutal rushes up the ice, but his ability to involve himself in controversy did not wain. In 1934, at the height of his career, he was responsible for one of the saddest events in NHL history, commonly referred to as the 'Ace Bailey Incident'.[135] At Maple Leaf Gardens on 12 December 1933, Shore was pushed against the boards by King Clancy of the Leafs. Shore then charged down the rink and smashed into Ace Bailey from behind, thinking he was Clancy, causing Bailey to tumble, crack his skull on the ice, and incur a partially disabling injury. Suspended from League play for approximately five weeks, Shore became the scourge of the NHL.[136] Bailey, injured too seriously to return to hockey, did mend well enough to show up at a benefit game, organized by Eddie Shore and others, to raise money for a trust fund. Held on 14 February 1934 at Maple Leaf Gardens before a capacity audience, an all-star team of Shore, Aurel Joliat, Charlie Gardner, Howie Morenz, 'Red' Dutton, Hooley Smith, Bill Cook, Lionel Conacher, Nels Stewart, Ching Johnson, and Allen Shields took on Bailey's teammates, the Toronto Maple Leafs, in an exhibition game.[137] The match started with Shore and Bailey shaking hands at centre ice while the crowd exploded with applause. Although this event was the result of a tragedy, it turned out to be one of the best marketing events ever for the NHL because it was an early precedent for the annual all-star game—which became an annual event in 1947.

Another great star of the era (who, incidentally, played in the benefit game for Bailey) was **Lionel Conacher** (1900–54). Nicknamed the 'Big Train' because of his hulking size and aggressive play, Conacher was a standout for several hockey clubs during his career.[138] He started his NHL tenure in 1925 with the Pittsburgh Pirates but was traded to the New York Americans in 1926; in 1930 he was traded to the Montreal Maroons. There he stayed until 1934, when he was traded to Chicago, where Conacher led the Black Hawks to their first Stanley Cup win. Traded again in 1935 back to the Maroons, he once again led his new club to a Stanley Cup championship. Conacher retired in 1937. Although he may have not been the most talented player at the time, he, like Eddie Shore, did much to popularize hockey in an era of rapid growth and, also like Shore, was a major drawing-card. His prowess in other amateur and professional sports made him one of Canada's most popular and recognizable athletes.[139] He was also an excellent football player (he

The NHL All-Stars and the Maple Leafs team that played the Ace Bailey Benefit Game on 14 February 1934. (Courtesy Imperial Oil Turofsky Collection, Hockey Hall of Fame, Toronto.)

led the Toronto Argonauts to a Grey Cup victory in 1921), a skilled baseball player (he played with the Toronto Maple Leafs in the International League in the late 1920s), an outstanding boxer and wrestler (he was once Canadian light-heavyweight champion), and a talented lacrosse and soccer player. Conacher's fame as the best all-round athlete of the period, rivalled only by Jim Thorpe in the United States, brought other sport fans to the early NHL arenas to view his athletic feats.

Lionel's younger brother **Charlie Conacher** (1909–67) was an instant star of the Toronto Maple Leafs in his first season of play in 1929.[140] Teamed with Harvey 'Busher' Jackson and Joe Primeau, Charlie became a member of the famous 'Kid Line', which terrorized goaltenders throughout the NHL in the early 1930s. Young Conacher won the NHL scoring title four consecutive seasons, from 1932 to 1936. He shared the title in 1932 with Bill Cook of the Rangers and in 1936 with Bill Thoms of the Leafs.[141] During his fourteen-year career—nine years with Toronto, one year with Detroit, and four years with the New York Americans—Charlie Conacher scored 225 goals and was three times selected as a first team all-star. One of the Leagues's fastest skaters, he was nicknamed 'The Human Express', an echo of his elder brother's sobriquet, 'The Big Train'.

Another of Charlie's other claims to fame during his stellar hockey career was his participation in the longest hockey game in the history of the sport (*New York Times*, 4 April 1933), along with Eddie Shore, Nels Stewart, and Dit Clapper of Boston, and Hap Day, King Clancy, Ace Bailey, Joe Primeau, Busher Jackson, and Red Horner of the Maple Leafs.[142] It was played in Toronto on 3 and 4 April 1933 and lasted some

6 hours and 50 minutes. At this time no points were awarded for a tie; therefore teams had to play until the tie was broken. The Maple Leafs and Bruins played three regular 20-minute periods, five extra overtime 20-minute periods, plus a sixth overtime period that lasted 4 minutes and 46 seconds. The game began at 7:00 p.m. and lasted until 1:50 a.m. on 4 April. It was witnessed by 14,500 exhilarated though tired fans—until this time the largest audience ever to witness an NHL game. At the end of the fifth overtime period, Frank Calder suggested that a flip of a coin should end the match, but Toronto refused. Luckily for the Leafs, diminutive Ken Doraty scored the winning goal in the initial stages of the sixth overtime period to win the game. The victory allowed Toronto to enter the final Stanley Cup playoffs against the New York Rangers, but the Leafs eventually lost.[143] Interestingly, Foster Hewitt announced the entire hockey game without a break on 'Hockey Night in Canada'. Thanks to his endurance, devoted hockey enthusiasts were able to listen to one of the most exciting games in NHL history.

One of the stars of the overtime game and one of the League's most popular fan attractions during the 1930s was **Francis 'King' Clancy** (1903–86). Born in Ottawa, he inherited his nickname from his sportsman father, Tom 'King' Clancy.[144] King Jr played amateur hockey in Ottawa at St Brigid's College, an early outpost for Irish-Catholic hockey players, but signed to play professional hockey with the Ottawa Senators in 1921 at age eighteen. He starred with the Senators in their Stanley Cup winning years of 1921, 1923, and 1927, and quickly became an NHL fixture.[145] Like Eddie Shore, Clancy was a paradox in motion. He was feisty, fast, and pugilistic on the one hand, but fun-loving, skilled, and soft-spoken on the other. As an unpredictable and gifted player, Clancy drew large crowds to watch his antics. He was called the NHL's 'King of Mirth and Merry'.

At the height of his hockey career, Clancy was traded in 1930 by the Ottawa Senators to Conn Smythe's new Toronto Maple Leafs. Smythe had wanted a *bona fide* star to lead his team in their new home, Maple Leaf Gardens. To get King, Smythe paid an unheard-of sum of $35,000, and was forced to give away forward Eric Pettinger and defenseman Art Smith. Termed the 'biggest player deal' of the era, the swap proved to be Conn Smythe's greatest coup. Clancy went on to be the inspirational leader of the Maple Leafs, while the other two players faded into hockey obscurity, along with the Ottawa franchise.[146] In his second year with the Leafs, Clancy proved his worth as he led the team to the Stanley Cup championship of 1932, securing for Conn Smythe his dream of a new hockey home, a new team, and a Stanley Cup victory. The King played until 1937, opting to retire and coach the Montreal Maroons in 1937–8. From 1939 to 1950 he was an official of the NHL. In 1953 he returned to the Leafs as coach—a colourful and argumentative one—but gave up the post in 1956 to pursue a less stressful career as a hockey administrator for the Leafs. Once quoted as saying, 'The time to quit is when it's no longer fun', Clancy never did relinquish his love-affair with hockey. As executive vice-president of the Maple Leaf Club during the eighties, and Harold Ballard's right-hand man, he was known as the Leafs' best public-relations device, the 'vice-president of making people happy'. In speeches he made fans believe that, even though hockey seemed brutal at times, it was fun, and that there were many positive aspects of the game.[147]

The construction of Maple Leaf Gardens was a significant milestone, not only in the history of the Toronto Maple Leafs, but in that of the NHL. It was built by Major **Conn Smythe** (1895–1980), an irascible and shrewd businessman.[148] Born in Toronto, he was captain of the University of Toronto Varsity team that won the 1915 Ontario amateur championship. He later coached the Varsity Grads to the 1928 Olympic title. He was then hired by the newly formed New York Rangers to assemble a team that could play for, and win, the Stanley Cup. While the Rangers won the Cup in 1928, Smythe was released by the New York management owing to differing views on running the team. In spite, Smythe immediately purchased the Toronto St Pats, hoping to make them an NHL contender. He renamed the team the Toronto Maple Leafs in 1929, as a token of his patriotism and of the country's close historical ties to hockey. Wanting to do justice to the fine group of players he had assembled, Smythe felt that he needed a larger arena, one that could seat at least 14,000 spectators. The Mutual Street Arena in Toronto had a capacity of only 8,000.[149] After scouting and abandoning two locations (on Fleet Street and the circular property of Knox College on Spadina Avenue), Conn Smythe and his friends—a veritable Who's Who of Toronto businessmen—approached the T. Eaton Co. about erecting a structure near Carlton Street. J.J. Vaughan, the head of Eaton's management, offered a patch of land one block north of Wood Street, but Smythe counter-proposed that an arena on Carlton Street would bring literally thousands of people past the doors of the Eaton's College Street store. Vaughan, believing this (it did not in fact happen), sold the Carlton and Church Street block to Smythe and agreed to purchase a significant amount of Maple Leaf Gardens' stock.[150] With this assurance, and with the backing of Sir John Aird's Canadian Imperial Bank of Commerce and the Sun Life Insurance Co., Smythe's plans began to unfold. The

Maple Leaf Gardens, Toronto, in 1932, the year after it opened. (Courtesy the Metropolitan Toronto Library, T 10161.)

addition of two prominent building contractors to the Gardens group, J.P. Bickell and Allan Thomson, secured the necessary assurances to start construction of an edifice that in the Depression few thought would ever be more than a pipe-dream. Yet Smythe and his politically influential band of capitalists were able to generate enough support and get the project underway in April 1931.

At various times upwards of 1,300 men were employed in building Maple Leaf Gardens—most of whom had been without work. Though a mammoth project, it was finished in an amazing six months. The building stands 13 storeys high and measures 350 feet (along Carlton Street) by 282 feet (along Church Street). The cost was approximtely $1.5 million, $200,000 of which had to be secured just prior to completion. Instead of making one more concerted bid for corporate donations, Smythe concocted a scheme whereby all the bricklayers, carpenters, masons, electricians, plumbers, and steelworkers would be paid their remaining wages in Maple Leaf Gardens' stock (valued at $10 a share), rather than cash. Considered a travesty at the time, the scheme eventually proved profitable. Within ten years the value of the common shares had increased ten-fold, making many of the previously disgruntled workers a significant amount of money on their forced investment.

The opening game in the Gardens on 12 November 1931—between the Leafs and the Chicago Black Hawks (won by the latter, 3–2)—was described for a radio audience by **Foster Hewitt** (1902–85), seated in the now-famous Gondola overlooking the rink. This was his first 'Hockey Night in Canada', which he opened with the words 'Hello Canada and hockey fans in the United States and Newfoundland'. (Hewitt's first broadcast of a game, however, was on 22 March 1923 from the Mutual Street Arena.)[151] With his distinctive high-pitched voice, his vivid descriptions of plays, and a style of delivery that aroused excitement and suspense, working up to the climax 'He shoots! He scores!', Hewitt imprinted the Leafs and the Gardens on more than a generation of Canadians and made his 'Hockey Night in Canada' an institution. The son of William A. Hewitt, sports editor of the *Toronto Daily Star* for thirty years, Foster Hewitt had been an intercollegiate boxing champion at the University of Toronto, but his first love was not the playing of sport. Rather he became a sportswriter for the *Star* and eventually the owner of radio station CKFH in Toronto, which broadcast 'Hockey Night in Canada' and made Hewitt a wealthy man. He broadcast thousands of hockey games, including national and international games and Olympic matches in Canada, the United States, and Europe. Almost singlehandedly he assisted in immortalizing the game of hockey, its heroes, and the Gardens in the minds of Canadians.

The opening of Maple Gardens was not only a milestone in the Leafs' history but also in the history of the NHL. The Gardens was soon the place where some of the League's most exciting games were played, and where some of the staunchest rivalries in hockey were contested. Over the next twenty years the Leafs would win the Stanley Cup seven times, three times consecutively (in 1947, 1948, and 1949). Their major rivals were the Montreal Canadiens (also known as L'Habitants—the H inside the C on the crest of the Canadiens' red, white, and blue sweater is for *Habitants*), the only other Canadian team in the NHL. Unfortunately their competitions played out a sad nationalistic drama between anglophones and francophones that had a sensational climax in the Montreal hockey riots of 1955, or 'L'Affaire Richard'.[152]

In 1955 **Maurice 'Rocket' Richard** (b. 1931) was the uncontested superstar of the NHL, 'Hockey's greatest goal-scoring machine'.[153] He even outplayed other Canadian-born stars, such as Ted 'Teeder' Kennedy, Gordie Howe, and Jean Beliveau. In a career that spanned eighteen seasons, he scored the most League goals (422), the most goals in a season (50 in a 50-game schedule), the most goals in a playoff series (12 in 9 games), the Leagues' most points (725), the most 'hat-tricks' in regular season games and playoff series, the most goals in a single playoff (5),[154] the most winning goals in playoff competition, the most points in one period (4), and the most overtime goals (4). Richard was one of the major reasons why the Canadiens won the Stanley Cup five consecutive times between 1955 and 1960, becoming the second Canadian 'dynasty' after the Leafs. L'Affaire Richard began in a game of 14 March 1955 with the Boston Bruins when Richard was high-sticked by Hal Laycoe of the Bruins. The fiery Rocket had a chance of winning the scoring title and was taking every opportunity to rush the opponent's net. Knowing this, the Bruins did everything in their power to prevent him from scoring. Unfortunately for Laycoe, his high-stick had drawn blood from Richard's scalp, which sent the superstar into a frantic rage. He attacked Laycoe with his own stick, breaking it across his back, then grabbed another stick to continue the attack until he was stopped by linesman Neil Thompson. Furious, Richard struck out at the official several times.[155] When the situation was brought under control, Richard was given two major penalties: one for fighting with intent to do bodily harm, and the other for abusing an official, which resulted in an automatic game misconduct. The latter penalty required that the president of the NHL review the circumstances of the infraction and interview Richard.

The League president at this time was **Clarence Campbell** (1905–84), an Edmontonian who had been a Rhodes Scholar, and was a retired Lieutenant-Colonel from the Canadian Army, a former NHL official, and an outstanding lawyer (who had served in the Nuremburg trials). He had met Richard before in connection with the Rocket's penalty fines and was noticeably impatient with the violent trends in Canadian hockey. The showdown between Campbell and Richard took on the dimensions of an English-French conflict, as Campbell was seen by French-Canadians simply as an enforcer of English-Canadian interests in the game.[156] The fallout from the incident showed how closely sport could, on occasion, reflect strains in society.[157] Campbell decided on a major form of punishment for Richard, presumably in an attempt to counter his critics for 'weak-kneed' management and to make a concerted effort to clean up the game. He suspended Richard for the remaining two games of the season and imposed a playing ban on him for the entire 1955 playoff schedule. This was viewed by francophones as a strike against French culture—even as a vendetta. Though the anglophone press commended Campbell's courage, the French-Canadian press rose against the striking down of their idol. Jean Pellerin, in *L'Idole d'un peuple: Maurice Richard*, explained the sentiment memorably:

> Monsieur Campbell, du haut de sa grandeur écrasait de sa botte anglaise Maurice Richard, et, en celui-ci chaque canadian-français se sentait écrasé. [Mr Campbell, from the height of his arrogance, squashed with his English boot Maurice Richard, and in him every French-Canadian felt himself squashed.][158]

Campbell's appearance on 17 March 1955 at a crucial end-of-season game in Montreal with Detroit was all that was needed to spark a scene of mob violence. Smoke bombs and rotten tomatoes showered the Forum where Campbell was sitting. Fearing for his life and that of his companion, he was spirited away by police. The game was cancelled and the violence spilled over into St Catherine Street. The rioting continued until the small hours of the next morning and fifteen square blocks surrounding the Forum were devastated. The violence ceased only when Maurice Richard pleaded over the radio, to all French-Canadians, to allow cooler heads to prevail. He had finally accepted the judgement of Campbell and wanted all others to do so as well. But since this point in time the rivalry between Toronto and Montreal has been a rallying point on which discussions of patriotism and nationalism have centred. The incident solidified in the minds of Canadians, both English and French, the close relationship hockey has in a culture that—in sport at least— is very much shared.

Even though there has always been a strong traditional French-Canadian component in the make-up of Les Canadiens, not all of their heroes have been exclusively French. Such early greats as George Hainsworth, Bill Durnan, Sylvio Mantha, 'Babe' Seibert, and Elmer Lach were all Anglophones, as was the Canadiens' greatest English-speaking member, **Howie Morenz** (1902-37). Hockey's most outstanding player of the first half-century, Morenz was born in Mitchell, Ontario.[159] He played amateur hockey in nearby Stratford and signed his first professional hockey contract with the Canadiens in 1923. Nicknamed the 'Canadien Comet', the 'Hurtling Habitant', the 'Mitchell Meteor', and the 'Stratford Streak', Morenz became an instant million-dollar box-office attraction through his reckless speed and his headlong rushes up the ice. Like Eddie Shore, Morenz was one of the NHL's leading stars. His notoriety earned him the reputation (along with Shore) as the the 'Babe Ruth of hockey' by sportswriters in the United States. Morenz's speed in his dashes up the rink established an important tradition among all future teams of the Canadiens, which any later applicant to the team would have to show he could come close to matching.[160] When Morenz exhibited his skill at the opening of Madison Square Gardens in 1925, the *New York Times* (16 December) reported:

> In the tiers of flag-draped boxes was a social registered representation which was something entirely new in New York's long history of events of sport. No sport in any man's town ever got the rousing greeting that Canada's great game got in Richards' new amphitheatre. This was no common or garden variety of sporting event. It assumed the importance of a Momentous Event. Much water will flow under the Brooklyn Bridge before New York witnesses a sporting carnival with so much fuss and ostentation which attended the introduction of pro hockey to Gotham. The Lobby looked like the foyer of an opera—furs, jewels, flashes of cerise, Nile greens. Immediately before the game's start, the teams lined up behind their national bands and paraded around the ice, the bands playing each nation's anthems at the conclusion of the march. The Canadiens skated like demons, winning of course, with Morenz flying for the full 60 minutes and scoring the third goal in their 3–1 win. The vast crowd proved anew that hockey is a game you can learn instantly—and enjoy—particulary with a Morenz to watch.

Howie Morenz played eleven seasons for Montreal before being traded to Chicago in 1935. Midway through the 1935–6 season he was traded again to the New York Rangers, who in turn traded him back to the Canadiens in time for the 1936–7 schedule. His return to Montreal was short-lived. In a game against Chicago on 28 January 1937, Morenz broke his leg crashing into the boards. In his convalescence in hospital he developed an embolism in one of his coronary arteries and died on 8 March 1937.[161] As a tribute to this player—who had scored 270 goals, won the Hart Trophy as the NHL's most outstanding player three times (1928, 1931, and 1932), and was twice named to the first all-star team— the Montreal Canadiens allowed Howie Morenz to lie in state at the Montreal Forum so thousands of his fans could pay their last respects. His funeral service packed 16,000 mourners into the Forum, and 200,000 lined the parade route to Côte-des-Neiges Cemetery. Although Anglophone by birth, he received the affections of the largely French-Canadian fans owing not only to his ability, but also to his total commitment to the ideals of skill, fair play, and pride, which Montreal teams have become known for.

Preceding Montreal's dominance of the NHL in the mid-to late-1950s, the Toronto Maple Leafs enjoyed a brief period of supremacy. Unlike Montreal, the Leafs did not have a Richard or a Morenz, a Beliveau, or a Geoffrion; they were essentially a team without a dominant player. But the players they had were all quality individuals who believed in the work ethic. To be on any Conn Smythe team a player had to give 110 per cent of himself at every game and practice. During their Stanley Cup winning years (1947–9), the Maple Leafs boasted Ted 'Teeder' Kennedy, Max Bentley, Howie Meeker, Frank McCool, Syl Apps, Nick Metz, Bill Ezinicki, Gus Mortson, Victor Lynn, Garth Boesch, Bill Barilko, and Turk Broda. **Ted Kennedy** (b. 1925), born in Humberstone, Ontario, first played organized hockey for the Port Colborne senior team prior to joining the Leafs in 1942–3. He fitted well into the tough-checking Leaf teams coached by 'Hap' Day (whose coaching career with the Leafs lasted from 1941 to 1950), and won the Hart Trophy in 1955, his last season.[162] **Max Bentley** (1920–84), born in Delisle, Saskatchewan, was a Smythe acquisition from Chicago in 1947. Smythe had given up four quality players (Bud Poile, Gaye Stewart, Gus Bodnar, and Bob Goldham) to get Bentley, who had been the NHL's leading scorer in 1946. While in Chicago, Max Bentley was teamed with his brother Doug, and Bill Mosienko, forming one of the most potent lines in the League—the Pony Line. Max won the Hart Trophy in 1946, the Lady Byng Trophy in 1943, and the Art Ross Trophy in 1946 and 1947. The Ross Trophy was presented to the NHL in 1946 by Arthur H. Ross, a governor, for the player who led the League in seasonal scoring.[163] **Turk Broda** (1914–72), a jovial and rollicking man in street clothes, was dead serious when he was goalie for the Leafs. His lifetime goals against the average of 2.56 ranks high among all NHL goaltenders and his 2.08 goals against average in the playoffs is still tops. Throughout his sixteen years as a Leaf (1936–52), Broda won the Vézina Trophy three times (1941, 1948, and 1951, sharing it with Al Rollins in the latter year), and recorded a total of 74 shutouts. **Syl Apps** (b. 1915)—from Paris, Ontario—was another notable Leafs player. An exceptionally gifted all-round athlete, he played hockey and football at McMaster University in Hamilton and went on to compete for Canada in the pole vault at the 1934 British Empire Games and the 1936 Berlin Olympics. Joining the Leafs in 1936, Apps was the *first* recipient of the Calder Trophy as the NHL's top rookie.[164] A quiet, modest type, he was an inspirational leader for the Toronto Maple Leafs. For most of his thirteen years on the Leafs, he was team captain and performed his duties admirably. He was a first-team all-star twice and a second-team selection three times, and the Lady Byng Trophy winner in 1941–2. Apps personified Smythe's commitment to team play, and with several 20-goal seasons carried out his boss's plan to spread the goal-scoring evenly throughout the forward ranks. Conn Smythe's vision of good goaltending and stalwart defence made the Leafs of the late 1940s an uncompromisingly disciplined and frustrating foe.

One of the greatest stars of the NHL, Gordie Howe, captain of the Detroit Red Wings, in a game with the Leafs in Maple Leaf Gardens, Toronto, in the early sixties: l. to r., Allan Stanley, Howe, Barry Cullen, and Johnny Bower. Howe's all-time scoring record for most goals and assists still stands. He played an unsurpassed thirty-two years of professional hockey. (Courtesy Imperial Oil Turofsky Collection, Hockey Hall of Fame.)

Before the Canadiens' 'dynasty' period of the late 1950s, another team rose to prominence and entered the record books: the Detroit Red Wings. Their roster (in 1950–5) was dotted with Canadian players who would later occupy places in the Hockey Hall of Fame, which was built at Exhibition Place in Toronto and opened in 1961 (but was unofficially begun in 1943). Three of the Wings' dominant players in the early fifties were Gordie Howe, Ted Lindsay, and Sid Abel. **Gordie Howe** (b. 1928), from Floral, Saskatchewan, holds the NHL's record (thirty-two years) for the longest professional hockey career—a remarkable feat. He played junior hockey in Saskatoon and Galt, Ontario, before turning professional with Omaha in 1945. The next year he jumped to Detroit and never looked back. While his career started slowly with 7, 16, and 12 goals in his first three years, his great strength and physical stamina allowed him, during the course of the rest of his career, to score 1,071 goals and have 1,518 assists for a total of 2,589 points—all-time records. Other career milestones for Howe in the NHL include most seasons (26)—six additional seasons were spent in the World Hockey Association

(WHA)—most games (including playoffs—1,924), most goals (869), most assists (1,141), and most points (2,010). As one of the pre-eminent stars of the game, Howe won the Art Ross Trophy six times (1950-4, 1957, and 1963), the Hart Trophy six times (1952, 1953, 1957, 1958, 1960, and 1963), and was an NHL all-star 21 times. Howe retired from Detroit in 1971 but returned to hockey in 1973 to join his two sons, Mark and Marty, with the WHA Houston Aeros. He finished his playing career in 1980 when he was 52, with the Hartford Whalers.[165]

As a member of the famed 'Production Line', Howe was supported by Ted Lindsay and Sid Abel.[166] **Ted Lindsay** (b. 1925) from Renfrew, Ontario, joined Detroit in 1944 and played left-wing opposite Howe, who played right-wing. **Sid Abel** (b. 1918), another Saskatchewan native, born in Melville, centred the Production Line. He joined the Red Wings in 1938. Between 1949 and 1952 the trio were considered the best offensive unit in hockey and contributed greatly to Detroit's Stanley Cup victories in 1950, 1952, and (minus Abel) in 1954 and 1955. Abel was the recipient of the Hart Trophy in 1949 and was selected a first-team all-star in 1949 and 1950, and a second-team all-star in 1942 and 1951. Lindsay won the Ross Trophy in 1950 for scoring, but was best known for his toughness and fearless checking. Interestingly, the architect of the Production Line, Jack Adams—Detroit's general manager—upon hearing of Lindsay's role in the formation of the NHL's players' union (Lindsay was its first president in 1957), traded him to Chicago. Few owners and general managers perceived a players' union as a constructive development in the game, owing to the destructive effect it would have on their control of the business aspects of hockey.

From 1955 to 1960 the Montreal Canadiens were an enormous force in hockey. The club was the first NHL franchise to win five consecutive Stanley Cups. While Rocket Richard, on their front lines, was the star of the Canadiens, a new young group of exceptional players fortified the dominance of the club. Under the coaching guidance of 'Toe' Blake (b. 1912)—the managerial wizardry of Frank Selke (1893–1985), and the prowess of Jean Beliveau, Bernie 'Boom Boom' Geoffrion, Doug Harvey, and Jacques Plante, the Canadiens secured an extended grip on NHL hockey supremacy.

Jean Beliveau (b. 1931), from Trois-Rivières, played his junior hockey with the Quebec Aces. Refusing to move up to the Canadiens for two years, he finally signed with them in 1953. The contract was touted as being the most lucrative ever signed by a Canadian (reported to be $100,000 per season for five seasons). 'Le Gros Bill' or 'Big Bill', as he was nicknamed, had an exemplary career.[167] In his eighteen seasons

Maurice Richard and Jean Beliveau holding the Stanley Cup in 1958. (Courtesy CanaPress Photo Service.)

with Montreal, Beliveau scored 507 goals and 1,219 points in 1,125 games. In 162 playoff games he scored 79 goals (second all-time) and a record 176 points. By 1956, when he won the NHL scoring championship (Ross Trophy) and the Hart Trophy (most valuable player), Beliveau had become the stately leader of the most powerful team in the history of the professional game. In 1971 his leadership landed him the vice-presidency of the Canadiens' franchise, owned and operated by Molson Breweries (Canada) Ltd.

Montreal-born **Bernie Geoffrion** (b. 1931), perhaps the most intense Canadien of the late 1950s, was accorded the nickname 'Boom Boom' for good reason.[168] Few players could match the strength and speed of his shot. Authorities likened it to the noise that jet aircraft make when breaking the sound barrier: Boom! Boom! In his fourteen seasons with the Canadiens, Geoffrion's high-spirited play earned him the distinction of being one of the game's highest-scoring players: 393 goals and 429 assists. He added 58 goals and 60 assists to his scoring totals in the playoffs. As a high scorer, Geoffrion won the Ross Trophy in 1954–5 and 1960–1, and was the second player, behind Maurice Richard, to score 50 goals in one season. Geoffrion won the Calder Trophy as top rookie in 1950–1 and in 1960–1 the Hart Trophy as the NHL's most valuable player.

Doug Harvey (b. 1924 in Montreal) rejected offers to play major-league football and baseball, opting to play senior amateur hockey for the Montreal Royals before joining the Canadiens in 1947–8. Unquestionably he was the best defenseman of his era, having the ability (much like Bobby Orr later on) to control the tempo of a game. His pinpoint passing, subtle playmaking, and dramatic offensive rushes made Harvey the first 'modern' defenseman. Although talented in the creation of goal-scoring situations, his stick and bodychecking skills were without equal at the time, and his leadership qualities—complementing those of Jean Beliveau—gave the Canadiens a solid generalship on and off the ice. Harvey was awarded the James Norris Trophy as the NHL's outstanding defenseman in 1955, 1956–8, and 1960–2—an unprecedented seven times.[169] (Norris (1879–1952), a former governor of the League, was the owner of the Detroit Red Wings and a long admirer of solid defensive hockey. The Norris Trophy recognizes the all-round ability of the game's best defensemen.) As hockey's most celebrated defenseman, Harvey was a first-team all-star seven times and scored 88 goals and 452 assists in 1,113 regular season games. He was traded in 1961 by Montreal—owing to his active involvement in the NHL players' association—to the New York Rangers, where he co-coached and played for one season. The last club he played for was the St Louis Blues and he ended his attachment to the professional game of hockey by briefly coaching the Los Angeles Kings in 1970.

Jacques Plante (1929–86) was the goaltender behind Doug Harvey's first line of defence. Born in Mont-Carmel, Quebec, Plante became a standout net-minder for the Canadiens during their first dynasty era and was accredited with introducing, on a permanent basis, the facemask into the equipment inventory of NHL goaltenders.[170] His roving style of play and his flopping, poke-checking technique became exciting trademarks at a time when conservative, defensive hockey was in vogue. Plante won the Vézina Trophy, as the League's outstanding goaltender, an unprecedented six consecutive times from 1955 to 1962. In the latter year he was awarded the Hart Trophy as the NHL's most valuable player and was a member of the first all-star team in 1956, 1959, and 1962.

Moreover, Plante was with the Canadiens' team when it won the Stanley Cup in 1953 and 1956 through to 1960. His 2.22 goals against average still stands as one of the best in NHL history.

After the Canadiens' dominance of the Stanley Cup between 1955 and 1960, a new hockey club appeared, with a new star, and it exhibited strong play until the NHL expanded in 1967. The team was the Chicago Black Hawks and their new superstar was **Bobby Hull** (b. 1939 in Pointe Anne, Ont.).[171] Like Wayne Gretzky of a later time, Hull was tagged at an early age as a sure-fire bet to star in the NHL. Always playing ahead of his age-group category, he starred in junior hockey at Hespeler (Cambridge), Woodstock, and St Catharines, Ontario, before joining the Chicago Black Hawks in 1957. Labelled the 'Golden Jet' because of his wavy blond hair and terrific speed, Hull terrorized NHL goaltenders with his innovative shooting technique—the slapshot. His deadly accurate slapshots recorded speeds of 187 km/h and were potent enough to break bones in the hands, feet, legs, chest, and faces of opponents. Bobby Hull was one of the NHL's strongest players ever. His strength translated into break-neck speed and crushing body-checking force. It was not uncommon to see players skate around him rather than incur the painful punishment of one of his body-checks—though Hull was never 'dirty' in his technique. The relative freedom he enjoyed at his left-wing position allowed him, in his sixteen NHL seasons, to score 610 goals and add 560 assists. In the playoffs he added 62 goals and 67 assists. He helped the Black Hawks to a Stanley Cup victory in 1961, their first since 1938, and was the first player to score 50 goals in a season (54 in 1965–6). He won the Ross Trophy three times; the Lady Byng Trophy once; the Hart Trophy twice; and the Lester Patrick Trophy, for his contribution to hockey in the United States, once. Hull made an indirect contribution to hockey in 1972 when he accepted a million-dollar contract to jump from the NHL to the Winnipeg Jets of the new World Hockey Association (WHA). As the most talked-about star of the WHA and as their media spokesperson, he did much to popularize the NHL's chief competitive hockey rival. Although in a different hockey association, Hull continued his prolific scoring ways in Winnipeg by adding to his totals 303 goals and 638 points in 411 games. Many of his teammates on the Chicago Black Hawks at this time were standouts in their own right. There was Stan Mikita,[172] the first Czechoslovakian-born player in the NHL and winner of the Ross Trophy in 1964, 1965, 1967 and 1968, and the Hart Trophy in 1967 and 1968; and there were the Canadians Glenn Hall, perhaps one of the NHL's most durable goaltenders, who played eighteen years and during that time won the Vézina Trophy three times;

and Pierre Pilot who, behind Doug Harvey, one of the League's best defensemen, was the recipient of the Norris Trophy three times and an NHL all-star on eight occasions.

The Toronto Maple Leafs' second dynasty team, coached by **George 'Punch' Imlach**, won Stanley Cups in 1962, 1963, 1964, and 1967. Imlach (1918–87), a general manager of exceptional quality who had a keen eye for talent, joined the Maple Leafs in 1958 after a mediocre career as a player-coach with the Quebec Aces.[173] He was a task-master who was capable of drawing talent from aging players. The Leafs' team that won the Stanley Cup in the mid-1960s overflowed with players considered by many to be past their prime: Johnny Bower, who began his career with Toronto at age 34 and went on to star for Imlach in the nets during the 1960s and 1970s; Tim Horton, who started his career with the Leafs in 1952 and was 32 when Imlach's team won the 1962 Stanley Cup; Terry Sawchuk, who was 33 in 1962 when he tended Toronto's goal with Bower; and there were many others—Allan Stanley, Marcel Pronovost, Bob Baun, Andy Bathgate, George Armstrong, Al Arbour, Bob Pulford, Eddie Shack, Floyd Smith, and Norm Ullman—who were well into their thirties during Imlach's reign as coach. Imlach did not believe in the adage 'You can't teach old dogs new tricks.' His veteran players continued to produce well into the twilight of their careers, always wanting to set an example for such fine young stars as 'Red' Kelly, Frank Mahovlich, and Dave Keon. **Red Kelly** (b. 1927), a trade-off from Detroit, was a stalwart defenseman and centreman for the Leafs. An earlier star with the traditionally strong St Michael's College team in Toronto, he scored 281 goals and added 542 assists during his nineteen-year NHL career. He later coached with Los Angeles, Pittsburgh, and Toronto. **Frank Mahovlich** (b. 1936), another St Mike's grad, won the 1958 Calder Trophy as the most outstanding rookie in the NHL. 'The Big M', as he was known, played twenty years in the League and gained six Stanley Cups—four with Toronto and two with Montreal, a club he joined in 1971. A smooth skater and famous for his big windups, he earned 533 goals and 1,103 total points in 1,181 regular season games. **Dave Keon** (b. 1940), another product of Father David Bauer's training at St Mike's, played eighteen years in the NHL before moving to the WHA for four years. A notably effortless skater who could 'turn-on-a-dime', he was the Calder Trophy winner in 1961. He centred a line with either Mahovlich and Bob Nevin or George Armstrong and Dick Duff. A four-time winner of the Lady Byng Trophy, Keon spent only 117 minutes in the penalty box during his long career. He was one of the early recipients of the Conn Smythe Trophy in 1967. Maple Leaf Gardens Ltd. presented the NHL with this award in 1964, to honour the most outstanding player in the NHL playoffs, in recognition of the contributions of Conn Smythe as a former coach, manager, president, and owner-governor of the Maple Leafs. The mid-1960s dynasty of the Leafs is well remembered for their mature talent and for their dogged determination and extraordinary team play.

The last dynasty of the NHL's 'original six' teams before expansion was that of the Montreal Canadiens from 1965 to 1969. The team won Stanley Cups in 1965, 1966, 1968, and 1969, but without many of the stars of the dynasty teams of the 1950s. By the mid-1960s only coach 'Toe' Blake, Jean Beliveau, Henri Richard, and Claude Provost remained.[174] **Lorne 'Gump' Worsley** and Charlie Hodge shared the goaltending duties in the later dynasty. Worsley, born in Montreal in 1929, enjoyed a standout career with the Canadiens and remained in hockey as a goaltender for twenty-four seasons.[175] In 1953 he won the Calder Trophy as the NHL's top rookie and shared the Vézina Trophy in 1965 and 1967 with Charlie Hodge and Rogatien Vachon respectively. Owing to the fact that the Canadiens of the mid-1960s were physically small—though the team boasted Henri Richard, Dick Duff, Yvan Cournoyer, Jim Roberts, Bobby Rousseau, and Jean-Guy Talbot—they were often taken advantage of by bigger and rougher opponents. Sam Pollock, Montreal's astute general manager, began to shop around for an 'enforcer'. John Ferguson (b. 1938), a capable player, was hired to act as an on-ice policeman, taking on opposing players who menaced the smaller Montreal forwards. As Pollock intended, now that the flashy and fleet Canadien stars had room to move, without annoyance from other teams' enforcers, they scored a greater number of goals and won games they would otherwise have lost if not for the Ferguson's 'protection', which helped the team to Stanley Cup supremacy. Ferguson's role signalled the beginning of a new era in professional hockey that saw physical play—which eventually degenerated into 'goon hockey'—become a *modus operandi* of nearly all NHL clubs.[176] Expansion in 1967 initially thinned the talent pool of the NHL. Although many skilled players entered the League by way of the American Hockey League (AHL), through the Central Hockey League (CHL), and the International Hockey League (IHL), other less-skilled players won their way into the NHL because of their ability to protect what few highly skilled players there were. As a result, between 1967 and the third NHL expansion of 1972 (Buffalo and Vancouver joined in 1970), teams were paying more attention to the quality of their 'enforcers' than they had at any other time in the history of the League.

Expansion did not always have negative connotations. In 1967 a new Canadian star arrived on the NHL horizon who would revolutionize the defenseman's role in hockey. His name was **Bobby Orr** (b. 1948), and at the age of eighteen, playing for the Boston Bruins in his first season, he exhibited a level of skill and maturity far beyond his years. Orr was the new hope for professional hockey. His advanced skills in skating, stick-handling, and shooting made hockey fans believe that the game was not going to turn into a gladiatorial exhibition—a show of little skill and much brutality. Orr, and his introduction to fans across North America by way of lucrative League-expansion television contracts, gave hope to a game that had been enveloped by negative criticism in the late 1960s. These expansion years were pivotal for the NHL, and for the professional game of hockey.

FROM GOON TO BOOM TO GRETZKY

The expansion of the NHL from six teams to twelve in 1967 signified a period of rapid growth for professional hockey. Television was credited with adding to the popularity of the game by reason of its improved ability to report on a wide number of issues. Players' lives were portrayed in greater detail, the competitive aspect of international hockey gained recognition, and 'goon' hockey of the period—individual acts of violence by players—titillated the masses. Through the greater range of television coverage, people more closely identified with both the positive and negative aspects of the sport and demanded to see more.

The six teams added to the NHL in the 1967 expansion were all American. The Oakland (California) Seals, the Los Angeles Kings, the Minnesota North Stars, the Philadelphia Flyers, the Pittsburgh Penguins, and the St Louis Blues were the new additions to a League that had been largely dominated by Canadian talent. The lack of Canadian franchise interest in the NHL moved the board of governors to add the Vancouver Canucks in 1970, along with another American team, the Buffalo Sabres. Further expansion in 1972 saw the New York Islanders and the Atlanta Flames added. The number of teams in the League reached eighteen in 1974 with the addition of the Kansas City Scouts and the Colorado Rockies (later the New Jersey Devils).[177]

Lobbying by Canadian interests for more teams from north of the 49th parallel fell on deaf ears. The board of governors (the owners) of the NHL was dominated by American interests at the time and all, except a few, felt that no Canadian city could generate adequate television or spectator revenue to make expansion in Canada a profitable venture. But the fortunes of several Canadian cities improved towards the end of the 1970s.

Two promoters who felt they could develop a league of equal stature to the NHL were Bill Hunter of Saskatoon and Ben Hatskin of Winnipeg. Hunter, a former owner of the Edmonton Oil Kings of the Western Canada Junior Hockey League (WCJHL) and Hatskin, a wealthy Winnipeg businessman who had been involved with the Winnipeg Esquires of the WCJHL, believed that by attracting numerous star players from the NHL and by mixing in a number of outstanding junior- and minor-league professionals, a hockey organization could be built to compete with the popularity of the NHL. In order to do this they agreed to offer sizeably lucrative contracts to NHL superstars, who in turn could provide them with large spectator interest and significant media coverage. Thus the World Hockey Association evolved. The lofty NHL did not consider the establishment of the WHA a real threat. Few hockey organizations could rival the secure though complex organization of the premier league in North America. But the possibility of a competitive league became credible when, on 27 February 1972, one of the NHL's brightest young goaltenders signed with the WHA. Bernie Parent saw his financial interests being best served by the Miami Screaming Eagles. The shock of his signing had barely wained when it was announced that another star of the NHL had jumped ship. Bobby Hull was enticed to the WHA by Haskin's own Winnipeg Jets franchise, which agreed to pay the 'Golden Jet' a million-dollar signing bonus, $250,000 a year for five years and $100,000 a year for another five years to act as a front-office executive. Hull's signing immediately gave the WHA credibility, and a flood of other NHL stars signed on. Many of those who joined the rival league were Frank Mahovlich with the Toronto Toros and Birmingham (Alabama) Bulls, Gordie Howe with the Houston Aeros, Gerry Cheevers with the Cleveland Cavaliers, Dave Keon with the Minnesota Fighting Saints and later the New England Whalers, Jacques Plante and Norm Ullman with the Edmonton Oilers, and Harry Howell with the Calgary Cowboys.[178] The threat of a rival league was now confirmed in the minds of previously doubting NHL administrators. Bill Hunter and Ben Hatskin had made good on their threats to wrest away from the older league considerable talent and money.

The WHA survived only seven years, with numerous Canadian cities hosting sucessful franchises. Its collapse in 1979, and the financial failure of the NHL Kansas City franchise in 1978, served to change the thinking of the NHL executives. Kansas City's downfall proved that not every location in the United States was ready to accept the introduction of ice hockey. Hence the pro-American political sentiments of NHL governors eased somewhat and the prospect of adding Canadian teams to the NHL became a real possibility. In the fall of 1979 four defunct WHA franchises were added to the NHL, three representing Canadian cities. The Edmonton Oilers, the Quebec Nordiques, the Winnipeg Jets, and the Hartford Whalers increased the NHL's total number of teams to 21. When the Atlanta Flames had trouble stimulating southern interest in hockey, the franchise was moved to Calgary. The Calgary Flames gave Canada seven teams in the NHL.

The relatively brief success of the WHA, and the concurrent expansion of the NHL through the late 1970s, had a considerable impact on the quality of play in the NHL—it weakened it. Teams scrambled to sign players who could strengthen them, but in reality they had lost a marginal amount of quality-control on talent. 'I'm not a drinking man,' said Conn Smythe, 'but I know if you pour too much water in your whisky, the whisky gets weaker'. And indeed the NHL and WHA talent pools of the early 1970s were thinned considerably as a result of rapid hockey expansion. So thin did they become, in fact, that the aesthetic quality of hockey, which novelist Ralph Allen called 'a tough but lovely form of art', was lost. Instead of loveliness, professional hockey became toughness.[179] The owners, unable to find players who could skate with the genuine stars, reached out to people who could knock them down. Big, rugged, tough guys, or 'goons' (as the most devoted fans called them) set out to intimidate the better quicker players and acted to protect their own team's stars from other similar 'goons'. What had been a game of finesse during the 1950s and 1960s had become a Kurt Vonnegut 'Battle of the Titans' in the 1970s. The definitive offensive play of the early seventies was to shoot the puck into the other team's zone and then observe who was big enough to go in and drag it out.

The team that understood the theory of 'goonism' best at this time was the Philadelphia Flyers, which quickly rose to the top of the expansion pyramid. Although their line-up had many fine players—Bobby Clarke, Bill Barber, and Rick MacLeish, to name a few—the Flyers were well endowed with 'enforcers': Bob 'Mad Dog' Kelly, who spent more than six hours in the penalty box in two years (1971–3), and Dave 'The Hammer' Shultz, who spent a complementary ten hours. By sheer intimidation coach Fred Shero had moved the Flyers from an expansion 'also-ran' to a team that, in 1973–4, became the first expansion club to wrest the Stanley Cup away from the 'original six'. Their brutal recipe for victory won out again in 1974–5, causing other clubs to move away from skilled play and towards physical intimidation. Boston recruited Ken Hodge and Wayne Cashman, the New York Islanders secured the services of Clark Gillies, the Maple Leafs boasted Bob Baun and Pat Quinn, the Canadiens had John Ferguson and Ted Harris, the New York Rangers had Reggie Fleming, the Chicago Black Hawks had Lou Fontinato, and the Vancouver Canucks unleashed Howie Young. Every team, it seemed, revelled in the fact that it had a fighter on its roster. But few clubs could match the 'Broad Street Bullies' of Philadelphia.

The 'goon era' of hockey had a significant effect on the lay person's perception of violence in the game. Most authorities felt that skill was being lost in the professional game in favour of violent play. And they thought it would have a devastating effect on young hockey players who, wishing to emulate their NHL heroes, might become too concerned about slashing, boarding, high-sticking, and butt-ending to concentrate on passing, skating, feigning, and scoring. For all intents purposes the knowledgeable men of hockey were right—the violence of the professional game did have a profound effect on pee-wee and bantam hockey in the post-expansion years. Building on Conn Smythe's adage, 'If you can't beat them outside in the alley, you can't beat them inside on the ice', minor-league coaches and officials became more tolerant of rough play from young hockey players. And parents, who had read *Hockey Is a Battle* (1970) by Punch Imlack and Scott Young and Bobby Hull's *Hockey Is My Game* (1967), became convinced that minor hockey was a testing-ground for masculinity. There was no room, they believed, for overt emotional sensitivity or cowardliness in the game. In fact, Hull went so far as to state:

> Hockey is no sport for cowards, aggression pays off, and not only in games won. The aggressive player not only makes a big contribution to the spectacle [of a hockey game], but he is also less liable to be hurt.[180]

In the 1970s the call of parents to their male offspring to 'hit "em"' rang out in arenas from coast to coast, often to the despair of less sanguinary coaches. Violence had definitely filtered down from the professional ranks of hockey to the minor-league levels—to the sanctioned approval of coaches and officials. One would have been hard-pressed to refute Dick Beddoes' example of a minor-league coach's 'pep' talk to his team, which was published in the Toronto *Globe and Mail* on 18 November 1970:

> If there is any blood on any sweaters, it is going to be on their sweaters— not ours . . . . I want you guys to hit these bums so hard, they will be scared to come back in the rink.

This era in minor hockey represented a 'black plague'. The violent tendencies of minor-league coaches and players translated into more frequent injuries. Although the Metropolitan Toronto Hockey League had as one of its aims to build 'good character and citizenship' among the young players,[181] a 1973 Toronto medical *Survey* of various minor sports showed that hockey produced more injuries among young Canadian males than did baseball, football, and soccer combined.[182] The doctors who did the research were convinced that the high-sticking habits of the minor hockey-league players was a major factor in the study's results. So intense was the criticism of violent tactics in minor-league at the time that politicians were moved to act in accordance with the general population's opposition to this trend.

In 1974 the Hon. René Brunelle, federal Minister of Community and Social Services, struck a task-force committee to investigate 'Violence in Amateur Hockey'.[183] Headed by Ontario's Attorney-General Roy McMurtry, the *Report*, to no one's surprise, found that children did emulate their NHL 'goon' heroes and that their parents were largely to blame in the reinforcement of violent acts of hockey behaviour. Moreover, and to the sickening astonishment of many Canadians, the study found that minor-league hockey coaches were teaching their young charges illegal techniques of charging and cross-checking. Convinced that something had to be done about violence in amateur hockey, the Canadian Amateur Hockey Association (CAHA), in association with the Canadian Department of National Health and Welfare, devised a plan to change hockey's minor-league approach. Coaching clinics and certification became imperatives in the mid-1970s for anyone aspiring to coach minor hockey. In essence a major transformation occurred.No longer were the older over-zealous minor-league coaches evident. Younger, better-conditioned, and, most importantly, better-trained coaches began to emerge. Many were university-trained and had played college hockey. But the transformation from old to new did not occur overnight. Certain external forces were needed to convince hockey 'kingpins' to alter their thinking about the violent direction of the game.

One of these forces, and perhaps the most important one, was the influence of Canada's participation in international hockey matches, particularly the 1972 Canada-USSR hockey series. This did much to alter Canadians' perception of how hockey should be played. The ultimate victory of Canada in the series of eight games (Canada won 4, USSR won 3, one was tied) did little to remove the indelible fact that hockey was being played elsewhere on a level with the NHL. This phenomenon was a shocking surprise to North America's premier professional hockey players. The views of Canadian team coach Harry Sinden were reported in the *New York Times*:

> . . . . the series had demonstrated to our professional players that hockey is being played well—or almost as well—in many parts of the world, particularly in the Soviet Union . . . . Referring to the contrasting styles of play between the two teams, Sinden added that the games had exposed the Canadians to 'a manner of puckhandling and passing that we don't see much of in the National Hockey League.'[184]

The rough play of the Canadians and their 'goon' tactics were perceived, by all who witnessed the matches, as an inferior style of play when compared with the fast-skating, crisp-passing, and well-disciplined tactics of the Russian team. As patriotic as Canadians felt about winning the first Canada-USSR hockey series, they were ashamed that the tactics used to steal victory were ones not inherent in the original ideals of the game. The excessively violent style of hockey in the NHL was suddenly no longer the style of popular choice. The NHL mode of play needed to be reformed. If Canadians wished to remain the supreme players of their 'national game' against foreign interests, the sooner they returned to skilled passing and disciplined play-making, the quicker they would regain pre-eminence in the sport. Hence professional, and even amateur, hockey in Canada went through a refurbishing in the mid-1970s. 'Goon' tactics wained in importance, and emphasis on skill and high-calibre play returned. This change took on a new and beneficial twist.

As a result of the 1972 Canada-USSR hockey series and the NHL's desire to recondition the professional game, owners and general managers began looking towards other countries to fill the obvious void for skilled players that rapid League expansion had left. Knowing that certain foreign countries were now playing hockey on a level almost equal to Canada, owners were less hesitant to sign talent from Sweden, Finland, and Czechoslovakia. As Peter Gzowski explained in *The Game of Our Lives*,[185] the importation of foreign players to the NHL in the post-1972 era became a 'Canadian sub-industry'. In 1973 the Maple Leafs signed from the Swedish national team Borje Salming, who quickly proved that he was not only one of the finer defensemen, but also that he and his countrymen were not 'chicken', which had been the NHL's conventional wisdom up to this point. The following year (1974) saw the Winnipeg Jets of the WHA sign two of Salming's former team-mates, Anders Hedberg and Ulf Nilsson. They were both great scorers, and when combined with Bobby Hull they formed one of the most productive forward lines in hockey. That same year the Toronto Toros assisted in smuggling Vaclav Nedomansky out of Czechoslovakia. And as well, both the NHL and WHA were beginning to hire well-coached graduates of American colleges. However begrudgingly, Canadian hockey enthusiasts began to recognize that non-Canadians, especially the Soviets, were playing the game as well as anyone, and playing it in a manner that was closer to the original ideals of hockey than were many of the Canadian-born players.

Since this period the quality of skilled play in the NHL has been improved by the addition of numerous foreign players: Kent Nilsson to the Atlanta (later Calgary) Flames, Peter and Anton Stastny to the Quebec Nordiques, Ulf Samuelson to the Philadelphia Flyers, Jari Kurri to the Edmonton Oilers, Mats Naslund and Petre Svoboda to the Montreal Canadiens, Pitre Sriko to the Vancouver Canucks, and Reijo Ruotsalainen to the New York Rangers, to name a few. Yet Canadians have had to wait almost two decades to witness the signing of a Soviet player to an NHL contract. Experts of the international game believed the Soviets would release one of their aging stars to the NHL for public-relations purposes—maybe a Vladislav Tretiak, a Boris Mikhailov, a Valeri Kharlamov, or an Aleksander Yakushev. But such a circumstance did not materialize owing to the importance of these stars to Soviet national and political interests. Instead, in 1989 Soviet hockey officials allowed a subnational team player, Sergei Priatkin of the Soviet Wings hockey club, to be their test case in the NHL.[186] A solid offensive and defensive player, Priatkin, under 'Glasnost' diplomacy, joined the Calgary Flames. He represented little risk to Soviet hockey interests. He was not a star in his own country, and if he failed in the NHL this would be viewed as a personal failure unrelated to the Soviet hockey system. In essence the Soviets had nothing to lose by sending him to the NHL and they had a substantial source of revenue to gain from this and possibly other transfers through NHL-Soviet player contracts that would see Canadian and American dollars going directly back to the Soviet Union to support its hockey program. But even this scenario would be of minor importance to the Soviets: their hockey system has been profitable for decades.

The Soviets had made their début in the international hockey arena in 1954 at the World Hockey Championships in Stockholm, Sweden.[187] By winning the world championship in 1954 on their initial attempt, they made clear that they wished to become the next reigning power in the sport. This fact they reasserted at the Winter Olympic Games in 1956 at Cortina, Italy. The Russians won the gold medal for the first time, beating out the United States (silver) and Canada (bronze). This was the first time (except for 1936, when the British team was mostly of Canadian servicemen) that Canada had lost an Olympic gold medal in hockey since the initial inclusion of the sport in the Winter Olympics in 1920 at Antwerp. Yet public recognition of Soviet hockey superiority remained unforthcoming in the next decade. At the 1957 World Championships in Moscow, the Russians suffered an embarrassing loss to Sweden in the finals. And again at the 1958 and 1959 World Championships in Oslo and Prague, Canada beat the Russians, serving to diminish the glitter that Soviet hockey had acquired at the 1956 Olympics. Insult was added to injury in 1960 at the Winter Olympics in Squaw Valley, California, when the United States beat Canada (silver) and the Soviet Union (bronze) for the gold medal. The Russians' play was anything but spectacular and it sparked a re-examination of their whole hockey system.[188] During their 'restructuring period', the World Hockey Championship became the prize of Canada in 1961 and Sweden in 1962. But starting in 1963, at the World Championships in Stockholm, the Soviets began a hockey campaign that, leading up to the 1972 Canada-Soviet series, saw them win seven consecutive World Hockey Championships (1963, 1965, 1966, 1967, 1969, 1970 and 1971) and win Olympic gold in 1964 at Innsbruck and in 1968 at Grenoble. The mighty Soviet hockey machine also won the 1972 Olympic gold medal in Sapporo, Japan, as a prelude to the Canada-Soviet hockey series. There was no doubt that the Soviet system rivalled that of Canada in producing winning hockey teams.

Canada's participation in the 1972 international series with the Russians was much anticipated because Canada had dropped out of world hockey competition in 1969 owing to disagreements with the International Ice Hockey Federation over the eligibility of players.[189] Therefore 1972 represented a critical point in hockey's future in Canada and a watershed for its continued popularity among Canadians—in the light of the growing controversy over 'goonism' and the apparent de-emphasis on skill in the NHL. Fortunately when Paul Henderson of the Maple Leafs scored the winning goal for Canada, with 34 seconds left in the final game, all matters of national pride and superiority resurfaced and Canada became once again the home of a superior brand of hockey. The professionals of the NHL had redeemed themselves and their sport against the Soviet 'amateurs', but had done so only up to the point where speed, passing, and teamwork supplanted 'goon' tactics and violent play.[190]

The reinvigoration of Canadian hockey has been tested every four years since 1972. The Canada Cup, which pits the Soviets and other foreign countries against Canada's best professional hockey players, has become an important thermometer recording supremacy in the game.

Seconds before this shot was taken Wayne Gretzky (of the Edmonton Oilers) and Mario Lemieux (of the Pittsburgh Penguins)—two of the best players in hockey—made the winning goal for Canada against the Soviet Union in the 1987 Canada Cup hockey tournament. Gretzky is on the left. (Photograph by Doug MacLellan courtesy the Hockey Hall of Fame, Toronto.)

In matches of 1976, 1984, and 1987, Canada was victorious. The Soviets won their only Canada Cup in 1981. While the NHL still holds a marginal advantage in skilled play, the Canada Cup has shown that other countries have improved the quality of hockey to near-NHL levels. The Soviet Union still dominates the major world hockey tournaments, but does so on a less-frequent basis than in the 1963-to-1972 period. Granted they have been strong in the Winter Olympic Games—winning in 1976, 1984, and 1988—but Czechoslovakia and Sweden have ousted them from World Hockey supremacy on several occasions (Czechoslovakia in 1975 and Sweden in 1976).

After the collapse of the WHA in 1979–80 and the addition of Winnipeg, Quebec City, Edmonton, and Hartford to the NHL, a return to a strong talent base and a certain amount of quality-control materialized.

More than ever, skilled play enjoyed a rebirth in the NHL led by the Montreal Canadiens in the late 1970s. They entered their third dynasty with **Guy Lafleur** (b. 1951), who emerged as a superstar in 1974–5 after mediocre NHL seasons in 1971, 1972, and 1973. The goal production of 'The Flower' jumped from 21 to 53 between 1971 and 1974, when it became evident that Montreal had an heir to Jean Beliveau, Maurice Richard, and Howie Morenz.[191]

The Lafleur-led Canadiens beat the Philadelphia Flyers for the Stanley Cup in 1975–6, sweeping the defending champions in four straight games. Between 1976 and 1980 Montreal teams, coached by hockey genius Scotty Bowman, won the Stanley Cup four consecutive times, each time averaging more than 125 points per season—an unprecedented number. During this period as well, Lafleur reeled off six consecutive seasons of 50 goals or more and combined with Steve Shutt and Peter Mahovlich (later Shutt and Jacques Lemaire) to create one of the highest-scoring trios in NHL history. The 'Habs' also enjoyed fine defensive play. Few NHL teams have ever been fortunate enough to have players of the calibre of Guy Lapointe, Larry Robinson, and Serge Savard. As well, few teams were able to boast about fine goaltending the way the Canadiens could with **Ken Dryden** (b. 1947) in the nets. His stoic resting pose against the butt end of his goalie stick—indicating that he was at the top of his game—threw shivers into many opposing forwards. But Montreal's strong defensive play was added to by two of the League's finest checkers, Bob Gainey and Doug Jarvis. Besides being able to score a large number of goals, the Canadiens sported an equally impressive defensive corps—key ingredients for a dynasty hockey team in the late 1970s.

The team that wrested the Stanley Cup from the Montreal Canadiens, and exhibited the necessary qualities of a strong defense and explosive scoring power, was the New York Islanders. Built to be a force in the NHL in a relatively short period by general manager Bill Torrey and coach Al Arbour, the Islanders went on to rejoice in their four consecutive Stanley Cups between 1979–80 and 1983–84.[192] In the League for just eight years prior to winning a Stanley Cup, the New York franchise shrewdly used the draft to build a team. Its first important pick was Denis Potvin in 1973, followed by two more Canadians, Clark Gillies and Bryan Trottier in 1974, Ken Morrow in 1976, and the Canadians Mike Bossy and John Tonelli in 1977, and Duane Sutter and Swede Tomas Jonsson in 1979. The later additions of Butch Goring and Billy Smith made the Long Island lock on the Stanley Cup a near-certainty.

Mike Bossy (b. 1957), like the Canadiens' Lafleur, was the focus of the Islanders' attack. The sharpshooter of the team, he had an ability to score goals by capitalizing on the hard work of his teammates. Bossy was selected 17th in the 1977 NHL draft, but soon improved his standing by scoring a record 53 goals as a rookie. His retirement in 1987 came after nine consecutive years of 50 goals or more, scoring more than 60 in four separate seasons.

Winning a record-breaking fifth Stanley Cup proved unattainable for the New York Islanders, just as it had been for the Canadiens four years earlier. In 1984 the Edmonton Oilers defeated the Islanders in a five-game final. There were five reasons why the Oilers won: Mark Messier, Glenn Anderson, Jari Kurri, Paul Coffey, and Wayne Gretzky. These five players symbolized a new definition of offence: skate fast, weave dizzyingly, shoot accurately. **Wayne Gretzky**'s unending repertoire of ingenious playmaking made him the single-most-feared player in the NHL. His wizardry with the puck even surprised his team-mates who, after scoring a goal, would wonder where the scoring pass came from. Gretzky's patented 'from-behind-the-net' passes were the secret ingredient in the Oilers' Stanley Cup victories in 1984, 1985, 1987, and 1988.[193] Few players have single-handedly contributed so much to the success of one team in the NHL as has Gretzky.

Gretzky (b, 1961 in Brantford, Ontario) was touted as a hockey prodigy from an early age. Under his father's guidance he, like so many other Canadian boys, mastered the skills of hockey on a backyard rink. He played minor hockey in the Brantford region, scoring over 350 goals as a pee-wee. He moved on to the Toronto Young Nats in 1976 and to the Sault Ste Marie Greyhounds Junior Hockey Club in 1977. In 1978, at the age of 17, he turned professional with the Indianapolis Racers of the WHA. He was traded to the Edmonton Oilers, also of the WHA, in 1979 after the Racers' owner Nelson Skalbania found it impossible to fill his rink and meet the high payroll demands of his hockey club. Gretzky's move to Edmonton was not by chance. The Oilers' owner Peter Pocklington had won the right to negotiate with Gretzky—called the 'Brantford Streak' or 'The Kid'—because he had beaten Skalbania at a card game. Pocklington accepted Gretzky's $800,000 salary demand and received, as a windfall, two additional players, Peter Driscoll and Eddie Mio.[194]

In his first season with Edmonton (1979–80), Gretzky tied for the NHL scoring lead with Marcel Dionne, won the Hart Trophy as the League's 'most valuable player', and the Lady Byng Trophy as the NHL's most 'gentlemanly' participant. In his second season (1980–1) he scored 164 points, breaking Phil Esposito's single-season record of 152 points and surpassing Bobby Orr's assist record of 102 with 109. The 1983 season brought him 212 points, including 92 goals—shattering Esposito's previous one-season record of 76 goals. Gretzky has won the Hart Trophy eight times in his nine NHL seasons and additionally has won the Art Ross Trophy seven times, the Lester B. Pearson Trophy for outstanding player as selected by the NHL Players' Association five times, and the Conn Smythe Trophy twice. Moreover, he has been selected an NHL all-star in all nine years (a first-team all-star in seven of those years), and has been the holder of over forty NHL individual records. The only man to rival his accomplishments in the near future might be Mario Lemieux, of the Pittsburgh Penguins, who won the Hart and Ross Trophies in 1988 with 70 goals.

In building the Edmonton team the Oilers' president, general manager, and coach, Glen Sather, had more than Gretzky to work with. Mark Messier, an Edmonton native, was an inspirational leader; Glenn Anderson was a high-spirited, tough-checking scorer; Jari Kurri was the 'soft-hands' forward who was as adept at scoring as he was in back-checking; and Paul Coffey was a rival of Bobby Orr for skating ability and scoring touch. As well, Grant Fuhr and Andy Moog provided Sather with stalwart goaltending. In the mid-1980s Messier, Anderson, Kurri, and Coffey were all 100-point scorers—a most potent scoring force in any league.

The biggest surprise in NHL trades occurred in August 1988, when Peter Pocklington, owner of the Edmonton Oilers, decided it was time to trade his 'established star', 'the franchise'. Wayne Gretzky was moved to owner Bruce McNall's Los Angeles Kings for an estimated $15 million.[195] The deal was publicized as being the 'Greatest Hockey Trade Ever' and the banner headline on the front page of the *Los Angeles Times* on 9 August 1988 was 'Gretzky Is a Man Who Will Be King'. He had for all intents and purposes finished his unparalleled career in Edmonton; but as a Los Angeles King he looked forward to contributing to the refurbishing of a relic NHL franchise. Making a Stanley Cup contender of a 'weak-sister' team might be his greatest accomplishment, and if anyone has the ability to do this, it is certainly Gretzky, 'The Great One'.

In the hearts and minds of Canadians, hockey has always been an inextricable part of the national culture. While the game has touched most people through radio and television, its omnipresence has been reflected in other ways. Hugh Hood, the Montreal novelist whose stated ambition was to write a fictional series of Proustian dimensions, took time out to write a worshipful book on Jean Beliveau. Mordecai Richler, who seems to be as devoted to following the Canadiens as he is to writing about his beloved St Urbain Street, has written widely about hockey. Rick Salutin wrote a play entitled *Les Canadiens* (1977), 'with an assist from Ken Dryden', and the singer Robert Charlebois wore a hockey sweater on the cover of his first album. When John Robert Colombo set about compiling the best-known Canadian images, he chose, among the grain elevators and Niagara Falls, Ken Danby's painting 'At the Crease'. And the game inspired a long poem by Al Purdy, 'Hockey Players', in which he calls hockey '. . . a Canadian specific / to salve the anguish of inferiority / by being good at something the Americans aren't . . .'[196] When Roch Carrier decided to portray the central interest of French-Canadian boyhood, he wrote his classic short story 'The Hockey Sweater':

> The winters of my childhood were long, long seasons. We lived in three places—the school, the church and the skating-rink—but our real life was on the skating-rink. Real battles were won on the skating-rink. Real strength appeared on the skating-rink. The real leaders showed themselves on the skating-rink. School was a sort of punishment. Parents always want to punish children and school is their most natural way of punishing us. However, school was also a quiet place where we could prepare for the next hockey game, lay out our next strategies. As for church, we found there the tranquillity of God: there we forgot school and dreamed about the next hockey game. Through our daydreams it might happen that we would recite a prayer: we would ask God to help us play as well as Maurice Richard.[197]

The boy's mother orders a new sweater for her son from the Eaton's catalogue and a Toronto Maple Leafs' sweater arrives.

Canadians grow up with hockey, playing it for fun and as a first experience of competition. Some stay with it, using it to gain an education and possibly a career and glory. Watching the game in arenas or on television is a leisure-time activity for an overwhelming number of Canadians. Indeed, Professor Tom Sinclair-Faulkner has observed that for many, hockey 'functions as a religion'—'that is, when one enters the hockey world, there is a tendency to treat its symbolic universe as ultimately meaningful so long as one is within that world'—though it does this, he says, 'at the expense of its own playfulness.'[198] There are many Canadians who take no interest in the sport, but even they have to admit that the national love of hockey is a fact of life, that it has somehow become entwined with our identity—with how we see ourselves and how others see us.

9
Women and Sport

Although in the 1980s women take part in almost every sport once reserved only for men, along with a few—ringette, netball, and synchronized swimming—that are reserved mainly for women, they have had to challenge ingrained customs that long prevented them from participation, competition, and leadership roles in sport. Scientific study of specific issues peculiar to women in sports has been used to determine the best training methods for them. No longer is there concern about the female athlete's entering endurance events, participating during her menstrual cycle, or using weight-training to increase her strength. Athletic equipment has been modified through the years to accommodate her slighter stature, and no longer is the woman athlete compelled to dress for decorum rather than to maximize her performance potential. These developments, and the acceptance of women as participants in most sports, are the salutary reflection of changing times; but they have not been won without much resistance and the prolonged efforts of women sports administrators and athletes.

One of the factors contributing to the restrictions against female participation in sports through the years has been traditional views of 'masculinity' and 'femininity'. It was generally believed that sport was a masculine activity, and therefore not to be pursued by females.[1] Those women who did participate were thought to be unfeminine and often were called 'Amazon athletes'. The accepted daily leisure-time activities of the frontier settlers and military personnel—for example, fishing, hunting, horseracing, canoeing, and snowshoeing—were pursued only by males.[2] Tied to the notion that sport activities were suitable only for them was the belief that strength, speed, and power—considered essential in sports—were exclusively male traits. In addition, Victorian attitudes towards women that were expressed in their clothes—long skirts, crinolines, tight corsets, hats, and gloves, all of which hampered movement—gave strength to the opinion that sports were not 'proper' activities for ladies, and there was the medical opinion that the physical demands of sport could be harmful to the female reproductive organs.[3]

Though the literature of early settlement abounds in examples of women who were forced by circumstances into strenuous physical activity, only such leisure pastimes as croquet and dancing, which required little physical exertion, were thought to be acceptable for them. When in the 1850s the innovative American feminist Amelia Bloomer popularized the 'bifurcated bags' that were named for her, women who wore these 'bloomers' began to experience freedom of movement without loss of dignity. One result was that by the time of Confederation horseback-riding and snowshoeing—which had previously been necessary activities of daily living—became acceptable leisure pursuits for women. And when the 'safety bicycle' was put on the market in 1885, women—comfortably clad in bloomers, which were 'ample and full below the knee'[4]—took to bicycling as an enjoyable outdoor pastime. However, as with any inroad women made into activities from which they had previously been excluded, there were divergent views about bicycling for women. A *Manitoba Free Press* editorial on 5 September 1898 appeared almost tolerant:

> Elderly ladies, in jaunty hats and irreproachable leggings, strike their miniature alarm bells with dowager-like demeanor and enter the stream of wheel life with all the nerve of veterans.[5]

But the Women's Rescue League of America in 1896 opposed the bicycling fad as disastrous:

> Whereas bicycling by young women has helped to swell the ranks of reckless girls who finally drift into the standing army of outcast women of the U.S., . . . therefore, be it resolved that [the] Women's Rescue League petition all true women and clergymen to aid in denouncing the present bicycle craze by women as indecent and vulgar.[6]

The bicycle craze nevertheless helped prepare Canadian women for their emergence as challenging sports figures in the early twentieth century. No longer prepared to view sport passively from the sidelines, women bicycled in the fresh air, dreaming of equality of opportunity not only in the sporting fields but in life. Their dress changed for participation, and so too did their aspirations. The new freedom encouraged them to strive for the more important issue of suffrage.

From the turn of the century American attitudes towards women in sport played a significant role in eastern Canada as Canadian women sought advanced degrees in major American universities, and women sport leaders in Canada looked for guidance from American professional organizations. (Also, the major sport publications were American.) American women physical educators were against aggressive competition in their schools and universities, fearing that girls would be injured. Therefore they established policies and procedures that limited the physical demands of competition and set standards that protected female participants. Community sport, however, was fostering more and more competition for girls in a variety of sports, and international records were being broken as girls excelled in their performances without negative consequences. Thus a chasm began to develop between educational and community sport, and between what was practised in physical-education classes and in community sport leagues.

Women physical-education teachers in Canada were first prepared in normal schools through summer courses,[7] followed by diploma courses in universities;[8] after 1941 university degree courses became available.[9] Several physical-education teachers associated with the early diploma courses in universities began to attend professional-association meetings in the United States and to pursue degree programs.[10] This close liaison in classes and at professional meetings strengthened the resolve of the Canadian women physical educators to develop better programs for girls and women in Canada, and of course their model was the American one with which they had become familiar.

> Basketball for girls and women was the bane of four generations of collegiate physical educators. Almost since its inception, basketball was the subject of vociferous debate among women physical educators. Convinced that the game's 'fighting features' developed aggressive characteristics that were not in harmony with proper behaviour expected of young ladies, collegiate physical educators launched a restoration campaign that spanned nearly two-thirds of a century. Attempts to control the roughness of the game through rule changes were initiated soon after the women began to play basketball. Perpetual rule changes confirm the persistence of women physical educators to regulate the physical demands of the game.[11]

In April 1923 the Women's Division of the National Amateur Athletic Federation was organized in the United States and women physical educators, led by Mrs Herbert Hoover, officially banded together to work for reforms in girls' and women's sport programs. A 'Platform'—advocating 'play for play's sake', the 'intrinsic' value of play, 'controlled' publicity, 'trained' women leaders, and minimized travel and commercialization—was first proposed at this meeting, and its philosophy guided girls' and women's sport for more than fifty years.[12] Thus rules were modified. Only women coaches and women's referees could lead, and separate women's organizations to set policies and procedures, to organize, conduct, and control girls' sport, were advocated to protect the female athlete from the abuses found in the men's games. This led to half a century of separate programs for boys and girls, men and women, in educational settings in the United States, and fostered a separate sport philosophy for women. In some states interschool sport for girls was discouraged between 1925 and 1935. These phenomena initiated the myth that, because it was separate and played under different rules, girls' and women's sport was inferior to boys' and men's, and a belief developed that girls were not serious participants.

One thing that fuelled this belief was the institution of the 'Play Day', which was developed by women physical educators to avoid all the hazards of overly aggressive play, the win-at-all-cost mentality, and commercialization, etc., associated with boys' and men's sport. Instead, on 'Play Day' teams were composed of many players to maximize participation, scores often were not recorded, and stress was laid on how you played the game rather than whether you won or lost. Sportsmanship and social interaction were all-important, and following their competitions the girls always socialized with the other team and enjoyed refreshments together.[13]

By the late 1920s these American attitudes were beginning to have an impact in some Canadian schools. Intramurals were preferred to interschool competitions and were sponsored to allow more girls to participate and to protect them from the injurious consequences of aggressive competition. It is interesting to note, however, that in the western provinces, where much of the physical education and sport was conducted by male teachers and coaches, and in many rural schools in Ontario and in community sport across the country, the girls and women enjoyed competition and often did not use the 'modified girls' rules'.[14] As in the United States, a split developed between educational and community sport. Girls who played in both systems began to question the rationale and need for the special regulations embodied in the 'girls' rules' practised in the school system, which did much through the years to perpetuate the opinion that girls were unable physically to play the game and needed to be protected from possible injury. The problem was finally resolved many years later when girls' rules were abandoned in the school system without the ill-effects expected by many.

Although basketball was the most popular team sport in most secondary schools and universities following its introduction at the turn of the century, most schools offered girls' tennis programs, some track and field, swimming (after pools were built in the 1920s), volleyball, and badminton. Interschool and intramural programs increased opportunities for participation between 1900 and 1939. Women physical-education teachers in the Canadian school system were concerned about the deleterious effects of aggressive competition and they modified their programs accordingly, but they did not, as had happened in many American states, curtail interschool sport.

The Women's Athletic Committee (WAC) of the Canadian Association for Health, Physical Education and Recreation (CAHPER) was organized in 1950 and adopted not only the same structure as the Division of Girls' and Women's Sports of the American Association for Health, Physical Education and Recreation, but also its philosophy, standards of conduct for sport, and training of women officials.[15] It would have been difficult, and perhaps even irresponsible, for these dedicated women in Canadian physical education to propose innovations in girls' and women's programs at this time, when all the 'professional', educational, and medical leadership in both countries advocated a conservative example in educational sport for girls and women.

The WAC was influential mainly in the Maritimes, Quebec, and Ontario; it was never a truly national organization because the women educators in eastern Canada had been influenced by their American colleagues. But there was no such influence in western Canada, where male physical educators had been much more influential in the development of girls' and women's sport. As well, in the West there were very few women physical educators, particularly in the universities, who gave leadership for women's sport. Although several meetings were held with women across the country in the late 1960s to try to develop a common national women's sport system, other influences were in effect—such as the national sport governing bodies, financed partially through Fitness and Amateur Sport grants, that initiated programs for their athletes, coaches, and officials—and it was no longer appropriate to pursue this course of action.

In community sport a different but equally influential attitude established long-lasting barriers to women's equal participation in sport. It was exhibited by nineteenth-century male sport leaders, notably the French patriot Baron Pierre de Coubertin, founder of the modern Olympics, which began in 1896. He espoused the view that women's sport was against the 'Laws of Nature' and therefore reserved the modern Olympic Games for men.[16] (Women were officially accepted into the Olympics in 1912, although unofficial competitions in golf and tennis occurred as early as 1900.)[17] This paternalism, emphasizing the biological differences between men and women, also characterized the attitude of doctors, educators, and legislators. The rules and regulations for sport perpetuated the view that girls and women were fragile, and inferior—physically and psychologically—to their male peers and should be pro-

Ethel Catherwood, 1930. (Courtesy the City of Toronto Archives, James Collection 8174.)

tected from the injuries that were bound to result from any exertion in sport. Women protested, of course, struggling at first to engage in a variety of sporting events and eventually to participate in local, national, and international competitions. A few American and Canadian writers, however, began to challenge this conservative paternalistic view and encourage women to participate in physical activity because it was natural and healthy.[18]

Sport changed significantly in the twentieth century, being inextricably related to the combined effects of changing patterns of urbanization, industrialization, and technological advancements.[19] Supported by the suffrage movement, which raised women's interest in their rights, education, and health, women began also to challenge entrenched male sport structures and dared—even though the rules were not welcom-

Myrtle Cook, 1926.
(Courtesy the
City of Toronto Archives,
James Collection 8172.)

ing—to compete in organized sport competitions. Demonstrated accomplishments by women who braved criticism without ill-effects have done more than anything else to induce society to favour their acceptance and participation.

The period 1920 to 1935 has been called the Golden Age of Sport for Canadian women.[20] There were more sporting opportunities, urbanization gave citizens more leisure time, and following the difficult war years there was a new and positive feeling about women's relationship to sport that was revealed both by their participation and by their evident interest as onlookers. Olympic-medal performances in track and field, combined with marathon swims and world-champion standing in speed-skating and basketball, introduced Canadian women athletes to the world and heralded changing attitudes that resulted in greater female participation in sport in Canada.

At the Olympic Summer Games of 1928 in Amsterdam, Canadian women athletes appeared in track and field and won world recognition for their performances.[21] Six women made up the team. The 4-x-100-metre relay team placed first, in the world-record time of 48.4 seconds;[22] members of the team were Florence Bell, Myrtle Cook, Bobbie Rosenfeld, and Ethel Smith, all from Toronto.[23] Other medal winners on the track were Bobbie Rosenfeld (silver) and Ethel Smith (bronze) in the 100-metre dash.[24]

Ethel Catherwood (c. 1909–37) of Saskatoon jumped 1.60 m. (just below the world record) and was widely acclaimed as a superb athlete;[25] the Canadian press dubbed Catherwood, who was a strikingly beautiful woman, the 'Saskatoon Lily'.[26] The Canadian women amassed thirty-four points, well ahead of the twenty-eight points of the second-place team from the United States.[27] When they returned to Canada a crowd of 200,000 jammed into Toronto's Union Station on Front Street.[28] More importantly, their success provided an impetus for the expansion of women's participation in many other sporting activities.

In the 800-metre event Bobbie Rosenfeld placed fifth and Jean Thompson fourth. Alexandrine Gibb, the dean of women sportswriters at the Toronto *Star* and manager of the women's team, reveals much about the co-operation demonstrated among the women team members:

> Remember, Miss Rosenfeld was not trained for this distance . . . . She was put in the 800 metres only to encourage Jean Thompson. On the stretch down the track [Rosenfeld] came from ninth position to close behind the seventeen-year-old Jeannie, and when she saw the latter falter coaxed the youngster to come on . . . . She refused to go ahead of the youngster . . . . [She] let Jean finish fourth, taking a fifth for herself.[29]

But the race was not without its problems. Of the eleven entrants only six finished, most of whom collapsed after crossing the finish-line.[30] The exhaustion suffered by some of the competitors was used as ammunition by opponents of women's participation in track-and-field events at the Games. The detractors found powerful voices in Coubertin and Pope Pius XI.[31] After Amsterdam a compromise was reached: women continued to participate in the Olympics, but the 800-metre race was withdrawn and was not re-introduced until the Rome Olympics of 1960. Dr A.S. Lamb, the manager of the 1928 Canadian Team, voted against women's participating in future Olympic Games. He had two reasons for voting as he did. First, he had consulted his male colleagues at the Games only to discover that none had an opinion one way or the other. But Lamb had strong views. He was against women's competing in strenuous events, believing that they were too highly strung and were not physically capable of such competition. Because medical opinion was not decisive and he felt that serious injuries might result, he clung to his conservative opinion. Lamb's vote, taken without consulting the Canadian women at the Games, was the subject of immediate controversy.[32] This may have been advantageous because it focused the issue, and challenged the Amateur Athletic Association and sport administrators to establish positions. The opinion of many athletes was similar to that expressed by Rosenfeld in a 1938 interview in *Maclean's*:

Bobbie Rosenfeld (right) racing c. 1928. (Courtesy Canada's Sports Hall of Fame, Toronto.)

Any girl who accepts and practices correct methods of training is capable of running 800 metres or continuing any other unusual athletic pursuit. The German and Japanese entries at Amsterdam did not experience any difficulty in the distance race, and even though I had not trained specially for it, there was no undue effort required to enable me to finish.[33]

Track and field was not the only sport in which women excelled in the golden years of the twenties and thirties. Jean Wilson (1910–33), who was born in Scotland and grew up in Toronto, won two Olympic medals in the demonstration sport of speed-skating in the Lake Placid Olympics of 1932. In the 1934 British Empire Games in London the swimmer Phyllis Dewar (1915-61) from Moose Jaw, Saskatchewan, won four gold medals: for 100-yard freestyle, 440-yard freestyle, 3-x-100-yard medley relay, and the 4-x-100-yard freestyle relay. Dorothy Walton (b. 1908), from Swift Current, Saskatchewan, won the All-England Championship in badminton in 1939. And the Edmonton Grads dominated the sport of women's basketball from 1915 until the team's dissolution in 1940.

Under the coaching of Percy Page, the Edmonton Grads' reign was unparalleled in team sport, both amateur and professional, male or female; they are reputed to have had a record of 502 victories and only 22 losses.[34] The Grads were a group of high-school girls who had been well coached in passing, dribbling, and shooting, and trained to play a simple game strategy with dedication, exemplary sportsmanship, and confidence. They set an example that dispelled the fears of many critics because they played a physically demanding game according to men's rules, and challenged the best in the world without negative consequences. Their long-time Canadian fan James Naismith, who invented the game of basketball in 1891 while a student at Springfield College, wrote to them in 1936 when he was seventy-five:

> Permit me to add my hearty congratulations to the many that must have poured in from your host of friends and admirers on this your twenty-first birthday. Your record is without parallel in the history of basketball. My admiration is not only for your record of clean play, versatility in meeting teams at their own style, and more especially for your unbroken record of good sportsmanship. My admiration and respect go to you because you have remained unspoiled by your successes, and have retained the womanly graces, notwithstanding your participation in a strenuous game. You are not only an inspiration to basketball players throughout the world, but a model of all girls' teams. Your attitude and success have been a source of gratification to me in illustrating the possibilities of the game in the development of the highest type of womanhood.[35]

The Edmonton Commercial Graduates Basketball Team in 1922. (Courtesy Don Morrow.)

The Edmonton Grads (wearing white jerseys) playing a French team on their 1936 European tour. Bloomers had now given way to abbreviated shorts. (Courtesy Don Morrow.)

When basketball was first introduced by Senda Berenson, Director of Physical Education for women at Smith College in Massachusetts, the year after it was invented by Naismith, the rules were modified to protect girls from the rough play experienced by boys. Personal contact was discouraged; the court was divided into three and each girl played only two-thirds of the full court; only two bounces were allowed before the ball was passed off to a team-mate. Berenson declared that basketball '. . . develops physical and moral courage, self-reliance, and self-control, and the ability to meet success and defeat with dignity.'[36] Basketball quickly spread across North America in both school and community facilities. Though played by thousands of girls, the special modifications—designed to protect 'fragile' girls from the physical demands of the play—endured until men's rules were adopted by women across Canada in 1970. But the Edmonton Grads had challenged the need for these sporting modifications for girls. Their coach was male; they played men's rules (thought to be too demanding physically for female athletes) and succeeded without undue stress; and more importantly they were viewed by society as still maintaining their femininity. Negative views had been expressed at various times during the thirties about the lack of femininity of female athletes,[37] and it was the exemplary reputation of the Grads and frequent articles by the leading women sports-writers of the day that helped to dispel such an image.[38]

In the years immediately following the Second World War—when Canadians were searching for new ideals, new standards, new models of behaviour—women were being encouraged to relinquish their wartime occupations and to resume their role as wives and mothers in the home. A feminine sport ideal appeared on the horizon in the form of Barbara Ann Scott, the eighteen-year-old Ottawa figure-skater who captured the European, World, and Olympic championships in 1948. Her athletic ability, however, was not emphasized or acknowledged as it deserved to be;[39] instead she was called by the newspapers of the day 'a tiny exquisite doll', 'a dainty blond dervish', or 'reigning queen of the blades'.[40]

Several years passed before it was acknowledged that female athletes could withstand the physical demands of sport. In 1954 the Toronto teenager Marilyn Bell shattered the myth of the 'fragile' female with her spectacular swim across the thirty miles of Lake Ontario. By the late evening of 9 September 1954 an estimated 100,000 people greeted her at the Canadian National Exhibition grounds in Toronto. Overnight she became a heroine, a household name, and established for all time a positive view of the physical capabilities of a well-conditioned female athlete. And as the first person to complete a swim across the lake, she set a standard for marathon swimming—one that in recent years has been repeated by several women.[41]

Abby Hoffman (b. 1947) in running, Marlene Stewart Streit (b. 1934) in golf, Beverley Boys (b. 1951) in diving, and Diane Jones (b. 1951) in the pentathlon have also added in a variety of sports to the prestige earned by women athletes. Supportive parental attitudes were an essential factor in developing their outstanding performances. Abby Hoffman's parents were unusually forward-thinking when, in 1950, they permitted their daughter to play hockey with and against boys, and encouraged her to try out for the Toronto hockey league, which permitted only boys on their teams. Abby—or 'Ab', as she was known— played the season as a boy until her birth certificate was checked when her team qualified for the playoffs. Then the story made headlines: 'Find Star Defenceman in Little League Girl, 9, But She Stays On Team'.[42] Abby enjoyed the attention, but gave up organized hockey after her team lost.

She turned next, without much success, to swimming, and at the age of fourteen to middle-distance running. Her career in track is unparalleled: she represented Canada at four Olympics, four Pan American

Abby Hoffman racing in the Montreal Olympics, 1976.
(Courtesy National Health and Welfare.)

Games, two Commonwealth Games, three World University Games, and at the Maccabiah Games. Her account of the 800-metre race at the Munich Olympics in 1972 describes both the ecstasy and the agony of competition, and is one of the best descriptions of the essence of competition:

> As we finished the first lap, I looked up and saw it was a very fast time. We were running in a tight group, struggling against each other, yet somehow joined together. As we headed into the back straightaway, over 60,000 spectators were screaming. But I didn't hear the noise. All I heard were the footsteps and breathing of the other runners. My eyes were riveted 10 metres ahead as I was drawn along in the pack.
>
> Even though the leader was only about 10 metres ahead of me, I was running last. I knew that was a mistake and that I had to move ahead.

On the back turn I tried to move up, but the group just stayed there. As we raced into the final stretch, my lungs were bursting. I turned on my last sprint of energy, but so did the others. I sprinted toward the finish, but I couldn't make up the ground, I finished barely a second behind the winner, but I was tied for seventh place. My time was 2:00.2, the fastest time of my life. I'd broken the previous Olympic record. The only trouble was that six other girls ran faster that day.

The Munich race was the greatest moment of my athletic career. Even though I didn't win a medal, I was thrilled to be part of a group who, competing against each other, were still pulled on and drawn together. We'd all broken the Olympic record. My dream had come true. It was exhilarating and I'll never forget it.[43]

Since retiring from competitive track, Abby Hoffman has played an influential role in sport as Supervisor of the Sports Services Section of the Ontario Ministry of Culture and Recreation (now the Ministry of Tourism and Recreation), and later as Director General of Sport Canada. Under her leadership the federal government has supported a women's program and has established a policy for women's sport that has been innovative and far-reaching. Hoffman has often spoken about her personal sporting experiences and has challenged girls and women to become active. Her thesis in many speeches has been that once a woman experiences the personal benefits of participation in sport or dance or exercise programs, such activity becomes an important part of her very being, and artificial social barriers will not stop her from continuing her involvement.[44] From 1980 to 1982 she wrote a *Chatelaine* fitness column that was factual and informative, concentrating on the physiological and psychological benefits to be derived from fitness programs without resorting to pictures of attractive, leotard-clad, thin performers that were featured in the usual magazine approach to women's fitness.

A new era for sport in Canada began when the federal government enacted the Fitness and Amateur Sport Act in September 1961, and became an important participant in defining new women's sport practices.[45] In a *Report of the Royal Commission on the Status of Women* of 1970 two recommendations addressed the issue of female participation in sports programs:

Recommendation 77: We recommend that the provinces and territories (a) review their policies to ensure that school programmes provide girls with equal opportunities with boys to participate in athletic and sports activities, and (b) establish policies and practices that will motivate and encourage girls to engage in athletic and sports activities.

Recommendation 78: We recommend that, pursuant to section 3(d) of the federal Fitness and Amateur Sport Act, a research project be undertaken to (a) determine why fewer girls than boys participate in sport programmes at the school level and (b) recommend remedial action.[46]

With regard to these Recommendations, the Canadian Advisory Council on the Status of Women (CACSW), in its report *What's Been Done?* (1980), listed the accomplishments of the Fitness and Amateur Sport Branch of the Ministry of Health and Welfare. In summary these included:

> . . . hiring one women's consultant responsible for defining the problems facing women in sport and designing programs to alleviate these problems. Programs have included (1) educational programs to ascertain the reason behind the lack of female participation and programs to alleviate the problem areas; (2) coaching programs for increasing the quality and quantity of women coaches; (3) promotional programs such as symposia, films and printed materials on women and sport; (4) establishment of an information retrieval center collecting and distributing needed materials on women in sport; (5) development of women officials for the 1976 Olympics and beyond.[47]

One Fitness and Amateur Sport project has had far-reaching ramifications. In March 1974 a National Conference on Women and Sport was held in Toronto, and significant recommendations were targeted to governments, sport agencies, educational authorities, status-of-women groups, and individuals.[48] In addition to the recommendations made and forwarded, this conference was important to women because for the first time they communicated as administrators, athletes, and coaches about their common problems; it established one of the first women's sport networks. Between 1974 and 1979 promotional materials were produced by the Sport Branch, but substantive change did not take place even when Iona Campagnolo became the first Minister of State Fitness and Amateur Sport and spent time defining the mandate of the Ministry. But in 1980 a 'women's program' was established, funded by lottery revenues, and several projects were launched that have had an ongoing influence in many areas that had been identified by women leaders as needing seed money for study, implementation, and emphasis.[49] These included a leadership survey; a planning workshop, which formed the Canadian Association for the Advancement of Women and Sport at McMaster University in 1981; a talent-bank feasibility study; an internship program designed to provide on-the-job training for national-calibre female athletes and ex-athletes;[50] a fitness program for inner-city women in Halifax; a post-mastectomy exercise program in Vancouver; and several promotional projects, including the publishing of a book of biographical sketches of outstanding Canadian women athletes.[51]

In concert with the initiatives undertaken by the Fitness and Amateur Sport Branch, a growing movement in Canadian society was to play an important role in redefining the components of sport from a woman's perspective, and that was feminism. Feminism—the theory that women should have political, economic, and social rights equal to those of men—inspired the movement that is winning such rights for women.[52] Sportswomen and physical educators were slower than many other Canadian women to embrace feminism, but several influences helped them to consider the issues facing women's sport from this perspective.

The Canadian Association for the Advancement of Women and Sport, founded in 1981, initially focused on research, communication, leadership, and advocacy, but in recent years it has acted as a catalyst for women's rights in sports.[53] Among several books on women in sport, Ann Hall's and Dorothy Richardson's *Fair Ball*[54] was the first to examine Canadian sport from a feminist perspective. Women leaders in universities, such as Dr Ann Hall at the University of Alberta, have also been influential in preparing graduate students to assume positions of influence in the sport milieu. Conferences with a feminist perspective on the issues facing women and sport—such as that held on the 'Female Athlete' at Simon Fraser University in March 1980—as well as studies such as the Canadian Interuniversity Athletic Union task force on the under-representation of women in the CIAU, and court challenges to eradicate discrimination in sport, all played an important part in cultivating a feminist attitude in sportswomen.[55] A recent publication by feminist researcher-writer Helen Lenskyi, *Women, Sport and Physical Activity: Research and Bibliography*, provides an excellent overview of research about women and sport, and suggests problems for future study.[56] Much more needs to be understood about sports and physical activity and their meaning in the lives of girls and women in Canada.

As soon as women joined together to examine the sport environment, they saw that change was necessary and decided that the emulation of the male model of sport would not meet their needs for better sport for women. But women have been by no means unanimous about what was desirable. Today many issues in sport need to be resolved to prepare women athletes for the 1990s. The issue of integrated *versus* segregated sport will be debated for years to come as women try to define equality of opportunity for girls and women in the world of sport. Both the federal government, through its women's sport policy, and CACWS have advocated integrated sport as the model to be pursued, but not all women participating in sport are sure this is the goal they seek. Answers to questions about leadership roles, about equitable budgets and the use of scarce facilities by female participants, and about systemic under-representation by women in leadership roles in sport organizations are basic if the concerns facing women now are to be resolved.

One issue that is not often discussed openly is the issue of lesbian athletes, coaches, and sport administrators.[57] Girls and women who participated in the so-called unfeminine sports—team sports rather than individual sports—often were suspect with regard to sexual orientation. Girls were encouraged by parents to choose individual sport that stresses agility, grace, and aesthetics rather than the 'masculine' traits of strength, speed, and muscular power. Since the 1920s innuendoes concerning lesbianism were often directed at women who participated in tradition-ally masculine sports and at women who failed to meet the feminine stereotype because of size, body type, or muscular development.[58] These homophobic attitudes have been a persistent problem for girls and women who have wished to take part in the sport of their choice; but more pervasive had been the hidden prejudice and innuendoes against women and coaches wanting to obtain leadership roles as national team coaches or national sport-organization administrators who were overlooked by hiring committees for positions because of their 'suspected' sexual pref-erence. The strength of the women's movement, the impact of the Charter of Rights, and demonstrated quality leadership by a few influential women have played a significant role in the last decade in challenging these discriminatory practices.

Human-rights legislation has been perceived as both a positive and negative method of achieving a better sport environment for girls and women, as sport administrators and athletes have turned to the courts to solve long-term sport inequities. In today's society the solutions for many problems seem more complex than at any other time in history. Now it appears almost easier to resolve sport inequities with words and arguments in the courts than on the playing-fields, where the realities of long-term underfunding and fewer playing opportunities actually exist. The biological differences between men and women are being researched, but their implications for sport participation are interpreted in various ways and the ramifications are not clear. Negative attitudes still plague the female athlete who wants to perform at her full potential in the sport of her choice.[59]

The struggle to redefine the opportunities for girls and women in Canadian sport presents a challenge to all sport administrators and par-ticipants. Debates will be waged and positions taken, but to expect a single model for girls' and women's sport in the near future is probably unrealistic. Many different approaches to redressing the inequalities will be pursued by women, both individually and collectively, as they work to improve the system in sport. Girls and women are participating in greater numbers in sport and fitness programs than at any previous time in our history, but many obstacles remain. The sport governing bodies and international organizations still offer fewer sport opportunities to women competitors.[60] There are still few female coaches and administrators in influential positions in national and international sport organizations. The budget discrepancies are still too apparent. Society has not yet fully accepted and embraced the vision of equal opportunity for women in sport as participants, coaches, and leaders. For example, many in our society cannot conceive that in the near future women will be playing on the same team in any sport with men in both amateur and professional sport, even though our courts have already ruled that discrimination in sport on the basis of sex is illegal.

Individual women athletes through the years have demonstrated that personal commitment and acceptance of sporting opportunities and challenges have changed the very nature of sport for girls and women. The stories of five athletes demonstrate how their sporting achievements provided new and unique experiences not only for themselves but for the women who followed them.

Bobbie Rosenfeld (1905–69). Fanny (Bobbie) Rosenfeld was born in the USSR and came to Canada as an infant, settling with her family in Barrie, Ontario. She participated and excelled in most sports, except swimming, but first became known as an outstanding sprinter when she participated in a small track-meet at Beaverton, Ontario, and beat Rosa Grosse, the reigning Canadian champion and eventual world record-holder. She played softball, won the Toronto grass-court tennis championships, and played on championship basketball and hockey teams.

In the Olympic Trials for the 1928 Games held in Halifax, dressed in her brother's 'Y' t-shirt and swim trunks and her father's socks, Rosenfeld set Canadian records in the broad-jump (18 ft. 3 ins.), the standing broad-jump (8 ft. 1 in.), and discus. Her greatest triumph, however, was at the Games themselves in Amsterdam. She placed second to Elizabeth Robinson of the United States in the 100-metre final; helped the 4-x-100-metre relay team win a gold medal with a world record of 48.2 seconds; and came fifth, behind team-mate Jean Thompson, in the 800-metre event.

Less than a year after returning from Amsterdam, Rosenfeld was stricken with arthritis and was bedridden for eight months; she then spent a year on crutches. In 1931 she returned to sport as a competitor, becoming the leading home-run hitter in a major softball league; and in the 1931–2 season she was the outstanding player in Ontario women's hockey. But owing to another bout with arthritis she retired from sport in 1933 and turned to a writing career as sports columnist with the Toronto *Globe*. In 1949 Rosenfeld was inducted into Canada's Sports Hall of Fame, and on 28 December 1949 she was named Canadian Woman Athlete of the Half-Century in a Canadian Press poll.

In her column, 'Sports Reel', Rosenfeld exhibited both her strong opinions and her cynicism about the sports stars of the day. Robert Fulford has written candidly about working with Rosenfeld on the *Globe and Mail*, where she was 'more tolerated than admired' as a writer. She received Hearst's New York *Journal-American* every day, 'and once she pointed out a Hearst columnist to me—"I steal my best aphorisms from him."'

> . . . Bobbie was the first lesbian I knew as such, and every day her moment of greatest happiness—happiness I could see her almost physically trying to hide, for reasons it took me years to understand—coincided with her companion's arrival to our office to pick her up after work. Once this lady mentioned that she and Bobbie were looking for a new apartment and needed two bedrooms—one for Bobbie's trophies.[61]

Rosenfeld retired in poor health from the *Globe and Mail* in 1966 and died three years later at the age of sixty-four.

Ada Mackenzie (1918–71) is frequently recalled as the first woman of Canadian golf and the queen of Canadian amateurs. For nearly half a century Mackenzie was out in front or near the front in Canadian women's competition. Her passion for the game was unfailing, and it is a true measure of her spirit and ability that she was still winning championships in the year she celebrated her seventy-eighth birthday—capturing the Ontario Seniors' title at the London Hunt Club in 1969.[62]

She was born in Toronto and was introduced to golf by her father. She won her first tournament at thirteen when she substituted for her mother. While a student at Havergal College in Toronto she played cricket, tennis, hockey, basketball, lacrosse, and excelled in diving and swimming. She won the Canadian waltzing championships in a skating competition in 1926.

During her golfing career, which lasted more than sixty years, Mackenzie won the Canadian Open five times, the Canadian Women's Seniors' Golf Championship eight times, ten Toronto and District Ladies' Championships, nine Ontario Ladies' Championships, two Ontario Sen-

*Ada Mackenzie, 1924.
(Courtesy Canada's Sports
Hall of Fame, Toronto.)*

ior Women's Championships, five Canadian Ladies' Closed Championships, and two Bermuda ladies' titles. 'Keeping active and busy has to be my key to success,' she once related near the end of her career. 'Some people have a tendency to over-indulge in sports. Not me. I treat athletics like recreation. Participation just adds to the fun. I wouldn't have the slightest notion of just how many tournaments I've won over the years.'[63]

Ada Mackenzie's contribution to golf was as important in the organizational sphere as in the player category. She experienced the restricted playing opportunities available to women in both tennis and golf clubs and determined to start her own club to give women more playing time and thus the opportunity to improve their game. After purchasing a rolling piece of land north of Toronto, at Thornhill, by organizing a bond issue to raise capital and issuing shares—$30,000 in six weeks, selling $100 memberships to 300 original club members to raise the money—she opened the Ladies' Golf and Tennis Club of Toronto in 1924. (This first course established exclusively for women provided, with satisfying irony, restricted hours for men.) She also initiated the Ontario Junior Ladies' Championships and donated a trophy for the tournament.

As player, organizer, and mentor to young players, Ada Mackenzie became synonymous with every aspect of the game of golf. She was also an innovator in women's golf apparel, which led to the establishment of Ada Mackenzie Ltd., a successful women's-clothing store now situated in the exclusive Yorkville shopping-district of Toronto. It was a rainstorm that first got her thinking about her own shop. At the American Women's Amateur Championship in 1927 she was leading in one match until a lashing storm broke out and thoroughly drenched her.

> 'I was wearing wool,' she explained. 'My sleeves were down over my wrists and the skirt was sloughing in the mud. It was just the completely wrong outfit. I lost the match but it was that experience that got me into the ladies' sportswear business.'[64]

A few months shy of her eightieth birthday, Ada Mackenzie finished sixth in the Canadian Senior Women's Golf Championships in Ottawa in 1971, the year she was elected to the Royal Canadian Golf Association Hall of Fame. Women's golf in Canada owes much to her innovations and long-term involvement in the sport.

Barbara Ann Scott (b. 1929). When the Olympic Torch cross-country journey to the 1988 Calgary Olympics was launched in St John's, Newfoundland, it was Barbara Ann Scott who carried the torch. Forty years after her gold-medal successes at the European, World, and Olympic figure-skating championships, Scott is still regarded as the queen of the sport and a symbol of sporting greatness, not to mention an ideal of the female athlete in Canada.

At six Barbara Ann began skating at Ottawa's Minto Skating Club, after receiving skates from her parents at Christmas. She progressed rapidly, winning the gold medal for figures at ten and, on her first try, also winning the Canadian junior championships. At nineteen she was to conquer all the major international events, culminating in the gold medal at the St Moritz Winter Olympics in 1948.

Prime Minister Mackenzie King sent her a cable expressing the feelings of Canadians: 'From one end of Canada to the other there is great rejoicing at the high honour you have brought to yourself and to our country', and further, he felt she had assisted Canadians in their darkest days of the Cold War following the Second World War, giving 'the courage and strength to help us through the gloom.'[65]

*Barbara Ann Scott, Olympic Women's Figure-Skating Champion,
St Moritz, 1948. (Courtesy the National Archives of Canada.)*

Scott, the gold-medal athlete, through media attention was turned
into an ideal for all Canadian females to emulate. She was portrayed as
tiny, dainty, doll-like, sweet, and a beauty, notably in a *Maclean's* article,
'Blonde on Blades'.[66]Even though the close of her 1947 four-minute free-
skating program included three double salchow jumps and changed
figure-skating forever,[67] her dedication, hard work, athletic ability, and
determination as she scaled the heights of international figure-skating
were minimized in favour of a 'sweetheart' public image that was reinforced by the playing of 'Let Me Call You Sweetheart' at receptions
across the country. The media treatment of this gifted young woman—
who went on to excel as an equestrienne, a pilot, and a business woman—
was later challenged.[68] But Barbara Ann Scott is still remembered as the
petite, smiling, flawless blue-eyed blonde on blades.

Marilyn Bell, the first swimmer to conquer
Lake Ontario, 9 September 1954.
(Courtesy Canada's Sports Hall of Fame.)

Marilyn Bell (b. 1937). In Toronto for a charity appearance in the summer of 1987, Marilyn Bell Di Lascio, when interviewed about her swim of Lake Ontario in 1954, said she remembered most the darkness and the eels, and she hated the eels. It seems only yesterday that 100,000 people stood on the shore of the lake at the Canadian National Exhibition grounds to welcome a sixteen-year-old-Toronto girl after she had conquered Lake Ontario.

Marilyn Bell was not known when she entered the lake in September 1954, but for several years she had been swimming long distances under the tutelage of Gus Ryder of the Lakeshore Swimming Club in Port Credit, winning the Lou Marsh Trophy as Canada's outstanding athlete in 1953. Eight weeks before her Lake Ontario swim she had become the first woman to finish the twenty-mile Atlantic City Marathon in New Jersey. The well-known American marathon swimmer Florence Chadwick had been invited by the CNE to swim the lake for a prize of $10,000.

Several Canadian marathon swimmers, including Marilyn Bell, felt they had been overlooked in this publicity venture and decided to swim along with the American, hoping to better her distance. Bell recalled: 'I don't think I was sure I could make it but I wasn't so sure Florence Chadwick could make it either. The challenge for me was to go one stroke further than the American. As corny as it sounds twenty-five years later, I did it for Canada.'

Chadwick was pulled from the water after twenty-six kilometres and Bell struggled on through the rain and the cold to victory. Because of strong currents and a northerly wind, she was swept off-course and swam further than the 51.5-kilometre distance across the lake. Her swim became front-page news. Both the Toronto *Star* and the *Telegram* ran extra editions, and radio stations gave hourly reports of her progress.

Marilyn Bell became an immediate celebrity, winning the $10,000 CNE prize and more than $50,000 in gifts from Canadians across the country. But determined to keep things in perspective, she proceeded to finish her education, while also accepting the challenges of attempting both the English Channel and the Straits of Juan de Fuca. On 31 July 1955 she completed the English Channel, crossing in fourteen-and-a-half hours—at the age of seventeen, the youngest swimmer ever to succeed. In August 1956, in her second attempt, she crossed the Straits of Juan de Fuca, the sixth person to do so.

She retired that year from marathon swimming, married another swimmer, Joe Di Lascio, and raised four children away from the public life she found distracting. More than any other athlete to date, Marilyn Bell demonstrated the potential of girls and women in physically demanding endurance events. In 1954 women were still not permitted to participate even in the 800-metre track events, not to mention middle-distance and distance events, such as marathons, because of possible deleterious consequences. By successfully swimming Lake Ontario, Bell showed that a well-trained female athlete could perform strenuously without ill-effects, with the result that more girls and women set their sights on marathons in both swimming and track and field. It was three decades later, however—in the Los Angeles Olympics of 1984—that women were first permitted to run the marathon.

Nancy Greene (b.1943). With parents and five siblings, Nancy Greene spent the winter months of her childhood on the ski-slopes of Red Mountain in British Columbia. She was challenged by her older sister Liz and concentrated her racing goals on beating her in local races. By the age of fourteen Nancy was having success, and within two years she was selected for the Olympic team. She watched Anne Heggtveit

Nancy Greene winning the World Cup in skiing, 1967,
at Grindelwald, Switzerland.

win a gold medal at Squaw Valley in 1960 and determined to do the same.

Nancy had to turn to the European circuit to gain the much-needed experience to challenge in both the World Cup and Olympic competitions. At this time the federal government did not give financial support for such training, and her hometown of Rossland, B.C., paid for her tour in the 1961 season.[69] She improved steadily and began to make an impression on the World Cup circuit, becoming a favourite of the press because of her forthright comments and fresh-faced appearance.

Greene won the World Cup in 1967 and was Gold Medallist at the Olympics in 1968. She also became the first female athlete to benefit commercially from her athletic successes. She entered the business world in her own way, as she recounts in her autobiography:

> I flew to Toronto to confer with lawyers and accountants and advertising agencies and personal managers and all the other people whom I needed to launch me into the business world. I was told that with all the success I enjoyed in my skiing career I was bound to make a good deal of money through endorsements, public appearances and all kinds of other commercial arrangements. It may sound slightly pompous, but the fact is I refused to become involved with anything I didn't approve of. My new managers agreed with my approach. And in the weeks that followed I became connected with a number of, I think, first-rate, responsible and decidedly Canadian organizations.[70]

As a direct result of the commercial benefits to be derived from sporting successes, Nancy Greene was one of the first Canadian female athletes to become a successful entrepreneur. Since her retirement in 1968 she has played an influential role in the development of sport, both as a member of the Task Force on Sport in 1969, which redefined the government's role in amateur sport at the federal level, and as the co-owner with her husband, Al Raine, of a ski resort at Whistler Mountain in British Columbia. Young skiers flock to this resort to seek advice from Nancy and Al Raine, who give willingly of their time and expertise to promote their favourite sport.

Through the years women's sport has changed dramatically. Women athletes have challenged the predominantly male sport establishment, entered competitions in a wide variety of sports, established new records, and often risked failure and ridicule in their struggle to develop equal sporting opportunities. Because of the stellar accomplishments of women, which opened so many doors for those who followed, today it is no longer peculiar for women to climb mountains, to run mega-marathons, to compete in senior-citizen competitions, or to embrace the joy of vigorous exercise as their right. There are still barriers to be lowered before true equality in women's sport is achieved, but so long as women are prepared to challenge, to participate, and to enjoy, progress will continue to be made.

10

Sport and Technological Change

Sport has always been directly influenced by the societal environment—the economic, religious, social, educational, and political conditions —that affects how people live their lives, spend their free time, and determine their values. During the nineteenth century such forces as urbanization, industrialization, and technological advancement moulded sport practices, influencing directly how Canadians spent their increasing leisure hours, and indirectly how they viewed sport. The impact of these forces in changing sport practices was complex and their effects cannot be discussed simultaneously. Several sports will therefore be examined individually, using examples to illustrate particular influences, followed by a more in-depth examination of combined influences on individual sport development, such as occurred in rowing, track and field, curling, golf, and basketball.[1]

As the population became concentrated in towns and cities, many factors were instrumental in changing sport. More people were available in one place to participate, but less space became available for play. Instead of a winter game of hockey or a curling match played on the plentiful large frozen inlets or lakes, with sometimes a day or several days given over to play—depending only on the desires of the agricultural settlers who through the years developed their own playing rules—confined spaces had to be set aside in parks, or in other open spaces within the city or its outskirts, to provide playing environments. Not only were specific spaces established for different sports, but it soon became necessary to establish playing rules, procedures, times of play, and to limit the numbers of participants and the length of the game because no longer were the players friends who had played together for years and had developed their own rules to suit their purpose. And there was no longer unlimited time for playing. The new definition of playing space, and the acknowledgement and ultimately the acceptance of the need for common sport regulations, fostered new sporting skills and competitive practices. Soon the same rules spread from community to community and were observed by all players despite home location.

Although travel was difficult and time-consuming, inter-city competitions developed and organizations were formed to promote each sport. Thus urbanization forced a fundamental structural and functional change in sport. It became institutionalized in sport clubs, which were usually formed for upper-middle- and upper-class males; elected executives were responsible for establishing rules of play and dictated the size of playing spaces, what equipment could be used, and who could play with whom.[2]

Industrialization not only changed society but affected sport as well. The building of canals to bypass rapids and falls began in the 1820s and by mid-century the St Lawrence was linked with Lake Ontario and (with the Welland canal bypassing the Niagara River and Falls) with Lake Erie; the Rideau Canal linked the Ottawa River at Ottawa with Lake Ontario at Kingston. Steamboats encouraged sport teams to travel by water. Their offer of excursion rates between Montreal and Toronto—return trips for the price of a one-way fare—attracted both players and spectators. Railways, however, had an even greater impact. In the 1840s the journey from Montreal to Quebec by coach took two to three days, and from Montreal to Toronto four days—limiting travel to those who had both the time and money. Railways had obvious advantages for Canada: they were more flexible than canals and did not freeze up in winter.[3] When the Guarantee Act (1849) offered financial help, many local railways started in Upper and Lower Canada and the Atlantic Provinces. By 1860 most major communities in Canada were connected by the Grand Trunk Railway, while the St Lawrence and Atlantic Railway joined Montreal with Portland, Maine. Completion of the Intercolonial Railway in 1876 joined central Canada with Nova Scotia and New Brunswick. Construction of the Canadian Pacific Railway through the incredibly difficult rock and muskeg of the Precambrian Shield, across the Prairies and through the Rockies, became one of Canada's greatest engineering feats. Finished in 1885, the CPR joined most regions of Canada, and introduced a method of transportation that promoted sporting competitions between widespread communities. The railways also courted sporting groups by offering them reduced rates.[4] Instead of taking four days to travel from Montreal to Toronto, the time was reduced to sixteen hours by 1863, and the introduction of the Pullman coach in 1879 made inter-town travel more comfortable. Baseball, cycling, curling, and rowing competitions all benefited from train travel.

Improved transportation within towns and cities also became important. A horse-drawn omnibus service was available in Toronto from 1849, but not until 1861 was the first horse-car street railway introduced by the Toronto Street Railway Company.[5] 'For the opening of the new grounds of the Toronto Base Ball Club in 1886, it was announced that the Metropolitan team from New York would play, and that the Street Car Company [would] signify their intention of granting transfer tickets, and doing their best to accommodate the public."⁶ Technological advancements in travel were the most significant influence on sport at this time. Without the railway, leagues would not have developed so quickly, nor would spectator increase in sport have been so dramatic. The expansion of the railway, linkages of communities by railway lines, more comfortable travelling accommodation, the reduction of travel time, and attractive excursion rates encouraged industrial workers as well as affluent citizens to participate as athletes and spectators—greatly swelling the sport community.

A Canadian communication system permitting rapid dissemination of information from sea to sea was also fully developed during the latter half of the nineteenth century, changing dramatically the way sports' results were distributed to eager fans. Before the development of the telegraph system, invented by Samuel F. B. Morse in the United States in the 1840s, information about sport results had often taken weeks to travel from the competition site to towns across the country, and often the information received was inaccurate. Letters sent by coach between Toronto and Quebec City took 16 to 18 days and news from England might not be received for two months. Few knew about competitions, and fewer still followed the events—sport was important only to the participants. This changed, however, when the telegraph system was fully in place; sport results were communicated across the country right after a competition—stimulating interest in the competition, the athlete and/or team, and also fostering spectator interest in the profit to be gained from gambling on the outcome. The completion of the Atlantic Cable in 1866 also brought British and European sporting results to Canada almost simultaneously with the end of the competition. The telegraph office quickly became the popular gathering place for sports enthusiasts eager to get the first word on an important competition from afar.

Another communication development in the latter half of the nineteenth century—the newspaper sports page, first introduced in 1855—resulted in a large daily audience eager to receive detailed information about the latest sporting event the day after a competition. Aided by the rapid availability of sport results from telegraph, and later telephone, transmission, a sports reporter in most major communities wrote a 'story' of the event for daily digestion. In 1874 there were 500 periodicals published in Canada; by 1900 this number had increased to more than 1,000.

The sports editor became important to newspapers by the 1870s and the sport page was the first page read by many. Initially wood-engravings were used to depict images of sportsmen; during the 1890s photographs took their place.[7] By 1900 the railway and the sport media had joined Canadians in a strong national bond and sport heroes helped solidify the link from Halifax to Vancouver. In addition, there developed a 'sporting industry' of workers—sports editors, reporters, photographers—whose prime responsibility became the promotion of sport, and at the turn of the century men were able to make a living directly from sport in an ancillary roll rather than as competitors.

On not such a grand scale as railway transportation or the communication systems, but certainly significant in their impact on society, were other technological advancements that also affected sporting practices. Elias Howe's sewing machine produced playing uniforms and other apparel such as mitts. The vulcanization of rubber in the 1830s by Charles Goodyear improved the elasticity and resiliency of rubber balls in the 1840s and of golf and tennis balls later in the century. The safety bicycle, the typewriter, the strand starting-barrier used in horse-racing, the camera, and the mass-production of sporting goods also influenced sport practices.

These inventions, and improved machinery and manufacturing techniques, produced balls, bats, and other sport equipment that met specific standards of size, weight, and shape, ensuring that all competitors had standardized equipment. Mass-produced sporting equipment was less expensive and more available to the average person; better equipment also led to improved performance skills.

Covered ice rinks were a Canadian innovation, the first such rink being reported in Quebec in 1852.[8] With this new facility, and the development of the spring skate (the separate blade was released by merely pushing aside a small lever), manufactured and patented by John Forbes of Dartmouth in 1865, indoor skating parties became popular with city residents; demonstrations, and soon competitions, of 'fancy skating' drew interested spectators to arenas. The discovery of electricity and the development of the incandescent bulb by Edison in 1879 made a major impact on urban social life. Electric light replaced the gas lights familiar in arenas and armouries of the time, changing sport from a daytime, usually out-of-doors activity, and making play possible inside or outside, during the day or at night. Winter sports were particularly affected.

The changing concept of time influenced the development of organized sport.[9] Agrarian 'time' of the pre-industrial period was determined by the rising and setting of the sun or by the tasks to be accomplished during a particular season; during the nineteenth century, however, an industrial system introduced a time concept characterized by the work-day and the work week, measured in minutes and hours. The day became divided into employer's time and other time—believed to be free time available for things other than providing the necessities of life, to which daily activities were dedicated in the former agrarian society. By Confederation year 'the mechanic, the employee, and the labourer' were participating with the élite of society in sporting activities.[10] When agitation produced shorter (though still long) working hours, workers were freed for recreational pursuits. By the mid-eighties Saturday after-noons were regarded as a time for sports, and the results of competitions were reported in Monday's paper. In the late 1890s the Toronto *Globe* had a separate sports page.

By the end of the nineteenth century many sports had written rules, standardized sport equipment was available for mass use, and people with increased leisure time could travel with relative ease and at mod-erate expense to participate in or watch their favourite events. Sport practices became established that were refined only in the twentieth century. Although dramatic changes have resulted in recent years—from television and air travel, for example—the foundation for sport orga-nization today was established in the nineteenth century.

ROWING

The importance of lakes and rivers in the growth of Canada and in the lives of Canadians made aquatic sports natural activities for them, par-ticularly rowing, the people's sport, and pleasure-sailing, the sport of the wealthy. The oldest sporting event in Canada is presumed to be the Newfoundland Regatta. On 6 August 1816 the *Royal Gazette and New-foundland Advertiser* informed its readers that 'a rowing match will take place on Monday next between two boats, on which considerable bets are depending—they are to start at half past one from alongside the prison ship.'[11] By the 1820s the races had shifted to 'the pond', Quidi Vidi Lake, where the Quidi Vidi Races are still held today.[12] While the wealthier Nova Scotia citizens, encouraged by both the military garrison and naval personnel stationed in Halifax, organized the first sailing regatta as early as 1826, Haligonians claim that their yacht club existed from 1837 (receiving royal patronage after the Prince of Wales' visit in 1860). In central Canada, from the St Lawrence River to Lake Superior, communities first looked to the waterway as an economic resource, but in the first half of the century yacht clubs were established in Cornwall,

Kingston, Belleville, Cobourg, and Hamilton, as well as Toronto, and regattas were held annually. On Toronto Bay, for example, spectators crowded the shore and boarded boats to get a front-row seat for these events. Public interest in sailing regattas declined, probably because sailing is much more interesting for the sailor than the spectator, who often was too far away from the competition to appreciate the race fully. But interest increased in rowing events because the excitement of this competition could easily be seen by spectators crowded along the length of the course. The gambling potential of rowing also enhanced its popularity with the Canadian public.

Rowing experienced a tremendous growth as a result of the industrial and technological changes that took place in the last half of the nineteenth century. The rower Edward 'Ned' Hanlan, called 'the Boy in Blue', became better known throughout the world in the early 1880s than any Canadian politician of the time. (See Chapter 2.) Early in his career, in 1875–6, a group of twenty upstanding men in the community formed an organization known as the Hanlan Club to look after all the details of racing, allowing Hanlan time to train for races. They purchased the best boat available, dynamically designed to streamline the craft, and added a rowing innovation—the sliding seat—which Hanlan popularized during a twenty-year reign of rowing in Canada, the United States, England, and Australia.

In reporting Hanlan's successes newspapers popularized rowing. They detailed every challenge, outlined the signing agreements, analysed the competitors, detailed their daily regimens and training programs, estimated the size of the crowd, asked how much money was bet, established the odds, were on hand to describe every aspect of the contest, and maintained interest between races with stories about the outstanding competitors. In England in May 1879, where Hanlan raced John Hawdon for the championship of the Tyne, the Newcastle *Chronicle* reported:

> Hanlan is undoubtedly one of the most finished scullers we have ever seen. His slide is exceptionally long, and he uses it to the fullest extent, thereby taking a grand sweeping stroke, which when he exerts his strength seems almost to lift the boat out of the water, even though it always travels gracefully on an even keel. If he had chosen he might have won the race by half a mile.[13]

The impact of technological change is well illustrated through Hanlan's career. The sliding seat enhanced his skill and gave him a longer pull and a faster time than that achieved by former scullers; a better appreciation of scientific knowledge was used by the boat-builders to trim the width of his scull, maximizing the principles of dynamics; the railway transported spectators at excursion rates to his events in the United States;[14] entrepreneurs popularized his feats with souvenirs to be sold for profit at each race; the telegraph transmitted immediate information about each race to an eager throng waiting in telegraph offices in both the United States and Canada; and newspapers, with their detailed coverage and their analysis of his every action, made Hanlan a national hero and sold many newspapers to eager sports fans. It is difficult to surmise what his stature might have been without these changes. To be sure, he would have rowed well, but the heightened awareness of his successes undoubtedly increased his reputation and popular appeal worldwide, not to mention the increased prize-money that accrued to him and his backers.

Professional rowing declined in the twentieth century and amateur rowing has never reached the appeal enjoyed during Hanlan's reign, although Canadians won medals in Olympic competitions in 1924, 1928, 1956, 1960, 1964, and 1984, and rowing regattas are annual events in various Canadian locations. The Royal Canadian Henley Regatta at Port Dalhousie, Ontario, and the Canadian National Exhibition Regatta at Toronto are two well-known longstanding annual events. The Royal Canadian Henley still has a large attendance of rowers and spectators from both Canada and the United States. Although the excitement and the gambling wins have subsided since the glory days of Hanlan, the individual dedication to rowing in clubs, universities, and schools continues to be stable.

TRACK AND FIELD

The premier Olympic sport of the twentieth century, track and field, began as an outgrowth of the Caledonia Games (the North American version of Scottish Highland Games) promoted by the Scots in Canada.[15] They were also aided by improved communications and transportation, permitting contestants to travel between Canada and the United States. Games were known to be held in Canada prior to 1838 but were probably not well established until after Confederation.[16] In Toronto in 1847 a typical Games involved a procession of members dressed in national costume who marched from the City Hall to the field for activities, including throwing the hammer, putting the stone, throwing the caber, and performing the leap and the 400-yard race. These activities were usually followed by social events and perhaps competitions for the bagpipe, Highland fling, sword dance, singing, etc., giving the Scots immigrants time to renew friendships and enjoy the camaraderie of their countrymen.[17]

In the 1860s and 1870s the Caledonia Games in Canada benefited from the growth of cities and their close proximity to the American border: the north-south affinity between Scottish communities in Ontario and New York State fostered interest and participation. Because many prominent Canadian politicians and businessmen were Scottish and patronized them, the Games became annual athletic and social events in Canada.[18] As their popularity grew, prize money increased, attracting many Canadians to the more lucrative American Games. The Caledonia Games became successful financially and from the sport perspective, but at the 1870 Annual Meeting in New York, members of both the American and Canadian Caledonian Society expressed concern about the lack of standardization of implement specifications, measurement procedures, and the rules governing competitions.[19] Without standardized equipment and rules for play, the competitions were not fair to each competitor. Increased industrialization helped solve the problem in the mass-production of equipment. For example, the hammer and caber, made to a specified weight, became available for practice and competition at reasonable cost.

The success of the Games continued during the later part of the century, but it was apparent that not only the Scots wanted to compete in athletic events. St Patrick's Societies, Ladies' Benevolent Societies, Irish Protestant Benevolent Societies, policeman's and fireman's associations, and factory groups began to feature athletic competitions as part of their annual picnics. At first each town or city used different equipment, different rules, and was willing to increase prize money to attract the best competitors. But that was to change as track and field matured.

About the 1880s, when British, American, and Canadian athletes competed against each other, standardized rules and equipment became a requirement for meets. The revival of the Olympic Games in 1896 brought to the attention of track-and-field enthusiasts the necessity of conducting all competitions under the same regulations, using standardized equipment. Another expressed concern was the issue of professional and amateur athletes competing against each other. The Amateur Athletic Association of Canada, formed in 1884, launched a strong movement to return sports to amateurism, to guard the 'gentlemanly' behaviour thought to be an essential ingredient of sportsmanship, and to regulate amateur competitions on the 'cinder track'.[20] It succeeded in achieving this goal in track and field and fifteen other sports that joined the AAAC, but not without difficulty, as some sports groups wanted more liberal rules to permit 'quasi-professional' practices at various times.[21] The AAAC organized track and field well and by 1900 the sport was maturing and developing a good system, particularly in Quebec and Ontario. Professionalism in the sport was no longer an issue because the AAAC controlled all track and field, and payment for performance had virtually disappeared.

Canada's athletes excelled in international competition. Between 1906 and 1912 William Sheering, Tom Longboat, Bobby Kerr, George Goulding, Walter Knox—to name just a few—established Canada's reputation.[22] There was a natural lull in activity during the war years, but during the 1920s track and field experienced increased popularity. Our women excelled in the 1928 Games and by doing so increased public awareness of the potential of females in sport: Ethel Catherwood and Fanny Rosenfeld became as well known as Percy Williams, who also excelled in the 1928 Olympic track events. For four decades Hamilton held an enviable reputation as the best city for promoting track and field. In 1930, without funding from either the provincial or federal governments, Hamilton hosted the first British Empire Games, building a stadium and swimming pool to provide facilities. Track and field reached its spectator zenith during the twenties and thirties, when every event attracted large crowds. In recent years they come out only for international competitions: the Pan Am Games in Winnipeg in 1967, the Olympics in Montreal in 1976, the Commonwealth Games in Vancouver in 1954 and Edmonton in 1978, and the FISU (World University) Games in Edmonton in 1983.

The most exciting and significant event in track occurred before thousands of Canadians and was observed around the world—on television screens or on film—in 1954 when Britain's Roger Bannister broke the 4-minute mile. On the last day of the Empire Games in Vancouver, Bannister and Australia's John Landry came home in less than four minutes, in a finish that surpassed expectation. At the sound of the starter's pistol laps. Then came one of the most memorable sequences in sport. Bannister, five yards back, headed into the final turn, sprinted past the Australian in a tremendous kick, and finished with a time of 3:58.8— five yards ahead of Landy.

Track and field had Canadian stars during the fifties and sixties—Bill Crothers, Bruce Kidd, Abby Hoffman—but there seemed to be a paucity of medals in Olympic competition during this period, followed by much soul-searching by track enthusiasts. Unfortunately, just when Ben Johnson seemed to be renewing interest in this sport and drawing large crowds at appearances in Canada, the United States, and Europe—at year-round indoor and outdoor meets—following his remarkable gold-medal performance in Rome in 1987, the track-and-field bubble burst when he was tested positive for steroids in Seoul in 1988. The Dubin Inquiry of 1988–9 has revealed many drug-related cheating practices. Following these disclosures sponsors—who had been enticed back into meet and athlete sponsorship—quickly withdrew their millions of dollars, and many wonder if track and field will ever recover its former stature and appeal in Canada.

CURLING

Another sport promoted in Canada by Scottish immigrants, curling benefited from the travel and communication developments of the nineteenth century. Edwin C. Guillet, writing about pioneer days in Upper Canada, shared a nineteenth-century French-Canadian farmer's impression of this new form of social activity:

> Today I saw a band of Scotchmen, who were throwing large balls of iron like tea-kettles on the ice, after which they cried 'Soop! soop!', and then laughed like fools. I really believe they ARE fools.[23]

Probably the most often-repeated curling impression, it does illustrate the indefatigable Scotch making the best of the severe Canadian winter by creating a playing-ground for sport. The first curling club was founded in Montreal, as Gerald Redmond recounts:

> A group of Scots who were identified chiefly with the fur trade desired to introduce to Montreal two favourite games of their native land, curling and golf. On January 27, 1807, they founded the Royal Montreal Curling Club at a banquet attended by fifteen charter members. Thus was born the oldest curling club in America . . . . The original members used the River St. Lawrence below what was then known as 'the port' for their rink. John Bude took a prominent part in founding the club and Thomas Blackwood, a partner of James McGill, was the first president.[24]

The Club rules for the first twenty members reflects two stereotyped attributes of the Scots—a love of frugality and whisky:

> The club shall meet at Gillies' on Wednesday, every fortnight at 4 o'clock to dine on salt beef and greens. The club dinner shall not exceed in cost seven shillings and sixpence a head, and any members infringing on this rule shall be fined four shillings . . . The losing party of the day shall pay for a bowl of whisky toddy to be placed in the middle of the table for those who may chuse [sic] it.[25]

Clubs developed in many Maritime and central-Canadian communities during the first forty years of the nineteenth century. Wooden 'stones', hand-made by Scottish enthusiasts,[26] were used until real stones were imported, and then Canadian stonemasons shaped granite stones. As would be expected, Montreal looked further afield for competition and accepted a challenge from Quebec, agreeing to play at Trois-Rivières;

> The Montreal players left the city on January 7 and 8, some by stage and other by their own sleighs, the first of them arriving in Trois Rivières around noon on January 9. The match took place the next day, with two rinks a side, and the final score was Quebec 31, Montreal 23. The eight Montreal players, as losers, paid £3 2s. 6d for the dinner afterwards, and a similar amount for transportation.[27]

Although initially players and promoters were predominantly Scottish immigrants, the success of curling and its rapid growth in Canada were partially due to its adoption by so many Canadians of different ethnic background, social position, and occupation. In 1855 the *Montreal Gazette* observed:

> Amongst the players we notice the Merchant and the Mechanic, the Soldier and the Civilian, the Pastor and his Flock, all on an equal footing, for the game of curling levels all ranks.[28]

While Montreal was the founding centre for curling and built the first indoor rink, it was soon overtaken by southern Ontario when Scottish settlers moved to this region. With the arrival of railways, equipment was more easily transported by train, travel time was greatly reduced, and comfort was increased. Thus competitions multiplied and factory workers too could play because less travel time was required. Railways recognized the business potential of curling excursions and offered reduced rates to teams travelling by rail, making curling a relatively inexpensive sport for Ontario citizens by the 1850s. In 1858 the first Grand East-West Bonspiel was held on Burlington Bay, with thirty-two rinks in attendance, while at the Don Valley Rink in Toronto a total of 168 participants and 42 rinks attended.[29] Keen rivalries developed between communities joined together by the train routes; for example, between Hamilton and Dundas, Paris and Galt, and Toronto and Scarborough. By 1884 the completion of the Port Hope, Lindsay and Beaverton Railway linked Port Hope, Millbrook, Peterborough, Beaverton, and Lindsay, and curling competitions increased in these small Ontario communities. Trophies established during this period are still in use today. As the Canadian Pacific Railway moved westward, with the final spike driven

A Notman composite of indoor curling in Montreal, 1905. (Notman Photographic Archives, 4201 view, courtesy the McCord Museum of McGill University.)

by Donald Smith (later Lord Strathcona) in the mountains of British Columbia in 1885, and more than 800 communities were linked together across the Prairies, curling became another binding western activity. Donald Smith himself participated in the sport and donated the Strathcona Cup to curling.[30] Clubs were started in Winnipeg by 1876, in Calgary by 1885, and in British Columbia by 1898. By the end of the century curling was a sport played from one coast to the other, and women were also participating.

International bonspiels increased by the 1880s. A competition between clubs in Toronto and three clubs affiliated with the Grand National Curling Club of the United States was held in Toronto in 1879.[31] The first tour of a Scottish curling team occurred in 1903. In less than two months they travelled 5,000 miles through Canada and the United States, playing 99 games with local teams.[32] This tour established Canada's curling credibility and promising future. When a Canadian team toured Scotland in 1908, they won 23 of 26 games, winning the coveted Strathcona Cup.

Artificial ice for curling was first used in Vancouver in 1912, and soon the indoor curling rink became the preferred location for the sport. Players and spectators grew rapidly as a result of the development of this new playing surface—until the Depression, when so many Canadians found themselves unemployed. However, since little equipment or expense was involved in curling, many turned to the sport to release their emotions and rid themselves of their fears about the future. It was at this time that curlers from the Prairie Provinces began to dominate the sport. Between 1927 and 1935 they lost the Canadian title—the Macdonald Brier Tankard—only twice.

Two phenomena in the twentieth century have significantly affected the popularity of curling in Canada: sponsorship and television. The W. C. Macdonald Company began sponsoring the Canadian Curling Championships by 1930, heading a long list of well-known Canadian companies that have generously sponsored this sport to gain greater sales of product and/or to attract business away from competitors. For example, Labatt's Breweries has traditionally sponsored pro-skiing, car-racing, and golf, while its rival Molson's has given financial support to cross-country skiing, powerboat racing, and curling. Air Canada's sponsorship of curling has been beneficial to both the sport and the sponsor—with curlers receiving free travel to international and national competitions. Each year's curling exposure on television dominates all other sports in February and March, and because Canadian curlers traditionally play for the championship at the World Tournament, Air Canada's sponsorship dollars are returned in good measure from the world-wide television exposure.[33] In 1974 it was estimated that '800,000—that's one in every 27 Canadians, participated in curling.'[34] In 1988 at the Calgary Olympics, where curling was merely a demonstration sport, the television audience was attracted to it, and the International Olympic Committee agreed to consider its inclusion in future winter games.

A story told about the Reverend Dr MacMillan, the Chaplain of the Halifax Curling Club in 1903, describes well how thoroughly curlers get caught up in this popular game:

> The Reverend's rink had met with great success throughout the year, and they were posted to play in the semifinals of the club competition on a Wednesday night, which happened to be the night of the weekly prayer meeting. The Reverend and his 'mate', an elder, were walking home, and the Reverend was grieving over the loss of his chance to play. The elder suggested a crack skip as a substitute for the match, but still the Doctor was despondent. Suddenly he brightened up and said: 'It's all right; I'll get my brother to be my substitute.' The elder was not so enthusiastic, and asked: 'Do you think he can play well enough?' 'Oh, no no!' replied the Reverend, 'he'll take the prayer meeting.'[35]

The Scottish immigrants could never have anticipated the success of the game in their adopted country. It has been, and continues to be, 'the social integrative' sport in Canada, enjoyed by thousands every winter evening. Although the French-Canadian farmer thought nineteenth-century curlers 'fools', they were neither fools nor foolish but rather people who recognized the necessity of leisure pursuits that provided enjoyment, physical activity, and social interaction—requisites for a healthy, happy life then as now.

GOLF

There is debate about when golf was introduced into Canada. Some sport historians suggest it was introduced by British officers in Quebec City and others say it was originated by Scottish sailors playing a three-hole game in Montreal.[36] Regardless of the exact time of introduction, golf, like curling, owes its growth and popularity to early Scottish businessmen. The Royal Montreal Golf Club—formed on 4 November 1873 by Scotsman Alexander Dennistoun—was the first club not only in Canada but in all of North America. Next was the Royal Quebec Golf Club, founded in 1874,[37] and the Toronto Golf Club in 1875. Inter-club competition between Quebec and Montreal began in 1876. The game moved westward with the railway in the nineties—clubs were formed in Winnipeg (1894), Fort Macleod (1895), Edmonton (1896), and Medicine Hat (1899). The Royal Canadian Golf Association was founded in Ottawa in 1894, organizing and conducting the first Canadian Amateur Championship the following year at the Royal Ottawa Golf Club. In 1894 membership in the RCGA was less than ten clubs, but by 1914 it had increased to 34 clubs and to 128 by 1936. In 1973 more than 846 clubs from coast to coast belonged.[38]

Because golf requires large tracts of land for play, the expense of preparing courses had to be borne by the membership, resulting in high golf fees.[39] Thus in the early years of the game's development, and for many years later, the time required to play eighteen holes and the expensive club and green fees meant that golf was played almost exclusively by members of the upper class.

Women became enthusiastic golfers as early as 1894. The Ottawa Golf Club had twenty-five 'lady' associate members, and the Toronto club had over one hundred members in its ladies' branch.[40] In 1896, a *Winnipeg Free Press* sportswriter commented:

> The number of the fair sex who play golf is small when compared to the men, but each day new recruits are enlisted. By many it is supposed that golf is a game requiring too much exercise to become popular among women, but a diligent inquiry as to facts would overthrow that theory . . . . At all tournaments of importance nowadays special competitions are arranged for the so-called weaker sex. As a general rule, women are not strong in long driving, but their direction is usually certain. In the short game they are wonderfully accurate.[41]

The Canadian Ladies' Golf Union was formed in 1913 and has been instrumental in serving the needs of golfing women ever since. At the Royal Montreal Golf Club women were paying annual dues of $3 and holding monthly competitions—complete with afternoon teas—throughout the golfing season. Uniform dress was expected: a dark skirt and red blouse for every day, and a white skirt and red blouse for competition days.[42]

Golf played a role in establishing more liberal sporting practices in Canada. During the nineteenth century the playing of 'skittles, ball, football, rackets or any noisy game' on Sunday was a punishable offense under the Lord's Day Act.[43] A case involving golfers helped to ease this law. On Sunday 26 May 1895, on the golf links at the Toronto Golf Club, four players were summoned by the county constable to appear before the magistrate, who fined them five dollars each. The men claimed they had 'a perfect right to play the game any day they pleased' and retained Dalton McCarthy, Q.C., to defend them. The case was argued before Chief Justice Armour, who asked, 'What is this golf?' The counsel for the defence explained that golf was a game played with a stick and one hits a little ball with it. Several days later the judge ruled that it was within the law to play golf on Sunday, giving his well-known judgement:

> This game of golf is not a game within the meaning of the law. It is not noisy. It attracts no crowds. It is not gambling. It is on a parallel, it seems to me, with a gentleman going out for a walk on Sunday and as he walks, switching off the heads of weeds with his walking stick.[44]

The case was dismissed and the golfers pursued the 'little ball' in peace.[45]

By the turn of the century golf was no longer the exclusive preserve of the upper class, and city, provincial, national, and international events were contested. By the 1920s club 'professionals' developed because golfers realized that lessons from someone who knew the game would improve their play. Professionals, called 'pros', were soon hired by most private clubs. A group of club 'pros' organized the Canadian Professional Golfer's Association (CPGA) at the Toronto Golf Club on 11 July 1911. It served a much-needed purpose—raising the level of play, providing tournaments, and increasing the competitive standard of professionals entered in the annual Canadian Open and giving 'pros' some prestige.

Golf professionals have always had a high position in their sport, unlike the very low status and regard that existed for professionals in most other sports at this time. P. D. Ross, of the Royal Ottawa Golf Club, donated the Ross Championship Cup to the CPGA in 1911 for annual competition among Canadian professional golfers. More recently many companies have sponsored the CPGA Championship—the House of Seagram, Labatt's Breweries Ltd., Peter Jackson Tobacco—and their funding has assisted a professional golfers' tour of Canada (providing good competition for young professionals) as well as business and educational programs, and the actual championship competition. In 1973 the prize money was $175,000. Since the rise of televised sports broadcasting in 1952, golfing competitions have been able to raise large amounts of money from television contracts. In the 1980s CPGA prize money rose to $425,000, attracting the best players in the world.

As the popularity of the game grew, there was also increased interest in the care and maintenance of the golf course. Two new occupations emerged—golf architect and greenkeeper. A group of prominent superintendents, who felt the need for a national organization, formed the Canadian Golf Superintendents' Association in 1966 at the Lachute Golf and Country Club, Quebec. Whether to use seed or turf, the number of unnatural hazards, the course layout—these and similar issues were frequently disputed. With the advent of improved golf clubs and balls, many golfers felt the game had become too easy and a reaction set in, with golf-course designers building 'ungainly and unnatural bunkers and traps all over the course without apparent reason.'[46] The increasing popularity of the game brought with it the need for a skilled industry to plan and maintain courses.

Canadian golf championships through the years have demonstrated outstanding Canadian talent. In its first decade the Canadian Open, the première golf tournament, starred George Cumming, the well-known 'pro' of the Toronto Golf Club, who worked there from 1900 to 1950;[47] brothers Charles and Albert Murray of the Royal Montreal and Outremont Clubs; Karl Keffer of the Royal Ottawa Golf Club; and George Knudson (1937–89), of the Buttonville Fairways north of Toronto, who was perhaps the best professional golfer Canada ever produced. Knudson was described by Jack Nicklaus as ' a million-dollar player and a 10-cent putter.'[48] (His inconsistent putting—he did not like to practise putting, preferring fairway shots that he could place with deadly accuracy—may have kept him from being considered among the greatest golfers of the century, such as Arnold Palmer, Sam Snead, and Ben Hogan.) As the quality of the competition in the Canadian Open increased, it became difficult for the club 'pro' to combine teaching and competition because of the time necessary to develop and maintain competitive skills, so professional golfers began to specialize in one occupation or the other to make their living. Professional Canadian golfers on the United States men's 'pro' tour have included Stan Leonard (b. 1915), who won three events in 1957–60, and George Knudson, who had won eight by the time he turned his attention to teaching in the late 1970s. On the women's tour Sandra Post (b. 1948), of Oakville, Ontario, won the Ladies' Professional Golf Association championship in her first year on the tour and more money than any other Canadian professional, male or female. It is amazing that Canadian golfers, who experienced a shorter playing season and fewer competitions than Americans, have been so successful in international competitions. (Some, who had enough funding, moved south to practise and play on American courses during the Canadian winter.) It has been observed that 'our best golfers may have been penalized by the Canadian environment, but that environment may well have had a good deal to do with the unusual moral and psychological resources they brought to the game.'[49]

Amateur golfers have also brought honours to Canada. George S. Lyon won the Canadian amateur title eight times between 1898 and 1914, and won the only Olympic golf event ever held, in 1904. C. Ross (Sandy) Sommerville, of the London Hunt Club, won the amateur title six times between 1926 and 1937; and Ada Mackenzie (1918–71), founder of the Ladies' Golf and Tennis Club in Thornhill, Ontario, won the Canadian Ladies' Amateur title five times between 1919 and 1935. (See pages 248–9.) They were later joined by top amateurs Marlene Stewart Streit (b. 1934) of Cereal, Alberta, eleven-time ladies' Canadian amateur champion, ladies' British Open amateur champion (1953), and United States women's amateur champion (1956); and Gary Cowan (b. 1938) of Kitchener, Ontario, winner of the United States men's amateur title in 1966 and 1971.

Golf—unlike curling, which has always been a democratic sport—is still mainly an upper-middle-class sport in Canada. With land costs always increasing, golf-club and playing fees escalating, and the length of time required to play eighteen holes, lower-income workers have not been able to afford the expenses associated with playing this sport in a private-club environment. However, some municipalities—for example, Edmonton, in 1907—have developed civic golf courses that enabled people to play for a nominal annual fee, or for pay-as-you-play green fees.[50] These facilities offer permanent green space and aesthetic park-like value within a city, in addition to community recreational opportunities.

The technological advances that have improved the sport of golf have been better-designed, mass-produced, and therefore less-expensive golf clubs and balls, and scientific advancements in perfecting the growing of grass and the care of greens. Television—besides giving rise to generous contracts and permitting large prizes—has popularized the game since the 1950s because it is particularly effective in focusing on the quiet, suspenseful moment of play and on the course of the ball. Games are transmitted year-round on television, and today golf is not only watched but played by millions of Canadians.

BASKETBALL

Basketball, another sport that Canadians took up in the twentieth century, was invented by a Canadian. James Naismith (1861–1936), raised in Almonte, Ontario, entered McGill University to prepare for the ministry, but changed his mind in his graduating year and became an instructor at the the YMCA International Training School in Springfield, Massachusetts (now Springfield College). (He later earned a medical degree from Colorado University and for forty years was associated with the University of Kansas as professor, physician, and director of physical education.) A young YMCA instructor, Luther Gulick, wanting to cultivate the play-instinct in physical training rather than perpetuate the emphasis on formal gymnastic exercise, challenged his students by speculating that perhaps a new game could be devised by recombining elements from existent games. Naismith was given the task of planning a new game for a class of men, some older than himself (he was thirty), who did not enjoy gymnastics but wanted something to do in the gymnasium that was more challenging than a children's game. After much thought, Naismith established four principles upon which the rules of basketball would be built: (1) no running with the ball; (2) no tackling or other rough body contact; (3) a horizontal goal above the players' heads; and (4) freedom of any player (while adhering to the no-contact requirements) to obtain the ball and score at any time.[51] Fastening two peach baskets to the balconies at each end of the gymnasium, about ten feet above the floor, he succeeded in inventing a new indoor game that recombined elements of other games. Naismith introduced this game with thirteen rules, and in December 1891 the first game of basketball was played. The peach-basket goals gave it its name.

The game was introduced into Canada by two members of Naismith's original basketball class, T.D. Patton and L.W. Archibald.[52] Archibald taught basketball in the YMCA of St Stephen, New Brunswick, in 1892, and that same year Patton taught the game in the Montreal Y.[53] It became very popular across the country and was introduced into physical-activity programs in many associations, educational institutions, and clubs. In 1902 the Toronto *Globe* described its growth:

> Hundreds of young men are now playing basketball who probably have a vague idea regarding its origin or realize that for so young a sport it has had a most unusual career. Started first as a game for members of the gymnasium classes of the Young Men's Christian Association, it has now attracted the attention of all classes of athletes as is seen from the scores of associations that now exist.[54]

In most YMCAs in eastern Canada, house leagues were organized, and so many members were interested in playing that junior, intermediate, and senior leagues, and later businessmen's leagues, were formed. Soon inter-city competitions began: a team from the Toronto Central YMCA played the Hamilton YMCA on 19 December 1895, winning 7 to 1.[55] The Y used basketball to improve life for railway workers across the country and to foster Christian-like leisure-time pursuits by organizing basketball leagues for them.[56]

Canada's most famous basketball team—a women's team officially called the Commercial Graduates Basketball Club—was the Edmonton Grads, which began in 1915 at the John MacDougall Commercial High School in Edmonton, with J. Percy Page as their coach. During their twenty-five years they played 522 games, some against men's teams, and lost only 20. This record is the best any Canadian team—male or female, amateur or professional—has accomplished.[57]

After the First World War basketball was the most popular winter indoor sport played in city, church, and university—in addition to the original YMCA leagues. Every area of the country embraced basketball, even during the Depression, when it was a popular activity of the unemployed because it required little equipment, and gymnasium facilities were always available. Commercial leagues developed, particularly in Southern Ontario. Men's basketball became an Olympic sport in 1936 and Canada's team won its only Olympic medal, a silver, that year in Berlin. Women's basketball became an Olympic sport at the Summer Games in Montreal in 1976 (Canadians have yet to be in the medals). Basketball has maintained its popularity in educational institutions, but to a lesser extent in the YMCA and other associations. Winter basketball games in universities, annual national championships for one weekend each spring, and Olympic competitions every four years have given limited television exposure to the game.

THE MASS MEDIA

It is interesting to look at how the perception and enjoyment of sport—which has never not been part of the life of Canadians, and began as small local endeavours with only local observers—has changed since the Second World War. Increased information about sports—in magazines, books, newspapers, and through formal study in higher education—has presented analyses, hypotheses about why sport is as it is, and projections about its future, thus increasing our understanding of sporting practices. Sport has been dissected, criticized, and extolled by journalists, media representatives, scholars, and sports fans. And beginning in November 1988 the Dubin Inquiry in Toronto examined all facets of amateur sport practices and embraced the very structure and function of sport in Canadian society.

Today there are specialized books on every aspect of Canadian sport, along with biographies and autobiographies (some ghost-written) of outstanding athletes. Since 1986 biographies of Debbie Brill, Ben Johnson, and Brian Orser have been snatched up by fans. In addition, books about teams, stellar performances, and major sporting events have been released quickly after the event.[58] Among several excellent sport books is *Canada's Sporting Heroes* (1974), by S.F. Wise and D. Fisher, which examines the social and cultural significance of Canadian sport in addition to assessing sport development, exceptional performances, and the athletes involved. Mention must also be made of the increase in sport articles appearing in popular magazines, trade journals, and scholarly journals, etc. Every aspect of sport seems to have a reading public, often with its own publication.

The computer has both enhanced the organization of written sports material and facilitated library searches. The Coaching Association in Canada began in 1975 the Sport Information Resource Centre, which exemplifies the changes that have taken place so rapidly in this area. First a library, specializing in sport literature, was established in 1975 at the National Sport and Recreation Centre in Ottawa to make available to Canadian coaches a comprehensive resource centre of international information about sport, physical activity, fitness, and sports medicine. Second, a ten-volume resource of all available sport literature—Sport Database (updated regularly)—was made available to coaches for a nominal fee. Third, by the 1980s online computer connections were established in university and municipal libraries for the coaches' research. Finally in April 1989 an advertisement was sent to each coach announcing the following:

> The publication of the CD-ROM product, called Sport Discus, brings together the wealth of information on sport, physical activity, fitness and sports medicine found in the SPORT Database with the ease and sophistication of CD-ROM technology. With SilverPlatter's powerful search and retrieval software, you can quickly locate the precise information you need.[59]

In just a decade the most comprehensive information about sport has been made available to coaches—first in a library, and then on a computer disk. No longer will Canada's geographical spread prevent any Canadian from receiving the most up-to-date information about a sport. In recent years the multiplication of sport-information sources—books/journals/films—combined with rapid computer technological advancements, have increased the availability of sport information beyond imagination. Computer enthusiasts suggest that soon baseball dug-outs and hockey-team benches will be supplied with a computer for coaches to check quickly their plays and calls with the statistics available from all games played.

During the last four decades communication and transportation—radio, television, and aeroplane travel—have radically changed sport, not only in Canada but world-wide. Today it is possible to travel in hours to every continent. The aeroplane has made it possible to conduct league play between different countries as easily as it was to have inter-city competitions a century ago. World competitors follow a newly established international circuit as they play each other. For example, tennis tournaments held in the United States, Canada, Britain, France, and Australia attract the same professional players. Such a schedule as Toronto one week, Sydney, Australia, the next, and Miami, Florida, the next has become the competitive norm; and although jet-lag is a common problem for globe-trotting athletes, participation in world-wide competitions has become an accepted way of making a living. Within Canada the relatively easy means of travelling and, perhaps more important, the subsidized travelling expenses borne by national sport organizations and/or sponsors, have dramatically changed sporting practices. Between 1915 and 1940 the Edmontons Grads travelled over 125,000 miles around the world. Their method of travelling was time-consuming, expensive, and not very comfortable. When setting out from Edmonton to London, Ontario, in 1922 for the Canadian championship they travelled by train; each athlete paid her own expenses (if gates were not sufficient to cover them) and sat up across the country because the club-car fare was too expensive. Before playing in the pre-Olympic basketball tournament in Europe, the Grads had to travel by train across Canada and then by steamship across the Atlantic. Today a comparable women's basketball team can travel by air, with relative ease and comfort, from Edmonton to London, England, or from Edmonton to Paris, on a weekend—leaving home on Friday night, playing a tournament, and being back at work on Monday morning. Air travel is regularly used by inter-university teams in the western provinces, by carded amateur athletes travelling to scheduled meets across the country, and by sport administrators and coaches who think nothing of travelling to Ottawa for a weekend sports-organization meeting. Air travel has not only reduced distance significantly but it has also encouraged people of moderate income within the work-force to stand for nomination in sport organizations. With government travel-assistance to National Sports Organizations executives, coupled with the convenience of air travel, the involvement of sport-volunteers has now been democratized.

Play-by-play broadcasts on radio brought hockey into Canadian homes every Saturday night. The first hockey broadcast was from Toronto's Mutual Street Arena on 8 February 1923, with Norm Allen calling the plays.[60] The next month, on 23 March 1923, Foster Hewitt—who as a reporter on the *Toronto Star* drew the assignment of covering an Ontario Hockey Association intermediate game at the same arena for the *Star*-owned radio station CFCA—broadcast the first of his famous play-by-play games. Some stories report that he shouted, 'He shoots! He scores!' during this first game; others suggest it was several years later, from the Maple Leaf Gardens, that he used these words to describe the game's ultimate moment. Making the first broadcast from the Gardens on 12 November 1931—from the Gondola, a box high above the ice—Hewitt became the voice of hockey for more than two decades, moving smoothly from the age of radio to the age of television. In 1957 he turned the microphone over to his son Bill, but at the age of seventy, in 1972, he was chosen to be the broadcaster of the USSR-Team Canada hockey series.

The technological phenomenon that has had the biggest impact on sport is television.[61] David Klatell and Norman Marcus have well described the impact of sport on the television reviewer:

> Sport transforms into dance, into song, into drama, into comedy, into news—often when one least expects it. It embodies aspects of ethnic, community, regional and national pride. It produces heroes and villains, rule-makers and law-breakers. It magnifies the striving accomplishments and tribulations of athletes raised high and fallen low. It is often candid, sometimes voyeuristic; often reassuring, sometimes disturbing. On some occasions, you can't turn away, on others you do so readily. Such moments are most special when they happen unexpectedly, when you want to call out to others, 'Hey, come in here and watch this!' How often does this happen in any other television program format?[62]

Today one can watch in the home events as they happen anywhere in the world. According to 1985 statistics provided by UNESCO, 1,598,000,000 radio sets and 735,441,200 television sets were providing news, entertainment, and sport events that appeared to take place in front of you.[63] Who will ever forget their excitement in 1972 when Paul Henderson scored the winning goal in the final game of the USSR-Team Canada hockey series, so far away in Moscow? In 1989 cable companies have introduced channels offering only sport programming—24 hours a day, seven days a week.[64] It would not be difficult to show a causal relationship between this increased exposure of talented athletes and the steadily declining numbers of amateur competitors in a sport such as hockey. Watching Junior B players in the local arena pales in comparison with seeing Wayne Gretzky play for the Los Angeles Kings on Hockey Night in Canada. Mainly as a result of television, the expectations of Canadian sport spectators have been raised, so that 'amateur' sport attracts large numbers of viewers only when élite athletes appear every four years in the Olympics. To the self-taught 'expert' home-viewer, local university and community sports are mediocre. The day when the Edmonton Grads, a women's amateur sporting event, could attract 6,792 spectators in 1930 has long since past.[65]

Revenues from television, in magnifying the amount of money previously gained from memberships and gates, have benefited both sport organizations and athletes. Television has necessitated better production of events—they must be staged to appeal to the large television audience. As a result of the impact of television a sophisticated new group of sport entrepreneurs has developed. Athletes hire managers, lawyers, and/or consultants to negotiate the best contract for them, and to help them with their speech, dress, and hair-style for television interviews; and sport-marketing consultants have become essential in a sport-business enterprise that so handsomely rewards talented athletes. Sport announcers, analysers, and commentators hired by television stations to bridge the gap between competition and spectator also benefit—world travel may be a job perk, association with athlete superstars is essential, escalating salaries are a reality, and personal stardom by association is always possible. Johnny Esaw is as recognized by the Canadian public as are the athletes he has interviewed on CTV since 1964.[66] As it seems to be true that television's appetite is insatiable, these sport-associated enterprises will continue to develop in sport's shadow.

Television sponsors of athletic events have reaped their own financial rewards. Entrepreneur Irving Ungerman is reputed to have gained substantially from this association: '. . . just about anything that's shown on closed-circuit TV in Canada comes through Ungerman's All Canada Sports Promotions.' In a Muhammed Ali boxing match, he is alleged to have paid $250,000 for the Canadian rights while grossing $1 million by showing the fight in only 24 centres across the country.[67] Television presentation of an excellent performance is also quickly parlayed into lucrative contracts, with corporations willing to link their product with the star athlete. Larry Heidebrecht, Ben Johnson's manager, said of this situation:

> The product is the image. It's strength, it's speed, it's being Number One in the world, but it is also being just Ben. He has a slight speech impediment, but his level of acceptance is such that it doesn't seem like some big flaw. It just makes him more human. We can identify with him. He could be any one of us, trying to succeed through hard work.[68]

Heidebrecht must have been a successful manager, because at his height Ben Johnson had endorsements in two countries, where he could not speak the language and would be seen only with the product in a television commercial: in Japan with an oil and gas company; with Visa, Johnson's Wax, Shueisha Encyclopedias, and Mazda automobiles; and in Italy with Diadora, endorsing a line of shoes and clothing at a salary of $1.6 million over five years, increasing to $1.75 million, contingent upon a gold medal at Seoul.[69]

The very possibility of being chosen for such million-dollar endorsements has inevitably brought about a change in the nature of amateur sport and in the attitude of some athletes, and their coaches, to their participation (quite apart from the effect it has had on professional sport). In this climate the former ideal of being sufficiently rewarded by a 'personal-best' performance, attained by honest hard work, seems to be receding—at least at the upper level of international championships, where business and profits have entered the picture. The Dubin Inquiry (see pp. 316–18) has revealed strong evidence that coaches, athletes, and even their doctors—eager to grasp a share of the million-dollar brass ring—have colluded in cheating with anabolic steroids and lied to themselves and others in order to achieve success. To restore the traditional moral and ethical standards that have so splendidly enhanced amateur sport in the past will require the pressure of public demand and an enormous effort of will on the part of everyone involved.

The sponsor/television/sport union has been attractive in Canada for many years—culminating in the great financial success of the Calgary Olympics. The Calgary Marketing Committee raised $454 million in revenue from corporations wanting to 'enhance their image through exclusive association with the Olympic Movement.'[70] For a minimum $2 million an 'Official Sponsor' held the most prestigious position; and an 'Official Supplier' contributed a minimum $500,000. Since the 1976 Games in Montreal, and particularly following the Los Angeles Games, this method of fund-raising has been attractive to both sport and the corporate sponsor. Otto Jelinek, then Minister of State for Fitness and Amateur Sport, was attracted to it and established the Sport Marketing Board to develop joint programs between Canadian corporations and the National Sport Organizations. Although some success has been achieved, the speedy abandonment of sponsors after Ben Johnson's Olympic disgrace may indicate that corporate sponsors will be hesitant in future to attach their corporate logo to sports organizations.[71]

Television's dominant influence on sport today is criticized for having a negative effect on viewers who watch sport, and on sport itself, by (i) turning the masses into passive spectators and away from being active participants; (ii) reshaping sport to satisfy TV's own needs, whims, and schedules; (iii) contriving artificial time-outs and excessive commercials; (iv) bullying sports administrators into altering rules; and (v) distorting the nature of games because it focuses on individuals and individualized plays—in baseball and soccer particularly, giving short shrift to the entire playing field; and inserting commercials at inappropriate times, often causing a team to lose momentum during an artificial and sometimes unwarranted time-out.[72]

The most serious concern with television has been the altering of rules. For example, originally golf scoring was based on 'match play', where the number of holes won, not the total number of strokes, determined the victor. But televised golf could not adapt to this: (i) no one could predict the game's duration, and (ii) a match could be decided at a hole where no cameras were mounted. The result was 'medal play', where players' total scores, or strokes, are put against those of all other tournament participants. If scores are deadlocked at the end of all regulation play, the tied players tee-off, usually at the fifteenth hole, and continue until a player wins one hole outright (instead of playing 18 holes the next day, as competitive golfers did before television entered the game).[73] Rules have also been modified in tennis, football, basketball, soccer, and baseball to accommodate the needs of television coverage. Conversely, sport has affected TV in its strict schedules. Often when games go into overtime even the National News is postponed to accommodate spectators wanting to watch the entire game. During the 1989 NHL playoff series the National News was seen at 9 p.m. instead of the regular 10 p.m., and as late as 11:30 p.m., in order to show complete games on the east- and west-coasts at game time.

The availability of international competitions in Canada from 1954 to 1988 has not only permitted exceptional Canadian television coverage,[74] but also personal involvement by Canadians through attendance—never before have Canadians been able to be spectators of such high-level competition in their own country. Highlights to date include: in 1954 England's Roger Bannister's 'miracle mile' against Australia's John Landry, viewed around the world as the four-minute barrier crumbled before millions at the Vancouver Commonwealth Games; the Montreal Olympics in 1976 and the Calgary Olympics in 1988 showed well-organized Games but no gold-medal home performances. It is ironic that at many of these media extravaganzas more television personnel were on hand than competitors. Gerald Redmond, citing information from an *Edmonton Journal* article of 20 July 1976, noted that in Montreal in 1976 'there were 7,886 reporters accredited to cover the Games (3,137 from newspapers and 4,749 from radio and TV) and a total of 6,934 athletes.'[75]

One of the most exciting, and then disheartening, TV spectacles at the Seoul Olympics of 1988 involved the Games' premier event—the 100-metre race featuring Canada's Ben Johnson and the American Carl Lewis. Canadians were glued to their television sets—first to cheer Ben to victory in an unbelievable world-record time, then in sadness to witness the Canadian press conference when the incidents associated with Johnson's positive drug test were revealed to the world media and the Canadian people 'live'. The resulting Inquiry was an unprecedented opportunity for Canadians to be educated about the Canadian sport system. Television (and print) coverage revealed the generally unknown world of the élite amateur athlete in track and field and weightlifting, the pressures and rewards of success in Olympic competition, and all the support personnel—coach, therapist, doctor, sports promoter, lawyers, etc.—along with the bizarre dimensions provided by the use of anabolic steroids. Never before in Canadian sport history has so much front-page and prime-time attention, analysis, and conjecture about amateur sport been directed by the media to mesmerized Canadians. While the sports community, in embarrassment, desired less coverage, the public discussed sport revelations with a passion. Some of this interest may have been generated by the sport, but much of it has been fostered directly by the persistence and voluminous information fed to the public by the media. Charlie Francis (Johnson's coach) and Jamie Astaphan (Johnson's sometime doctor) have joined Ben Johnson as well-known and recognized names and faces; drug names, training methods, and sprint times have become common knowledge. It is alleged that many Canadians watched the Inquiry in place of their usual 'soap'—perhaps an example of the medium's becoming the message.

The interior of the Olympic Oval on the campus of the University of Calgary. Its dimensions are approximately 200 metres—roughly equivalent to the length of two Canadian football fields—by 90 metres. It encloses two international-sized ice surfaces, a speedskating track, and (not visible) a permanent 450-metre running track.

MODERN TECHNOLOGY

Scientific advancements and research in the sport field have changed significantly our understanding and appreciation of what happens in sport. Sport laboratories are used regularly by sport scientists to replicate competition environments. Altitude issues, of great importance at the Mexico Olympics in 1968, were studied in laboratories to advise athletes and coaches about training methods to be used when required to run so high above sea level. The Canadian bobsled team worked with engineers to design a new bobsled to maximize speed and minimize the 'drag effect' experienced in this sport. In hockey, safety measures have prompted the improvement of face-masks and visors for players susceptible to eye injuries; and in football plastic has been used in helmet construction to provide better protection for the head. The use of computers in score-boards has revolutionized the scoring methods used previously in swimming and diving meets—the computer has replaced many people and the results are more accurate. Video cameras have enhanced training methods and athlete understanding in almost every sport. A study of the change in athletes' clothing also demonstrates the application of scientific knowledge. Manufacturing expertise, combined with financial resources, has refined clothing to the point where it can create an important competitive advantage. Karen Percy has discussed skiing with only latex ski-wear in final runs because the difference between the winning and losing time may be .001 secs.; she said wearing long underwear to keep warm could be the reason for her skiing .001 secs. too slow in the 1989 Canada Cup race.[76] The engineering feats in constructing the Olympic Oval in Calgary demonstrate the challenge and innovations that now go into preparing facilities for every Olympic Games. This $40-million building won four prestigious design awards recognizing its architecture, construction, and structural engineering.[77] Because of the Oval, the XV Olympic Winter Games represented the first time in Olympic history that speed-skating events were held indoors.

Toronto's SkyDome opened on 3 June 1989, establishing another technological first—a retractable roof. The SkyDome is spectacular:

> St. Paul's Cathedral would fit inside. So will 60,000 people. The stadium will suck up enough power to light a city of 25,000 homes. Its roof weighs 11,000 tons. They've poured enough concrete for a sidewalk from here to Montreal. The $17-million [sic] video-screen scoreboard is more than 100 feet long. Its image is probably sharper than the TV in your den. For $1,000 a night you can watch a game from your hotel room. And on and on and on.[78]

The SkyDome astroturf field-surface has an added underpad that is designed to reduce injuries. But such technological achievements do not prevent some people from asking why $60-million from the public coffers should help to defray the cost of SkyDome when housing, education, medical, and food-bank services are in financial crisis. The pressure for stadiums to accommodate the apparently insatiable demands of fans for entertainment, and of promoters for profits, has been rationalized by city politicians and business people as an ambitious project essential in a 'world-class' city—which is what boosters call Toronto, thus immediately reducing its world-wide significance. Toronto's SkyDome is a prime example of sport's being subverted by the excesses of commercialism.

Futurists suggest that the day will come when stadiums will have a television set at each seat so that spectators can watch slow-action replays, computers for them to calculate the odds of a play's being successful, and headphones to hear conversations with journalists and coaches in the press gallery and the dug-out or on the team-bench respectively. At the 1976 Olympic Games in Montreal sportswriters were given individual television sets, allowing them to communicate with the media headquarters and to survey events taking place at different venues while watching in person one event.

Changes in sport environments and technological advancements have been used by sportsmen to invent new games and sports—parachute-jumping, skate-boarding, ski-boarding, frisbee-throwing, water-skiing, snowmobiling, and windsurfing. Computers and simulation techniques used in the space program have been adapted to the sport environment; for example, in 1989 a demonstration of windsurfing instruction on a machine simulating conditions found on waters in a windy lake was advertised to teach a person to windsurf in a few minutes, compared with the three-to-four hours that are necessary for instruction in water.[79]

Technological advancements have also been stimulated by need. Ron Foxcroft, internationally known Canadian basketball official from Hamilton, Ontario, spent four years and several thousand dollars designing a new referee's whistle. For several years he had been dissatisfied with the traditional whistle (with a small round pea in a hollow barrel) that seemed not to work just when a critical foul needed to be 'blown down'. After years of experimentation he designed a whistle without the traditional 'pea'. This 'failsafe' whistle, the Fox 40, has been adopted as the official whistle by amateur and professional basketball and soccer leagues.

The new knowledge, goods, and services resulting from technological change and scientific advancements have enabled men and women to seek the challenge of pitting themselves against the elements in relatively unknown regions of the world. To give one example, Vancouver photographer Patrick Morrow describes in his book *Beyond Everest: Quest for the Seven Summits* (1986) his decision after reaching the summit of Mount Everest (elevation 29,028 feet/8,848 m) in Asia, on 7 October 1982 (the second Canadian to do so): to stand atop the highest peak of each of the world's seven continents. He had accomplished two before the Everest climb; on 9 June 1977 he stood atop Mount McKinley (elevation 20,320 feet/6,194 m) in Alaska; on 9 February 1981 he scaled Mount Aconcagua (elevation 22,831 feet/6,959 m) in South America; on 25 July 1983, with his new wife Baiba (Auders) Morrow, an occupational therapist at the Ottawa Children's Hospital, and writer Jeremy Schmidt, he climbed Mount Elbrus (18,481 feet/5,633 m) in the USSR; on 17 August 1983, with Jeremy Schmidt and his future wife Wendy Baylor, Morrow successfully climbed Mount Kilimanjaro (19,340 feet/5,894 m) in Africa; on 9 November 1985, with a party of ten he conquered Vinson Massif (16,067 feet/4,897 m) in Antartica; and finally, once again with his wife Baiba on the team, he conquered the Carstensz Pyramid (16,023 feet/

Aerial view of the SkyDome in downtown Toronto, taken before the start of a baseball game in the first week of June 1989, shortly after it opened. (Photograph by Norm Betts, courtesy Canada Wide Feature Services Limited and the Toronto Sun.)

4,884 m) in Australia on 7 May 1986. Every adventure was spectacular and changed forever the climbers' lives. In his book Morrow uses words such as staggered, drained, barren, fantastic, towering, immense, and ethereal to describe the effort made and the impressions experienced. Describing being at the top of Vinson's first icefall, he wrote:

Exhausted physically and mentally from months of logistical problems and affected by the altitude, I felt somewhat like an inebriated penguin stumbling about the slopes. To make matters worse, the sun shone 24 hours a day, and my internal clock was having trouble keeping track of what time it was. Finally, I stashed my watch until the climb was over.[80]

Equipment and supplies on each trek were chosen from the latest designs: lightweight telemark skis, plastic sleds to move gear, lightweight down-filled clothes capable of providing warmth at minus 30 degrees F (34 degrees C), a 16-pound video-camera, a specially made reinforced box tent, a hanging single-burner stove that burned a special mixture of butane and propane and could be safely used inside the tents, and dehydrated high-calorie foods.

Skateboarding is another, more accessible, example of a 1980s sport around which an entrepreneurial infrastructure has grown.[81] Skateboards are expensive—the board costing as much as $100, wheels $52 per set (two sets are required for each board), 'trucks' $60, and 'rails' $10. But a skateboarder, to be in a group, must purchase specially designed decals for the board, skateboard-shoes ($84), pants ($60), tee-shirts with skateboard designs on the front and back ($25), elbow- ($30) and knee-pads ($60), and wear a skateboarder's helmet ($30) and haircut. A monthly California skateboard magazine, *Thrasher*, and demonstration video-tapes of the 'star' skateboarders use up any extra change a teenager may have after equipping him- or herself for participation on city streets.

It is difficult to believe that Canadians will turn away from conventional sports, but it is curious that such non-conventional activities as skateboarding, freestyle skiing, windsurfing, mountain-climbing, and travelling through the North West Passage in a sailboat have attracted so many young Canadians in recent years. Sports enthusiasts appear to be turning towards individual, environmentally safe activities. With the inextricable linkage of sport and technological change, the whole concept of sport may be altered as sportsmen harness the latest scientific advancements to an ever-widening spectrum of leisure pursuits.

11

Canada at the Olympic Games

There were many attempts in the nineteenth century to revive the Greek Olympic Games,[1] but it took the imagination, organizational ability, passion, and persistence of the Frenchman Baron de Coubertin (1863–1937) to accomplish this dream in 1896. Coubertin believed that two powerful forces for good—'Hellenic Completeness' and the ideals embodied in English sport—could work together to promote world peace. He not only idealized the Greek practices and dreamed of reviving the ancient Olympic Games but, having visited England, he had become enthusiastic about Thomas Arnold's Rugby School Experiment, which included sports for all pupils. This developed into what became known as 'Muscular Christianity', but Coubertin emphasized the 'muscular' more than Christianity. His view of the potential good to be gained from reviving the ancient Olympic movement was based on combining the holistic Hellenic concept of unity of character, intellect, and the body with the discipline and sportsmanship promulgated through Arnold's public school in Rugby, England. Coubertin also developed an idealistic vision in which the youth of the world would compete together in sport as a pacifist enterprise. With this goal in mind, he organized in 1894 an International Athletic Congress at the Sorbonne in Paris. Seventy-nine delegates, representing world sporting societies and academic institutions, sat through the eight-day conference and, remarkably, approved Coubertin's plans unanimously.[2]

The International Athletic Congress had split into two committees: one to discuss amateurism and professionalism, the other to consider the revival of the Olympic Games. Elaborate resolutions about amateurism, and a proposal that 'international sport competition should be held every fourth year on the lines of the Greek Games',[3] were presented to the delegates along with a proposal for organizing an International Olympic Committee (IOC), which was duly formed and of which Coubertin became secretary-general. The practices that were established at this first IOC have been followed to the present day. It was planned as an independent organization divorced from nationalism. Each member

Strongman Étienne Desmarteau,
Canada's first Olympic gold medallist,
who won the 56-pound throw at the
St Louis Games, 1904. (Courtesy Don Morrow.)

was to be selected by the IOC and represent himself rather than a country—the committee alone could choose members from each country. 'The very fact that this Committee is self-recruiting', Coubertin stated, 'makes it immune to all political interference and it is not swayed by intense nationalism.'[4] Although this method of recruitment was open to criticism, it was important for members to have international ideals without political ties, and be financially capable of accepting nomination, since all travel and meeting expenses were to be borne by individual members. They represented, without exception, upper-class males. It was from this background of privilege that the Olympic Games were revived.

The first Games opened in Athens on Sunday, 5 April 1896, in a period when Greece was experiencing political and military strife and was bankrupt. A private benefactor contributed $390,000 towards the cost of building the stadium, and $100,000 came from interested Greek merchants to help Athens host these first Games.[5] They have been held every four years since, excluding the war years, and in 1924 Winter Games were introduced. Coubertin had a noble motive in wishing to revive the ancient Olympic Games: he abhored brutality, over-specialization, and the desire for material gain in sport, and fought for their elimination. His goals may not have been totally realized. But the staging of these Games every four years undoubtedly contributed to better communication and understanding in the world community; and today, when they are televised world-wide, the Games have created a universal bond.

It was not lack of athletic talent in Olympic sports but financial difficulties that prevented Canadians from participating as a team in 1896. At the Paris Olympics in 1900 a Canadian graduate student at the University of Pennsylvania, George Orton (1873–1958) from Toronto, was chosen to participate on the American team and won the gold medal in the 2500-metre steeple-chase—which was naturally credited to the United States.[6] In St Louis in 1904 a gold medal was won by a six-foot-one, 225-pound Montreal policeman, Étienne Desmarteau (1877-1905), throwing the 56-pound weight.[7] Only eight countries were represented at the St Louis Olympics, which were overshadowed by a World's Fair, but Desmarteau was the only non-American to win a gold medal in track and field and the first athlete to win an Olympic medal for Canada.[8]

The IVth Olympiad was officially opened in Shepherd's Bush Stadium in London, England, on 13 July 1908. John Howard Crocker (1870–1959), serving as team manager, accompanied Canada's first official Olympic athletes to London. Canadians were entered in athletics, cycling, gymnastics, wrestling, rowing, fencing, tennis, shooting, and swimming. The Canadian team returned with 8 medals—1 gold, 1 silver, and 6 bronze—and a positive quote from *The Times* after the closing of the Games:

> The Canadian Olympic athletes furnish a good example of the combination of physical excellence with other qualifications which make athletics a higher thing than they may sometimes appear to be on the surface. The bearers of the red maple leaf have shown throughout these Games a dogged pluck and a cheerfulness in the face of disappointment which the representatives of none of the other nations have surpassed.[9]

These words reflect a standard and behaviour on the part of the Canadians that contrasted with that of other teams, particularly the Americans, who protested loudly about many of the British referees' decisions. The IVth Olympic Games, dubbed the 'Battle of Shepherd's Bush', were

Tom Longboat running against Alfred Shrubb in a marathon race at Hanlan's Point Stadium, Toronto Island, c. 1910, before 22,000 spectators. (Courtesy Don Morrow.)

fraught with many controversies, some of which involved Canadians. The best-known Canadian controversy involved **Tom Longboat** (1887–1949), from Ohsweken, Ontario, the Onondaga runner who had captured most marathon crowns in North America, including the Boston Marathon. Longboat had fallen under the questionable influence of two Toronto promoters who were more interested in making money through his feats than in training him to continue to excel in marathon running. Although Tom's eligibility was challenged, he was allowed to compete. He was expected to win easily, but collapsed at the twentieth mile outside the stadium. Many rumours circulated: he had been doped; he was 'yellow' and quit; he had been partying the night before the race and had been drunk; his trainer had won $100,000 on his defeat.[10] Crocker reported to the Canadian Olympic Association: 'Longboat should have won his race. His sudden collapse and the symptoms shown seem to me to indicate that some form of stimulant was used contrary to the rules of the Games.'[11] Although the COA discussed Crocker's Report at their annual meeting following the Games, further information was not available. There was controversy with managers about his self-developed method of training, but he stuck to this and had many successes. He bought up his contract in 1911 and the next year he set a record of 1:18:10 for fifteen miles. He served as a dispatch runner in France during the First World War.

Canadians took great pride in Hamilton's Bobby Kerr (1882-1963), who won a gold medal in the 200-metre and finished third in the 100-metre sprint. Like Longboat, he was favoured to win, and did in fine fashion. Although controversy, a lack of goodwill among the competing nations, and much rainy weather plagued the London Games, Canadian athletes returned home well satisfied with their first appearance in this international sport scene and were committed to returning in four years.

In 1912 George Hodgson (1893–1983) and George Goulding (1885–1966), who excelled in swimming and walking respectively, won gold medals for Canada in Stockholm at the Vth Olympiad. At these Games the IOC awarded the VIth Olympiad to Berlin. In 1914, however, the First World War began, and the official IOC records note succinctly, 'Sixth Olympic Games, Berlin 1916—Omitted'. Coubertin's goal for the Games of providing a pacifist alternative to war was crushed by the reality of a world war. Perhaps it was unrealistic to think that a sporting event among the youth of the world would have the power to change political forces that so often resulted in wars, but Coubertin firmly believed in this possibility. It was a personal affront to him each time the 'real' world interfered with his Olympics.

The 1920 Games were awarded to Antwerp, Belgium, where the Olympic Flag was introduced: five interlocking rings, three above and two below, in blue, yellow, black, green, and red on a white background. These colours were chosen because at least one of them appears in the flag of every nation in the world. The five rings signify the five major continents: Europe, Asia, Africa, Australia, and both North and South America.[12]

In 1924 the Olympics Games were once again held in Paris. Canada gave lacklustre performances, but the introduction of Winter Games, held at Chamonix in the French Alps, brought Canada the first of many gold medals in hockey. The 1928 Games in Amsterdam, however, were special in many ways for Canadian athletes. A large team of 116 included women for the first time as official competitors. Ethel Catherwood of Saskatoon won the gold medal in high-jump; and Canada's 400-metre women's relay team—composed of sprinters Bobbie Rosenfeld, Florence Bell, Ethel Smith, and Myrtle Cook—not only won the gold medal but

Percy Williams winning the 100-metre race, Amsterdam, 1928. (Courtesy Canada's Sports Hall of Fame.)

set a world record in the preliminary race and broke it again in the finals. In the women's 100-metre race Bobbie Rosenfeld and Ethel Smith placed second and third, although many believed that Rosenfeld finished ahead of Elizabeth Robinson from the United States and should have been awarded the gold. The team of only six Canadian women earned two gold, two silver, one bronze, and had one fourth- and one fifth-place finish. The Canadian women placed first in the unofficial Olympic medal count. (See also pages 236–8.)

Our men also excelled in 1928. Jim Ball (b. 1903) of Winnipeg finished second in the 400-metre final;[13] Vancouver's **Percy Williams** (1908–82) was the gold medallist in the 200-metre and 100-metre sprints; and his 1600-metre relay team came third. One of the most dramatic sports photographs of the 1928 Games, if not ever, was that of Percy Williams crossing the finish line in the 100-metres. This photograph has often been used to portray the total concentration and effort of an athlete in action.

Nineteen-year-old Williams was frail, owing to a childhood bout of rheumatic fever that, the doctors had said, damaged his heart. He was discovered by a Vancouver coach, Bob Granger, at a high-school track meet when the 125-lb. Williams easily beat the Vancouver sprint champion. Using dubious training methods, according to present-day knowledge, Granger prepared Williams for his Olympic challenge in two events: instead of warming up on the track, Williams lay in the locker-room covered with blankets, to preserve body heat. Above reproach, however, was Granger's strategy for running the race: he guided his man to two victories in each meet leading up to the 1928 Olympics. Much of this strategy involved Granger's knowledge of each opponent, and his advice about how to run well enough to win while still conserving energy during the heats and finals. At the 1928 Olympics, Williams ran three heats to qualify for the 100-metre final; on the day following this race and his gold-medal effort, in order to qualify for the 200-metre he ran two heats. In the second heat, knowing the competition well and that only two would qualify for the final, Granger advised Williams to stay with the lead and place second. He did this and, again following Granger's detailed advice, he won the final race—even though he was running against new and fresh athletes—and a second gold medal of the Games. The pressure was great, but with Granger's guidance Williams approached each race with dedication and determination and excelled, helping to establish the 1928 track-and-field team as our best. Canadians idolized him.

The 1932 Games were held in Los Angeles in the throes of a world Depression, which makes the final audit of a million-dollar surplus extraordinary. Many innovations occurred at these Games. The organizing committee guaranteed that it would feed, house, entertain, and locally transport every competitor for $2 per day. To make this possible the first Olympic Village was designed to house and feed the athletes in close proximity to the Olympic competitive sites, and free bus service supplied transport everywhere. Five-hundred-and-fifty cottages, each accommodating four athletes, were built among the Los Angeles hills. The Village experiment became popular with teams, providing medical and dental facilities, entertainment, and an environment in which athletes from many different countries could meet. This innovation satisfied many of Coubertin's original dreams of making the sporting event a catalyst for developing the sort of friendships among the youth of the world that would lead to world peace. It was a successful venture that has since become an essential part of Olympic planning.

Other innovations included electric photo-timing,[14] the victory stand, and after each event was completed the playing of the appropriate national anthem while the flag of the winner's country was unfurled—for 1,500 athletes from thirty-four nations and over 100,000 spectators.

The Depression seriously affected the Canadian Olympic Committee's ability to raise funds to prepare for these Games, and each athlete assumed personal responsibility for his or her expenses. There were 127 athletes representing Canada at the Opening Ceremonies on 30 July 1932, which were heralded around the world by enthusiastic reporters:

> There was little chance for argument when it came to picking the most impressive and colourful column. Canada drew by far the greatest round of applause and justly deserved this tribute. The Canadians wore striking

red and white uniforms, the crimson blazing forth brilliantly in the mid-summer sunlight. Numbering approximately 160 marchers, the Maple Leaf delegation filed past the Tribune of Honor amid the roar of the multitude.[15]

Gold medals were won by Duncan McNaughton (b. 1910) in high-jump with a height of 1.97 metres (6 ft. 51/2 in.) and by Horace 'Lefty' Gwynne (b. 1912) in bantamweight boxing. Canadian athletes also won 4 silver and 8 bronze medals in sports as varied as track and field, wrestling, rowing, and yachting. The female athletes did not match their Amsterdam performances. They were outclassed in nearly every competition they entered—fencing, swimming, cycling, lacrosse, and track and field—and were not represented in the popular sports of field hockey, gymnastics, waterpolo, and equestrian sport.[16] In a wonderful display of male chauvinism they were praised only for their beauty, with no reference to athletic ability—a form of admiration that has often been repeated in Olympic accounts and speeches since that time:

> The Canadian girls are undoubtedly the prettiest and most wholesome looking group of girls who have arrived for the competition. They constitute a denial of the general idea that a woman athlete must be built like a baby grand piano and have a face like a hatchet. Their ages range from 16 to 21, and they are here to show the world that Canada has some splendid young women who are good-looking and who know how to conduct themselves.[17]

Hilda Strike (1910–1989), of Montreal, returned from Los Angeles with two silver medals, one the result of a very close race in the 100-metre with Stella Walsh. A native of Poland, Stella Walsh was born Stanislawa Walasiewiczowna. Although a United States resident at the time of the 1932 Games in Los Angeles, she competed for her homeland and won the gold medal in the 100-metres. This result became more interesting when in late January 1981 her body was discovered in Cleveland, Ohio, shot in an apparent robbery attempt. The story of her tragic death received little attention, and few eyebrows were raised when her autopsy report revealed male sex organs. But it was of interest to Hilda Strike Sisson, living in the Laurentians with her husband. In 1983, in an interview with Tom West, then Curator of Canada's Sports Hall of Fame, she recalled:

> She [Stella Walsh] didn't stay in the hotel with us. I don't remember ever seeing her, except when she was with her male coach. She would come in her sweatsuit and leave like that. She was an awful lot stronger than all of us. I don't ever think she would have got through if they [the officials] had found out.[18]

Hilda was only 5 ft 4 in. tall and weighed barely 105 lbs. If the sex-test had been in place in 1932 she undoubtedly would have won the gold medal in the 100-metres because the runners were so close officials clocked the identical time of 11.9 seconds. Hilda Strike Sisson died in January 1989, never having received her legitimate gold medal. Stella Walsh was probably not the only male in Olympic history who competed as a female. Several world-class athletes retired suddenly when the sex-test procedure was introduced at the Mexico Olympics in 1968.

When the IOC announced that the 1936 Games would be held in Berlin, Heinrich Bruning was Chancellor of Germany under a centrist coalition; but when the Games were actually held, the Nationalist Socialists were in power and Aldolf Hitler was Chancellor. To be sure, the Games were not what the IOC had expected. The XIth Olympiad— Berlin 1936—will always be known as the 'Nazi Olympics' because Hitler and his Nazis were very much in evidence, and to many oppressively so. One other name stood out at these Olympics, that of James Cleveland 'Jesse' Owens, the four-time American gold medallist.

Hitler wanted to impress the world with the magnificence of the Games, and the world *was* impressed. The facilities, especially the Olympic stadium itself, were monumental, and the pageantry, which can still be vicariously experienced in Leni Riefenstahl's documentary film *Olympia*, was extraordinary. The social and cultural activities available for tourists left them well satisfied, and spectators at the Games appreciated the successful organizational ability of the Germans—some may have left feeling that National Socialism was not the horror they had imagined from reading their own country's newspaper reports. These were the first Olympic Games to be broadcast and televised. A closed-circuit television system to halls throughout the country allowed over 160,000 people daily to watch the transmissions from the four main Olympic sites.[19]

Jesse Owens achieved remarkable performances: four gold medals, and in the finals he either equalled the record (in the 100-metre dash) or set new Olympic records (400-metre dash, broad-jump, and 400-metre relay). One of the leading British journals observed: 'The German spectators, like all others, have fallen completely under the spell of the American Negro Jesse Owens, who is . . . the hero of these Games.'[20]

Many stories circulated after these Games about Hitler's failure to congratulate Owens, the black American, on his outstanding track-and-field performances. Early in the Games the German leader had invited the first two German medal winners to his box to congratulate them. But, so the story goes, he did not congratulate Owens or any of the other black athletes who, it was suggested, proved the fallacy of the theory of Aryan supremacy. The American press played up this story from every position. Richard D. Mandell, in *The Nazi Olympics* (1971), gives the facts:

> Count Baillet-Latour, president of the International Olympic Committee, sent word to Hitler that he was merely a guest of honour at the Games. He should congratulate all or none. Hitler chose to congratulate none— in public at least. (Thereafter, he did warmly felicitate German victors, in private however.) So when Jesse Owens won the final of the 100-metres the next day, August 3, he was not publicly greeted by Hitler—nor was any other winner on that or any of the following days.[21]

A few Canadian performances were outstanding. Hamilton's Betty Taylor (1916–77) twice equalled the Olympic record in the women's 80-metre hurdles and then won the bronze medal in a final so close that photo-finish equipment was needed to decide the placings. A second McMaster University student, Syl Apps (b.1915), later a well-known professional hockey player, earned one point in the pole vault, though not a medal. James Worrall (b.1914), a Canadian who served more than twenty years on the IOC, ran the hurdles on the track-and-field team. Our only gold-medal performance came from Frank Amyot (1904–62), the powerful Ottawa paddler, in the 1,000-metre single canoeing event.

The Second World War necessitated cancelling the XIIth Olympiad (Tokyo/Helsinki, 1940), and the XIIIth Olympiad (London, 1944). But in 1946, soon after the end of the war, the Games were awarded once again to London. The indomitable spirit of the British was evident in the organization of the XIVth Games as they struggled against scarce building materials and the rationing of food, clothing, and many other essentials.

Canadians did not perform well in the Summer Olympics of 1948, but in the winter Games at St Moritz, Barbara Ann Scott (b. 1928) won gold, and the heart of all Canadians. If any female athlete could dispel the 'piano-leg' image of the woman athlete, it was this fair-haired, well-coached, and disciplined figure-skater from Ottawa. The Royal Canadian Air Force Flyers, Canada's hockey representative, also brought home the gold medal, but overall 1948 was not a stellar year in Olympic sport for Canada.

Helsinki had been offered the 1940 Olympiad after Tokyo was banned from holding the Games because of the Sino-Japanese War, but the war delayed Finland's opportunity to be host until 1952. These Games, re-garded as one of the happiest in history, closely resembled Coubertin's dream. Forty-three nations won medals at the XVth Olympiad, and Canada's standing was twenty-fourth, with a single gold medal in clay-pigeon shooting for a seventeen-year-old Saskatoon boy, George Patrick Genereux (b. 1935). Although Canadian athletes did not excel, they were again described as the best-dressed team.

In 1952 the USSR entered the Games for the first time since 1912 and began the domination of Olympic medals that has continued to the present day: 22 gold, 30 silver, and 17 bronze medals, a total exceeded only by the United States. The Soviet entry to the Games introduced the question of 'state amateurism'. American sports officials complained that Soviet athletes were being supported by the state. Soviet officials replied that the athletes were in military and/or academic institutions and were not reimbursed for athletic performances. IOC President Avery Brundage scoffed at the American suggestions and pointed out that most American athletes were scholarship athletes at universities.[22] This was the beginning of discussions in the sporting environment about escalating cold-war issues.

In 1956 significant future problems for our hockey teams began. At the VIIth Olympic Winter Games at Cortina d'Ampezzo in the Italian Alps, the Kitchener-Waterloo Dutchmen were beaten by the USSR (2 to 0) and by the United States (4 to 1), and finished third. Canadian hockey had traditionally been represented only by gold; to win a bronze was unheard of—a national disgrace. Another tradition began at these contests, however, when Lucile Wheeler (b.1935) placed third in downhill skiing, winning Canada's first Olympic medal for that sport.

Melbourne won the bid for the XVIth Olympiad by one vote in 1949. Had the problems of hosting the Games in Australia been known before the vote, another city would have been chosen. The most serious problem, and one that broke an Olympic rule, was an Australian law on quarantine. As a result, the equestrian events were moved to Sweden and held between 10 and 17 June 1956. Our equestrian team in the three-day event placed third to Great Britain and Germany. John Rumble, Jim Elder (b. 1934), and Brian Herbinson became household names as Canadians basked in reflected glory from these young riders.

Irene MacDonald (b. 1933) finished third in the 3-metre springboard diving, Gerry Ouellette (b. 1934), a Windsor marksman, scored a maximum score of 600 to win the small-bore rifle prone event, and teammate Gilmour Boa (b. 1924), shooting 598, won the bronze medal. Not often have two maple-leaf flags been raised at the awards ceremonies in a single event. In rowing, Canada won gold medals in the fours, and silver medals in the eights. Frank Read (b. 1911), from the University of British Columbia, who coached both crews to these victories, has been credited not only with excellent coaching but also with inspiring these young men to believe in their abilities and to dedicate themselves to their sport. So, although the prestige sports of track and field and hockey seemed less successful than anticipated, Canadian athletes excelled in the lesser-known sports of diving, shooting, rowing, and riding.

The Rome Olympics in 1960 have been described as the most glamorous of the Games to date. Athletic prowess was outstanding, and 100 records were broken. Once again Canada's athletes did not fare well. Although 97 competitors travelled to Rome and participated in 13 different sports, Canada returned with only one silver medal in rowing. Even in the winter Games at Squaw Valley our hockey team did not play well and won only the silver medal. Fortunately for Canadian pride, Barbara Wagner (b. 1938) and Bob Paul (b. 1937) captured the gold medal in pairs figure-skating, Donald Jackson (b. 1940) won the bronze medal in men's figure-skating, and Anne Heggtveit (b. 1939) captured the gold in the women's slalom skiing.

In Japan in 1964, at the XVIIth Olympiad in Tokyo, Canadian athletes fared better: gold medals were won by Roger Jackson (b. 1942) and George Hungerford (b. 1944) in the rowing coxless pair, silver medals were captured by Bill Crothers (b. 1940) in the 800-metre run, Doug Rogers (b. 1941) in judo, and Harry Jerome (1940–82) in the 100-metre sprint. The Tokyo Games were known as the 'friendly' Games and many have credited this to the smiling Japanese people who organized the first Olympic Games in Asia with attention to detail and an attitude of making every visitor welcome and eager to return. This they accomplished, although at one point it appeared that politics would have a detrimental effect on the Games. Indonesia had been suspended by the IOC for refusing to admit competitors from Israel and Taiwan to the fourth Asian Games in 1962, which it hosted. Therefore ineligible for the Tokyo Olympics, Indonesia decided to hold its own GANEFO Games (Games of the New Emerging Forces) in Jakarta in 1963, and persuaded the People's Republic of China to take part. Before these Games were held, the IOC warned that no person taking part in these Games would be eligible for participation in Toyko. The Indonesians and the North Koreans took no notice of the IOC edict and travelled to Japan, hoping that the Japanese could persuade the IOC to change its stand. Although the Japanese Organizing Committee would have welcomed these teams, they were unable to participate and had to return empty-handed to their own country. Once again sport and politics created tension just prior to Opening Ceremonies.

At the winter Olympics in Innsbruck, Austria, the team of Vic Emery (b. 1933) won the gold in 4-man bobsled for Canada. In Mexico four years later only one gold medal was won at the Summer Games: the equestrian Prix des Nations was captured on the last day of competition by Jim Day (b. 1946), Jim Elder, and Tom Gayford (b. 1928). Nancy Greene (b. 1943) became the heroine of the Winter Games, capturing the gold in women's giant slalom. Unfortunately Canadian teams were once more complimented for their parade uniforms but seldom for their athletic prowess. Officials in Sport Canada were beginning to question the policy that was funding élite sport, Olympic teams, and national sport-developmental programs, but was not producing the medals anticipated. 'The next Game!' became the oft-repeated promise of coaches and sport administrators responsible for teams' performance.

The 1972 Summer Olympiad returned to Germany, the scene of the infamous 'Nazi Olympics' in 1936, but the city was Munich not Berlin. The Games opened in a joyous mood. For the first time the Federal Republic of Germany and the German Democratic Republic (GDR) had separate teams and the GDR had the opportunity to shine in 'amateur' sport performance by displaying to the world the results of their ten-year sport plan. The star of the gymnastics competition was the petite Olga Korbet, who seemed to be weightless in her manoeuvres on the uneven bars. The Munich Games might have been recorded as an outstanding celebration of the Olympic movement, but tragedy suddenly struck.

In the predawn hours of 5 September a small group of Palestinian terrorists approached the fence ringing the Olympic Village, clambered over it, and made their way to 31 Connollystrabe, a street named for a man and woman whose marriage symbolized sport's ability to bring people together.[23] The Palestinians knocked on the door and pushed their way into the apartment. While the terrorists rounded up their hostages, Gad Tsorbari escaped and alerted the police. At a little after 5:00 a.m. the Palestinians announced their demands: freedom for 234 prisoners in Israel and for the German terrorists Andreas Baader and Ulrike Meinhof. At 9:00 a.m. they threw Moshe Weinberg's mutilated body into the street.

The German officials set the terms of negotiations with the terrorists and arranged for the move of both the terrorists and their Israeli hostages to Fürstenfeldbruck airfield at 10:00 p.m. They planned a rescue mission at the airport but it was mismanaged. Forty minutes later, when the shooting stopped, three of the terrorists and all the hostages were dead, and three terrorists were apprehended.

The IOC had to decide if the Games should continue. To do so despite the atrocity seemed heartless, callous; to abort the celebration would be to fulfil the aspirations of the terrorists. It was announced that the remainder of the afternoon's events would be cancelled. A memorial service would be held at 10:00 a.m. the next day, and then the Games would continue. IOC President Brundage spoke with passion at the service:

> Every civilized person recoils in horror at the barbarous criminal intrusion of terrorists into peaceful Olympic precincts. We mourn our Israeli friends[,] victims of brutal assault. The Olympic flag and the flags of all the world fly at half mast. Sadly, in this imperfect world, the greater and the more important the Olympic Games become, the more they are open to commercial, political and now criminal pressure. The Games of the XX Olympiad have been subject to 2 savage attacks. We lost the Rhodesian battle against naked political blackmail. We have only the strength of a great ideal. I am sure that the public will agree that we cannot allow a handful of terrorists to destroy this nucleus of international co-operation and good will we have in the Olympic Movement. The Games must go on and we must continue our efforts to keep them clean, pure and honest and try to extend the sportsmanship of the athletic field into other areas. We declare today a day of mourning and will continue all the events one day later than originally scheduled.[24]

Brundage was the best person to deliver this address to those attending the Munich Games. For sixty years he had been involved in the Olympic movement as athlete, administrator, spokesman, leader, and trustee. He shared the the dream of Coubertin and the vision of a better world the Games inspired.[25]

The tragedy spoiled the satisfaction of winning medals for all the athletes. Canada's swimmers Bruce Robertson and Leslie Cliff won silver in 100-metre butterfly and 400 individual medley respectively; bronzes were won by our 4-x–100-metre men's freestyle relay team, by Donna-Marie Gurr in the 200-metre backstroke, and by Paul Côté, John Ekels, and David Miller in solo-class yachting.

The tragic event at Munich made the IOC realize that security would henceforth be an important element and necessitate a large expense in the planning responsibilities of future Games.

Canada had its first chance to host the Games in 1976, in Montreal. These competitions were well administered and memorable. Some of the performances were outstanding: Jack Wszola (Poland), Lasse Viren (Finland), and John Walker (New Zealand) became well-known performers; the women swimmers from the German Democratic Republic dominated, and Romania's gymnast Nadia Comaneci thrilled crowds in the Montreal Forum. The media hype surrounding decathlon medal-

winner Bruce Jenner illustrated that the public wished to know everything about him and would buy papers and watch television to see him
and his wife Chrystie. Canadian athletes provided the hometown crowd
with some excellent sporting feats: silver medals were won by Greg Joy
(b. 1956) in high-jump, John Wood (b. 1950) in 500-metre C1 canoeing,
Micheal Vaillancourt (b. 1954) in equestrian jumping, Cheryl Gibson (b.
1959) in the 400 individual medley in swimming, and by our men's 4-
x–100 medley relay team; bronze medals were won by Nancy Garapick
(b. 1961) in 100-metre and 200-metre backstroke, Shannon Smith (b. 1961)
in 400-metre freestyle, Becky Smith (b. 1959) in 400 individual medley,
and by our women's 4-x–100-medley relay and 4-x–100 relay teams.
Canada was the first hosting country not to win a gold medal.

Outstanding performances, however, were overshadowed for Canadians by serious administrative and political problems that tarnished the
memory of these Games and gave Canada a very large black eye in the
sporting world. Although Mayor Jean Drapeau entered the Olympic
Stadium to a standing ovation on opening day (17 July), less positive
attention surrounded his every decision both before and after the Games.
On a trip to Lausanne, Switzerland, on Expo 1967 business, the mayor
came across, quite by accident, the headquarters of the IOC. Following
a tour of the museum he determined to hold the 1972 Games in Montreal.
By February 1966, with his administrative assistant Gerry Snyder, he
travelled 45,000 miles in 30 days to visit IOC members to convince them
that Montreal would be a perfect city for the Games.[26]

The 1972 Games went to Munich, but Drapeau worked diligently to
win the 1976 Games—all the IOC delegates were flown to Montreal to
attend Expo 67, all expenses paid.[27] In May 1970 the vote, on the second
ballot, was Montreal 42–Moscow 28. He had won the Olympic bid with
the argument that Montreal would be the saviour of the Games; they
wouldn't cost the taxpayers a cent and, above all, Montreal would put
on a 'modest Games'. Mayor Drapeau stated: 'The Montreal Olympics
can no more have a deficit than a man can have a baby.'[28] He suggested
that the 'modest' total cost would be $124 million, maximum. But when
a committee began work on a realistic budget, the projection was announced at $310 million.[29] The final cost has been estimated to be more
than $1.5 billion.[30] A few months before opening day the Quebec gov-
ernment, fearful of the escalating costs—not to mention the disarray
with facility and financial plans—took control.

Mayor Drapeau had paid little attention to financial detail, relying on
the private sector to provide funding. By selling the rights of 'official
supplier', the organizing committee had hoped to finance the major

expenditures. For example, Coca Cola paid $1.3 million plus all the free Coke the athletes could drink in order to become an 'official supplier', Pitney-Bowes paid $350,000, and Adidas shoes paid $500,000.[31] The Quebec government legalized sports lotteries to help finance the Games. These ventures would have sufficed if the Olympic organizing committee (COJO) had had complete control, but unfortunately that was vested in Mayor Drapeau and a few City Hall assistants. Labour unions manipulated the out-of-control system to their advantage, costs escalated from the time of the bid until the Games opened, and many people profited who contributed nothing.

Following the Games, the Commission of Inquiry into the Montreal Olympics, headed by Superior Court Justice Albert Malouf, cited the wrong-doings associated with the Games and identified those individuals responsible for the problems. The Report was officially released to the public in four volumes on 5 June 1980. The Montreal *Gazette* summarized the following major mistakes, according to the Commission:

Failing to set a cost limit either in the organization of the Games or the building of Olympic installations.

Mayor Jean Drapeau's assuming the role of project manager even though 'he was entirely lacking in the required aptitudes and knowledge.'

Selecting French architect Roger Taillibert, who directed the realization of his grandiose and complex design for the Stadium from 3,000 miles away and was not subject to constraints of cost or feasibility.

Building a 25-million-dollar Olympic rowing basin which now is seldom used and has become a 'real white elephant.'

Constructing a 75-million-dollar Velodrome without any relation to Olympic requirements or the city's needs after the Games.

Including expensive fountains and raised walkways as well as superfluous space in the planned mast in the Olympic Stadium.

Plunging ahead with a plan for the Olympic Village before private financing was secured; leaving COJO, the Olympic organizing committee, to pick up the cost overruns.

Choosing an Olympic Village without a call for tenders or competition.

Misleading provincial government authorities about costs of Olympic construction work.

Allowing unions to take advantage 'shamelessly' of the confused construction situation.

Allowing Regis Trudeau and Associates to get out of their Olympic contracts with a no-damage-action agreement, even though they had not completed work on a parking lot, and 3 million dollars had to be spent to repair what they had done.[32]

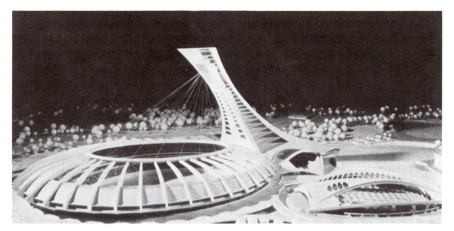

A model of Roger Taillibert's interconnected design for Montreal's 1976 Olympic sport facilities—stadium, swimming pool, and velodrome—which were not finished in time for the Games. As of 1988 a large awning made of tolar reaches from the 168-metre mast to the stadium, supported by 25 steel cables. The cause of a scandalous amount of overspending, 'the Big O' has been called 'the Big Owe'.

Longstanding political problems festered before the opening ceremonies, resulting in many vacant seats in the VIP section of the stadium; 30 flags were absent from the spectacular flag display of participating countries. As these Olympic Games drew near, the Canadian government alerted the IOC to potential problems with athletes from the Republic of China (Taiwan).[33] Canada had instituted a one-China policy in 1970, recognizing the People's Republic of China (PRC) as the only legitimate representation for all China, and requested that the Taiwanese delegation compete without reference to the word 'China'. Lord Killanin, President of the IOC, replied on 8 June that the Canadian position was in 'complete conflict with Olympic principles'. Both parties were adamant in their positions, causing considerable concern that the Games might be cancelled if Canada did not relent. Nothing was done until 9 July, just eight days before the opening ceremonies, when several Taiwanese team members were refused entry at the United States/Canada border.

The United States government opposed the Canadian stand, and the press unleashed scathing attacks on the Trudeau government.[34] The IOC submitted a compromise plan to Canada—that Taiwan would march as 'Taiwan-ROC' behind a flag bearing the Olympic rings.[35] The Taiwanese delegation opposed this, demanding to march and compete under its own flag, and as the Republic of China.[36] On 11 July the IOC executive board capitulated and announced that it would submit a resolution to the full session of the IOC that Taiwan should compete as Taiwan under the Olympic banner. At the IOC general session the executive-board resolution was approved by the full body in a vote totalling fifty-eight in favour, two against, with six abstentions.[37] The Taiwan team withdrew from the Games. Lord Killanin and the Canadian government officials were diametrically opposed on the Taiwan situation. Forgotten in these recriminations was the individual athlete, denied the opportunity to compete in his or her sport, after a lifelong commitment to training. *Sports Illustrated* alluded to this controversy with humour:

> Sports buffs who seek the ultimate in Olympic memorabilia should pick up a pair of the athletic shoes that the Hanover chain sells under the brand name 'Pony.' On the underside of the tongue of many of Hanover's Ponies is a label that reads, 'Official Shoe of the Canadian Olympic Team.' The inside heal is stamped, 'Made in Taiwan.'[38]

A second political issue concerned the IOC position with regard to South Africa, which had been banned from the Olympic movement since 1964 but still participated in sporting exchanges with several countries. Using persuasion rather than legislation, the IOC tried to cut off all sporting contacts between Olympic member nations and South Africa. When, in May 1976, New Zealand sent a rugby team to tour South Africa, African, Eastern European, and Caribbean countries threatened to boycott the Montreal Games.[39]

The boycott threat was important to track-and-field fans because it involved a classic confrontation between the two top-milers in the world—Tanzania's Filbert Bayi and New Zealand's John Walker. After all the attention given to the Taiwan incident, the New Zealand issue was devastating. On 9 July, Tanzania said it would not compete if New Zealand competed.[40] Forty-eight hours before the opening of the Games, fifteen African countries sent Killanin an ultimatum: send New Zealand packing or they would boycott.[41] The IOC did not give in to the African demands and thirty countries boycotted.[42]

Other serious problems that concerned training were discussed informally among coaches and athletes at the 1976 Games: they included blood-doping, drugs, steroids, and bizarre restrictive diets. A Soviet fencer was sent home when he was caught cheating during his competition.

Montreal will be remembered differently, depending on personal perspective. Killanin's wife was convinced that a heart attack he suffered was brought on by the pressures of Montreal;[43] Montreal taxpayers, still paying for the Games, will remember the financial chaos; the IOC will remember the 1976 Games as the acknowledged beginning of the acceptance of sport's commercialization, through both television and sponsorship; and many Canadians would say with pride that the Olympics showed the world how well Canada could put on a sporting spectacle.

When Afghanistan was invaded by the USSR in December 1979, it unintentionally became the catalyst for the most blatant sport-politics clash in modern Olympic history. The invasion caused a Moscow-Washington conflict, and American President Jimmy Carter called for a massive Western boycott of the 1980 Moscow Games.[44]

Initially, Prime Minister Joe Clark announced that Canada was unlikely to withdraw from the Games.[45] The COA position, announced three days later, was also non-supportive of the boycott. COA President Richard Pound, in a Montreal interview, stated that the COA would defy a government decree to boycott the Games unless the athletes' safety was in doubt. He warned that Clark could not make a boycott decision because 'the Association acts independently from the government'.[46]

President Carter called Prime Minister Clark, and within a week Clark declared that Canada would boycott the Games if the USSR did not remove its troops from Afghanistan by 20 February.[47] The issue became blurred, however, and was stalled because Clark's government fell and the Liberals under Pierre Elliott Trudeau were returned to power in an election on 18 February; and because, although the Olympic Trust had announced that enough money had been raised to send a team to Moscow,[48] its members were being pressured by multinational corporations with head offices in the United States to support the boycott and they threatened not to release the funds if athletes were to be sent to the 1980 Games in Moscow.[49] The Liberal government decided to support the boycott. External Affairs Minister Mark MacGuigan, and Fitness and Amateur Sport Minister Gerald Regan, met with the IOC Canadian members Richard Pound and James Worrall to deliver this message. Following the meeting, Pound stated: 'The COA would then reconsider its position and do whatever the government told it to do with regard to the boycott.'[50] Twenty-four athletes from nineteen sports made a presentation to the COA to support sending athletes to Moscow, but when the COA voted on 27 April 1980, the boycott was supported by a count of 137 to 35. Thus Canadians did not participate in the first Olympic Games held in an Eastern Block country. More importantly, the COA demonstrated that sport and politics were interrelated on many levels and that to suggest otherwise would be naïve.

Politics were again to have a significant effect in 1984 at the Summer

Sylvie Bernier, winner of the gold medal in diving at the 1984 Olympics. (Courtesy the Athlete Information Bureau, Canadian Olympic Association.)

Olympics in Los Angeles. On 8 May, just two-and-a-half hours after the transcontinental Olympic torch relay began its journey to Los Angeles, the Soviet Union announced that it would not attend. Within a few days Bulgaria, East Germany, Vietnam, Mongolia, Czechoslovakia, Laos, and Afghanistan followed suit. These countries were later joined by Cuba, Ethiopia, Hungary, North Korea, Poland, and South Yemen.

The Soviets withdrew on the grounds that their athletes would be endangered by 'anti-Soviet hysteria'.[51] The following statement from the Soviet National Olympic Committee was released: 'The cavalier attitude of the U.S. authorities to the Olympic Charter, the gross flouting of the ideals and traditions of the Olympic movement are aimed directly at undermining it. In these conditions, participation of Soviet sportsmen in the Games of the XXIIth Olympiad in Los Angeles is impossible.'[52] International Olympic officials openly stated that they deplored the boycott. The Los Angeles Organizing Committee defended their security arrangements and again declared that all athletes would be welcomed in Los Angeles. Los Angeles organizers visited the IOC; IOC President Samaranch visited Moscow; and Peter Ueberroth, President of the Los Angeles Olympic Organizing Committee (LAOOC), visited Cuba in unsuccessful attempts to persuade these countries to attend the 1984 Olympics.[53] Only Romania broke with the Soviet Union in accepting the invitation to attend. Despite the boycott, the LAOOC announced that a record number of 142 countries would participate. This total exceeded by 20 the previous high of 122 countries at the 1972 Munich Games.[54]

Because of this boycott, Canadian hopes for a record-shattering medal total had been buoyed. Performances of the country's swimmers, divers,

The speedskater Gaetan Boucher, bronze-medallist at the 1984 Winter Olympics. (Photograph by Tim O'Lett, courtesy the Athlete Information Bureau, Canadian Olympic Association.)

canoeists, rowers, yachtsmen, track-and-field athletes, boxers, wrestlers, cyclists, gymnasts, weight-lifters, and shooters exceeded all expectations. Gold medals were won by pistol-shooter Linda Thom (b. 1943); by Alex Baumann (b. 1964), Victor Davis (b. 1964), and Anne Ottenbrite (b. 1966) in swimming; by diver Sylvie Bernier (b. 1964) and rhythmic gymnast Lori Fung (b. 1963); and by canoeist Larry Cain (b. 1963) and kayak pairs Hugh Fraser (b. 1952) and Alwyn Morris (b. 1957). Canadian athletes assaulted the waters, tracks, and rings of competition. They climbed the medal platform with unprecedented regularity and the Canadian identity crisis seemed to fade with every first-, second-, and third-place finish. Some have suggested that the medals were tarnished because of the boycott, but Canada's young athletes would never believe this. The Los Angeles results, however, gave a false sense of accomplishment to Canadian sport administrators and coaches who were directing sport development that could not be tested until all the nations of the world next met in Olympic competition.

The Olympic fever reached a peak in Canada once again in February 1988 when Calgary hosted the most successful Winter Games in Olympic history and showed that Canada could not only produce an Olympic spectacle but make it financially viable. The Organizing Committee Chairman, Frank King, reported on 1 March 1988 that $557 million had been raised for the Games and they had cost only $525 million, resulting in an unprecedented $32 million profit.[55] The $557 million in revenue had come from $326 million in television rights, $40 million from tickets, $89 million from sponsors and licences of official Olympic products, $52 million from government contributions, and $16 million in interest. These revenues should be offset against the close-to-$500 million the federal, provincial, and city governments spent on building facilities for the Games.[56]

The Calgary Games will be remembered with pride by Canadians for many memorable moments: the moving torch relay that wound its way across Canada with runners from every corner of the country; the spectacular and innovative opening ceremonies; the laser show in Olympic Square each evening, which became the backdrop for spontaneous Olympic parties among all peoples of the world; and, to be sure, the medals won by Canadians Karen Percy (b. 1966), Brian Orser (b. 1961), and Elizabeth Manley (b. 1965). For three weeks in February, Canadians worried about high winds in Calgary; watched spellbound as hapless Eddie (The Eagle) Edwards risked life and limb and came dead last in the 70-metre and 90-metre ski-jumps;[57] empathized with the Battle of the Brians and commiserated with the Canadian skater Brian Orser for winning the silver medal instead of the expected gold that was won by American skater Brian Boitano; were captivated by the effervescence and almost flawless skill of another Canadian skater, Elizabeth Manley, and were enthralled by the suspense that surrounded her winning a silver medal against two formidable rivals; shed tears with American speed-skater Dan Jansen, whose sister died of leukemia just before his spec-tacular tumble on the curve in the 500-metre; prayed that the highly trained security squad would not have to perform; and heaved a sigh of relief at the closing ceremonies. Every Canadian caught the Olympic fever.

The Calgary Games set the stage for positive anticipation for the Seoul Olympics. In two successive Olympiads the Games had made a profit— a great leap forward from the billion-dollar deficit resulting from the Montreal Games. Television contracts once again swelled the coffers of the IOC,[58] and to maintain the calibre of competition expected in several sports, the IOC, through more lenient international sport-federation regulations, admitted professional athletes. In soccer, for example, it was feared that if professional soccer players were declared ineligible, the television network would not pay high fees to broadcast the com-petitions. (Many Olympic observers believe that admitting professionals in selected sports is the precursor to open Olympic competitions.) The issue of boycotts had been thoroughly discussed by the members of the IOC—new rules were introduced to penalize countries boycotting—and there was every expectation of the biggest representation of both coun-tries and athletes at the 1988 Games in Seoul. The Olympic movement seemed to have weathered once again controversies and problems that had plagued it so often.

The 1988 Summer Olympics in Seoul were the first Games in sixteen years not to be tarnished by a boycott: the major sporting nations of the world were prepared to challenge for gold.[59] Seoul was to be a special Olympics because it was being held in Asia, in a country that had been ravaged by war only a few years before; its hosting of the Olympics, providing both facilities and technological equipment that were state-of-the-art, was an indication to the world that South Korea would soon be a modern industrial nation to be reckoned with in the world economic markets. Olympic visitors were unexpectedly welcomed by a highly educated populace in a country that is a leading builder of ships, pro-ducer of steel, and developer of personal computers.

The Koreans were determined to have a peaceful Games, but there was serious concern for three reasons. First, South Korea still remained at war with North Korea thirty-five years after a truce supposedly ended

Carolyn Waldo—who won the gold medal in synchronized swimming at the 1988 Olympics—carries the Canadian flag at the opening ceremonies in Seoul. (Courtesy the Athlete Information Bureau, Canadian Olympic Association.)

their conflict. Second, the Japanese Red Army, which has contributed to world terrorism, was resurgent and threatening to disrupt the Seoul Games. And finally, South Korea's radical university students were making headlines in pitched street-battles with police. Six days before the Games opened, IOC President Juan Antonio Samaranch said he was convinced security measures were solid. More than 100,000 police and military personnel—including the normal complement of 42,000 US servicemen permanently stationed in Korea—were prepared throughout the country. But security was not to be Seoul's problem. A week before the opening a percipient pre-Olympic article—'Olympic Dream or Nightmare?', by the senior sports writer with the London *Observer*, Hugh McIlvanney—identified the real problems facing the Seoul Olympics:

There may be any number of athletes who perform superbly while remaining clean, but does anyone believe that there will not be massive use of drugs in Seoul, that for example, the big battalions of the United States, the Soviet Union and East Germany will go into battle without very heavy pharmaceutical armament at their disposal?[60]

At a press conference on 13 September 1988 the IOC Medical Committee stated they anticipated a drug-proof Games. Dr Park Chong-se, a member of the Games' official testing laboratory, issued a warning to all: 'We are 100 per cent confident we will catch any athlete using drugs and we are also 100 per cent certain no one will be able to challenge the results.'[61] It was expected that more than 6,000 analyses would be conducted on a total of about 2,000 urine samples taken from athletes—including all the medallists—during the seventeen-day event. There are more than 3,700 banned substances on the IOC's list, falling into five general categories: stimulants, narcotics, anabolic steroids, beta-blockers, and diuretics. The control centre was equipped with $3 million worth of equipment from the Hewlett-Packard Company.

As soon as the competition ends, the top-four finishers, plus other athletes selected at random, are sent to the doping-control station at the event site. Athletes are closely monitored until they have given a urine sample so that nothing can be tampered with. Canadians were particularly interested in dope-testing because four Canadian weightlifters tested positive and were not allowed to compete in Seoul; and Sports Minister Jean Charest said at a press conference: 'We want to clean this thing up, we want to find out what the problem is in their federation.'[62] In addition, Canada had co-sponsored, with the IOC, the First Permanent World Conference on Antidoping in Sport in Ottawa, on 26–9 June 1988,[63] and had prepared 'The International Antidoping Charter' for presentation to the IOC in Seoul.[64]

The South Koreans were well prepared. In 1987, during the Asian Games, facilities of highest quality had been tested under competition conditions; the security system was ready; and the doping-control centre functioned 24-hours a day to ensure that the athletes were clean. Everything was in place for the world's greatest sporting event.

Symbolism characterized the Opening Ceremonies of the XXIVth Olympic Games on 17 September 1988. Spectators paid up to $250 US for tickets to the opening, which featured a 22-metre Olympic cauldron that would hold the flame of Hera for two weeks. Early in the ceremonies the cauldron had been a sculpture of a sacred birch—the Korean symbol of unity. The sculpture fell away, revealing its futuristic pillar. As the cauldron was lit, jets painted the air with the Olympic rings, and a fly-past trailed a ribbon of the Games colours—red, green, blue, yellow, and black. More than 13,000 dancers, musicians, athletes, and taekwondo fighters, and 76 colour-clad parachutists—forming the five Olympic rings in mid-air and floating to earth on the grass field at the bottom of the stadium's cauldron—participated in the three-hour drama. The most moving scene of all was a moment of utter silence near the end of the ceremony, when a seven-year-old boy named Yoon Tae-oong, born the day the Games were awarded to Seoul, rolled a metal hoop across the empty field with a Y-shaped stick. The hoop represented the circle of the world, symbolizing the harmony of heaven and earth and mankind, which is at the very heart of Korean existence. The Opening Ceremonies seemed to be more thoughtful than the extravaganza designed for Los Angeles television-viewers four years earlier, reflecting the goals of peace, fair play, and harmony among nations envisaged by Coubertin.

There were many moments for Canadians to be proud of during the sixteen days of competition and not all occurred on the podium. Philippe Chartrand (b. 1963), the 23-year-old gymnast from Laval, Quebec, tore ligaments in his knee during the team competition but competed in two more events, enduring great pain, to help the Canadian team increase points. Lawrence Lemieux (b. 1955), a Vancouver sailor, was in second place in a race on the stormy waters off Pusan when he noticed a fellow yachtsman from Singapore in distress. He diverted course, dove off his boat, and pulled the struggling sailor to safety. IOC President Samaranch presented him with a special medal of honour that in the long run may be more meaningful than the silver he might have won had he continued on course, disregarding his competitor in distress. Ben Johnson (b. 1961), a Jamaica-born Toronto resident, won a gold medal in the 100-metre race, which he ran in 9.79 seconds. Egerton Marcus (b. 1965), the Toronto middleweight, fought gamely with a broken right hand. During an interview with CBC-Radio, after winning a silver medal, he cried because he felt that by not winning a gold medal he had let his country down. **Dave Steen** (b. 1959), from Burlington, won a bronze medal in the decathlon, one of track-and-field's premier but most strenuous events. In the 1,500 metres (Steen would willingly have foregone this event because nine other tough events came before it in the competitive cycle) he edged out living-legend Daley Thompson of Great Britain, exerting a supreme effort because he entered the final day in eleventh place. He was eighth when he headed into the final event, the 1500-metre race, which won him the bronze medal. Intelligent, personable, articulate, and a superb athlete, Steen is a natural to personify sport integrity to the youth of the nation who are looking for a sport hero. In winning the bronze medal for the decathlon (without the use of the notorious anabolic steroids), Steen accomplished what no other Canadian had done before him. Frank McLaughlin (b. 1960) and John Millen (b. 1960) won a bronze medal in the Flying Dutchman. Carolyn Waldo (b. 1964) won a gold medal in solo synchronized swimming, and with her duet partner Michelle Cameron (b. 1962) won a second gold in the pairs. Boxer Lennox Lewis (b. 1965) won a gold in super-heavyweight and Ray Downey (b. 1968) a bronze in light middleweight. The men's 4-x–100-metre medley relay team (silver), the women's 4-x–100 medley relay team (bronze), and the dressage team in the equestrian competition (bronze) added to Canada's medal count.

A record number of countries (161) and athletes (9,627) competed in a record number of sports (23) for a record number of gold medals (237).[65] Unfortunately the Seoul Olympics will not be remembered for these records, however, but rather for other things: for the fiasco when Korean boxer, bantam-weight Byun Jong-il, sat in the ring for an hour after two Korean coaches and a trainer assaulted New Zealand referee Keith Walker when their athlete lost a contentious bout; and above all for the sensation that was caused when Ben Johnson (and nine other athletes) tested positive for drugs.[66] Many years from now the Seoul Olympics will only be remembered as the 'drug' Olympics. Although drug-testing of all sports had been initiated at the 1968 Games in Grenoble and Mexico City, drug-usage reached epidemic proportions in Seoul. The potential commercial benefits of a gold-medal performance seem to spur athletes to gamble not only with their careers but with their lives by taking banned substances on the chance the drug would make the difference between winning—and thus collecting millions of dollars in sponsorship—and losing.

Since **Ben Johnson** set a world 100-metre record in Rome in 1987 he had been regarded as a superstar. Articles were written about him and corporations, anxious to share in his glory, paid millions of dollars to sponsor him in his athletic pursuits. But at the same time allegations were made by opponents that he could not have run so fast—in 9.87 seconds—without artificial aid. In Tokyo, in March 1988, his Olympic preparation—to confirm his ability, and to pluck the gold medal from outspoken American challenger Carl Lewis—was threatened when he injured his hamstring during an indoor 60-metre race. Controversy surrounded him when he left his coach Charlie Francis on a track tour in Europe and travelled to St Kitts in the Caribbean to confer with and receive medical attention from his doctor and friend Mario (Jamie) Astaphan.

Ben Johnson running a relay race in the Junior Track and Field Championship at Sudbury, Ontario, August 1980. (Photograph by Claus Andersen.)

While Carl Lewis was recording some fast early-season times—including a very windy 9.78 seconds at the US Olympic trials—Johnson was quietly preparing for his first competition of the season, the Canadian Championships. He ran an impressive 9.90 seconds, supported by an illegal tail-wind. Immediately a pre-Olympic Johnson *vs.* Lewis confrontation was designed by Larry Heidebrecht and Joe Douglas, agents for Johnson and Lewis respectively. The 100-metres would be run in Zurich for a reported $300,000 fee for each athlete. The CBC televised the race live across Canada. Carl Lewis, 1984 Olympic champion, passed Johnson with a time of 9.93 seconds and Johnson finished the event in third place in 10.00 seconds. A few days later he lost to Calvin Smith and Dennis Mitchell in a Cologne meet. These unexpected losses were unsettling for Johnson supporters and the Canadian public at large; many wondered if the fastest man on earth would be healthy enough to run at Seoul. Johnson withdrew from other European meets and returned to Canada to train and prepare for the Olympics.

The rivalry between Johnson and Lewis reached a fever-pitch as they arrived in Seoul. Police escorts were required to protect them as they moved through the Kimpo International Airport. Each held a press conference in Seoul, hoping that this would satisfy the eager press corps; but, as would be expected, they were followed everywhere and training became difficult. Reporters were asking, about Johnson: 'Have the scars healed, the torn muscle fibre in the hamstring and the hurt at losing twice in his comeback mended?'[67]

Carl Lewis ran all-out in the Olympic preliminaries, while Johnson finished only second and third, but well enough to qualify for the finals. In the final race Lewis drew lane 3 and Johnson was in lane 6. Johnson seemed oblivious to all around him; he was last to settle into the blocks, concentrating on the task before him. Johnson's explosive start put him ahead at the first thirty metres of the race. Five metres from the finish, Johnson looked over at the trailing Lewis and, realizing he had won, raised his right hand, declaring he was first. In 9.79 seconds Johnson had beaten his arch-rival Lewis, who ran his best time, 9.92, shaving .04 seconds from his world record. Johnson had showed all those who doubted his ability that he was indeed world champion and Olympic gold medalist. He ran around the track, carrying the Canadian flag high overhead, but showed little emotion.

In Canada the headlines told the story the next day, on Saturday, 24 September—'BEN'S PURE GOLD', 'Big Ben Strikes Gold', and 'Toast of the track world.'[68] Prime Minister Mulroney spoke to Ben by telephone and talked to him on the CBC on 'The National'. 'We are all proud of you,' he said, expressing the feelings of most Canadians that night.[69] Canada hadn't won a gold in the 100-metre event since 1928. Our swimmers had not performed well at Seoul, anticipated medals were not forthcoming,[70] but now Canada had the big one, the special one, and Johnson had set a remarkable new world record as well. Canadians celebrated.

On Tuesday the 27th the headlines announced a stunning revelation: 'Johnson Stripped of Gold', 'DISGRACED!'[71] At 10:05 a.m. Seoul time the IOC stripped the gold medal from Ben Johnson because a banned drug, Stanazolol, had been detected in his urine. There was shock, anger, sadness, and disbelief that he had cheated to win. 'It runs so contrary to the ethic of the Games that one feels tainted by association,' wrote one reporter.[72] Later in the day the International Amateur Athletic Association suspended him from competition for two years. Fitness and Amateur Sport Minister Jean Charest said Johnson would be denied federal funding for life and Prime Minister Brian Mulroney called the athlete's disgrace 'a moment of great sorrow for all Canadians.'[73]

While Johnson vehemently denied that he had used anabolic steroids, his track associates became the focus of attention as a rationale for this occurrence was sought. Astaphan was alleged to have given Ben the steroid on St Kitts as he recuperated from his hamstring injury.[74] Charlie Francis, Johnson's coach, went into hiding—and hired well-known lawyer and diplomat Roy McMurtry to represent him. Francis was suspended with pay by the Canadian Track and Field Association. Many felt he was the key to unlocking whatever truth would be revealed about this most scandalous drug episode in Olympic history. Although Francis remained silent, Astaphan swore, in a television interview on 'The Journal', that he had not given steroids to Johnson. Nevertheless the College of Physicians and Surgeons of Ontario launched an official investigation of him.[75]

The Toronto *Sun* published a well-written letter from Ben to the people of Canada stating categorically that he had not taken an illegal drug. When it appeared, distrustful sport fans believed that the *Sun* not only got the scoop with Ben's personal story but also 'ghost-wrote' the cleverly worded letter. The drug Stanazolol is not an 'illegal' drug; rather it is a banned drug as listed by the IOC; thus Johnson may have taken this drug and at the same time not perjured himself in this letter.

Jean Charest announced that on the recommendation of the Prime Minister, by Order-in-Council, a Commission of Inquiry would be called, with Mr Justice Charles Dubin of the Ontario Court of Appeal as Commissioner.[76] It opened on 15 November 1988, in the ballroom of Toronto's Royal York Hotel. With the ability to subpeona witnesses and records, and the power to demand testimony under oath, Dubin promised a very broad inquiry, and one that would delve into almost every element of the drug problem. In his opening remarks he outlined the areas to be addressed by the Commission:[77]

• To inquire into and report on the recent cases involving our Canadian athletes who were to or did compete in the 1988 Olympic Games in Seoul, South Korea.

• To conduct a thorough investigation into the extent, if any, of the use of drugs and banned practices by Canadian athletes who are governed by provincial, federal and international sports federations.

• With respect to prohibited drugs, initially to concentrate on anabolic steroids, which can be taken by injection or by pill form.

• To inquire into whether any of our athletes are engaged in blood doping, soda-loading, or the use of beta blockers and diuretics.

• To inquire into the role of provincial, federal, and international sports agencies, their funding of athletes, and the steps being taken by them to eliminate the use of prohibited drugs and banned practices.

• Hearing from the International Olympic Committee and the Canadian Olympic Association about the efforts being made by them to eliminate the use of such drugs and banned practices.

• To inquire into the use of anabolic steroids, their effect on the athlete, both as to performance and health, and to the potential harm that may result to both male and female athletes who use them.

• To inquire into the supply of anabolic steroids in Canada and their method of distribution and, in that light, consider the adequacy of the regulation of anabolic steroids under the Food and Drug Act.

• To inquire into the validity and the adequacy of testing policies and procedures to detect such anabolic steroids and other banned practices.

• To inquire into in detail and step-by-step all the facts and circumstances into the alleged use of banned drugs by Canadian athletes who were to or did participate in the Seoul Olympics, and all aspects of those events will be carefully reviewed.

• To inquire into what is transpiring in other countries participating in international competition and into their efforts to eliminate the use of prohibited drugs and banned practices, and whether there is a level playing field for our athletes who participate in such competition, and, if that cannot be accomplished, what should Canada's future participation be in such competitions.

• To inquire into the responsibilities for doping violations, if such violations are occurring. The responsibility is obviously not that solely of the athlete, and we will, therefore, inquire into the responsibilities of the self-governing sports federations, both national and international, and of coaches, trainers, physicians, agents, and the like.

• To inquire whether there are pressures being placed on our young men and women athletes to tempt them to cheat, a course of conduct that is the antithesis of athletic competition and even at the risk of their own health

Aided by legal assistants, the Royal Canadian Mounted Police, and a panel of sport, medical, and scientific experts, Dubin began a significant event in the history of Canadian sport, during which he hoped 'in the end, a healthy climate of athletic competition can be created to further its very objectives.'[78] Many questions surfaced: What would happen to the records if Johnson were found to have been taking drugs throughout his career? Were athletes from other countries also using drugs to win medals? Are all the track-and-field records artificially inflated? Who in the sport bureaucracy knew about this drug usage in track and field and weightlifting? Had they condoned its use or just turned a blind eye? If we can't win without drugs should we compete in international sport events? Can the Olympic Games survive?

Much soul-searching by athletes, coaches, and sport administrators at every level of competition has resulted in an examination of past practices and motivations as the use of drugs in amateur sport has now come into the open. The Dubin Inquiry has cost $1.41-million from its beginning to 31 March 1989 and an additional $2.33-million was budgeted by the federal government to cover costs from 1 April up to its conclusion.[79] Two track-and-field leaders, Cecil Smith, Executive Director of the Ontario Track and Field Association, and Bruce Kidd, former Olympic runner, in published comments have fixed blame for this problem—Smith blaming the bureaucrats in Sport Canada for pushing for more medals[80] and Kidd the IOC for 'how they unwittingly add to the pressure to win at any cost.'[81]

But as Dubin said in his opening remarks, 'A Royal Commission should look to the future and not harken to the past.' Although there has been confirmation that drugs were widely used in both Canadian track and field and weightlifting, and allegations that this is a world-wide problem, there is high expectation among the sporting community for recommendations that will take amateur sport in Canada back to the high road.[82] Canada has never ranked among the super-powers in Olympic competition, but as a nation it has been well represented by young men and women athletes striving to do their best fairly. The issue of drug-use by national athletes had not been sufficiently heeded by sports leaders, who apparently turned a blind eye as efforts increased to better the medal collection. On several occasions weight-lifters and field athletes had tested positive for drugs and not been allowed to compete for their country.[83] But it took a positive test at the Seoul Olympics for Ben Johnson, 'the fastest man on earth', to make Canadians pause and reconsider why athletes were cheating in their attempt to win medals in international competition, to seriously examine the role of television and sponsorship payoffs, and to question the pressures placed by society on athletes representing their country in the world arena. Too often the Olympics have been called the 'War without Weapons'—an egregious image for the traditionally pacifist Games.[84] But the use of drugs does seem to have become a weapon to win an ideological war. Canada has taken a leading role in investigating this drug issue in sport. No doubt it will also initiate a system of random short-notice testing to try to stop drug use among Canadian athletes. Canada could play a world-wide leadership role to eradicate this cancer from international sport.

Unfortunately for the health and safety of the athlete, cheating with drugs has serious ramifications and must be excluded from sport practices if the modern Olympics are to survive. Nothing will turn off commercial sponsors and television viewers faster than the perception of unfairness. This is the most critical issue that has yet been faced by the IOC. It must try to keep the use of drugs by athletes from getting worse. If world-wide random short-notice testing of all sports is required, the necessary funding must be found. A major breakthrough occurred in November 1988, at IOC meetings in Moscow, when the United States, the Soviet Union, and East Germany—all sport super-powers—agreed to work toward the elimination of drugs from sport. This first step was important because it demonstrated that members of sport organizations and governments were concerned about both the health of the athletes and fairness—two essential ingredients in sport. In April 1989 the IOC announced to the International Sports Federations that they would be conducting unannounced-spot-drug test of international athletes. The huge expense anticipated was justified to save the Games.

To date the testimony from the Dubin Inquiry has shocked many and sent warnings around the world. Both weight-lifters and track-and-field athletes and coaches have described in great detail the methods followed to cheat with drugs—athletes had illegally transported drugs to and from Canada for their personal use, and paid many dollars for them. Coaches had hired doctors who advised their athletes to use steroids, believing that—because so many athletes from other countries were doing so—this was the only way to win medals. At the Dubin Inquiry, Charlie Francis said he felt that without steroids his athletes would lose the equivalent of two metres in time to steroid users. Both male and female Canadian track-and-field athletes, including humbled Ben Johnson, have acknowledged long-term drug usage. The daily television (and extensive print) coverage of the Inquiry has made the use, and abuse, of steroids in sport common knowledge among Canadians. The long-term consequences of this is yet to be seen, but in the short term it seems more Canadians have turned to steroid usage for narcissistic reasons.[85] If the Olympic Games are to survive, the honest effort of everyone involved will be required to restore the ethical principles that formed the foundation of the Olympic movement. But the haunting question remains: after Seoul, and the testimony of the Dubin Inquiry, is this too much to expect?

THE AMATEUR ISSUE

Among the persistent problems facing the IOC, the most long-lasting has been who should be eligible to compete in the Olympic Games. Coubertin realized that amateurism in the nineteenth century was a controversial problem and used this issue to invite international sportsmen to Paris in 1894 to discuss it, but his real purpose was to revive the Olympic Games.[86] When the world sport leaders, all upper-class males, met at the athletic congress on 22 June, the following resolutions regarding amateurism were passed.

1. Any infraction of the rules of amateurism disqualifies as an amateur. A disqualified amateur may be reinstated on proof of ignorance of the law, or of good faith.
2. The value of objects of art given as prizes need not be limited. Whosoever obtains money by means of the prizes he has won loses his qualification as an amateur.
3. Gate money may be divided between societies, but never between competitors. Teams may have their travelling expenses paid by the societies to which they belong.
4. Betting is incompatible with amateurism. Societies should prevent or restrict betting by every means in their power, and especially by opposing any official organization of betting in the grounds in which competitions are held.
5. The committee considers that the tendency of all sports should be toward pure amateurism, and that there is no permanent ground in any sport to legitimate money prizes.
6. As regards horse-racing, pigeon shooting, and yachting, the general definition of amateur does not for the moment apply.[87]

The amateur issue has never been satisfactorily resolved through definition or compliance measures. It was examined again by the International Olympic Committee and modified in 1902, 1908, 1912, 1921, and 1925. Two major issues of amateurism were discussed at Prague in 1925, when delegates from the IOC, the National Olympic Committees, and the International Sports Federations were present. The following statement regarding amateurism and eligibility for all athletes at the Olympic Games was agreed upon:

1. *Amateurism*
The amateur status as defined by the respective international Federations shall apply to athletes taking part in the Olympic Games.
    At the same time, all athletes taking part in the Games must comply with, as a minimum, the following conditions:
    A. Must not be a professional in any branch of Sport.

B. Must not have been re-instated as an Amateur after knowingly becoming a Professional.

C. Must not have received compensation for lost salaries.[88]

In order to personalize the amateur rule and gain the athletes' compliance, the IOC also ruled that all participants in the Olympic Games must declare their amateur qualifications by signing the following statement: 'I, the undersigned, declare on my honour that I am an amateur according to the Olympic Rules of amateurism.'[89] This was the beginning of the athlete's oath of amateurism, which has been signed by participating Olympic athletes since 1925.

In May 1934, at a conference of delegates of the International Sports Federations and an IOC sub-committee on amateurism, the following definition of an amateur was unanimously approved.

An amateur is so called who practices sport solely for the love of it and for its own pleasure, without any intention from a spirit of greed [or] of obtaining any direct or indirect profit. Every International Federation shall regulate and control the applications of this fundamental principle.[90]

Through the years the amateur concept was determined and defined by men of privilege protecting sport for themselves and their peers, in a fashion befitting the conduct and behaviour of a British gentleman. The ideal Olympic athlete was characterized as an honest man of his word, with the 'ability to play solely for the love of it'. If you were not able to play as an amateur, if you needed money to support you while you participated, you were classed as a professional and were ineligible.

It was not until governments and entrepreneurs began to intrude into the sports arena, seeking national prestige and economic profit, that more liberal definitions were contemplated by the IOC. 'Sport and politics do not mix', became the IOC rallying call and concern. However, the Nazis in 1936 were oblivious and attempted to use the Olympics to promote their cause, and equipment manufacturers were eager to join the lucrative Olympic movement. These external pressures intensified and forced the IOC, following the Second World War, to look seriously at their restrictive amateur definition.

During the 1952 Olympics in Helsinki, Avery Brundage was elected president of the International Olympic Committee, a position he held for twenty years. During this period he became known throughout the world as the leading advocate for amateurism. (As IOC vice-presidennt in 1948 he prevented Barbara Ann Scott from accepting the yellow Buick convertible presented to her by the City of Ottawa—a stand that earned an attack from Trent Frayne.)[91] Many felt Brundage protected the amateur ideal far too long and thus had to turn a blind eye to increasing eligibility irregularities. During the 1950s the amateur status of athletes in Communist countries, who were known as 'state' amateurs, was questioned, and there has been continuous debate about whether they are professionals or amateurs. Also suspect were athletes in the United States receiving athletic scholarships while attending colleges and universities. To clarify the rules regarding these types of abuses, the following interpretative paragraph was added to the official rules for the Olympic Games in 1956:

> PSUEDO AMATEURS
>
> Individuals subsidized by government, educational institutions, or business concerns because of their athletic ability are not amateurs. Business or industrial concerns sometimes employ athletes or sponsor athletic teams for their advertising value. The athletes are given paid employment with little work to do and are free to practice and compete at all times. For national aggrandizement, governments occasionally adopt the same methods and give athletes positions in the Army, on the police force or in a government office. They also operate training camps for extended periods. Some colleges and universities offer outstanding athletes scholarships, and inducements of various kinds. Recipients of these favours which are granted only because of athletic ability are not amateurs.[92]

In 1960 the infamous Rule 26 defined an amateur as 'one who participated and always has participated solely for pleasure and for the physical, mental, and social benefits he derives therefrom, and to whom participation in sport is nothing more than recreation without material gain of any kind, direct or indirect.'[93] This led to a problem for the IOC in distinguishing between the ideal and reality. Too many 'amateurs' were perjuring themselves when they agreed to the Olympic regulations. Something had to be done. Although the IOC held several more commissions, and drafted new regulations defining those who were eligible and those who were not, it was frustrated by the interpretation used by individual international sports federations, by individual national Olympic committees, and by the changing sport environment throughout the world. In 1971 the IOC decided to eliminate the term 'amateur' from Article 26 of the IOC Charter, and henceforth defined status in terms of eligibility. In 1972 it approved the concept of 'broken time'—financial reimbursement of athletes for the time lost away from a job during attendance at athletic training-camps. By 1981 IOC President Juan Antonio Samaranch had completed the shift in emphasis away from defining an amateur by concentrating on defining a professional. In 1984, for example, ice-hockey players were defined as those athletes who had played in more than ten games in the National Hockey League. In tennis, professionals were deemed to be those players who were older than twenty, regardless of whether they had ever won prize money. Thus great inroads were made in opening the Olympic Games to qualified athletes, and the concept of 'amateur' had been forgotten.

Commercial interests became an increasingly important factor in defining amateurs and professionals after the Second World War, when sporting-goods manufactureers turned to élite athletes to model their products. The most blatant problem was evident in Alpine skiing, where leading athletes were receiving (under the table) money and were openly advertising skiing equipment at victory ceremonies.[94] This created a serious problem for the advocates of amateurism because so many 'amateur' athletes were receiving funding to assist with the training and travel expenses required to become first-class. In addition, the media paid handsomely for television rights because public interest in the Olympic Games is high, and television networks have learned that sport is profitable.[95] Meanwhile 'state amateurism', commercialism in sport, the necessity to court sponsors, and media exposure have placed increasing pressures on the individual athlete to perform well.

Changing attitudes towards amateurism have had an impact not only on Canada's Olympic Association but also on our coaches and athletes. In the 1930s Dr Arthur Lamb and Dr John Howard Crocker were staunch advocates of a rigidly defined and administered definition of an amateur.[96] Lamb, in a paper prepared for Canadian Olympic Association discussion in 1930, coined the word 'shamateurism' to describe the all-too-prevalent tendency of many athletes to flout amateur regulations. On every sporting occasion he spoke passionately about living within the letter and the spirit of the eligibility rules, and admonished anyone who deviated from his ideal. This 'amateur' perspective influenced the Canadian Olympic Association for the first half of the century. But Canadian sport leaders, administrators, government officials, and athletes learned quickly that increased funding was important if more athletes were to compete and more medals were to be won in Olympic competitions. New rules were adopted to take advantage of the liberalization of the amateur definition. The Canadian government (Sport Canada), through its athlete-assistance program, now subsidizes its élite athletes with monthly financial support.[97] Our 'state athletes' may not be rewarded as well as some in other countries, but now Canadian amateur-sport interests are attempting to take every advantage of the more liberal definition of 'amateur'.

As a code of conduct and as a philosophical concept the original ideal of amateurism has collapsed. Rather than promoting honesty, virtue, and good sportsmanship the present amateur code seems to encourage hypocrisy, dishonesty, and corruption. So much time has been spent on this issue that other important concerns have not been addressed. Future issues facing the IOC will be as demanding and as difficult to resolve as the amateur issue has been, and will include: the organizational ability of the IOC to provide competitions in a variety of sports for the best (amateur and professional) athletes in the world; the increasing commercialization of the Games and their manipulation by television; the increasing interrelationship of sport and politics; the ever-increasing financial and technical logistics of having all the sports at one site in a two-to-three-week period; and, with regard to the athletes themselves, the training methods used and the dependence of so many on drugs. The old ideals—engaging in sport for the love of playing the game and the spirit of fair play—have lost their value both financially and politically. As winning has become more and more important in terms of rewards, so has the ambition to better a competitor by fair means or foul.

By 1988 the Games were no longer focusing on the young athlete but had also become a vehicle for many exploitative interests, both commercial and political. The world-wide participation in the events has burdened the competitions with a heavy commercial overload, and the many boycotts inflicted on recent Games have placed individuals in a secondary position to national interests. The world's outstanding amateur athletes will surely demand a treatment that excludes such non-athletic pressures. As the International Olympic Committee approaches the twenty-first century and is confronted by further changes in thinking and practice, it is hoped that the original intention of providing a viable forum for displays of exceptional skill by all the youth of the world, whose loyalties are to sport itself, will be protected.

12

Government Involvement
in Fitness and Amateur Sport

Before the government became interested in fitness and amateur sport Canada, like many other countries, relied on volunteer associations to organize, administer, and fund sport. Even coaches were volunteer. Amateur sport in Canada in the early twentieth century was a middle-class pheneomenon, excluding members of the working class who lacked both time and money to participate at anything but the local or neighbourhood level. Serious athletes, coached by volunteers, who took part in sports in their spare time for no remuneration, had to be able to pay for their training and competitive expenses. Performing to the best of their ability in international competitions, some even won medals. There was little knowledge of training methods, and research in sport and fitness was very limited. Physical fitness as a concept was not well known and few people exercised regularly. Although many Canadians participated in sports and recreation for social reasons, they did not appreciate, nor were they interested in, the health benefits to be derived from regular physical activity. In the 1950s joggers on our city streets were a rarity; sports clubs were popular, but aerobic classes, nautilaus gyms, and the fifteen-minute workout were unheard of.

In the sixties and seventies, however—as a direct result of government interest, and particularly funding—many changes occurred. Bill C-131, *An Act to Encourage Fitness and Amateur Sport*, was introduced in the House of Commons on 18 September 1961 by the Hon. J.W. Montieth, then Minister of National Health and Welfare. Speaking on the project of resolution on 22 September 1961, Monteith stressed how pleased he was, in the face of more sombre matters on the international scene, to introduce this measure relating to 'a matter which is wholly dedicated to the greater benefit and enjoyment of the people of Canada'.[1] Pointing out that the thinking behind the proposed bill was not of recent origin, he acknowledged the efforts and contributions of agencies, organizations, and institutions, as well as of 'outspoken champions of fitness and amateur sports' who had repeatedly urged federal-government involvement.

Many influences combined to create the new and favourable climate of opinion that led to the Bill. A forerunner was the National Fitness Act, proclaimed on 1 October 1943 but repealed on 15 June 1954.[2] In 1958 the Canadian Sports Advisory Council's Brief, 'Concerning the Problems Arising from Physical Fitness Deficiencies in Canada',[3] submitted to the Government of Canada, was well received. Focusing on specific sport and fitness issues—such as national prestige, defence, production, health status, culture, fitness as a benefit to the economy, and evidence of physical-fitness deficiencies—it contained six strong recommendations to the federal government. It was widely circulated among Members of Parliament, government departments and agencies, sport governing bodies, and agencies active in the fields of sport and fitness. The protection of national security and maintaining a healthy population were both attractive arguments for government intervention in this field.

On 30 June 1959 the Duke of Edinburgh delivered a speech before the Canadian Medical Association in which he referred to 'physical fitness deficiencies' among Canadians and to the relationship of sports and games to 'national prestige'.[4] Since the language used by the Prince was similar to that contained in the Canadian Sports Advisory Council Brief, he may also have been influenced by it. He challenged the medical profession to become involved in addressing these deficiencies, and this served as a rallying call to Members of Parliament. President John F. Kennedy too was influential through his widely publicized belief in the importance of physical fitness for the realization of his country's potential as a nation and for the full development of each citizen.[5] In addition, fitness research data were available in both Canada and the United States that gave additional objective support to the need for government intervention in physical-fitness programs to raise the level of national health.[6] Finally, the writers of Bill C-131 were influenced by the joint conference of the Canadian Medical Association and the Canadian Association for Health, Physical Education and Recreation in March 1961. This pointed out the many gaps in knowledge about the effects of participation in physical activity and drew attention to the need for undertaking or assisting research on fitness and its relation to growth, development, athletic performance, specific disease morbidity, ageing, well-being, and health.

There was strong support from sporting organizations and interested individuals who articulated the concern of many Canadians about the country's declining reputation in international sport, specifically in Olympic and World Cup hockey competitions. They had urged Members of Parliament during the 1950s to suggest that the government offer assistance to Canadian 'ambassadors of sport'[7], an idea that was echoed in newspapers across the country. Prime Minister John Diefenbaker, invited to visit the Canadian team at the Pan-American Games in Chicago in the summer of 1959, became convinced of the advantages of the government's becoming involved in these international sporting events. Meanwhile, through increased television coverage the public was watching repeated Canadian hockey losses at international tournaments, and wondering why we were failing when the Eastern Block countries were becoming so successful at the game.[8] Members of Parliament began to receive more and more complaints from constituents about the lack of gold medals in Canada's national sport. Was this a signal of a corresponding loss in national prestige? And 1960 represented a stage in the social-assistance practices of Canadian governments—Canadians now welcomed government financial support such as 'baby bonuses'. The situation was much changed from 1943, when the National Physical Fitness Act—enacted to promote physical activity to ensure Canadian's preparedness for war—was soundly criticized by Canadians who did not want the government to dictate their voluntary participation in fitness programs. All these factors—but especially our hockey decline, which bruised our national ego, and the changed attitude of Canadians towards the social-welfare environment—convinced the government that it was time to enact legislation in the areas of fitness and amateur sport.

The official reports of the debates that took place in the House of Commons and the Senate in September 1961 clearly indicate that all parties welcomed the initiative taken through Bill C-131. In addition to Monteith, who introduced and moved the three readings of the Bill, as many as twenty-four MPs and six Senators spoke at length on the proposed legislation—its objects and powers, its scope, advantages, and shortcomings, its implications and consequences.[9] The various presentations revealed the Members' depth of understanding and their appreciation not only of the nine separate but interrelated objectives of the proposed legislation but also, and especially, of the spirit and the idealism behind the entire Bill. Unanimity on the latter, in both the House and the Senate, is strikingly evident from the following excerpt from Monteith's first reading:

> . . . we look on [Bill C-131] as a people's program, with all that implies. In other words, not only will its full implementation rest at the grass roots level, but in its development we will welcome the advice and suggestions

of all who have an interest in furthering the fitness of the people of Canada, in bringing to our sports activities the qualities that will not only produce champions, but will also provide opportunities for as many Canadians as possible to enjoy and benefit from healthy participation in sport and recreational activity[10]

Lester B. Pearson, Leader of the Opposition, spoke about amateur sport on 18 September 1961 supportively, though somewhat incoherently:

> . . . amateur sport . . . has two aspects. There is the domestic aspect and the international aspect. It is perfectly true that the achievements of a nation in amateur athletics, amateur sport, in its domestic aspect leads to achievement in the international side of amateur sport which does do something for a nation's morale, its confidence and its prestige. It may be unfortunate, but it is true that the prestige of a country can be affected by failure in this field, though it should not be nearly as important as in other fields . . . . all the publicity attached to international sport and the fact that certain societies, particularly the communist societies, use international sport, as they use everything else, for the advancement of prestige and political purposes, it is a matter of some consequence that we in Canada should do what we can to develop and regain the prestige we once had, to a greater extent than we now have in international competition.[11]

Bill C-131 was adopted unanimously in the House of Commons on 25 September and in the Senate on 27 September 1961. Royal assent was granted on 29 September and the new legislation was in force on 15 December.[12] The provisions of the Act were expressed in vague, general terms, leaving room for interpretation of the government's intention during the early years of its implementation.

Objects and Powers:
3. The objects of this Act are to encourage, promote and develop fitness and amateur sport in Canada, and, without limiting the generality of the foregoing, the Minister may, In furtherance of such objects,
    (a) provide assistance for the promotion and development of Canadian participation in national and international amateur sport,
    (b) provide for the training of coaches and such other personnel as may be required for the purposes of this Act;
    (c) provide bursaries or fellowships to assist in the training of necessary personnel;
    (d) undertake or assist in research or surveys in respect of fitness and amateur sport;
    (e) arrange for national and regional conferences designed to promote and further the objects of this Act;
    (f) provide for the recognition of achievement in respect of fitness and

amateur sport by the grant or issue of certificates, citations or awards of merit;

(g) prepare and distribute information relating to fitness and amateur sport;

(h) assist, co-operate with and enlist the aid of any group interested in furthering the objects of the Act;

(i) co-ordinate federal activities related to the encouragement, promotion and development of fitness and amateur sport, in co-operation with any other departments or agencies of the Government of Canada carrying out such activities; and

(j) undertake such other projects or programmes, including the provision of services and facilities or the provision of assistance therefore, in respect of fitness and amateur sport as are designed to promote and further the objects of the Act.[13]

The purpose of the Act was to provide access to sport and fitness for all Canadians. The immediate effect was felt in the form of unprecedented stimulus to the agencies active in the fields of fitness, recreation, and sport across the nation. For example, volunteers, who for years had paid all their own expenses to promote their sport, suddenly found the government willing to reimburse them when attending coaching clinics and planning meetings, or taking their teams to compete in national competitions.[14] As this new-found financial assistance led to a huge amateur-sport boom in the early seventies, the already well-organized and politically shrewd sports groups gained significantly. However, the spirit and principles behind the objects and powers of the Act were not immediately implemented by the government.

It provided for the establishment of a National Advisory Council (NAC) to advise the Minister on matters referred to it, or on any other matters relating to the Act's objectives. There was also provision for the appointment of public servants to administer it. As the Council and the bureaucrats were established, each assumed the role of advising the Minister, often differing on an issue. The Minister turned increasingly to his bureaucrats for advice, but bureaucratic attempts to become more actively involved in advising the Minister on policy were resented by the NAC.[15] In 1968 the disagreement came to a head. The Minister chose to strengthen the sport bureaucracy within his ministry, took a more active role in defining sport policy and programming, and restricted the NAC to long-range planning rather than giving it the executive role it had sought. From this time on, policy-making power—both to interpret and to implement the Act—shifted dramatically from the sport, recreation, and fitness volunteers on the NAC to the small core of professionally trained public servants.

It was originally envisaged that a cost-sharing agreement between the federal and provincial governments to distribute the $5 million available through the Act would be effective in developing mass-sport and physical-fitness programs across the country at the grass-roots level. This was not easily achieved in the 1960s and did not bring the high-profile results expected by the federal government. The federal-provincial agreements for the allocation of sport and fitness resources were not understood, because many sport and fitness practitioners were unaware of the procedure for allocating funds in each province; as a result, these funds were not being fully used. Federal-provincial relations deteriorated even more in the 1970s as the provinces protected their own territory, forcing the federal government to look for a different program-delivery system. As well, in the first ten years of the Act the government recognized that international medal results were not as plentiful as had been anticipated. In this area of élite sport development—the training of world-class athletes—sport bureaucrats realized that the sport-governing bodies staffed by dedicated volunteers were unable to deliver programs, even when assisted with increased financial resources, because they lacked an administrative infrastructure.

Nevertheless, during the first decade following the enactment of Bill C-131 the magnitude of the accomplishments and positive changes that occurred across Canada were impressive. Funding was used for conferences and seminars held for coaches and administrators, and for graduate studies undertaken by many physical-education scientists;[16] research laboratories were established at several universities to study both sport and fitness[17] and there was an increase in sport competitions for Canadian athletes. These accomplishments, dynamic in themselves, were also consequences of the momentum created in the post-war period by swift industrial, technical, and socio-economic growth in all Western nations; by the concomitant broadening of concepts and aspirations regarding personal development and well-being; and by the undeniable world-wide phenomenon of competitive sport as a socio-economic-political activity and system with a life and power of its own, being brought into the homes of the world by television.

Though the original intention was to balance the respective interests of sport and fitness, in the end the objects and powers of the Act, as well as the government's eventual supportive role in its application, were phrased so as to favour élite sport (that is, national and international amateur sport). This may have resulted from outside pressures brought about by the increasing cultural and political significance of high-performance sport, both nationally and world-wide, coupled with the perennially slower development and less-well-organized delivery system for fitness in Canada. The Hon. John Munro, Minister of Health and Welfare, was responsible for the Fitness and Amateur Sport portfolio. A lover of sport, he appreciated not only the publicity value of amateur sport[18] but realized that major revisions were required for the Act to be implemented with the funding and results proposed by the legislators. He identified the need for 'priorities and planning'.[19] As well, during the 1968 election campaign Prime Minister Trudeau, recognizing the potential of sport to act as a unifying force in Canadian society—at a time when separatist views were being discussed both in Quebec and in Western Canada—committed his government, if elected, to studying sport and strengthening it. These initiatives led to an independent investigation of fitness and amateur sport by a task force that proved instrumental in shaping increased governmental involvement, particularly in élite sport in the seventies and eighties.

Public debate has been a trade mark of the evolution of the federal government's policies on fitness and amateur sport. Since 1968 concerns have been expressed incessantly, and various solutions have been proposed and tested, both within and outside government, about the purpose, continuity, coherence, extension, and improvement of fitness and amateur-sport services generally. The steady flow of national conferences, briefs, committee and task-force reports, as well as Green and White Papers, indicates not only the persistence of problems and conflicts, and the proliferation of policy initiatives, but also the government's uncertainties and hesitations in clarifying its own position—its legitimate role and responsibilities—regarding present and future needs.[20]

The following reports and conferences served to direct government fitness and amateur-sport initiatives between 1968 and 1981:

1968 'A Look at the Future in Fitness and Amateur Sport' (National Advisory Council)[21]

1969: *Report of the Task Force on Sports for Canadians* (Rae, Desruisseaux, Greene)[22]

1969: *Leisure in Canada* (Montmorency Conference on Leisure)[23]

1969: *A Report on Physical Recreation, Fitness and Amateur Sport in Canada* (Ross and Associates)[24]

1970: 'A Proposed Sports Policy for Canadians' (Munro)[25]

1971: 'Sport Canada, Recreation Canada' (Munro)[26]

1972: 'The 1972 Master Plan for Federal Action in Physical Recreation and Sport Excellence'[27]

1972: The 1972 National Conference on Fitness and Health[28]

1973: 'Game Plan'[29]

1974: The Lalonde Report: *A New Perspective on the Health of Canadians*[30]

1974: *Report of the National Conference on Employee Physical Fitness*[31]

1974: *Report of the National Conference on Women and Sport*[32]

1977: *Toward a National Policy on Amateur Sport: A Working Paper* (Campagnolo)[33]

1979: *Toward a National Policy on Fitness and Recreation* (Campagnolo)[34]

1979: *Partners in the Pursuit of Excellence: A National Policy on Amateur Sport* (Campagnolo)[35]

1981: *A Challenge to the Nation: Fitness and Amateur Sport in the '80's* (Regan)[36]

With exceptions listed above, the majority of the 'policy' papers and other reports that have been produced since the beginning of the seventies have paid little attention to matters of fitness, physical recreation, and mass participation in sports. Government intervention has been notable, however, in the promotion of élite sport. This can be accounted for by a 1969 Task Force Report, and by the Olympic and Commonwealth Games hosted by Canada in 1976 and 1978 respectively. Further elaboration of the impact of these events will help to explain the course of government involvement in the seventies and eighties.

The 1969 *Report of the Task Force on Sports for Canadians* made far-reaching recommendations that were welcomed by Trudeau and Munro. When enacted they shaped the future federal role for élite amateur sport as announced in the 'Proposed Sports Policy for Canadians',[37] in which Munro organized the Fitness and Amateur Sport Branch into two separate but complementary divisions: Sport Canada and Recreation Canada. The Task Force legitimized government involvement in sport for its own sake, stating that 'Sport is too important, both objectively as a bringer of national benefits, and subjectively, in the minds of the Canadian people, to be smuggled into government politics as merely another phase of physical fitness.'[38] Sport and fitness were identified as being important for national unity, and to assist every Canadian in coping with the pressures of the time. Munro talked persuasively about a 'new [government] administrative policy which would put the pursuit of international sport in its proper prospective, as a consequence and not as a goal of mass participation.'[39] He was therefore encouraged to establish a larger and more influential Directorate for Fitness and Amateur Sport, overseen by bureaucrats with expertise in sport and fitness who would assume a more direct control over sport organizations.

Other Task Force recommendations resulted in the creation of arm's-length agencies to be funded by the federal government but that were not considered part of the bureaucracy because they would be administered by 'independent' boards of directors (often with federal-government appointments to oversee the government's long-term goals for sport and fitness). Since their formation in the early seventies these agencies have played an important role in shaping both sport and fitness. The National Sport and Recreation Centre was organized in Ottawa in September 1970 to provide office space and support services to the national sport organizations.[40] Initially thirty-three sports moved into the Centre, thereby transferring their administration from 'the kitchen tables' of volunteers to the offices of professional executive directors. The Centre contributed significantly to the planning that was essential to promote a higher level of performance among our national athletes—a serious concern as Canada approached the hosting of the Olympic and Commonwealth Games.

Hockey Canada was formed to deal primarily with Canada's poor showing in international competitions and with the jurisdictional control of hockey in Canada. Actually announced before the Task Force Report was tabled, which illustrated the Minister's concern about the sport, Hockey Canada was intended to organize national teams and to negotiate players' rights with the National Hockey League. Although it has been fraught with political problems associated with negotiating with the NHL and the Canadian Amateur Hockey Association, not to mention the International Hockey Federation—which would not allow Canadian professional athletes to compete—its prestige has grown through the years and it has shown results with the international successes achieved in 1987 at the Canada Cup, the Izvestia Tournament in the USSR, and at the Junior World Championship.

Sport Participation Canada (PARTICIPaction) was organized to encourage Canadians to improve their physical fitness. The mass-media and marketing techniques (promotional methods similar to those used by companies to sell soap) were used to promote this program, with excellent results. One fifteen-second television commercial caused quite a stir: with humour and some exaggeration, a 30-year-old Canadian was portrayed as being only as fit as a 60-year-old Swede, a comparison that was not based on research data but was designed simply to show that there was much room for improvement in the fitness levels of Canadians. To the consternation of Recreation Canada Director Cor Westland, this comparison became widely quoted as a genuine statistic.[41] PARTICIPaction is now well known across Canada. A 1978 survey revealed that 79 per cent of Canadians were aware of it and that 72 per cent believed it was effective.[42] By 1980 these figures had risen to 87 per cent and 85 per cent respectively.[43] PARTICIPaction's arm's-length relationship with the federal government has enabled it to generate private-sector financing and to acquire public-service time in both the print and television media that was estimated in 1978 to total $8 million in free advertising.[44] On the fitness side PARTICIPaction has been the most visible, successful, and effective arm's-length agency.

The Coaching Association of Canada (CAC) was the fourth arm's-length organization established to solve a problem that had long been recognized by many in amateur sport: the need to develop better coaches if our national athletes were to excel. The CAC administers a national coaching certification program and a national coaching apprenticeship program, and has played an active role in communicating with coaches through its in-house publications *Coaching Review* and *Coaching Science Update*, as well as in co-ordinating the establishment of the Sport Information Resource Centre (SIRC), a centralized documentation service. Since its inception in 1970 the CAC has had an important effect: more coaches, from the local church league to Canada's national teams, are more knowledgeable about their sport and are better prepared to coach Canadian athletes.

The allocation of subsidies to national sport organizations and the above-mentioned arm's-length organizations (representing in many cases 80 per cent of their operating budgets) strengthened the government's intervention. Ten years after the enactment of Bill C-131 the federal government's fiscal commitment to fitness and amateur sport was about $6 million. The next year, in 1972–3, following the Task Force Report recommendations and their implementation by Munro, it suddenly jumped by about 83 per cent to $11 million, with two-thirds of the funding going to amateur sports. Six years later, in 1978–9, the funding more than tripled (to $35 million), this time with as much as three-quarters being allotted to the development and support of élite sport (now called high-performance sport). In 1985–6, out of a total budget that had practically doubled in seven years to a record high of $67 million, the percentage of the overall government funding for fitness had dropped to an all-time low of only about 15 per cent. In contrast, between 1983 and 1986 a number of Cabinet decisions and federal-provincial agreements, particularly regarding lotteries, resulted in a supplementary federal commitment of $237 million: to the 'Best-Ever Winter Program' ($200 million for the 1988 Calgary Winter Olympic Games) and to the 'Best-Ever Canadian team performance' (about $37.5 million towards the development of Canada's 1988 Summer Olympic team for Seoul).

The sport side of the Fitness and Amateur Sport mandate (Sport Canada) has prospered not only as a result of the implementation of the

Task Force recommendations and significant increased funding, but also as a result of the necessity of planning for, and preparing teams to compete in, the Olympic Games in Montreal in 1976 and the Commonwealth Games in Edmonton in 1978. Sport Canada bureaucrats and sports governing-body volunteers capitalized on these events to increase budgets and personnel and to organize and implement long-range plans stimulated by Game Plan '76, a planning exercise—sponsored by the Canadian Olympic Association, the Olympic Trust, the federal and provincial governments, the Coaching Association of Canada, and the sports governing bodies—to produce excellent results in Montreal, and to develop amateur-sport programs of a calibre sufficient to increase Canada's chances of winning medals at international competitions.

Recreation Canada, which changed over time to concentrate on fitness and became known as Fitness Canada, suffered from the lack of a mobilizing high-profile event and failed to create the developmental opportunities enjoyed by Sport Canada. In 1972 Munro was succeeded as Minister of Health and Welfare by the Hon. Marc Lalonde, whose interest in health promotion, outlined in the book *A New Perspective on Health of Canadians*,[45] did much to rationalize and enhance the role of Fitness Canada. Lalonde was fearful of escalating health-care costs and was committed to encouraging every Canadian to participate in physical activity to promote a healthier population. He attempted to move the responsibility for health care from the government to the individual Canadian, who would be encouraged to choose to live a healthier life by improving his or her diet, learning to cope with stress, and engaging in a personal fitness regimen. Fitness Canada, together with Health Promotion, a program within Health and Welfare, accepted educational responsibilities for delivering this message to Canadians. Thus a new *raison d'être* and social responsibility for Fitness Canada developed. Although its progress has been less apparent than Sport Canada's during the past fifteen years, important achievements have been made (initiated, supported, and/or financed through Fitness Canada) that continue to have a real impact on the fitness movement in Canada and even abroad: the creation of PARTICIPaction in 1971;[46] the realization of the unique Canadian Fitness Survey in 1981, and the wide distribution of its reports;[47] the creation of the Canadian Fitness and Lifestyle Research Institute in 1985;[48] and the institution of National Physical Activity Week, of the PARTICIPaction Challenge, and of various employee-fitness initiatives and in-service training opportunities, and services for both fitness leaders and management volunteers. Though this legitimate role of Fitness Canada—the promotion of a healthy lifestyle—was endorsed, it did not result in increased funding.

Following the Montreal Olympics in 1976 the government seemed even more enamoured with international sport. In 1977 Iona Campagnola, the high-profile Sport Minister, circulated a Green Paper entitled 'Towards a National Policy on Amateur Sport: A Working Paper' and followed this with a cross-Canada tour accompanied by her Sport Canada bureaucrats to consult with the sport community about the future of élite sport. This was Canadians' first opportunity to debate sport policy with the government, and there were high expectations that their expressed concerns would be translated into action. Unfortunately cynicism was the reaction of the sport community when, in 1979, the White Paper failed to include their recommendations. Because it failed to act as a united, single voice in responding to the Green Paper, the sport community lost an opportunity to gain back some of the control for amateur sport that had been increasingly assumed by the government.[49] In the same year a promised Green Paper addressing the Fitness and Recreation plans for the federal government was also circulated. Before these initiatives were completed Trudeau called a federal election and Campagnola was defeated. Joe Clark led a minority Conservative government until Trudeau's liberals defeated it in February 1980.

From 1979 on—when first the Conservatives, then the Liberals, and then again the Conservatives assumed power[50]—there was a period of 'swinging-door' leadership by Fitness and Amateur Sport Ministers: seven different ministers were in charge in five years, few of whom were in office long enough to have any impact. The bureaucrats in Ottawa therefore acquired more opportunity to exercise control of sport, and as a result paid even less attention to the concerns of Canadians about fitness programs. But in the eighties the federal government's role in amateur sport, as it had emerged in the seventies, was strengthened through the initiatives of Minister Gerald Regan's White Paper, *A Challenge to the Nation: Fitness and Amateur Sport in the 80s*, which emphasized the government's intention to promote high-performance sport in Canada. To that end centres were established, many at Canadian universities; an enhanced athlete-assistance program was launched to enable athletes to commit time to competing and training while pursuing an education; the 'Best Ever 88' program, initiated in 1982, allocated $25 million towards the attainment of 'the best performances ever' in the ten winter Olympic sports at Calgary in February 1988; and finally a comprehensive women's program was organized to help women athletes meet their sport potential.[51] Sport Canada's planning, its clearly delineated policy and programs, and its successes have in no small measure been due to the commitment and dedication of three Directors: Lou Lafaive, Roger Jackson, and Abby Hoffman. All three demonstrated their ability to make things happen for sport: they established high standards for athletes and their sport organizations, capitalized on opportunities available, and raised the level of performance in international sport.[52] Under them, however, the government gained more power in determining national sport policy and practices, while the national sport organizations lost control, almost becoming government puppets.[53]

Sport Canada's Athlete Assistance Program clearly illustrates the planning, control, accountability, and performance-enhancement expectation developed by its administrators within Sport Canada. It was recognized that if athletes were to perform better in international competitions—win more medals—it was necessary for them to spend longer and longer periods training and competing, and that no longer was it possible for athletes to hold full-time jobs while preparing to win medals. As the International Olympic Committee's eligibility rules were liberalized to permit payment for lost time (time spent away from the job to train and/or compete), Sport Canada recognized that funding athletes directly was essential. Criteria were established—based on competitive performance—to determine the funding for each athlete.[54] Athletes were given a classification of an A, B, C, or D card in Olympic sports, and a C card in non-Olympic sports; for example, placing as top 8th or 16th in the world rated the A and B cards respectively. The 1986–7 remuneration was $650 per month for two years for A-carded athletes, $550 per month for B-, $450 per month for C-, and $300 per month for one year for D-carded athletes. In addition, if there was a demonstrated need, additional funding could be made available for extraordinary training costs, child care, special equipment, moving and travel expenses, and facility rentals. Students had their university and college tuition, books, and incidentals paid. In return, the athletes were obliged to sign a contract with Sport Canada. This reinforced and increased the pressure on athletes to train full-time, and to compete at their maximum to maintain their funding.[55] Although this assistance has 'relieved athletes of the financial burden of training and competition', their pressures—increased time-commitment for scheduled training and major competitions out of the country, rigorous training methods similar to assembly-line work—have suggested to some that athletes are actually underpaid government workers.[56] The dilemma faced by those in leadership roles in Sport Canada, the Canadian Olympic Committee, and the National Sport Organizations (NSOs) is how to set standards to challenge athletes to achieve their potential while assisting them with their financial burdens, and yet not manipulate them unreasonably for national prestige.

Upon taking office in the fall of 1984 as Minister of State for Fitness and Amateur Sport in the Conservative government, the Hon. Otto Jelinek was faced with a rather bemused constituency, because he was the eighth minister to represent them in five years. Nevertheless many and varied unresolved issues and concerns were brought to his attention. An Olympic athlete in figure-skating in 1960, he was quick to realize that certain policies within his Branch had become problematic and did not accurately reflect Canadians' increased awareness of personal fitness, domestic sport opportunities, and élite sport at the international level. During his first years as Minister, Jelinek set the stage for an extensive and co-ordinated review, involving the federal and provincial governments and the agencies and individuals directly concerned with fitness affairs throughout Canada. His new and bold attempts at consultation, identification and analysis of issues, initiation and maintenance of co-operation, delivery of programs and services, and promotion of the fitness message, had had no equivalent since the enactment of the Fitness and Amateur Sport Act in 1961. The fitness community took in earnest the federal government's new commitment to fitness as it was expressed in Jelinek's annual report for 1984–5:

> As far as fitness is concerned, I believe that it has, for too long, taken a backseat to its sporting partner. While it is exciting and certainly essential to have world champions, it is equally necessary to have a fit nation.[57]

The years between 1985 and 1987 were punctuated by a series of major initiatives, forums, and Canada-wide consultations that attracted general attention and successfully mustered the co-operation and involvement of the various partners in the fitness community:

1985 (May) The first Federal-Provincial Ministers' Conference on Fitness,[58] followed by six Federal-Provincial-Territorial Task Forces on Fitness.[59]

1985 (December) The Canadian Symposium on Youth Fitness (International Youth Year Symposium).[60]

1986 (June) The Canadian Summit on Fitness.[61]

1986 (October) The Jasper Talks: Strategies for Change in Adapted Physical Activity in Canada.[62]

1986–87 The Minister's Advisory Committee on a Structural Framework (for fitness).[63]

1987 (Summer) 'Fitness . . . the Future! Achieving the Vision' (a discussion paper prepared by the Minister of State).[64]

1987 (Fall) The national round of consultations on the structural options for fitness described in the above ministerial document.

1987 'Fitness . . . the Future! Achieving the Vision' (provincial meetings).

A unique opportunity was presented to the fitness community when Michel Bédard, the Director of Fitness Canada, envisaged and committed resources to a national grass-roots planning process to determine future goals for fitness. This involved selecting a planning committee whose responsibility it was to communicate (by both questionnaire and personal visits) with the Canadian fitness community to ascertain the existing fitness issues, to plan a national conference that would consider these issues and explore the future of fitness in the Canadian context, and to write a report that would guide government fitness initiatives into the next century.[65] Bédard often advised the planning committee that this was 'an opportunity to dream'. Nevertheless, this rare consultation process, initiated through Fitness Canada, involved Canadians in advising the government about their fitness future. At the Canadian Summit on Fitness in June 1986, a utopian ideal for the future of fitness was developed by the delegates:

> The vision of fitness by the year 2000 depicts a society that values well-being as a fundamental and an integral part of day-to-day life. Canadian social structures, the family, the schools, the workplace, the health care system, will all enthusiastically embrace and reward daily physical activity and behaviour which contribute significantly to health and well-being. Regular physical activity and optimal well-being will be ingrained as important and widely accepted values in Canadian Society.[66]

This rhetoric generated a ground-swell of activities in the form of ever-more-numerous and urgent calls for expanded activities, programs, and services in fitness. The challenge appears to be threefold:

1. Reaching the fitness goals for the year 2000 entails first a marked extension and democratization of traditional quality services—such as providing fitness programs to low-income families unable to pay for them, and addressing the needs of the elderly, the handicapped, and native people. Fitness has traditionally been a 'pay-as-you-play' phenomenon reserved for the middle- and upper-income Canadians. It also requires innovative ideas, approaches, and products with an emphasis on practicality—for example, providing subsidized day-care facilities for the single-parent participant, rock music to attract the over-weight teenager to an aerobics class, and social activities to attract the widow to participate in fitness classes.

2. The fitness community was convinced that the federal government should not abandon fitness through 'privatization' but rather strengthen its Fitness Canada role to promote and develop the well-being and health of the entire Canadian population through 'active living'.

3. The Fitness and Amateur Sport Act needs to be rewritten to ac-knowledge the new view of fitness as expressed at the Fitness Summit. The Act has been permissive in allowing the federal government to undertake a wide range of activities and provide support in many areas. But it is also outdated: several structures and processes that are reflected in it are either not in use or have been significantly altered, and the relative values, benefits, and contributions of sport and fitness are not adequately expressed. The equality objective of development and fund-ing for both sport and fitness has never been achieved. In a revised Act it would be important, through legislation, to achieve a reasonable bal-ance of services and returns to the taxpayer in matters pertaining to both sport and fitness.

For two years following the Summit, Jelinek and his staff in Fitness Canada, and ministerial committees, considered the implications of the privatization of fitness, the structural changes that would be necessary, and even considered rewriting the Act. There were plans to implement these objectives in the spring of 1988, but many in the fitness movement aggressively expressed their opposition to total 'privatization' and chal-lenged the government to accept its responsibility as protector of the underprivileged in Canadian society. At the same time they acknowl-edged that increased private-sector involvement and funding in the fit-ness movement would be welcomed. Jelinek was replaced by Jean J. Charest, however, on 31 March 1988, and the 'privatization of fitness'[67] and the proposals for new legislation were moved to the back-burner.

In February 1987 Jelinek had established a Task Force of people active in a variety of national sport organizations to make recommendations in three broad areas: goals, directions, and priorities; principles and financing; and the co-ordination of agencies. The Federal Sport Task Force Report, *Toward 2000*, was unveiled in August 1988.[68] Six themes permeate its goals and recommendations:

1. The need for a holistic integrated approach to the development of the Canadian sport system.

2. Sport development based on models and systems for the devel-opment of athletes.

3. National sport organizations as the key agencies in the Canadian sport system.

4. The need for strong federal-government leadership in sport.

5. Shared leadership in the Canadian sport system.

6. Leadership development and education.[69]

The Report had two drawbacks: the model emulates the sport system of the German Democratic Republic and it would be difficult to establish

The Honourable Jean Charest discusses his new responsibilities as Minister of State, Fitness and Amateur Sport with his predecessor, the Honourable Otto Jelinek, March 1988. (Photograph by Scott Grant.)

their socialist goals in democratic Canada; secondly, the necessity for co-operation and linkages between the federal government and both the provincial governments and the provincial educational authorities has still not been achieved after many attempts because each level of government and their educational authorities jealously protect their own jurisdictions. Furthermore, the Report could not have appeared at a less advantageous time. Our athletes did not live up to expectations at the Seoul Olympics and many Canadians have questioned the merit of government funding for amateur sport. Furthermore, the drug scandal associated with the stripping of the gold medal from Ben Johnson, record-holder in the 100-metre sprint, has caused many Canadians to question the ethics of amateur sport. Winning gold medals by cheating with drugs is the antithesis of the purpose of sport, and since the Seoul Games—

which took place the month after the Report was issued—many in Canada have questioned our very participation in international sport if drug usage is necessary to be competitive. Great interest will be given to the government-initiated Dubin Commission inquiring into the use of drugs and of banned practices intended to increase athletic performance.[70] Sport officials both inside and outside government hope that a new path for sport is recommended that will return sport to a higher plane.

Many issues remain to be decided in fitness and amateur sport. A new or revised Act will do much to indicate the future role of the federal government in these areas. Looming ominously on the horizon is the possibility that the Conservative government might still bring about the 'privatization' of fitness as it tries to reduce the deficit. In amateur sport there is concern because much of the recent funding for sport initiatives, such as the 'Best Ever 88' program, did not come from operating budgets and could therefore be reduced or even eliminated following the next round of NSO quadrennial planning after the Seoul Olympics, and as a result of recommendations resulting from the report of the Dubin Inquiry.[71] As well, many in the sport community fear that new national sport-organization initiatives to test athletes for drug usage on an ongoing basis will cost so much that sport-programming expenditures will be reduced even further, thus making significant gains in international competitions improbable if not impossible.[72] On the fitness side, where funding has been weak, there is fear that the social-responsibility function of the government to achieve a 'vision' for fitness by the year 2000 could be jeopardized if fitness programs have to depend solely on the private sector for support. Thus both sport and fitness enthusiasts are campaigning for a more equitable allocation of government commitment and resources in any new legislation. As we approach the year 2000 both sport and fitness communities have high aspirations, but whether the government and society will support them fully is an open question.

What has been the sport and fitness benefit of government involvement? Government funding for sport has democratized sporting opportunities—no longer is sport a middle- and upper-class phenomenon. (This has not happened to the same extent in fitness because it has nothing like the same funding.) On the one hand, government funding has stabilized and improved the quality of the administrative and technical capabilities of the NSOs and fitness agencies. More than 200 professional administrators are working full time at Place R. Tait McKenzie in Ottawa to improve sport—a far cry from the volunteers scattered across the country, working in his or her spare time. But on the other hand, by accepting 80 per cent of their total funding from the government, sport organizations have given up to government their autonomy, authority, and control. While Place Tait McKenzie is the envy of many countries, the COA had to acquiesce in the government's dictating the Moscow boycott in 1980. Neverthless government funding has accomplished a great many things, including more programs for the disabled, national coaching schools, state of-the-art facilities and equipment for international athletes such as those at the Calgary Olympics, and regular athlete testing at university laboratories across the country, the results from which influence training programs.

Government funding to fitness organizations such as PARTICIPaction and the Canadian Lifestyle and Research Institute has greatly stimulated interest and participation in fitness programs. In 1972 only 3 per cent of Canadian adults were physically active, but by the 1980s the federally funded Canadian Fitness Survey revealed that 56 per cent of Canadians over the age of 10 were physically active in their leisure time. In May 1983, 600,000 Canadians took part in the Great Canadian PARTICIPaction Challenge and by 1987 this project involved 250 communities and over 3.5 million registered participants. The rate of success with government funding has been significant, but in the fitness area much still needs to be accomplished.

Although there was a slight reduction in the Fitness and Amateur Sport budget in April 1989,[73] the relationship between the government and both sport and fitness will continue in the foreseeable future and its complexity will no doubt continue to increase. It has often been suggested, in many forums, that there is need for an independent organization situated between government and both sport and fitness. Perhaps with a new Act this will be achieved.

Notes

1. MONTREAL; THE CRADLE OF ORGANIZED SPORT

[1]S.F. Wise and D. Fisher, *Canada's Sporting Heroes* (Don Mills, Ontario: General Publishing Company Limited, 1974), pp. 13–14.

[2]Information on the Montreal Curling Club is synthesized from R. Wayne Simpson, 'The Influence of the Montreal Curling Club on the Development of Curling 1807–1857', unpublished Master of Arts thesis, University of Western Ontario, 1980.

[3]*One Hundred and Fifty Years of Curling, The Montreal Curling Club 1807–1957* (Montreal: privately printed, 1957), pp.15–17.

[4]Alan Metcalfe, 'The Evolution of Organized Physical Recreation in Montreal, 1840–1895', *Histoire Sociale/Social History*, Vol. XI, No. 21 (May 1978), p.144. Heavy reliance was placed on this seminal article for background information on the chronological development of Montreal sport.

[5]As quoted in P.C. McIntosh, *Physical Education in England Since 1800* (London: G. Bell and Sons, 1968), p.70.

[6]See P.L. Lindsay, 'The Impact of the Military Garrisons on the Development of Sport in British North America', *Canadian Journal of History of Sport and Physical Education*, Vol. 1, No. 1 (May 1970), p.33. Material on the Montreal garrison was gleaned from this article.

[7]*Montreal Gazette*, 29 August 1844, cited in Lindsay, 'A History of Sport in Canada 1807–1867', unpublished Ph.D. dissertation, University of Alberta, 1969, pp. 425–427.

[8]Ibid.

[9]Robert D. Day, 'The British Army and Sport in Canada: Case Studies of the Garrisons at Halifax, Montreal and Kingston', unpublished Ph.D. dissertation, University of Alberta, 1981, pp.404–5.

[10]Alan Metcalfe, 'Organized Sport and Social Stratification in Montreal, 1840–1901', in *Canadian Sport: Sociological Perspectives*, edited by R.S. Gruneau and J.G. Albinson (Don Mills: Addison-Wesley (Canada) Ltd., 1976), pp. 78–9.

[11]Material on snowshoeing is extracted from Don Morrow, 'The Knights of the Snowshoe: A Study of the Evolution of Sport in Nineteenth Century Montreal', in *Journal of Sport History*, Vol. 15, No. 1, Spring 1988, pp. 5–40.

[12]*Montreal Gazette*, 16 January 1873.

[13]H.W. Becket, *The Montreal Snow Shoe Club, Its History and Record* (Montreal: Becket Brothers, 1882), pp.44–5. This 521-page book is an excellent period piece on Montreal snowshoeing.

[14]Morrow, op. cit., p.22.

[15]Information on the Victoria Skating Rink was taken from D. Rosenberg, D. Morrow, A.J. Young, 'A Quiet Contribution: Louis Rubenstein', *Canadian Journal of History of Sport*, Vol. 12, No. 1 (May 1981), pp. 51–65.

[16]The photograph is in the Notman Archives at the McCord Museum of Canadian History in Montreal. It is reprinted on the cover of *Fact and Fiction: Canadian Painting and Photography, 1860–1900* (Montreal: Plow and Watters Ltd., 1979).

[17]P.L. Lindsay, 'George Beers and the National Game Concept: A Behavioral Approach' in *Proceedings of the Second Canadian Symposium on the History of Sport and Physical Education* (Windsor, 1972), pp.27–44.

[18]Alan Metcalfe, *Canada Learns to Play: The Emergence of Organized Sport, 1807–1914* (Toronto: McClelland and Stewart Ltd.,

1987), pp.182–3.

19B. Schrodt, R. Baka, G. Redmond, *Sport Canadiana* (Edmonton: Executive Sport Publications Ltd., 1980), p.23.

20Lindsay, 'A History of Sport in Canada 1807–1867', pp. 168–81.

21G. Redmond, *The Sporting Scots of Nineteenth Century Canada* (Toronto: Associated University Presses, 1982), pp. 214–18. See also *The Royal Montreal Golf Club, 1873 to 1973* (Montreal: privately published, 1973).

22Redmond, op. cit., pp. 214–18.

23Lindsay, 'A History of Sport in Canada 1807–1867', pp. 264–6.

24*Montreal Gazette*, 11 June 1867, as cited in ibid., p.268.

25Lindsay, 'A History of Sport in Canada 1807–1867', p.267.

26Don Morrow, *A Sporting Evolution: The Montreal Amateur Athletic Association, 1881–1981* (Montreal: Graphics Group, 1981), pp. 37–41.

27Don Morrow, 'The Powerhouse of Canadian Sport: The Montreal Amateur Athletic Association, Inception to 1909', in *Journal of Sport History*, Vol.8, No.3 (Winter, 1981), pp.21–2.

28Material on the MAAA is synthesized from ibid. and from Morrow, *A Sporting Evolution*.

29*Montreal Daily Star*, 15 December 1883.

30Metcalfe, 'Evolution of Physical Recreation in Montreal', p.160.

31Ibid., pp.161–4.

32Don Morrow, 'A Case Study in Amateur Conflict: The Athletic War in Canada, 1906–1908', *The British Journal of Sports History*, Vol. 3, No.2 (September 1986), 173–90.

2. RUBENSTEIN, HANLAN, AND CYR

1This section on Rubenstein is based upon D. Rosenberg, D. Morrow and A.J. Young, 'A Quiet Contribution: Louis Rubenstein', in *Canadian Journal of History of Sport*, Vol. 13, No. 1 (May 1982), pp. 1–18.

2*Illustrated Police News*, 28 February 1885.

3*Montreal Gazette*, 19 February 1885.

4Rubenstein Scrapbook, n.p., property of the YMHA, Montreal.

5*Montreal Gazette*, 23 February 1889.

6See *Montreal Gazette*, 8 February 1883, and 23 January 1885.

7Ibid., 8 February 1883.

8Ibid., 26 January 1886, for example.

9A copy of the circular was printed in the *Montreal Gazette* on 1 November 1887.

10The list was published in the *Gazette* on 18 January 1888.

11*Montreal Gazette*, 22 February 1884.

12*Spirit of the Times*, 27 February 1886, and the *Montreal Daily Star*, 5 February 1886.

13*Montreal Gazette*, 23 January 1888 and 31 January 1889.

14Ibid., 23 February 1889. Compare Donald Jackson's title, nearly 100 years later: 'King of the blades'.

15Ibid., 15 January 1889.

16Ibid., 7 March 1888.

17Ibid., 30 December 1889.

18Ibid., 15 March 1890.

19Ibid., 14 March 1890.

20*Montreal Daily Star*, 10 February 1891.

21*Montreal Gazette*, 30 January 1895.

22Ibid., 14 February 1890.

23Ibid.

24Ibid., 14–18 February 1890.

25B. Postal et al., *Encyclopedia of Jews in Sport* (New York: Block Publishing Co., 1965), p. 341.

26No copies of this book have been found. The only reference to it was in one newspaper article written near the end of Rubenstein's athletic career.

27*Annual Reports of the Montreal Amateur Athletic Association*, 1884 to 1887.

28*Montreal Gazette*, 1 April 1899.

29Don Morrow, *A Sporting Evolution: The Montreal Amateur Athletic Association, 1881 to 1981* (Montreal: Graphics Group, 1981), p. 47.

30*Montreal Daily Star*, 6 February and 12 December 1895.

31Ibid., 20 February 1897.

32Ibid., 2 February 1907, and 6 February 1909.

33Ibid., 24 June 1911.

[34]*Annual Report of the M.A.A.A.*, 1912–1913.

[35]*Montreal Daily Star*, 5 January 1916.

[36]S.F. Wise and D. Fisher, *Canada's Sporting Heroes: Their Lives and Times* (Don Mills: General Publishing Co., 1974), p. 214.

[37]Personal interview with Rabbi Charles Bender, 19 December 1980.

[38]See, for example, the *Montreal Gazette*, 1 August 1888 or 17 March 1898.

[39]Frank Andrews, *Rejoice We Conquer* (Toronto: New Line Fraternity, 1960), pp. 13–14.

[40]*Montreal Gazette*, 6 January 1931.

[41]A.E. Cox, 'A History of Sport in Canada, 1868 to 1900', unpublished Ph.D. dissertation, University of Alberta, 1969, p. 286. Information on early rowing leading up to Hanlan's exploits are taken from this source unless otherwise indicated.

[42]B. Flood, *Saint John: A Sporting Tradition* (Saint John: Neptune Publishing Company, 1985), pp. 15–17.

[43]Robert S. Hunter, *Rowing in Canada* (Hamilton: Davis-Lisson Ltd., 1933), pp. 13–17.

[44]Flood, op. cit., p. 33.

[45]Hunter, op. cit., p. 27.

[46]The Toronto *Globe* and *Telegram* carried daily messages about American centennial festivities and Canadian contributions to displays or ceremonial occasions.

[47]Frank Cosentino, 'Ned Hanlan—Canada's Premier Oarsman: A Case Study in Nineteenth Century Professionalism' in *Canadian Journal of History of Sport and Physical Education*, Vol. 5, No. 2 (December 1974), p. 8. Background information on Hanlan was derived from this source, together with Hunter's work cited above.

[48]Cosentino, op. cit., p. 8.

[49]Hunter, op. cit., pp. 29–30. Cosentino relies on Hunter for the allegation.

[50]'Sketches of the Champion Oarsmen: Hanlan and Courtney' (Montreal: Callehan and Co., Printers, 1878), 37 pages.

[51]Hunter, op. cit., p. 29.

[52]Cosentino, op. cit., p. 10.

[53]The *Mail*, Toronto, 2 October 1878.

[54]H. Roxborough, 'The Boy in Blue', in *Great Days in Canadian Sport* (Toronto: The Ryerson Press, 1957), p. 15.

[55]The *Mail*, Toronto, 4 October 1878.

[56]Cosentino, op. cit., p. 10.

[57]Hunter, op. cit., p. 30.

[58]Cosentino, op. cit., p. 11.

[59]The *Globe*, Toronto, 15 July 1879.

[60]Pierre Berton, 'Ned Hanlan and the Golden Age of Sculling', in *My Country: The Remarkable Past* (Toronto: McClelland and Stewart, 1976), pp. 204–5.

[61]J. Batten, *Champions* (Toronto: New Press, 1971), p. 53, as cited in Cosentino, op. cit., p. 12.

[62]The *Globe*, Toronto, 19 August 1879.

[63]Ibid., 14 July 1879.

[64]Race events were culled from a variety of sources, including Hunter, Cosentino, and Berton.

[65]Hunter, op. cit., p. 33.

[66]Ibid.

[67]Cosentino, op. cit., p. 15.

[68]A. Brown, 'Edward Hanlan, The World Sculling Champion Visits Australia' in *Canadian Journal of History of Sport and Physical Education*, Vol. XI, No. 2 (December 1980), pp. 1–44.

[69]Ibid.

[70]The *Globe*, Toronto, 28 April 1883.

[71]Berton, op. cit., p. 211.

[72]Cosentino, op. cit., pp. 16–17.

[73]B. Weider, *The Strongest Man in History: Louis Cyr* (Toronto: Mitchell Press Ltd., 1976), 104 pages. Weider is also the author of *Les Hommes Forts du Québec* (Montreal: Editions du Jour, 1973), 242 pages. The latter work focuses primarily on Cyr. These two sources, plus newspaper articles written at the time of Cyr's death in 1912, are relied upon for most of the information on Cyr.

[74]Weider, op. cit., pp. 3–13.

[75]S.F. Wise, 'Sport and Class Values in Old Ontario and Quebec' in *In His Own Man: Essays in Honour of A.R.M. Lower*, edited by W. H. Heick and R. Graham (Montreal: McGill-Queen's Press, 1974), p. 96.

[76]Weider, op. cit., p. 31, and Wise and

Fisher, *Canada's Sporting Heroes*, p. 141.

[77]Wise and Fisher, op. cit., pp. 63–7.

[78]Wise and Fisher, op. cit., p. 141.

[79]David R. Norwood, 'The Sport Hero Concept and Louis Cyr', unpublished Master of Human Kinetics thesis, University of Windsor, 1971, p. 40.

[80]*Le Devoir*, 11 November 1912.

[81]*Montreal Daily Star*, 7 May 1896, as cited in Norwood, op. cit., pp. 42–3.

[82]Weider, op. cit., p. 76.

[83]Norwood, op. cit., p. 39.

[84]Calgary *Herald*, 24 December 1891.

[85]Weider, op. cit., pp. 89–93.

[86]*Le Devoir*, 11 November 1912.

[87]Norwood, op. cit.

3. LACROSSE AS THE NATIONAL GAME

[1]M.A. Salter, 'The Relationship of Lacrosse to Physical Survival Among Early North American Indian Tribes' in *Proceedings of the Second World Symposium on the History of Sport and Physical Education* (Banff, Alberta, June 1971), pp. 95–106.

[2]M. Jette, 'Primitive Indian Lacrosse—Skill or Slaughter' in ibid., pp. 107–26.

[3]Both Salter's and Jette's works cited above attest to the skills required and the values that were believed to be a component of lacrosse. By far the most definitive source on early Indian lacrosse that underscores its nuances and skills is Stewart Culin's *Games of the North American Indians* (New York: Dover Publications Inc., 1975), pp. 562–616.

[4]Culin, op. cit., pp. 562–3.

[5]Ibid., p. 563.

[6]Ibid., p. 564 and H.H. Roxborough, *One Hundred—Not Out: The Story of Nineteenth Century Canadian Sport* (Toronto: Ryerson Press, 1966), pp. 12–13.

[7]*Tewaarathon (Lacrosse): Akwesasne's Story of Our National Game* (produced by the North American Indian Travelling College, 1978), p. 20.

[8]P.L. Lindsay, 'A History of Sport in Canada, 1807–1867', unpublished Ph.D. dissertation, The University of Alberta, 1969,

p. 114.

[9]Ibid., p. 115 and see *supra*, Chapter 1.

[10]Don Morrow, *A Sporting Evolution: The Montreal Amateur Athletic Association 1881–1981* (Montreal: Graphics Group, 1981), pp. 14–25.

[11]The photograph is by Notman and depicts ten players in high button shirts, bow-ties, white trousers, and peaked caps.

[12]Lindsay, op. cit., p. 117.

[13]See Alan Metcalfe, 'Sport and Athletics: A Case Study of Lacrosse in Canada, 1840–1889' in *Journal of Sport History*, Vol. 3, No. 1 (Spring, 1976), pp. 1–5.

[14]*Montreal Gazette*, 23 August 1860.

[15]Ibid., 28 August 1860.

[16]Goal-Keeper, *The Game of Lacrosse* (Montreal: M. Longmore Co., 1860).

[17]*Montreal Gazette*, 15 September 1860.

[18]As cited in Christina A. Burr, 'The Process of Evolution of Competitive Sport: A Study of Senior Lacrosse in Canada, 1844 to 1914', unpublished M.A. thesis, University of Western Ontario, 1986, Appendix A, p. 255.

[19]Text of a speech delivered by George N. Beers, grandson of Dr George W. Beers, to the Merit Awards Banquet at the Canadian Lacrosse Association Annual Convention in Vancouver, B.C., 24 November 1973. Mr Beers cites his grandfather's birth year as 1841 but most historical sources list it as 1843.

[20]P.L. Lindsay, 'George Beers and the National Game Concept: A Behavioural Approach' in *Proceedings of the Second Canadian Symposium on the History of Sport and Physical Education*, Windsor, Ontario (May, 1972), pp. 27–8. Lindsay's article on Beers is the basis of the information used here to determine Beers' influence in promoting lacrosse.

[21]See W. George Beers, 'A Rival to Cricket', *Chambers Journal*. Vol. 18 (6 December 1862), pp. 366–368; 'The Voyageurs of Canada', *British American Magazine* Vol. 1 (1863), pp. 472–9; 'Canada in Winter', *British American Magazine'* Vol. 2 (1864),

pp. 166–71.

[22]Roxborough, *One Hundred–Not Out*, p. 173.

[23]*Montreal Gazette*, 8 August 1867.

[24]The convention concept was discussed in the *Montreal Gazette* as early as 29 July and 12 August 1867. See Burr, 'A Study of Lacrosse in Canada', p. 60 and p. 102.

[25]*Montreal Gazette*, 30 September 1867.

[26]Lindsay, 'A History of Sport in Canada, 1807–1867', p. 123.

[27]Roxborough, *The Story of Nineteenth Century Canadian Sport*, p. 16.

[28]Culin, op. cit., p. 563.

[29]G.W. Beers, *Lacrosse: The National Game of Canada* (Montreal: Dawson Brothers, 1869).

[30]Ibid., pp. 57–8. In Beers' article 'Canadian Sports', *Century Magazine*, Vol. 14 (May-October 1877), p. 507, he also states: 'The game of lacrosse, which was adopted as the national game of Canada on the 1st of July, 1859 . . . .' This 21-page article romanticizes and promotes lacrosse, snowshoeing, and tobogganing as the quintessential Canadian sports.

[31]See, for example, K.G. Jones and T.G. Vellathottam, 'The Myth of Canada's National Sport', *Journal of the Canadian Association for Health, Physical Education and Recreation*, Vol. 41, No. 1 (September-October, 1974), pp. 33–6. Douglas Fisher examined every major Canadian newspaper and all relevant parliamentary documents between 1860 and 1870 and found no mention of lacrosse's being enacted as a national game. See ibid., p. 35.

[32]Lindsay, 'A History of Sport in Canada', p. 130, emphasis mine.

[33]*Montreal Gazette*, 8 August 1867. According to the *Gazette* editor, 'For a half dollar person can obtain an outfit unlike ricket', Ibid., 1 August 1867. Lindsay, 'A History of Sport in Canada', p. 125. *Montreal Gazette*, 23 October 1867, as cited in ibid., p. 126. Lindsay, 'A History of Sport in Canada',

p. 130.

[37]Beers, 'Canadian Sports', p. 512.

[38]A.E. Cox. 'A History of Sports in Canada, 1868–1900' unpublished Ph.D. dissertation, University of Alberta, 1969, p. 138.

[39]Alan Metcalfe, *Canada Learns to Play: The Emergence of Organized Sport, 1807–1914* (Toronto: McClelland and Stewart Ltd., 1987), p. 196. The discussion on the Shamrocks is based on Metcalfe's discussion of them on pp. 196–203.

[40]Ibid., p. 197.

[41]Burr, op. cit., p. 76.

[42]*Montreal Gazette*, 13 September 1875.

[43]Burr, op. cit., p. 84.

[44]Metcalfe, op. cit., p. 201.

[45]See *Montreal Gazette*, 4 October 1869 and 16 October 1876. Cited in Burr, op. cit., p. 110.

[46]*Laws of Lacrosse and Constitution of the National Lacrosse Association of Canada*. Revised and adopted 7 June 1878 (Toronto: Robert Marshall, 1878), p. 23.

[47]Burr, op. cit., pp. 78–9.

[48]Metcalfe, 'Sport and Athletics', pp. 6–15.

[49]'Hints to Players by a Native', *Canadian Magazine*, Vol. 1 (July-December, 1871), pp. 120–4 and 248–54.

[50]W.K. McNaught, *Lacrosse and How to Play It* (Toronto: Robert Marshall, 1873). A prominent Toronto player, McNaught copied Beers' text and issued it under a different title. In 1883 he was elected president of the NALA.

[51]W.G. Beers, 'The Ocean Travels of Lacrosse', *Athletic Leaves* (September 1888), p. 42.

[52]Don Morrow, 'The Canadian Image Abroad: The Great Lacrosse Tours of 1876 and 1883' in *Proceedings of the Fifth Canadian Symposium on the History of Sport*, Toronto (August 1982), pp. 10-21.

[53]*Montreal Herald* press clipping, 1875, in the Montreal Amateur Athletic Association Scrapbook, Vol. 15, p. 124.

[54]MAAA Scrapbook, press clipping, p. 165.

[55]Ibid., p. 176.

[56]Ibid., p. 166.

[57]Ibid., p. 161.

[58]See, for example, the Toronto *Globe*, 2 June 1876. In boxing fashion, this article provided the heights and weights of all of the lacrosse players on the tour.

[59]Ibid., 13 July 1876.

[60]*Montreal Gazette*, 1 May 1876.

[61]MAAA Scrapbook, Vol. 15, p. 192.

[62]Beers, *Lacrosse: The National Game of Canada*, pp. 42–3.

[63]The *Globe*, Toronto, 28 April 1883.

[64]*Montreal Gazette*, 14 August 1883, and Beers, 'The Ocean Travels of Lacrosse', pp. 42–3.

[65]The *Globe*, Toronto, 29 June 1883.

[66]Ibid.

[67]See *Sessional Papers*, Vol. 8, under the report of the Canadian Minister of Agriculture.

[68]The *Globe*, Toronto, 18 August 1883.

[69]*Laws of Lacrosse*, amended 10 April 1885 by the NALA, cited in Morrow, *A Sporting Evolution*, pp. 209–10.

[70]H.H. Allingham, 'Lacrosse in the Maritime Provinces', *Dominion Illustrated Monthly* (1892), pp. 225–33.

[71]Metcalfe, *Canada Learns to Play*, pp. 204–5.

[72]Burr, op. cit., pp. 121–22.

[73]Metcalfe, *Canada Learns to Play*, p. 207.

[74]Ibid.

[75]The *Globe*, Toronto, March 29, 1902.

[76]Cox, op. cit., p. 144.

[77]*Mainland Guardian*, New Westminster, 28 September 1890, as cited in Cox, op. cit., p. 145.

[78]Burr, op. cit., p. 157.

[79]The *Globe*, Toronto, 8 July 1911.

[80]J.A.P. Day, 'The 1908 New Westminster Salmonbellies', *Proceedings of the First Canadian Symposium on the History of Sport and Physical Education*, Edmonton, Alberta (May, 1970), p. 225. For greater ease of handling the ball, the Salmonbellies also used a shorter lacrosse stick than most teams.

[81]Burr, op. cit., pp. 135–41.

[82]Ibid., p. 141.

[83]Don Morrow, 'A Case Study in Amateur Conflict: The Athletic War in Canada', *The British Journal of Sports History*, Vol. 3, No. 2 (September 1986), pp. 177–86.

[84]Burr, op. cit., pp. 198–209.

[85]Metcalfe, *Canada Learns to Play*, pp. 207–8.

[86]T. G. Vellathottam and K. G. Jones, 'Highlights in the Development of Canadian Lacrosse to 1931', *Canadian Journal of History of Sport and Physical Education* Vol. 5, No. 2 (December 1974), pp. 46–7.

4. SPORT AND PHYSICAL EDUCATION IN SCHOOLS AND UNIVERSITIES

[1]Norman O. Brown, *Life Against Death: The Psychoanalytic Meaning of History* (Middletown, Connecticut: Wesleyan University Press, 1959), p. 31, brackets mine.

[2]W.T. Newham and A.S. Nease, *The Professional Teacher in Ontario: The Heritage, Responsibilities and Practices* (Toronto: The Ryerson Press, 1965), p. 1, 19.

[3]J. G. Althouse, 'The Ontario Teacher: An Historical Account of Progress, 1800–1910', Doctor of Pedagogy dissertation, University of Toronto, 1929, pp. 1–18.

[4]J.G. Hodgins, *Documentary History of Education in Upper Canada*, Vol. 5 (Toronto: Warwick Brothers and Rutter Printers, 1897), p. 272.

[5]E.C. Bockus, 'The Common Schools of Upper Canada, 1786–1840', unpublished MA thesis, McGill University, 1967, p.122.

[6]J.G. Hodgins, *The Establishment of Schools and Colleges in Ontario, 1792–1910*, Vol. 2 (Toronto: Printed and published by L. K. Cameron, 1910), p. 143.

[7]Ibid., Vol. 1, p. 9. The 'Old Blue School' merged with Upper Canada College in the late 1820s and 1830s. The original 6-acre plot of land owned by the Home District School was given to Upper Canada College as its permanent site.

[8]Hodgins, *Documentary History of Education in Upper Canada*, Vol. 1, p.293

[9]Susan E. Houston, 'Politics, Schools and Social Change in Upper Canada Between

1836 and 1846', unpublished MA thesis, University of Toronto, 1967, pp. 16–50.

[10]A. Egerton Ryerson, *The Story of My Life*, ed. by J.G. Hodgins (Toronto: William Briggs, 1883), pp. 342–3.

[11]Peter L. Lindsay, 'A History of Sport in Canada, 1807–1867', unpublished Ph.D. dissertation, University of Alberta, 1969, pp. 197–218.

[12]Ibid., p. 40. 'The primary and dominant motive of his life was religious,' wrote Ryerson's principal biographer, C.B. Sissons in *Egerton Ryerson: His Life and Letters*, Vol. 1 (Toronto: Clarke Irwin and Company Limited, 1937), p. 3.

[13]See C.B. Sissons, ed., *My Dearest Sophie: Letters from Egerton Ryerson to His Daughter* (Toronto: The Ryerson Press, 1969), p. 3, p. 75 and p. 87, for examples.

[14]Ibid., p. 83.

[15]Ryerson considered Arnold 'one of England's most distinguished and enlightened educationists.' Egerton Ryerson, ed., *Journal of Education for Upper Canada*, Vol. 6, No. 1 (January 1853), p. 16.

[16]See J.A. Mangan, *Athleticism in the Victorian Edwardian Public School* (London: The Falmer Press, 1981) and J. A. Mangan, *The Games Ethic and Imperialism: Aspects of the Diffusion of an Idea* (New York: Viking Penguin Inc., 1985), especially pp. 142–67.

[17]Hodgins, *The Establishment of Schools and Colleges in Ontario*, Vol. 6, pp. 161–2.

[18]Hodgins, *Documentary History of Education*, Vol. 10, p. 6.

[19]Ibid., p. 245.

[20]N.F. Davin, *The Irishman in Canada* (Toronto: Maclear and Co., 1877), pp. 620–2.

[21]*Annual Report of the Superintendent of Education for Upper Canada*, 1853, p. 113, and *Annual Report of the Superintendent of Education for Ontario*, 1869, p. 67.

[22]F. H. Johnson, *A Brief History of Canadian Education* (Toronto: McGraw-Hill Company of Canada Ltd., 1968), p. 78.

[23]A. Marling, *A Brief History of Public and High School Textbooks Authorized for the Province of Ontario 1846–1889* (Toronto: Warwick and Sons, 1890), p. 36

[24]A selection of these and other articles is reprinted in F. Consentino and M. Howell, *A History of Physical Education in Canada* (Don Mills: General Publishing Company Ltd., 1971), pp. 73–98.

[25]Egerton Ryerson, ed., *Journal of Education for Upper Canada*, Vol. 10, No. 8 (August 1857), pp. 115–16.

[26]See ibid., Vol. 15, No. 8 (August 1862), pp. 113–14 for three articles pertaining to military drill and military training.

[27]Ibid., Vol. 19, No. 10 (October 1866), pp. 145–54.

[28]Ibid., Vol. 30, No. 7 (June 1877), pp. 89–90.

[29]Hodgins, *The Establishment of Schools and Colleges in Ontario*, Vol. 1, p. 26.

[30]Ibid., Vol. 8, No. 2 (February 1855), p. 29.

[31]Hodgins, *op. cit.*, pp. 86, 94.

[32]P. L. Lindsay, op. cit., p. 335.

[33]Ibid., p. 342–4.

[34]A. E. Cox, 'A History of Sports in Canada, 1868–1900', unpublished Ph.D. dissertation, University of Alberta, 1969, p. 391.

[35] See G. Redmond, *The Sporting Scots of Nineteenth Century Canada* (Toronto: Associated University Presses, 1982), pp. 159-213.

[36]Althouse, op. cit., p. 179.

[37]W. N. Bell, *The Development of the Ontario High School* (Toronto: University of Toronto Press, 1918), p. 159 and p. 146.

[38]Ontario Archives, Department of Education, Record Group 2, Series p, p-2, Coole No. LV, Box 50, Physical Culture.

[39]*Annual Report of the Minister of Ontario for the Province of Ontario*, 1889, p. 195.

[40]See, for example, G.M. Shutt, *The High Schools of Guelph* (Toronto: University of Toronto Press, 1961), p. 36 and p. 66.

[41]James L. Hughes, *Manual of Drill and Calisthenics* (Toronto: W.J. Gage and Company, 1957), p. 274.

[42]C. E. Phillips, *The Development of Education in Canada* (Toronto: W.J. Gage and

Company, 1957), p. 274.

[43]They were Lieutenant-General Sir Sam Hughes (later, federal Minister of Militia), Major-General John Hughes, and Brigadier-General William St. Peter Hughes. L. Pierce, *Fifty Years of Public Services: A Life of James L. Hughes* (Toronto: Oxford University Press, 1924), p. 122.

[44]E.B. Houghton, *Physical Culture* (Toronto: Warwick and Sons, 1886).

[45]*Annual Reports of the Minister of Education for Ontario*, 1887, 1889, and 1899.

[46]Houghton, op. cit., p. 13.

[47]Houghton, op. cit., p. 220.

[48]E.T. White, *Public School Text-Books in Ontario* (London: The Chas. Chapman Co., 1922), p. 71.

[49]*Proceedings of the Ontario Education Association*, 1890–1908.

[50]J.D. Wilson, R.M. Stamp, and L-P. Audet, eds., *Canadian Education: A History* (Scarborough: Prentice-Hall of Canada Ltd., 1970), p. 318.

[51]*Minutes and Proceedings of the Dominion Educational Association*, 1892, p. 224.

[52]*The Educational Journal*, Vol. 6 (1892), p. 173.

[53]W.B. McMurrich and H.N. Roberts, *The School Law of Ontario* (Toronto: The Goodwin Law Book and Publishing Office, 1894), p. 300.

[54]*Annual Reports of the Minister of Education for the Province of Ontario*, 1891 to 1897.

[55]Ontario Archives, Department of Education, Record Group 2, Series p, p–2, Select Files, 1885–1913, Box No. 38.

[56]*Regulations of the Education Department, Province of Ontario* (Toronto: L.K. Cameron, 1907), pp. 10–11.

[57]F. Consentino, *Canadian Football: The Grey Cup Years* (Toronto: The Musson Book Company Ltd., 1969), p. 13.

[58]T.A. Reed, *The Blue and White: A Record of Fifty Years of Athletic Endeavour at the University of Toronto* (Toronto: University of Toronto Press, 1944) pp. 90–2.

[59]Reed, ibid., p. 188 and H. Roxborough, *One Hundred—Not Out: The Story of Nineteenth Century Canadian Sport* (Toronto: The Ryerson Press, 1966), pp. 140–1.

[60]Cox, op. cit., pp. 400–2.

[61]R.J. Moriarty, 'The Organizational History of the Canadian Intercollegiate Athletic Union Central (C.I.A.U.C.) 1906–1955', unpublished Ph.D. dissertation, Ohio State University, 1971.

[62]Ibid., pp. 107–8.

[63]H. J. Savage, 'American College Athletics' Bulletin No. 23 of *The Carnegie Foundation for the Advancement of Teaching* (Boston: The Merrymount Press, 1929), p. 25.

[64]F. Cosentino, *Canadian Football*, pp. 26–59.

[65]See, for example, the Toronto *Globe*, 17 October 1922.

[66]Toronto *Telegram*, 27 October 1930.

[67]Queen's won 3 consecutive Grey Cup championships between 1922 and 1924. See Cosentino, *Canadian Football*, pp. 55–9.

[68]K. Jones, 'Sport in Canada 1900–1920', unpublished Ph.D. dissertation, University of Alberta, 1970, p. 423.

[69]See G.J. Burke, 'An Historical Study of Intercollegiate Athletics at The University of Western Ontario 1908–1945', unpublished M.A. thesis, University of Western Ontario, 1979, pp. 103–8.

[70]Jones, op. cit., pp. 420–33.

[71]J.A. Morris, *Prescott 1810–1967* (Prescott: St. Lawrence Printing Company, 1967), p. 77.

[72]K. Beattie, *Ridley: The Story of a School*, Vol. 1 (St Catharines: Ridley College, 1962), p. 318.

[73]*Debates of the House of Commons*, Vol. 90, 1909, pp. 3200–1.

[74]E.A. Hardy and H.M. Cochrane, eds., *Centennial Story: The Board of Education for the City of Toronto 1850–1950* (Toronto: Thomas Nelson and Sons Ltd., 1950), p. 281.

[75]Ibid.

[76]*Annual Report to the Minister of Education for Ontario*, 1911, p. 254.

[77]Don Morrow, 'The Strathcona Trust in

Ontario, 1911–1939', *Canadian Journal of History of Sport and Physical Education*, Vol. 8, No. 1 (May, 1977), pp. 72–90.

[78]See Yvette Walton, 'The Life and Professional Contribution of Ethel Mary Cartwright, 1880–1955', unpublished M.A. thesis, University of Western Ontario, 1976.

[79]'Physical Education', *The Canadian Encyclopedia* (Edmonton: Hurtig Publisher, 1985), Vol. III, p. 1406.

[80]R.S. Lappage, 'Selected Sports and Canadian Society 1921–1939', unpublished Ph.D. dissertation, University of Alberta, 1974, pp. 228–40.

5. SPORT BETWEEN THE WARS
[1]Keith L. Lansley, 'The Amateur Athletic Union of Canada and Changing Concepts of Amateurism', unpublished Ph.D. thesis, University of Alberta, 1971, p. 205.

[2]Percy Williams, telephone interview conducted in Vancouver, 15 May 1970.

[3]The *Globe*, Toronto, 7 July 1925.

[4]Williams interview, 15 May 1970.

[5]Nancy Howell and Maxwell L. Howell, *Sports and Games in Canadian Life—1700 to the Present* (Toronto: Macmillan of Canada, 1969), p. 199.

[6]J. Novil Marks, 'Pigskin Feud', *Maclean's*, 1 October 1937, p. 40.

[7]Frank Cosentino, *Canadian Football: The Grey Cup Years* (Toronto: The Musson Book Company Limited, 1969), p. 111.

[8]*Chronicle Herald*, Halifax, 1 September 1925.

[9]Ibid., 3 September 1928.

[10]Ibid., 25 November 1972.

[11]Ibid., 19 December 1927.

[12]Ibid., 18 April 1975.

[13]*Port Arthur News Chronicle*, 7 November 1935.

[14]Ibid., 22 November 1935.

[15]Ibid., 25 November 1935.

[16]Ibid., 7 January 1936.

[17]Ibid.

[18]See Brian and Phil Backman, *Bluenose* (Toronto: McClelland and Stewart Ltd, 1965), and Michael C. Sultzback, 'Canadian Schooner *Bluenose*', unpublished

M.S. thesis, Dalhousie University, 1978.

[19]H.H. Roxborough, 'Cash or Character', *Maclean's*, 15 April 1928, p. 18.

[20]Ibid.

[21]Ibid.

[22]J. Lewis Brown, 'Senior Football and Sham Amateurs', *National Home Monthly*, September 1937, p. 22.

[23]Ibid., p. 55.

[24]Frederick Edwards, 'Bootleg Amateurs', *Maclean's*, 1 November 1930, p. 7.

[25]Ibid., p. 48.

[26]Ralph Allen, 'Enter the Paid Amateur', *Maclean's*, 1 November 1940, p. 29.

[27]Lou E. Marsh, 'How Amateur Are Canadian "Amateurs"?', *Maclean's*, 15 October 1925, p. 16.

[28]H.H. Roxborough, 'Is Worship of Mammon Killing Amateur Sport?', *Maclean's*, 15 February 1928, p. 6.

[29]The *Globe*, Toronto, 22 November 1935.

[30]Keith L. Lansley, 'The Amateur Athletic Union of Canada and Changing Concepts of Amateurism', unpublished Ph.D. thesis, University of Alberta, 1971, p. 231.

[31]Ralph Allen, op. cit., p. 24.

[32]Archie Wills, 'Patrick of the Puck', *Maclean's*, 1 April 1928, p. 12.

[33]Ibid.

[34]*Vancouver Sun*, 15 March 1921.

[35]Frederick Edwards, 'Is Pro-Hockey a Career?', *Maclean's*, 1 June 1928, p. 10.

[36]Ted Reeve, 'Hockey's Frozen Assets', *National Home Monthly*, February 1933, p. 16.

[37]Frederick B. Edwards, 'High Hat Hockey', *Maclean's*, 15 December 1927, p. 53.

[38]The *Globe*, Toronto, 15 April 1929.

[39]Reeve, op. cit., p. 16.

[40]Edwards, 'High Hat Hockey', p. 53.

[41]*Winnipeg Free Press*, 21 January 1933.

[42]Elmer W. Ferguson, 'Red-Ink Hockey', *Maclean's*, 15 November 1938.

[43]*Winnipeg Free Press*, 28 September 1931.

[44]Ferguson, op. cit., p. 14.

[45]J. Lewis Brown, 'Tragedy and Glamour in Hockey', *National Home Monthly*, January 1939, p. 4.

[46]Reeve, op. cit., p. 16.

47Ibid.
48Brown, op. cit., p.33.
49C.J. Carroll, 'Can Baseball Come Back?', *Maclean's*, 15 May 1937, p. 23.
50The *Globe*, Toronto, 25 July 1933.
51Frank Cosentino, 'A History of Canadian Football, 1909–1968', unpublished MA thesis, University of Alberta, 1969.
52Howell and Howell, op. cit., p. 201.
53*Chronicle Herald*, Halifax, 15 August 1938.
54Ibid., 5 September 1938.
55*Winnipeg Free Press*, 9 December 1935.
56Ibid., 3 July 1933.
57*Le Devoir*, 29 May 1933.
58*Winnipeg Free Press*, 17 September 1934; 1 July 1935.
59Ibid., 13 August 1932.
60Material for this section is based on Richard Browne, 'The Concept of the 6-Day Cycling Show-Circus in the 1930s: The Star Showman, "Torchy" Peden', *Canadian Journal of History of Sport*, Vol. XVII, No. 29 (December 1986), pp. 85–96, and Henry Roxborough, 'King of the Six-Day Cyclists' in *Great Days in Canadian Sport* (Toronto: The Ryerson Press, 1957), pp. 149–59.
61Roxborough, op. cit., p. 155 and p. 157.
62Bob Ferguson, *Who's Who in Canadian Sport* (Toronto: Summerhill Press Ltd., 1985), p. 195.
63Browne, op. cit., p. 88.
64*Vancouver Sun*, 2 May 1936.
65Wilfred Kesterton and John S. Moir, 'Communications' in *The Canadians 1867–1967*, ed. by J.M.S. Careless and R. Craig Brown (Toronto: Macmillan of Canada, 1967), p. 531.
66H.H. Roxborough, 'He Shoots, He Scores!', *Maclean's*, 15 December 1937, p. 14.
67Wills, op. cit., p. 12.
68*Winnipeg Free Press*, 14 November 1931.
69The *Globe*, Toronto, 20 September 1926.
70Ibid., 23 February 1926.
71Ibid., 25 June 1925.
72Ibid., 13 November 1931.
73Ibid., 16 November 1931.
74*Chronicle Herald*, Halifax, 26 January 1935.
75Ibid., 1 February 1932.
76Cosentino, op. cit., p. 114.
77*Winnipeg Free Press*, 8 November 1930.
78J. Norvil Marks, 'Prairie Kick-off', *Maclean's*, 1 October 1931.
79J. Lewis Brown, 'Pigskin Warfare', *National Home Monthly*, November 1939, p. 56.
80*Winnipeg Free Press*, 21 November 1932.
81Ibid., 21 November 1932.
82The *Province*, Vancouver, 7 May 1938.
83Ibid. 3 March 1934.
84J. Lewis Brown, 'Salute to Winter Sport', *National Home Monthly*, December 1938, p. 39.
85*Globe and Mail*, Toronto, 24 September 1931.
86H.H. Roxborough, 'Golf Incorporated', *Maclean's*, 1 June 1930, p. 42.
87Rolf Tonning Lund, 'A History of Skiing in Canada Prior to 1940', unpublished MA thesis, University of Alberta, 1971, p. 343.
88Ibid.
89The *Globe*, Toronto, 11 April 1927.
90*The Canadian Encyclopedia* (Edmonton: Hurtig Publishers, 1985), Vol. II, p. 1035.
91*Globe and Mail*, Toronto, 4 July 1938.
92Ibid., 6 August 1938.
93Ibid., 21 September 1938.
94*Chronicle Herald*, Halifax, 10 April 1933.
95Ibid., 16 November 1936.
96Ibid., 17 August 1936.
97*Globe and Mail*, Toronto, 30 September 1938.
98*Vancouver Sun*, 31 January 1925.
99Ibid., 17 October 1925.
100Ibid., 8 November 1927.
101*Winnipeg Free Press*, 18 September 1926.
102*Chronicle Herald*, Halifax, 5 May 1936.
103*Winnipeg Free Press*, 25 September 1922.
104Ibid., 7 May 1927.
105C. Howard Hopkins, *History of the Y.M.C.A in North America* (New York: Association Press, 1951), p. 590.
106The *Globe*, Toronto, 17 January 1921.
107Ibid., 24 March 1926.
108*Winnipeg Free Press*, 14 April 1928.
109*Chronicle Herald*, Halifax, 25 April 1927.

[110]*Vancouver Sun*, 9 April 1923.

[111]*Chronicle Herald*, Halifax, 6 April 1925.

[112]Reet Nurmberg, 'History of Competitive Gymnastics in Canada', unpublished M.A. thesis, University of Alberta, 1970, p. 381.

[113]Kevin G. Jones, 'Sports in Canada—1900 to 1920', unpublished Ph.D. thesis, University of Alberta, 1970, p. 478.

[114]Minutes of the 39th Annual Meeting of the Amateur Athletic Union of Canada held in Saint John, N.B., 9–11 December 1926.

6. BASEBALL

[1]David Q. Voigt, *American Baseball: From the Gentleman's Sport to the Commissioner System* (University Park: Penn State Press, 1983), Vol.I, pp. 5–8.

[2]Ibid.,p. 8. These rules were actually written for the Club by Alexander Cartwright in 1846.

[3]The letter, and a discussion of its significance, is published by N.B. Bouchier and R.K. Barney in 'A Critical Examination of a Source on Early Ontario Baseball: The Reminiscence of Adam E. Ford', *Journal of Sport History* (Spring, 1988), pp. 75–90. Most of this section is based on this publication.

[4]William Humber, *Cheering for the Home Team: The Story of Baseball in Canada* (Erin, Ontario: The Boston Mills Press, 1983),p. 28. Lindsay cites 1859 as the date of the first recorded game in Hamilton: P.L. Lindsay, 'A History of Sport in Canada, 1807–1867' (unpublished Ph.D. dissertation, The University of Alberta, 1969),p. 80. Given the known existence of at least 4 teams in 1859—the Burlington Club, the Barton Club, the Hamilton Maple Leafs, the Canadian Pioneer Club of Toronto—an earlier date seems more logical. Lindsay goes so far as to call Hamilton 'the baseball centre of North America' during this period.

[5]Bryan D. Palmer, *A Culture in Conflict: Skilled Workers and Industrial Capitalism in Hamilton, Ontario 1860–1914* (Montreal: McGill-Queens University Press, 1979), p. 53.

[6]Ibid.,p. 52. Palmer remarks that baseball was almost a 'matter of course' at union picnics and that whole teams would turn out at funerals of a fellow team member as a kind of 'bond of solidarity cementing the working-class community.' Ibid.,p. 54 and p. 36. His deduction that scores of 73–4 and 58–35, common during the 60s and 70s, were strong evidence of 'raucous' affairs and much 'merriment' shows a lack of understanding of the nature of baseball of the time. Batters could wait for the pitch of their choice, fielders were inept and without gloves, and the emphasis was on base-running and scoring.

[7]Lindsay, op. cit., p. 80.

[8]William Humber in 'Cheering for the Home Team: Baseball and Town Life in 19th Century Ontario', *Proceedings of the Fifth Canadian Symposium on the History of Sport and Physical Education* (University of Toronto, August 1982),p. 192.

[9]See the *Ingersoll Chronicle*, 20 July 1882, 12 July 1884, 16 July 1885, 17 June 1886, and 26 July 1889 for accounts of middle-class games.

[10]*Woodstock Sentinel*, 3 September 1875. Examples abound of this level of competition in this paper, through to the mid–1880s in Woodstock.

[11]*Hamilton Spectator*, 29 September 1864.

[12]Lindsay points out that baseball, among other games, was prohibited in Montreal's public parks by an 1865 municipal ordinance that carried a five-dollar penalty for infractions. It is likely that baseball was perceived as a children's game that was a nuisance activity within the serenity of a public park.

[13]Alexander J. Young, *Beyond Heroes: A Sport History of Nova Scotia* (Hantsport, Nova Scotia: Lancelot Press, 1988), p. 95.

[14]The *Globe*, Toronto, 17 August 1867.

[15]The same *Brampton Times* excerpt is quoted in W. Perkins Bull, *From Rattlesnake Hunt to Hockey: The History of Sports in Canada and of the Sportsmen of Pell 1798–*

1934 (Toronto: George J. McLeod Ltd., 1934),p. 324 and p. 327. Brampton never did develop as a nineteenth-century baseball town. Lacrosse was its dominant sport in the last third of the century.

[16]Humber, *Cheering for the Home Team*, p. 28.

[17]*New York Clipper*, 19 June 1869.

[18]Humber, 'Baseball and Town Life', pp. 194-5.

[19]*Hamilton Spectator*, 11 August 1864. The citizens of Woodstock donated American silver dollars that were melted down and crafted in 1864 into an elegant ball of regulation size. The Silver Ball is pictured in the *Star Weekly*, 19 July 1924.

[20]Sleeman Papers, University of Guelph. One newspaper article in the 1880s actually suggested renaming the town Sleemanville.

[21]*Guelph Evening Mercury*, 5 August 1869.

[22]Alan Metcalfe, *Canada Learns to Play: The Emergence of Organized Sport, 1807–1914* (Toronto: McClelland and Stewart, 1987), p. 86.

[23]'Club Rules', 1874, in Sleeman Papers.

[24]*The Globe*, Toronto, 6 April 1877.

[25]'Canadian Base Ball Association Constitution, By-Laws, Playing Rules, Championship Code, 1876, in William Bryce, *Canadian Base Ball Guide for 1876* (London, Ontario: Bryce, 1876), pp. 37–42. This *Guide* was a promotional device contrived by the CBBA.

[26]Unidentified clippings contained in the Sleeman Papers, 1886. Humber, in *Cheering for the Home Team*, p. 47, briefly describes the tour, but his statistics on games played and fan appeal are inflated.

[27]Tecumseh Baseball Club of London Minute Book, June 1868 to May 1872. This Minute Book is very formally written by the secretary of the Club, whose object was to 'impart, foster and perpetuate the game of Base Ball and to advance the interests of its members' (page 2). The team was scheduled to practise 3 days per week at 5:00 p.m. and the Club paid all necessary expenses during match games (players' expenses, equipment, umpire, and scorer). Most of the Minute Book entries are very businesslike committee-meeting items—definitely an indication of increasing organization creeping into baseball.

[28]Sleeman Papers and selected issues of the 1876–1880 *London Advertiser*.

[29]The author is indebted to Frank Dallier for his newspaper research covering the *London Free Press* and the *London Advertiser* for 1876 to 1878.

[30]Humber, *Cheering for the Home Team*, p. 40.

[31]The general trend in baseball, not Englehart's specific part in it, has been paraphrased from R. Gruneau, *Class, Sports, and Social Development* (Amherst: University of Massachusetts Press, 1983), pp. 116–17. Gruneau's remarks were pointed specifically at Canadian professional baseball. He noted that the entrepreneurial orientation 'crystallized' after 1910. I would argue it happened much earlier, even with Sleeman's role; it may have proliferated after 1910.

[32]*London Daily Advertiser*, 27 May 1876.

[33]Ibid., 2 September 1876.

[34]The *Globe*, Toronto, 12 September 1876, cited in A.E. Cox, 'A History of Sports in Canada 1868–1900', unpublished Ph.D. dissertation, The University of Alberta, 1969, p. 46.

[35]*London Daily Advertiser*, 18 May 1876.

[36]Ibid., 4 May 1878.

[37]Ibid., 11 July 1878.

[38]Ibid.

[39]Metcalfe, op. cit., pp. 88–89.

[40]See ibid., p. 86.

[41]See Cox, op. cit., pp. 54–5, for a description of the leagues in Ontario and Quebec that popped in and out of existence as late as 1895 to 1900.

[42]Brian Flood, *Saint John: A Sporting Tradition* (Saint John: Neptune Publishing Co., Ltd., 1985), p. 71. This source is heavily relied upon for Maritime baseball history in this chapter.

[43]Ibid., p. 74.

[44]Ibid., pp. 75–80 and p. 125.

[45]Cox, op. cit., p. 53.

[46]Flood, *Saint John*, p. 78.

[47]Ibid., pp. 121–9.

[48]H. Charles Ballem, *Abegweit Dynasty 1899–1954: The Story of the Abegweit Amateur Athletic Association* (Summerside, P.E.I.: Williams and Crue, 1986), p. 53.

[49]M. Mott, 'The First Pro Sports League on the Prairies: The Manitoba Baseball League of 1886', *Canadian Journal of History of Sport* (December 1984), pp. 62–3. Winnipeg baseball history is based upon this article.

[50]Ibid., 62–9.

[51]Humber, *Cheering for the Home Team*, p. 69.

[52]Barry Broadfoot, *The Pioneer Years 1895–1914: Memories of Settlers Who Opened the West* (Toronto: Doubleday Canada Limited, 1976), p. 337.

[53]Humber, *Cheering for the Home Team*, p. 53. Humber cites the formation of the Crescents team in 1868 at St. John's, P.Q., but there is no documentation of baseball games in Quebec (outside of Montreal) at that early period.

[54]Metcalfe, op. cit., pp. 94–5.

[55]*Annual Reports of the MAAA, 1886 to 1889.*

[56]Bull, op. cit., p. 327.

[57]Ibid., p. 337.

[58]Ibid., pp. 338–42.

[59]Metcalfe, op. cit., p. 166.

[60]W.A. Hewitt, *Down the Stretch: Recollections of a Pioneer Sportsman and Journalist* (Toronto: The Ryerson Press, 1958), p. 122.

[61]Louis Cauz, *Baseball's Back in Town: A History of Baseball in Toronto* (Toronto: Controlled Media Corporation Publication, 1977), p. 17.

[62]Cox, op. cit., p. 53.

[63]*Saturday Night*, 22 June 1895, p. 6.

[64]Kevin G. Jones, 'Sport in Canada, 1900–1920', unpublished Ph.D. dissertation, the University of Alberta, 1970, p. 36.

[65]Paul O'Neill, *The Oldest City: The Story of St. John's Newfoundland* (Don Mills: Musson Book Co., 1975), Vol. 1, p. 331.

[66]Ballem, op. cit., pp. 90–1.

[67]Flood, op. cit., p. 130 and pp. 164–5.

[68]Young, op. cit., Vol. 1, p. 104.

[69]Ibid., p. 107.

[70]Humber, *Cheering for the Home Team*, pp. 69–73.

[71]Ibid., pp. 79–80.

[72]Jones, op. cit., pp. 43–7.

[73]Ibid., pp. 53–5.

[74]The *Globe*, Toronto, 24 May 1917.

[75]Metcalfe, op. cit., pp. 85, 88. Metcalfe used the cities of Halifax, Montreal, Toronto, Winnipeg, Edmonton, Vancouver, and Victoria in his sample.

[76]E. Janice Waters, 'A Content Analysis of the Sport Section in Selected Canadian Newspapers 1927 to 1935', unpublished M.A. thesis, University of Western Ontario, 1981, pp. 24–52.

[77]Hewitt, op. cit., p. 123 and Cauz, op. cit., p. 35.

[78]Cauz, op. cit., p. 36.

[79]Cauz, op. cit., p. 35.

[80]*Saturday Night*, 16 May 1908, p. 11.

[81]*Saturday Night*, 15 May 1909, p. 10.

[82]Hewitt, op. cit., p. 135–6.

[83]*Saturday Night*, 1 June 1912, p. 6.

[84]*Saturday Night*, 16 May 1908, p. 11.

[85]Harvey Frommer, 'Jackie Robinson as a Montreal Royal', *Fifth Canadian Symposium on the History of Sport and Physical Education* (University of Toronto, August 1982), pp. 122–8. For a complete discussion of Robinson's time with the Royals, see Jules Tygiel, *Baseball's Great Experiment: Jackie Robinson and His Legacy* (New York: Oxford University Press, 1983), pp. 99–143.

[86]A fine reminiscence of the Royals in the 1940s and later by Mordecai Richler, 'Expansion: Up from the Minors in Montreal', is included in Daniel Okrent and Harris Lewine, eds., *The Ultimate Baseball Book* (Boston: Houghton Mifflin Company, 1988).

[87]This passage is gratefully drawn from William Humber's *Cheering for the Home Team*, Chapter 7.

[88]Humber, ibid., p. 106.

[89]Tygiel, op. cit., p. 143; Sam Maltin in the Pittsburgh *Courier*, 12 October 1946.

[90]I am grateful to William Dendy for providing information on the Stadium.

[91]Louis Cauz's valuable book, *Baseball's Back in Town*, was the source for much of the information in the following passage on the Leafs in the 1930s and after, and on the Blue Jays

7. FOOTBALL

[1]*Football Rules* (Rugby: H. King & Co. (printers), n.d.).

[2]Thomas Hughes, *Tom Brown's Schooldays* (London: Blackie and Sons Ltd., 1857), p. 73.

[3]'Playing Rules of McGill University', 1874, reproduced from original document.

[4]John Allen Krout, *Annals of American Sport* (New Haven: Yale University Press, 1929).

[5]A.C. Kingstone and C.A.S. Boddy, 'Characteristics of Canadian Football', *Outing*, vol. 27, December 1892, p. 250.

[6]Minutes of the CRU Annual Meeting, 1906.

[7]Minutes of the first meeting of the CRU (reorganized), 19 December 1891.

[8]Minutes of the CRU Annual Meeting, 1897.

[9]See F. Cosentino, *Canadian Football: The Grey Cup Years* (Musson Book Co., 1969).

[10]The *Globe*, Toronto, 22 September 1909.

[11]Spalding Athletic Library, Vol. 1, no. 8, *Official Football Guide, 1911* (Canadian Sports Publishing Co. Montreal), p. 57.

[12]*Football Hall of Fame*: letter from Hanbury-Williams to D.B. Macdonald, 2 April 1909 (emphasis his).

[13]The *Globe*, Toronto, 1 December 1909.

[14]Ibid., 23 November 1910.

[15]Ibid., 28 November 1910.

[16]Ibid., 14 September 1912.

[17]Ibid., 19 November 1912.

[18]Ibid., 17 January 1921.

[19]Minutes of the CRU Annual Meeting, 13 January 1912.

[20]The *Globe*, Toronto, 25 April 1921.

[21]Edmonton *Bulletin*, 20 September 1921.

[22]Deacon White, article in the Edmonton *Bulletin*, 5 December 1921.

[23]Frank Cosentino and Don Morrow, *Lionel Conacher* (The Canadians Series, Toronto: Fitzhenry and Whiteside), p. 18.

[24]*Winnipeg Free Press*, 9 December 1935.

[25]Ibid., 4 December 1935.

[26]Warren Stevens: letter to the writer, 15 March 1968.

[27]Brian Timmis: interview with the writer, 15 May 1968.

[28]Tony Allan, *Grey Cup Cavalcade* (Winnipeg: Harlequin Books, 1959), p. 20.

[29]The *Herald*, Hamilton, 3 November 1931.

[30]The *Globe*, Toronto, 3 November 1931.

[31]Al Ritchie, 'That Forward Pass', *Maclean's*, 1 November 1931.

[32]*Winnipeg Free Press*, 9 November 1932.

[33]Joe Ryan: interview with the writer, April 1968.

[34]The *Globe*, Toronto, 2 March 1936.

[35]Jim Coleman: article in the *Globe and Mail*, Toronto, 25 February 1946.

[36]*Globe and Mail*, Toronto, 29 November 1948.

[37]Ted Reeve, *Grandstand Quarterback* (Toronto: Longmans Green and Co., 1955), p. 127.

[38]*Globe and Mail*, Toronto, 24 January 1956.

[39]Ibid., 23 January 1956.

[40]*Time*, 30 November 1962.

[41]Ibid.

[42]Ibid.

[43]Ibid.

[44]Minutes of the CFL Meeting, 29 November 1963.

[45]Frank Cosentino, *Canadian Football: The Grey Cup Years* (Toronto: Musson Book Co.), 1969.

[46]*Toronto Star*, 16 February 1973.

[47]Hugh Bremner, London CFPL editorial, 9 April 1974.

[48]Dalton Camp, *London Free Press*, 13 March 1974.

[49]Earl McRae, *The Canadian Magazine*, n.d., 1975.

[50]Ontario Human Rights Commission, Toronto: 26 June, 10, 11, 12, 17 July 1979.

[51]The *Sun*, Toronto, 15 December 1988.

8. HOCKEY

[1] Alice B. Gomme, *The Traditional Games of England, Scotland and Ireland* (New York: Dover Publications, 1964), p.16.

[2] Henry Roxborough, *One Hundred—Not Out; The Story of Nineteenth Century Canadian Sports* (Toronto: Ryerson Press, 1966), p. 137, as cited in Peter L. Lindsay, 'A History of Sport in Canada, 1807–1867', unpublished Ph.D. dissertation, University of Alberta, 1969, p. 41.

[3] Lindsay, op.cit., p. 41.

[4] John Arlott, ed., 'Hurling', *The Oxford Companion to Sports and Games* (Oxford: Oxford University Press, 1976), pp. 449–52.

[5] 'Hurling', *Encyclopedia Britannica* (Chicago: William Benton, 1970), vol. XI.

[6] *Novascotian*, Halifax, 26 December 1833.

[7] As cited in Lindsay, op. cit., p. 42.

[8] Cited in the *Montreal Gazette*, 1 January 1941. Also cited in N. Howell and M. Howell, *Sports and Games in Canadian Society, 1700 to Present* (Toronto: Macmillan, 1969), p. 33.

[9] Ibid.

[10] As cited in Foster Hewitt, *Hockey Night in Canada* (Toronto: Ryerson Press, 1968), p. 3. Also noted in Lindsay, op. cit., p. 43. The CAHA Report is also mentioned in J.W. Fitsell, *Hockey's Captains, Colonels and Kings* (Erin, Ont.: Boston Mills Press, 1987), p. 20.

[11] Roxborough, op. cit., p. 138.

[12] *Kingston Chronicle and Gazette*, 2 January 1839. On 15 January 1840 it stated this was the second year for the playing of shinty, 'the noble and manly game'.

[13] Ibid., 16 January 1841.

[14] Ibid., 25 January 1843.

[15] The *Globe*, Toronto, 12 October 1863. Bowes' involvement in Toronto sport is documented in Robert Wayne Simpson, 'The Elite and Sport Club Membership, 1827–1881', unpublished Ph.D. dissertation, University of Alberta, 1987, *passim*.

[16] Simpson, op. cit., p. 329.

[17] The *Globe*, Toronto, 2 November 1863.

[18] *Montreal Gazette*, 23 October 1843.

[19] Lindsay, op. cit., pp. 24–40.

[20] See Ian F. Jobling, 'Sport in Nineteenth-Century Canada: The Effects of Technological Changes on Its Development', unpublished Ph.D. dissertation, University of Alberta, 1970, *passim*.

[21] 'Hockey, Ice', *The Canadian Encyclopedia* (Edmonton: Hurtig Publishers, 1985), Vol. II, pp. 823–4.

[22] Arlott, op. cit., pp. 453–4.

[23] *Montreal Gazette*, 3 March 1875.

[24] 'Hockey, Ice', op. cit., p. 823. Also referred to in Fitsell, op. cit., p. 33.

[25] Hewitt, op. cit., p. 11, and Ken Dryden, *The Game* (Toronto: Macmillan, 1983), p. 12.

[26] *Montreal Gazette*, 22 December 1936.

[27] Fitsell, op. cit., p. 39.

[28] These rules and their evolvement generally coincide with those outlined by Roxborough in *One Hundred—Not Out*, p. 141.

[29] For dates of formation of these two early hockey clubs, see Allan Cox, 'A History of Sport in Canada, 1868–1900', unpublished Ph.D. dissertation, University of Alberta, 1969, p. 230.

[30] Ibid., p. 229. McGill team members F.W. Robertson, R.F. Smith, and W.L. Murray were recognized as devising and codifying the earlier rule drawn up by J.G.A. Creighton.

[31] Ibid., p. 231.

[32] Fitsell, op. cit., p. 40.

[33] As documented in Alan Metcalfe, *Canada Learns to Play: The Emergence of Organized Sport, 1807–1914* (Toronto: McClelland and Stewart, 1986), p. 63; also in Charles L. Coleman, *The Trail of the Stanley Cup* (Montreal: National Hockey League, 1966), p.v.

[34] The *Globe*, Toronto, 13 December 1898.

[35] Ibid., 14 and 15 January 1888.

[36] Ibid., 17 February 1888.

[37] See Cox, op. cit., p. 233.

[38] Foster Hewitt, *Down the Stretch* (Toronto: Ryerson Press, 1958), p. 179.

[39] Cox, op. cit., p. 233.

[40] For references to these developments,

see the *Globe*, Toronto, 14, 15, and 22 January 1891.

⁴¹Cox, op. cit., p. 240.

⁴²The *Globe*, Toronto, 27 February 1897.

⁴³*Fredericton Reporter*, 23 December 1896.

⁴⁴Much of this information was drawn from N.J. Woodside, 'Hockey in the Canadian NorthWest', *The Canadian Magazine*, January 1896, p. 244.

⁴⁵Ibid.

⁴⁶Cox, op. cit., p. 237.

⁴⁷*Calgary Herald*, 4 January 1893.

⁴⁸*Edmonton Bulletin*, 29 November 1894.

⁴⁹For instance, see the *Medicine Hat Times*, 12 December 1895, for a description of an initial ice-hockey contest. Medicine Hat was a siding-stop for the Canadian Pacific.

⁵⁰Cox, op. cit., p. 238.

⁵¹*Regina Leader*, 25 January 1894.

⁵²Metcalfe, op. cit., p. 64. Also see B. Zeman, *88 Years of Puck Chasing in Saskatchewan* (Regina: Saskatchewan Sports Hall of Fame, 1983) and G. Zeman, *Alberta on Ice* (Edmonton: Westweb, 1985).

⁵³Quoted in Frank Cosentino, 'A History of the Concept of Professionalism in Canadian Sport', unpublished Ph.D. Dissertation, University of Alberta, 1973, p. 158.

⁵⁴As P.D. Ross (later a noted newspaper publisher) played hockey with Arthur Stanley in the Rideau Rebels Hockey Club, he was not, strictly speaking, an impartial trustee. He remained a trustee, however, for 56 years, until his death at 91.

⁵⁵For an in-depth discussion of the ramifications of the Montreal Amateur Athletic Association's refusal, see Don Morrow, 'The Little Men of Iron: The 1902 Montreal Hockey Club', *Canadian Journal of History of Sport*, May 1981, pp. 51–65.

⁵⁶Coleman, op. cit., p. xviii. See also the *Montreal Gazette*, 23 February 1894.

⁵⁷Cosentino, op. cit., p. 161. To date there have been only seven trustees of the Stanley Cup: John Sweetland, P.D. Ross,

William Foran, Mervyn Dutton, Cooper Smeaton, Brian F. O'Neill, and Judge Willard Estey.

⁵⁸See D. Diamond and J. Romain, *Hockey Hall of Fame: The Official History of the Game and Its Greatest Stars* (Toronto: Doubleday, 1988), p. 20, and Coleman, *The Trail of the Stanley Cup*, pp. 5–6.

⁵⁹Cox, op. cit., p. 240.

⁶⁰The *Globe*, Toronto, 9 December 1895. Arenas that were constructed specifically for ice hockey were barely large enough to contain the rink itself; therefore players were always in danger of hitting the outside walls.

⁶¹Coleman, op. cit., p. 5. Coleman says Merritt was hockey's finest goaltender in the nineteenth century.

⁶²Cox, op. cit., p. 242.

⁶³See editorial in the *Toronto Star*, 26 December 1902.

⁶⁴For a case study on the Pittsburgh example, see Frank Cosentino and Don Morrow, *Lionel Conacher* (Don Mills: Fitzhenry and Whiteside, 1981).

⁶⁵All the information on the definitions of what an amateur was is taken from the author's lecture notes and from ideas presented in K. Lansley, 'The Amateur Athletic Union of Canada and Changing Concepts of Amateurism', unpublished Ph.D. Dissertation, University of Alberta, 1971, *passim*.

⁶⁶Ibid. The Amateur Athletic Association of Canada would consider the reinstatement of professionals back to amateur status.

⁶⁷See Coleman, op. cit., pp. 45–8.

⁶⁸Cosentino, op. cit., pp. 196–204.

⁶⁹Ibid., p. 206.

⁷⁰For an excellent description of this American league, and professional hockey in general at this time, see Eric Whitehead, *Cyclone Taylor: A Hockey Legend* (Toronto: Doubleday, 1977), *passim*. In particular see Chapter 2, 'Houghton', pp. 34–53.

⁷¹See Roxborough, *The Stanley Cup Story*, p. 27.

[72]Diamond and Romain, op. cit., p. 46.

[73]Coleman, op. cit., p. xxvii.

[74]See Ron Lappage, 'The Kenora Thistles: Stanley Cup Champions', a paper presented at the 6th Canadian Symposium on the History of Sport and Physical Education, University of Western Ontario, London, June 1988, *passim*.

[75]Roxborough, *The Stanley Cup Story*, p. 32.

[76]The *Globe*, Toronto, 29 December 1900, and 9 January 1901.

[77]See Cosentino, op. cit., p. 227.

[78]Whitehead, op. cit., pp. 60–1.

[79]Ibid., pp. 106–29. This is substantiated in the 'Hockey' entry in *The Canadian Encyclopedia*, Vol. II, p. 824.

[80]For details of the first professional contract, see the *Toronto Star*, 13 November 1906.

[81]Coleman, op. cit., pp. 134–5.

[82]Ibid., pp. 178–9.

[83]Cosentino, op. cit., p. 236. The Renfrew team was called both the Creamery Kings and the Millionaires, names inspired by the business and success of their owner, Ambrose O'Brien, who was both the owner of a dairy and a multi-millionaire.

[84]Frank Selke, *Beyond the Cheering* (Toronto: McClelland and Stewart, 1962), p. 28.

[85]See Scott Young, *O'Brien* (Toronto: Ryerson Press, 1967), *passim*.

[86]Diamond and Romain, op. cit., p. 45.

[87]Cosentino, op. cit., pp. 236–7.

[88]The Ontario Professional Hockey League continued to operate until 1911, but it was continually struggling to make ends meet.

[89]*Ottawa Citizen*, 29 December 1910.

[90]Cosentino, op. cit., pp. 242–3.

[91]The material on the Patricks is drawn from Eric Whitehead, *The Patricks: Hockey's Royal Family* (Toronto: Doubleday, 1980), *passim*.

[92]See Roxborough, *The Stanley Cup Story*, p. 54.

[93]Whitehead, *The Patricks*, pp. 103–5.

[94]Ibid., p. 107.

[95]Coleman, op. cit., p. 243.

[96]Cosentino, op. cit., p. 244.

[97]Coleman, op. cit., p. 327.

[98]Cosentino, op. cit., p. 249.

[99]Coleman, *The Trail of the Stanley Cup*, p. 407.

[100]Whitehead, op. cit., p. 143.

[101]*New York Times*, 6 February 1925.

[102]Coleman, op. cit., p. 487.

[103]Dick Irvin, *Now Back to You Dick: Two Lifetimes in Hockey* (Toronto: McClelland and Stewart, 1988), p. 25.

[104]*New York Times*, 27 September 1925.

[105]Ibid., 26 September 1926.

[106]Ibid.

[107]Coleman, op. cit., vol. 2, p. 8.

[108]Irvin, op. cit., p. 25.

[109]*Fort Qu'Appelle Times*, 8 March 1988.

[110]Ernest V. Heyn, *Twelve More Sport Immortals* (New York: Bartholomew House, 1951), p. 245.

[111]Diamond and Romain, op. cit., p. 86.

[112]Coleman, op. cit., vol. 2, p. 89.

[113]Ibid.

[114]Ibid.

[115]*New York Times*, 26 August 1938.

[116]Coleman, op. cit., vol. 2, pp. 372–3.

[117]Diamond and Romain, op. cit., pp. 44–5.

[118]Robert Al Styer, *The Encyclopedia of Hockey* (New York: A.S. Barnes, 1973), p. 300.

[119]*New York Times*, 7 December 1925.

[120]Coleman, op. cit., p. xxvi.

[121]'Hart Trophy', *The Canadian Encyclopedia*, Vol. II, p. 796.

[122]Diamond and Romain, op. cit., p. 41.

[123]Whitehead, op. cit., p. 127.

[124]*New York Times*, 9 March 1925.

[125]Styer, op. cit., pp. 303–4.

[126]*Montreal Star*, 25 March 1926.

[127]The *Globe*, Toronto, 23 March 1937.

[128]John Robert Colombo, *Colombo's Canadian References* (Toronto: Oxford University Press, 1976), p. 9.

[129]*Canada's Hockey Heritage* (Toronto: Hockey Hall of Fame, 1964), p. 58.

[130]Ibid.

[131]*New York Times*, 29 September 1929 and 28 September 1930.

¹³²Heyn, op. cit., p. 247.

¹³³Neil Scully, 'Memories of Mr. Hockey', *Springfield Indians' Magazine*, n.d., p. 32. Family *Scrapbook* in the possession of Allan Shore, Regina, Saskatchewan.

¹³⁴Ibid.

¹³⁵Kyle S. Crichton 'Flash and Fury: Career and Accomplishments of Eddie Shore', *Collier's*, 24 February 1934, p. 22.

¹³⁶*New York Times*, 5 January 1934.

¹³⁷The *Globe*, Toronto, 14 February 1934.

¹³⁸Don Morrow, 'Lionel Pretoria Conacher', *Journal of Sport History*, vol. 6, no. 1 (1979), pp. 5–37.

¹³⁹See a concise history of his career and sporting life in Frank Cosentino and Don Morrow, *Lionel Conacher* (Don Mills, Ont.: Fitzhenry and Whiteside, 1981). Conacher was voted Canada's outstanding athlete of the first half-century.

¹⁴⁰Diamond and Romain, op. cit., p. 71.

¹⁴¹Coleman, op. cit., Vol. 2, p. 631.

¹⁴²The *Globe*, Toronto, 4 April 1933.

¹⁴³*New York Times*, 14 April 1933.

¹⁴⁴Fitsell, op. cit., p. 145.

¹⁴⁵Robert Collins, 'The King of Maple Leaf Gardens', *Reader's Digest*, November 1976, pp. 194–202.

¹⁴⁶Anne M. Logan, *Rare Jewel for a King: A Tribute to King Clancy* (Erin, Ont.: Boston Mills Press, 1986), pp. 37–9.

¹⁴⁷The *Globe*, Toronto, 9 November 1986.

¹⁴⁸Scott Young, *Conn Smythe: If You Can't Beat 'Em in the Alley* (Toronto: McClelland and Stewart, 1981), *passim*.

¹⁴⁹Hewitt, *Hockey Night in Canada*, p. 94.

¹⁵⁰The T. Eaton Co. not only gave the land option to Maple Leaf Gardens Inc. but it also bought $25,000 worth of stock. The land was sold to Smythe's group for the then huge sum of $350,000—a deal by today's standards. See also Stan Obodiac, *Maple Leaf Gardens: Fifty years of History* (Toronto: Kendall Hunt Publishing, 1981), p. 12.

¹⁵¹Diamond and Romain, *Hockey Hall of Fame*, p. 76. Corroborated in Hewitt, *Hockey Night in Canada*, pp. 214–15, and Irvin, *Now Back to You Dick*, pp. 107–9.

Although Hewitt became the most popular hockey broadcaster of the era, he was not the first. Pete Parker of Regina was the inaugural hockey broadcaster, giving a live play-by-play of the game between the Regina Capitals and the Edmonton Eskimos on 14 March 1923.

¹⁵²Jean R. Duperreault, 'L'Affaire Richard: A Situational Analysis of the Montreal Hockey Riot of 1955', *Canadian Journal of History of Sport*, May 1981, pp. 66–83.

¹⁵³Trent Frayne, 'Hockey's Greatest Scoring Machine', *Maclean's*, 1 November 1951, pp. 18–19 and 57–8.

¹⁵⁴Richard scored them against the Maple Leafs and the press reported the event as 'Richard 5, Toronto 1'.

¹⁵⁵See M. Richard and S. Fischler, *The Flying Frenchman: Hockey's Greatest Dynasty* (New York: Hawthorn Books, 1971).

¹⁵⁶Sidney Katz, 'The Strange Forces Behind the Richard Hockey Riot', *Maclean's*, 17 September 1955, p. 11.

¹⁵⁷*Montreal Star*, 17 March 1955; *Le Devoir*, 18 March 1955.

¹⁵⁸Jean-Marie Pellerin, *L'Idole d'un peuple: Maurice Richard* (Montreal: Les Éditions de l'Homme, 1976), p. 92.

¹⁵⁹He was voted the distinction in a 1950 Canadian Press poll. See Dean Robinson, *Howie Morenz: Hockey's First Superstar* (Erin, Ont.: Boston Mills Press, 1982).

¹⁶⁰Claude Mouton, *The Montreal Canadiens: An Illustrated History of a Hockey Dynasty* (Toronto: Key-Porter, 1987), p. 41.

¹⁶¹*Montreal Star*, 9 March 1937.

¹⁶²R. Wayne Simp , 'The China Wall: Fact or Fiction?', ,roceedings of the 6th Canadian Symposium on the History of Sport and Physical Education (University of Western Ontario, London, June 1988).

¹⁶³See front cover of Stan Obodiac, ed., *The Leafs: The First 50 Years* (Toronto: McClelland and Stewart, 1976).

¹⁶⁴Coleman, op. cit., vol. 3, p. xxx.

¹⁶⁵'Howe, Gordie', *The Canadian Encyclopedia*, Vol. II, p. 841.

¹⁶⁶'Lindsay, Ted' and 'Abel, Sid,', ibid., Vol. II, p. 1010 and Vol., I. p. 43.

[167]Gary Ronberg, 'Grand Jean, A Mighty Man Is He: Montreal vs. Boston Bruins in the East's Stanley Cup Finals', *Sports Illustrated*, 5 May 1969, pp. 24–7.

[168]Peter Axthelm, 'One More Boom or Bust for the Boomer', ibid., 14 November 1966, pp. 42–52. Also J. Bolet, 'Boom Boom', *Colliers*, 20 December 1952, pp. 48–9 and 'Boom Boom on Top', *Time*, 27 December 1954, p. 41.

[169]Coleman, op. cit., vol 3, p. xxxi.

[170]Ibid., pp. 792–3.

[171]J. Atwater, 'Golden Hawk of Hockey: B. Hull', *Saturday Evening Post*, 1 January 1966, pp. 56–9.

[172]'NHL's Stan Mikita, All-Star Center', *Sports Illustrated*, 2 September 1968, p. 37.

[173]Scott Young, *Hockey is a Battle: Punch Imlach's Own Story* (Toronto: Macmillan, 1969), *passim*.

[174]Diamond and Romain, op. cit., p. 116.

[175]B. Surface, 'Lonely Hero of Hockey: G. Worsley', *Reader's Digest*, November 1972, p. 65.

[176]See, for instance, Clive Cocking, 'Goon Hockey', *Weekend* (Toronto *Globe and Mail*), 24 January 1976, pp. 4–6.

[177]'National Hockey League', *The Canadian Encyclopedia*, Vol. II, p. 1195.

[178]Kevin Lowe and Stan Fischler, *Champions: The Making of the Edmonton Oilers* (Scarborough, Ont.: Prentice-Hall, 1988), pp. 61–77.

[179]Bill Surface, 'Blood and Ice', special to the *New York Times*, 2 February 1969.

[180]Bobby Hull, *Hockey Is My Game* (Don Mills, Ont.: Longmans, 1967), p. 96.

[181]As quoted in Jim Crerar, 'Leave the Hockey to the Kids', *Maple Leaf Gardens Programme* (n.d.), p. 48; on file at the Hockey Hall of Fame, Toronto, Ontario.

[182]*Hospital for Sick Children (Toronto) Cross-Canada Survey of Sports Injuries*, as reported in the *Catholic Register*, 8 May 1976.

[183]William McMurtry, 'Investigation and Inquiry into Violence in Amateur Hockey', *Report* submitted to the Honourable René Brunelle, Minister of Community and Social Services, 21 August 1974, Ottawa, Ont.: Queen's Printer, 1974.

[184]*New York Times*, 29 September 1970.

[185]Peter Gzowski, *The Game of Our Lives* (Toronto: McClelland and Stewart, 1981), p. 88.

[186]*Globe and Mail*, Toronto, 31 March 1989.

[187]See Jim Coleman, *Hockey Is Our Game* (Toronto: Key-Porter, 1987), *passim*.

[188]Mark Mulvoy, 'Red Faces in Canada: Russia-Team Canada Match' *Sports Illustrated*, 11 September 1972, pp. 16–19, and J. Paré, 'A Survival Plan for Canadian Hockey', *Maclean's*, January 1973, p. 6.

[189]'Canada Withdraws from World Hockey', *World Affairs*, February 1970, pp. 12–13.

[190]D. Fisher, 'Hockey Series That Challenged Canadians' View of Themselves', *International Perspectives*, November/December 1972, pp. 13–20.

[191]Tom Murray, 'Main Man in Montreal: Guy Lafleur', *Sport*, November 1975, pp. 13–20.

[192]Lowe and Fischler, op. cit., pp. 173–7.

[193]Ibid., pp. 93–5.

[194]Walter Gretzky and Jim Taylor, *Gretzky: From the Backyard Rink to the Stanley Cup* (Toronto: McClelland and Stewart, 1984), *passim*.

[195]*Globe and Mail*, Toronto, 11 August 1988.

[196]Extract from 'Hockey Players' in *Collected Poems of Al Purdy* (Toronto: McClelland and Stewart Limited, 1987), pp. 54–6; first published in *The Cariboo Horses* (1965).

[197]From Roch Carrier, 'The Hockey Sweater' in *The Hockey Sweater and Other Stories*, translated by Sheila Fischman (Toronto: House of Anansi Press Limited, 1979).

[198]Tom Sinclair-Faulkner, 'A Puckish Reflection on Religion in Canada' in Peter Slater (ed.), *Religion and Culture in Canada/Religion et culture au Canada* (Waterloo, Ont: CCSR, 1977).

9. WOMEN AND SPORT

[1]Even in 1988 women are still challenged with this view. See *Stroke* by national team-rowers Heather Clarke and Susan Gwynne-Timothy (Toronto: James Lorimer & Company, 1988), p. xii.

[2]Nancy Howell and Maxwell Howell, *Sports and Games in Canadian Life: 1700 to the Present* (Toronto: Macmillan of Canada, 1969), pp. 3–56 Only one reference to women is made in this chapter : 'The Montreal *Gazette* of October 16, 1860, carried the following: "Calisthenics: Mr. C.D. Dearnally . . . proposes forming classes of young ladies and gentlemen for instruction in this graceful accomplishment" ', p. 4.

[3]See Wendy Mitchinson, 'Historical Attitudes Towards Women and Childbirth', *Atlantis*, 4, 2, Part 2 (Spring 1979), pp. 13–34, and Angenette Parry, 'The Relation of Athletics to the Reproductive Life of Women', *American Journal of Obstetrics* 66 (September 1912), pp. 348–9.

[4]Sidney H. Aronson, 'The Sociology of the Bicycle', *Life in Society*, ed. Thomas E. Lasswell et al. (Chicago: Scott, Foresman and Company, 1965), p. 62.

[5]*Manitoba Free Press*, 5 September 1898.

[6]*The Inland Sentinel*, 10 July 1896. Cited in A. Hall, 'The Role of the Safety Bicycle in the Emancipation of Women', *Proceedings of the Second World Symposium on the History of Sport and Physical Education* (Banff, Alberta, 31 May–3 June 1971), p. 248.

[7]Helen Gurney, *Girls' Sports A Century of Progress in Ontario High Schools* (Don Mills: An OFSAA Publication, n.d.), p. 14.

[8]Yvette Walton, 'The Life and Professional Contribution of Ethel Mary Cartwright, 1880–1955', unpublished M.A. thesis, University of Western Ontario, 1976, p. 22.

[9]Frank Cosentino and Maxwell Howell, *A History of Physical Education in Canada* (Toronto: General Publishing Company Ltd., 1971), p. 44.

[10]Iveagh Munro, 'Challenging Years', in *A Fair Shake*, ed. Margaret Gillett and Kay Sibbald (Montreal: Eden Press, 1984), p. 323–4.

[11]Paula Welch, 'Interscholastic Basketball: Bane of Collegiate Physical Educator'. Paper presented at the North American Society for Sport History Annual Convention, University of Maryland, College Park, Maryland, May 1978, p. 1.

[12]National Amateur Athletic Federation. Platform Women's Division, Revised, April 1931, in Gurney, op.cit., p. 35.

[13]Play Days were still popular in Canadian universities in the late fifties and early sixties. Part of the competitive season of the McMaster University basketball team in 1964 was the West-Gu-Mac Play Day, involving teams from the University of Western Ontario, the University of Guelph, and McMaster University. Following a peaceful round-robin competition in a variety of sports, everyone gathered for a social time to eat donuts and drink coffee and juice together.

[14]Mary E. Keyes, 'The History of the Women's Athletic Committee of the Canadian Association for Health, Physical Education and Recreation, 1940–1973', unpublished Ph.D. dissertation, Ohio State University, 1980, p. 41.

[15]Keyes, op.cit. p. 25. It would have been difficult for the WAC to have operated had not such members as Dorothy Jackson, Gladys Bean, and Helen Gurney not been classmates, colleagues, and friends with American women physical educators, and thus familiar with the purpose, organization, structure, and on-going work of this American organization. When rating boards were established in Canada, U.S. Nationally Rated Officials conducted the rating sessions.

[16]Uriel Simri, *Women at the Olympic Games* (Israel: The Wingate Institute for Physical Education and Sport, 1979), p. 12.

[17]Betty Spears, 'Women in the Olympics: An Unresolved Problem', in *The Modern Olympics*, edited by Peter J. Graham and Horst Ueberhorst (Cornwall, N.Y.: Leisure Press, n.d.), p. 66.

[18]See R. Tait McKenzie, *Exercise in Education and Medicine*, 3rd. ed. (Philadelphia: W.B. Saunders, 1923), p. 278; Tait McKenzie, 'Report on Physical Education at McGill', 1892, cited in Margaret Gillett, *We Walked Warily* (Montreal: Eden Press, 1981), p. 103; Grace Ritchie, 'Discussion' in *National Council of Women of Canada Yearbook, 1895* (Montreal:John Lovell, 1896), pp. 116–17; and Bernard Macfadden, *Macfadden's Encyclopedia of Physical Culture* (New York: Macfadden Publications, Inc., 1926), p. 1043.

[19] See Alan Metcalfe, *Canada Learns to Play: The Emergence of Organized Sport, 1807–1914* (Toronto:McClelland and Stewart, 1987), pp. 47–98; K. Jones, 'Sport in Canada, 1900–1920', unpublished Ph.D dissertation, University of Alberta, 1970; P. Lindsay, 'A History of Sports in Canada, 1807–1867', unpublished Ph.D. dissertation, University of Alberta, 1969.

[20]Jean Cochrane et al., *Women in Canadian Life: Sports*. (Toronto: Fitzhenry & Whiteside, 1977), p. 35. Women did emerge as international figures in this period—in track and field, for example—but if a quantitative analysis is made of women's involvement, the post-war period in the forties and fifties may be a more appropriate time to mark the beginning of the Golden Age.

[21]Barbara Schrodt, 'Canadian Women at the Olympics: 1924 to 1976', in *Her Story in Sport: A Historical Anthology of Women in Sports*, ed. Reet Howell (West Point N.Y.: Leisure Press, 1982), p. 273. Canadian women athletes at the Olympics first won world-wide recognition with the outstanding performances of the 1928 track-and-field team, and this often overshadows the fact that these girls were not the first to represent Canada. That honour probably belongs to Cecil Smith. As a fifteen-year-old figure-skater, she was the only female member of the Canadian Olympic team that attended the first Winter Games in Chamonix, France, in 1924.

[22]Simri, op.cit., p. 66.

[23]Ibid., p. 274

[24]Ibid.

[25]Ibid., p. 66.

[26]Cochrane, op.cit., p. 41.

[27]Frank Cosentino and G. Leyshon, *Olympic Gold: Canada's Winners in the Summer Games* (Toronto: Holt, Rinehart and Winston of Canada, Ltd., 1975), p. 93.

[28]Ibid., p. 94.

[29]S.F.Wise and Douglas Fisher, *Canada's Sporting Heroes* (Don Mills: General Publishing Company, 1974), p. 80.

[30]Schrodt, op. cit., p. 274.

[31]David McDonald and Lauren Drewery, *For the Record: Canada's Greatest Women Athletes* (Rexdale: John Wiley & Sons Canada, Limited, 1981), p. 12.

[32]John D. Eaton, 'Dr. A.S. Lamb—His Influence on Canadian Sport', *Proceedings of the First Canadian Symposium on the History of Sport and Physical Education*, Edmonton: University of Alberta, 13–16 May 1970, pp. 424–5.

[33]McDonald, op.cit., p. 12.

[34]McDonald, op.cit., p. 60

[35]McDonald, op.cit., pp. 56–7.

[36]J.P. Paret, 'Basket-Ball for Young Women,' *Harper's Bazaar*, 20 Oct. 1900, p. 1563.

[37]Elmer W. Ferguson, 'I Don't Like Amazon Athletes', *Maclean's Magazine*, 1 August 1938, pp. 9, 32.

[38]Sportswriters such as Myrtle Cook ('In the Women's Sportlight, 'Montreal *Daily Star*, 1929 to 1955) and Bobbie Rosenfeld ('Feminine Sports Reel', later 'Sports Reel', *Globe and Mail*, 1938–59) tried to change the negative view of the female athlete.

[39]Graham Cox, 'Barbara Ann Scott: The Girl Who Changed Figure Skating Forever', *Winners: A Century of Canadian Sport* (Toronto: Grosvenor House Press Inc., 1985), pp. 28–9. Cox is convinced that Scott changed figure-skating from the 'basic gliding and swooping' of Sonja Henie to a more 'athletic style' because Barbara Ann included in her 1947 World

Championship four-minute free-skate 'three double salchows, three double loop jumps in succession' that gained her the perfect 6.0 mark from two judges. Although little attention was given to this by the press of the time, her performance changed the expectations for female skaters. Jumps that had previously been performed only by men became an expected part of women's free-skating.

[40]McDonald, op.cit, p. 69.

[41]For example, between 1974 and 1978 Cindy Nicholas crossed Lake Ontario in record time, crossed the English Channel in a record two-way crossing-time, and concurrently was a student pursuing a law degree. By the summer of 1987 swimming Lake Ontario seemed commonplace when Vicki Keith swam around Lake Ontario in aid of Muscular Scelerosis; in 1988 she swam across each of the Great Lakes raising money for Variety Village.

[42]Toronto *Star*, 8 March 1956.

[43]Fred McFadden, *Abby Hoffman* (Don Mills: Fitzhenry &Whiteside Ltd. 1978), pp. 38–9.

[44]Abby Hoffman, presentation at 'A Renaissance in Sport and Fitness, a Toronto Conference organized by the Ontario Women's Intercollegiate Athletic Association', 1983.

[45]Keyes, op. cit., pp. 81–99.

[46]*Report of the Royal Commission on the Status of Women* (Ottawa: Information Canada, 1970), pp. 185–7.

[47]*What's Been Done?* A Report by the Advisory Council on the Status of Women, March 1974, p. 15.

[48]*Report: National Conference on Women and Sport*, Toronto, 24–6 May, 1974.

[49]Following the 'Female Athlete Conference', held at Simon Fraser University in March 1980, the women's sport consultant from Fitness and Amateur Sport, Susan Vail, invited a group of women (Betty Baxter, Abby Hoffman, Dorothy Richardson, Ann Pompa, Rose Mercier, and Mary Keyes) to work with her in promoting programs for women. The 1980 program-initiatives were the result of this planning process.

[50]Many national players have discussed their competitive and post-competitive problems. Books such as Heather Clarke and Susan Gwynne-Timothy's *Stroke*, (1988) about women rowers, and *Jump* (1986), Debbie Brill's autobiography, suggest strongly that a new view to accommodate women in high-performance sport is required.

[51]Compiled from personal notes from the Women's Program Advisory Committee meetings 1980–1, and summarized by Susan Vail, Women's Program Consultant, Sport Canada.

[52]*Webster's New Twentieth Century Dictionary*, Second Edition (World Publishing Company New York, 1962).

[53]CAAWS, for example, acted as a friend of the court in the Justine Blainey case, and clarified the human-rights issues. Justine Blainey challenged the Ontario Minor Hockey Association and the Ontario Women's Hockey Association in an Ontario Human Rights Commission Appeal because she was denied the opportunity to play on a boys' hockey team in Toronto. The Commission ruled in her favour, thus permitting her to play on a boys' team, and at the same time designated women's ice hockey a 'special program', thus protecting it from boys playing on a girls' team. Both CAAWS and the Sport Canada Women's Policy recommend integrated sport (boys and girls playing on the same team).

[54]M. Ann Hall and Dorothy A. Richardson, *Fair Ball Towards Sex Equality in Canadian Sport* (Ottawa: The Canadian Advisory Council on the Status of Women, 1982).

[55]Several Human Rights Legislation cases have been taken to Human Rights Commissions for resolution. In addition, several female athletes have challenged discrimination against their participation in sport through the courts, e.g.

Bannerman *vs.* the Ontario Rural Softball Association, Cummings *vs.* the Ontario Minor Hockey Association, Blainey *vs.* the Ontario Minor Hockey Association. This is still a controversial issue that has not been satisfactorily debated and resolved among women sports leaders.

[56]Helen Lenskyj, *Women, Sport and Physical Activity: Research and Bibiliography* (Ottawa: Minister of State Fitness and Amateur Sport, 1988).

[57]This issue was brought forward spontaneously at the second meeting of CAAWS held at McMaster University in 1982. Several women in attendance, not wanting to be associated with a 'lesbian cause', withdrew also from active support of the new organization. Others took an active stance and argued that feminism was important for the future development of sport, but that lesbianism was a personal sexual preference and should not be associated with or promoted in the sporting context.

[58]Lenskyj, op.cit., p. 40.

[59]Although Justine Blainey was granted the opportunity to play on a boys' hockey team in Toronto by a Human Rights Ruling in December 1987, parents of boys playing on the team she joined were opposed to this ruling and petitioned the Metropolitan Toronto Hockey League to challenge it.

[60]Of the 21 new sports accepted into Olympic competition in April 1989, the majority were women's sports. IOC President Samaranch acknowledged that the rationale for adding even more sports to the already crowded Olympic schedule was to give more equality to the women athletes. CBC Interview, 27 April, 1989.

[61]Robert Fulford, *Best Seat in the House* (Toronto: Collins Publishers, 1988), pp. 31–2.

[62]L.V. Kavanagh, *History of Golf in Canada* (Toronto: Fitzhenry and Whiteside Limited, 1973), p. 122.

[63]Ibid., p. 123.

[64]Ibid.

[65]Trent Frayne, *The Best of Times: Fifty Years of Canadian Sport* (Toronto, Key Porter Books, 1988), p. 49.

[66]Douglas Howe, 'Blonde on Blades', *Maclean's*, 15 February 1947.

[67]Cox, op.cit., p. 28.

[68]Susan Swain, 'Barbara Ann—Are You Still Happy?', *Chatelaine* (November 1975), pp. 51, 74, 76, 78, 80–2, 84,85, and David McDonald and Lauren Drewery, *For The Record: Canada's Greatest Women Athletes* (Rexdale, Ontario: John Wiley & Sons Canada Ltd., 1981), p. 67.

[69]Nancy Greene, *Nancy Greene: An Autobiography* (Don Mills: Pagurian Press, 1971), p. 60.

[70]Ibid., p. 168–9.

10. SPORT AND TECHNOLOGICAL CHANGE

[1]Several sources were used for this summary of nineteenth-century sport and technological change. See S.F. Wise and D. Fisher, *Canada's Sporting Heroes* (Toronto: General Publishing, 1974); Maxwell L. Howell and Reet A. Howell, *History of Sport in Canada* (Champaign, Illinois: Stipes Publishing Co., 1985); Peter Lindsay, 'A History of Sport in Canada, 1807–1867' (unpublished doctoral dissertation, University of Alberta, 1969); Allan E. Cox, 'A History of Sport in Canada, 1868–1900' (unpublished doctoral dissertation, University of Alberta, 1969); Kevin G. Jones, 'Sport in Canada, 1900–1920' (unpublished doctoral dissertation, University of Alberta, 1970); Ian F. Jobling, 'Sport in Nineteenth Century Canada: The Effects of Technological Changes on Its Development' (unpublished doctoral dissertation, University of Alberta, 1970); Gerald Redmond, *The Sporting Scots of Nineteenth-Century Canada* (Toronto: Associated University Presses, 1982); and Alan Metcalfe, *Canada Learns To Play: The Emergence of Organized Sport, 1807–1914* (Toronto: McClelland and Stewart, 1987).

[2]See Richard S. Gruneau, 'Sport as an Area of Sociological Study: An Introduction to Major Themes and Perspectives' in *Canadian Sport Sociological Perspectives*, eds. Richard S. Gruneau and John G. Albinson (Don Mills: Addison-Wesley (Canada) Limited, 1976), p. 18. Gruneau diagrammatically presents the socio-historical development of sport from a play form (unorganized and unstructured), through the games phase (systematization, regulation, and transmission) to sport (institutionalization, legitimation, bureaucratization, and rationalization).

[3]*The Canadian Encyclopedia*, Vol.III (Edmonton: Hurtig Publishers Ltd., 1985), p. 1791.

[4]T. Williams, 'Cheap Rates, Special Trains and Canadian Sport in the 1850's', *Canadian Journal of the History of Sport*, XII, 2 (December, 1981), pp. 84–95.

[5]Ian F. Jobling, 'Urbanization and Sport in Canada, 1867–1900', in *Canadian Sport Sociological Perspectives*, op. cit., p. 67.

[6]Ibid., p. 68.

[7]The *Globe*, Toronto, accumulated sports photographs between 1860 and the 1890s. When the photographs began to appear in newspapers during the nineties the *Globe* published a Saturday supplement, beginning in 1896, containing this collection.

[8]Peter L. Lindsay, 'The Pioneer Years Prior to Confederation', in Howell and Howell, op.cit., p. 62.

[9]Metcalfe, 1987, op. cit., pp. 49–54.

[10]*Hamilton Times*, 10 July 1863.

[11]Wise and Fisher, op. cit., p. 83.

[12]They are still held on this August weekend. Newfoundlanders were given a half-holiday from work because there was such keen interest in the race and in the money waged on its results. 'Respectable' people were said to avoid the events because of the nature of the festivities. Governor Sir Herbert Murray refused to attend in 1897 'because it was not patronized by the best people.' Wise and Fisher, op. cit., p. 83.

[13]Roxborough, op. cit., p. 180.

[14]A railway spur line was even built along the shore parallel to the race course at Mayville, N.Y., in 1879 for spectators to follow the race between Hanlan and Courtney.

[15]See Roxborough, *One Hundred—Not Out*, op.cit.; Redmond, *The Sporting Scots*, op. cit.; Wise and Fisher, *Canada's Sporting Heroes*, op. cit.

[16]The Prince Edward Island Caledonia Club was organized in 1838 and still has annual Games with athletics, dancing, and piping. Redmond, op. cit., p. 160–2.

[17]Redmond, op. cit., p. 166.

[18]Sir John A. Macdonald, Canada's first Prime Minister, regularly attended these Games.

[19]Redmond, op. cit., p. 187.

[20]First Annual Report of the Amateur Athletic Association of Canada, 1884, p. 6.

[21]A Montreal contingent withdrew from membership in 1906 because many of the lacrosse competitions they sponsored were semi-professional. These members wanted the amateur code redefined to permit play between professionals and amateurs without loss of amateur status for the amateur athlete. The Montreal group withdrew, forming the Amateur Athletic Federation of Canada, which waged war with the AAAC for many years.

[22]See Chapter 11, 'Canada at the Olympic Games', for details about these athletes.

[23]John McNair, *The Channel Stane, or Sweeping Frae the Rinks*, 4 vols. (1883–85), 1: 73–73, as quoted in Edwin C. Guillet, *Pioneer Days in Upper Canada* (Toronto: University of Toronto Press, 1970), pp. 208–9.

[24]*Montreal Star*, January 1934, cited in Redmond, op. cit., p. 108.

[25]As quoted in John A. Stevenson, *Curling in Ontario, 1846–1946* (Toronto: Ontario Curling Association, 1950), p. 23. Social activities and alcoholic refreshments following a game are still an important curling tradition.

[26]James Young wrote that the curlers in Galt 1836–37 'made blocks out of the maple tree, putting in pieces of iron as handles'. James Young, *Early History of Galt and the Settlement of Dumfries* (Toronto: Hunter, Rose and Co., 1880), p. 127.

[27]Redmond, op. cit., p. 112.

[28]*Montreal Gazette*, 10 January 1855.

[29]The *Globe*, Toronto, 9 February 1859.

[30]Ibid. p. 130. The Strathcona Cup was to be used for international competition between Canada and Scotland.

[31]The *Globe*, Toronto, 13 February 1879.

[32]The Scottish team won 47, lost 49, and drew 3.

[33]On CBC Sports in 1989 the men's championship in Saskatoon was televised 11–18 March; the following week the world juniors in Markham, Ontario; the following week, 25 March, Canadian junior finals in Winnipeg, Manitoba; men's and women's world championships in Milwaukee the following week. 'Wittman needs his photographic memory', *TV Times*, 25 February 1989, p. 48.

[34]Jack Ludwig, 'Rocks of All Ages', *Maclean's*, February 1974, p. 26.

[35]G. W. Bowie, 'An Affectionate Look at Curling in Canada', *Proceedings of the First Canadian Symposium on the History of Sport and Physical Education* (Edmonton, Alberta: University of Alberta, 13–16 May 1970), p. 207.

[36]See Roxborough, *One Hundred—Not Out*, op. cit., p. 105; Howell and Howell, op. cit., p. 50.

[37]L.V. Kavanagh, in *History of Golf in Canada* (Toronto: Fitzhenry and Whiteside Limited, 1973), p. 1, states that the Quebec club was founded in 1874. But William Perkins Bull, in *From Rattlesnake Hunt to Hockey* (Toronto: The Perkins Bull Foundation, George J McLeod Ltd., 1934), p. 191, says it was founded 'two years later' than the Montreal Club, founded in 1873—which would make the date 1875.

[38]L.V. Kavanagh, op. cit., p. 1.

[39]The Mississauga Club, which opened in 1906 with a membership of 60 and an annual playing fee of $15, occupied 200 acres of land that cost $12,000. William Perkins Bull, op. cit., p. 188.

[40]'Ladies' golf is the term used for the female golf-club members. In recent years at many golf clubs energetic arguments have been voiced by feminist members who would prefer the term 'women's' golf, but few clubs have changed their terminology.

[41]*Winnipeg Free Press*, 4 September 1896, cited in Howell, op. cit., p. 131.

[42]Kavanagh, op. cit., p. 9–10.

[43]Statutes of Canada, 1845, pp. 263–4.

[44]Bull, op. cit., p. 183.

[45]Ibid.

[46]Ibid., p. 18.

[47]George Cumming won the Canadian Open in 1905 and was runner-up in that tournament on four occasions (1906, 1907, 1909, 1914). Also in 1905, he tied for the lowest eighteen-hole score in the U.S. Open, finishing in eighth place. In 1914 he won the Canadian PGA Championship and three other times tied for runner-up spot (1912, 1919, and 1924).

[48]Kavanagh, op. cit., p. 112.

[49]Wise and Fisher, op. cit., p. 260.

[50]Kavanagh, op. cit., p. 147.

[51]*New York Times*, 29 November 1939, cited in B. L. Webb, *The Basketball Man: James Naismith* (Lawrence: The University Press of Kansas, 1973), p. 62.

[52]Letter from J. H. Crocker to Dr James Naismith, 11 December 1930.

[53]H. C. Cross, *One Hundred Years of Service with Youth: The Story of the Montreal Y.M.C.A., 1851–1951* (Montreal: Southam Press, 1951), p. 175.

[54]The *Globe*, Toronto, 27 December 1902.

[55]The *Globe*, Toronto, 20 December 1895.

[56]Murray C. Ross, 'The Toronto Y.M.C.A. in a Changing Community 1864–1940', unpublished M.A. thesis, University of Toronto, 1947, p. 234.

[57]Wise and Fisher, op. cit., p. 77.

[58]See James Christie, *Ben Johnson: The Fastest Man on Earth* (Toronto: McClelland

Bantam Inc., 1988); Brian Orser with Steve Milton, *Orser: A Skater's Life* (Toronto: Key Porter Books Limited, 1988); Debbie Brill with James Lawton, *Jump* (Vancouver: Douglas & McIntyre, 1986); Peter Gzowski, *The Games of Our Lives* (Toronto: McClelland and Stewart, 1981); Trent Frayne, *The Best of Times: Fifty Years of Canadian Sport* (Toronto: Key Porter Books Ltd., 1988); Wendy Bryden, *Canada at the Olympic Winter Games* (Edmonton: Hurtig Publishers Ltd., 1987); and *XV Olympic Winter Games Official Report* (Edmonton: The Jasper Printing Group Ltd., 1988).

59The announcement of Sport Discus by SilverPlatter Information, Inc. For $1,250 Sport Discus on CD-ROM can bring the resource of an international library into the homes of coaches in every corner of the country.

60Donn Downey, 'Foster Hewitt Broadcast Was Voice of Hockey', *Globe and Mail*, 22 April 1985.

61For primary sources consulted see: Everette E. Dennis and Huntington Williams III, eds., 'Sports and Mass Media', *Gannett Centre Journal*, Vol. 1, No. 2, Fall 1987; William O. Johnson, Jr. *Super Spectator and the Electric Lilliputians* (Boston: Little, Brown, 1971); David A. Klatell and Norman Marcus, *Sport for Sale: Television, Money and Fans* (New York: Oxford University Press, 1988); Roger Noll ed., *Government and Sports Business.* (Washington, D. C.: Brookings Institute, 1974); Benjamin G. Rader, *In Its Own Image* (New York: Macmillan, 1984).

62David Klatell and Norman Marcus, op. cit., p. 5.

63'Television and Radio', *1989 Britannica Book of the Year* (Chicago: Encyclopaedia Britannica, Inc., 1989), p. 363.

64TSN is a popular television network dedicated to sport broadcasting.

65David McDonald and Lauren Drewery, *For the Record: Canada's Greatest Women Athletes* (Rexdale: John Wiley & Sons Canada, Limited, 1981), p. 56.

66E. McRae and R. MacGregor, 'Executive Sweat: Gentlemen, Players and other People Who Make Sport', *The Canadian*, 29 January 1977, pp. 4–9.

67McRae and MacGregor, op. cit., p. 6.

68James R. Christie, *Ben Johnson: The Fastest Man on Earth* (Toronto: McClelland-Bantam Inc., 1988), pp. 133–4.

69Ibid.

70*XV Olympic Winter Games: Official Report*, op. cit., p. 327. Corporations not only made financial, product or service contributions, they also undertook activities that enhanced the visibility of the Olympic Movement. $90 million was generated from 169 corporations, including 21 sponsors, 30 suppliers, 40 licensees, 27 contributors, and one donor.

71Lou Lafaive, President of the Sport Marketing Board, has been vocal in commenting about this sport-funding concern. It was discussed at length at the COA meeting in April 1989 and prompted many Executive Directors from the NSOs to propose their own slate of nominees to the COA Board, hoping to open the COA coffers. Roger Jackson, the incumbent President, was re-elected to a fourth term by only one vote and commented that he had gained opposition because he did not want to spend the capital in the short term to assist NSOs with their declining financial situation.

72Don Kowet, 'For Better or For Worse,' *TV Guide* 26 (1 July 1978), pp. 2–4, 6.

73Wilbert Marcellus Leonard II, *A Sociological Perspective of Sport* 3rd. ed. (New York: Macmillan Publishing Company, 1988), p. 429.

74Commonwealth Games, Vancouver (1954); Pan Am Games, Winnipeg (1967); Olympics, Montreal (1976); Commonwealth Games, Edmonton (1978); FISU Games, Edmonton (1983); and Winter Olympics, Calgary (1988). These events raised the level of spectator appreciation of the techniques of élite-sport arm-chair critics developed while watching these events. In recent multi-sport presentations the networks presenting the Games have used sport films, sport memorabilia, and sport heritage in the months leading up to the event to 'educate' the viewing public. The 'Road to Seoul', prepared by CBC researchers and reporters, gave pertinent information to TV viewers about Seoul, about the Olympics, about past Canadian Olympic performances of note, and biographical profiles of the Canadian team preparing to participate

[75]Redmond, op. cit., p. 345.

[76]CBC interview following the Canada Cup race, February 1989.

[77]XV Olympic Report, op. cit., p. 145.

[78]Christian Belpaire, 'Edifice Rex', Toronto, May 1989, p. 28.

[79]Global News, 16 April 1989.

[80]Patrick Morrow, Beyond Everest: Quest for the Seven Summits (Camden East: Camden House Publishing, 1986), p. 141.

[81]Personal interview with Stephen Kelly, 30 April 1989.

11. CANADA AT THE OLYMPIC GAMES

[1]G.Redmond, 'Prologue and Transition: the "Pseudo-Olympics" of the Nineteenth Century', in Olympism, ed. J. Segrave/D. Chu (Champaign, Illinois: Human Kinetics Publishers, Inc., 1981), pp. 20–1.

[2]J.A. Lucas, 'Baron Pierre de Coubertin and the Formative Years of the Modern International Olympic Movement, 1833–1896', unpublished doctoral dissertation, University of Maryland, 1962, pp. 99, 176–8.

[3]J.A. Lucas, 'The Genesis of the Modern Olympic Games' in Olympism, p. 26.

[4]P. de Coubertin, 'Olympism and the IOC'. Address to the Olympic Congress, Prague, 29 May 1925, Bulletin du C.I.O., January 1951, pp. 15–16.

[5]It is interesting to note that many in the sporting world want to return the Games to Greece in 1996 to celebrate the 100th anniversary of the Olympic Games re-

vival. The European community is rumoured to have contributed more than $3 billion to help construct new facilities.

[6]Steeplechases were held in 1900 (two races), 1904, and 1908, but none were over obstacles or at distances comparable with the existing event (3,000 metres). No steeplechase event was held in 1896, 1906, or 1912. Guinness Book of Olympic Records (Toronto, 1988), p. 174.

[7]This event was dropped from Olympic events after 1920. In Henry Roxborough, Canada at the Olympics (Toronto, 1963), p. 25, Étienne is alleged to have thrown 34' 4", but this writer could not find an official record of the throw, and Roxborough does not document the source of his information.

[8]George Seymour Lyons (1858–1938), of Toronto, was an accomplished athlete who played football, soccer, baseball, curling, lawn-bowling, cricket, and was a Canadian record-holder in the pole-vault. In the 1904 Olympics he won the gold medal in golf, the only time this event was held in Olympic competition. But few Olympians regard golf as a recognized Olympic sport, and this is not recorded in the Guinness Book of Olympic Records.

[9]The Times (London), 31 July 1908.

[10]John Howard Crocker, Report of the First Canadian Olympic Athletic Team (1908), pp. 11–12.

[11]Ibid., p. 4.

[12]Henry Roxborough, op. cit., p. 57.

[13]The Rt Hon. Philip Noel-Baker, writing about the Amsterdam Olympics, observed that Jim Ball made every mistake imaginable in placing second. 'Ball apparently forgot that, as was the practice in the 400 metres in those days, he could break from the lanes in the back straight. Instead, he carried on in his lane and must have run several yards further than anyone else. Ball was beaten only by inches, and photos show him at the tape looking so wildly and so abstractedly over his left shoulder that that alone must have cost him his first place.' The Olympic

Games: 80 Years of People, Events and Records, ed. Lord Killanin and John Rodda (Don Mills, 1976), p. 51.

14Hand-timing remained official, but the system was used as a back-up.

15*New York Times*, 31 July 1932.

16Ibid. Hilda Strike won a second in the 100-metres, as did the 400-metre relay team of Mary Frizell, Mildred Fizzell, Lillian Palmer, and Hilda Strike. *Guinness Book of Olympic Records* (Toronto, 1988), pp. 186, 191.

17Roxborough, op.cit., p.83. Ethel Catherwood, who died in April 1988, refused interviews following the 1928 Games because the press were more interested in her beauty than in her athletic performance. Unfortunately the stereotype of the 'baby grand piano' image persisted well past the 1932 Games.

18Tom West, 'Hilda Strike: Should 1932 Gold Be Hers?', *Champion*, April 1983, p. 11.

19The importance of television to the survival of the Olympic Games must not be forgotten. Since 1936 it has become a major influence—a source of revenue for both the IOC and the organizing committee, but also a communication phenomenon that links, for two or three weeks every four years, spectators worldwide to see not only the athletic feats but the pageantry surrounding the games, which often seems more real than the athletic events.

20'Olympic Games', the *Spectator*, London, 7 August 1936.

21Richard D. Mandell, *The Nazi Olympics* (New York, 1971), p. 228.

22*Speeches of President Avery Brundage: 1952–1968* (Lausanne: Comité International Olympique, 26 January 1964, 61st Session of IOC, Innsbruck), pp.73–4.

23These details on the Munich massacre are taken from Serge Groussard's *The Blood of Israel*, trans. Harold J. Salemson (New York: William Morrow, 1975).

24Allan Guttmann, *The Games Must Go On* (New York, 1984), p. 254.

25Ibid.

26See Brian McKenna and Susan Purcell, *Drapeau* (Markham, Ontario: Penguin Books Canada Ltd., 1981), p. 262.

27The research Drapeau did was masterful: there were dossiers on each IOC delegate, the views of each were recorded, with their likes and dislikes in food and drink. Nothing was left to chance the second time around.

28*New York Times*, 15 October 1974.

29*Sports Illustrated*, 45 (3), 19 July 1976, p. 34.

30A thorough discussion of the many problems associated with the Games that resulted in a billion-dollar overrun is discussed from a Montreal councillor's perspective in Nick Auf der Maur, *The Billion-Dollar Game* (Toronto, 1976), and from the mayor's perspective in Brian McKenna and Susan Purcell, *Drapeau* (op. cit.).

31*New York Times*, 15 October 1975.

32*The Gazette*, Montreal, 6 June 1980, p. 7.

33The re-emergence of the People's Republic of China (PRC) in sport began with their participation in the table-tennis world championships in Japan in 1971. In 1971 the United Nations recognized the PRC and expelled Taiwan. This facilitated the re-examination of the PRC by the sporting world. Overtures were made early in 1973 by the Japanese Olympic Committee to request the IOC to admit the PRC for membership. China would not join, however, if Taiwan maintained membership. The PRC was a member of only two federations, table-tennis and ice hockey, and had to acquire membership in at least five recognized federations whose sports were on the Olympic program, and to establish an Olympic committee. By April 1975 the PRC was a member of 9 federations and had applied for IOC membership. The IOC was reluctant to make a decision. The PRC claimed jurisdiction over all China, including Taiwan, but would not accept dual membership. On the other hand, the Taiwan committee had been a member for more than twenty years and was not opposed to dual-membership.

[34]The American press was much more negative than the Canadian press; but several Canadian papers, including the Southam chain, condemned the government. New York Times, 11 July 1976; Los Angeles Times, 11 July 1976.

[35]Globe and Mail, Toronto, 11 July 1976.

[36]Ibid.

[37]Canadian Embassy, Public Affairs Division, 'Olympics and Taiwan', Canada Report, no. 4, 22 July 1976, p. 2.

[38]Sports Illustrated, 16 August 1976, p. 7.

[39]The Times (London), 4 May 1976.

[40]Globe and Mail, 10 July 1976.

[41]Sports Illustrated, 45(4), 26 July 1976, p. 17.

[42]Olympic Review, statement of vice-president Mohamen Mzali, no. 107–8 (September-October 1976), pp. 463–4.

[43]Lord Killanin, My Olympic Years (London, Secker & Warburg, 1983), p.120.

[44]Globe and Mail, 5 January 1980.

[45]Ibid., 8 January 1980.

[46]Ibid.

[47]Ibid., 28 January, 1980.

[48]Edmonton Journal, 28 March 1980.

[49]Globe and Mail, 3 April 1980.

[50]Ibid., 3 April 1980.

[51]This view is too simplistic. The Soviet-led boycott probably had several causes: retaliation for President Carter's boycott of the 1980 Moscow Olympics; fear of demonstrations against, and defections by, Soviet athletes; the tensions in American-Soviet relations; and concern over the athletic ability of their team. All of these factors are more plausible than the single explanation given in the Soviet communication.

[52]'Special Report—Are the Olympics Dead?', Newsweek, 21 May 1984, p. 18.

[53]Peter Ueberroth, Made in America (New York, 1985), p. 286.

[54]The Los Angeles Olympic Organizing Committee. News Release, 3 June 1984.

[55]Kevin Cox, 'Olympic Committee Reports $32-million profit', Globe and Mail, 2 March 1985.

[56]Ibid.

[57]Ian Buruma, 'Playing For Keeps,' The New York Review of Books, 10 November 1988, pp.44–50. Buruma felt Eddie Edwards exemplified Coubertin's Olympic ideal: just to take part was enough, winning was irrelevant. But many at Calgary felt Eddie denigrated the Olympic goal of excellence. Abby Hoffman, Director-General of Sport Canada, felt he should not have been allowed to participate and that minimum standards should be met by all athletes wanting to compete.

[58]NBC paid $300 million for the Seoul Games and ABC paid a record $309 million for the US broadcasting contract for the 1988 Calgary Games. Richard Pound revealed that perhaps $430 million(US) would be made from the 1992 Barcelona Olympics. Globe and Mail, 24 November 1988. When the contract was signed in early 1989, NBC guaranteed $401 million (US).

[59]North Korea, Cuba, Ethiopia, Albania, Nicaragua, and the Seychelles did not send athletes to Seoul. Thus six of the 167 invited nations were not represented. Cuba's boxers and baseball players, and Ethiopia's marathon runners, are world-class athletes and were missed in their competitions.

[60]Hugh McIlvanney, 'Olympic dream or nightmare? Drugs, violence, politics and crass commercialism have combined to erode the pinnacle of sport', London Observer, 11 September 1988.

[61]'Security measures impress Samaranch', The Sunday Star, Toronto, 11 September 1988.

[62]'Ottawa Probes Steroid Abuse', Hamilton Spectator, 16 September 1988.

[63]Conference Report, First Permanent World Conference on Antidoping in Sport, Ottawa, Canada, 26–9 June 1988.

[64]The Charter prepared in June was accepted by the IOC and sports ministers

around the world at a meeting of the IOC in Moscow in November. All agreed to try to eliminate drug usage in sport. *Globe and Mail*, 25 November 1988.

[65]'Symbols abound in Seoul', *Hamilton Spectator*, 17 September 1988.

[66]Rumours circulated, following the Olympics, that several more positive test-results had been discovered in Seoul, but that the IOC had suppressed the information to protect the image of the Games. On 17 November 1988 the first of a series of articles appeared in the *New York Times* alleging that 'as many as 20 other athletes tested positive and were not disqualified'. Dr Park Jong Sei, director of the Seoul drug-testing lab, is quoted as saying he voted in the minority to disqualify an athlete who had tested positive. He would not identify any of the athletes with positive tests in Seoul who were not disqualified, other than to say one was an American and the others 'mostly Europeans'. Michael Janofsky and Peter Alfano, 'Experts Claim Half Olympians Used Drugs', *Globe and Mail*, 18 November 1988.

[67]John Kernaghan, 'Medal Mission', *Hamilton Spectator*, 15 September 1988.

[68]*Saturday Star*, Toronto, 24 September 1988; *Hamilton Spectator*, 24 September 1988; *Sunday Star*, Toronto, 25 September 1988.

[69]'Only Canadian Hearts Raced Faster Than Mighty Johnson', *Hamilton Spectator*, 24 September 1988.

[70]Prior to the opening of the Games, the COA was predicting 18 medals. On every occasion COA officials reminded the Canadian public not to expect as many medals as were won at Los Angeles because all nations were to be at Seoul and competition would be tougher for the Canadian athletes.

[71]*Globe and Mail*, 27 September 1988; *Hamilton Spectator*, 27 September 1988.

[72]John Kernaghan, 'A Nation's Heart Broken by Ben's Fall From Grace', *Hamilton Spectator*, 27 September 1988.

[73]*Hamilton Spectator*, 27 September 1988.

[74]'Astaphan Supplied Steroids, Story Says', *Globe and Mail*, 29 September 1988.

[75]Press Release, The College of Physicians and Surgeons of Ontario, 30 September 1988.

[76]'Commission of Inquiry Into the Use of Drugs and Banned Practices Intended to Increase Athletic Performance'.

[77]Justice Charles Dubin, Opening Remarks, 'Commission of Inquiry Into the Use of Drugs and Banned Practices Intended to Increase Athletic Performance' held at the Royal York Hotel, Toronto, 15 November 1988.

[78]Ibid.

[79]'Dubin inquiry bill 3.74m', *Hamilton Spectator*, 29 April 1989.

[80]Cecil Smith, 'The Inside Track', *Athletics*, January 1989, p. 26.

[81]Bruce Kidd, 'Olympic Views', *Athletics*, January 1989, p. 8.

[82]It would be unfortunate for sport, and the athletes who participate, if the results of this investigation do not improve sport practices and change the 'win-at-all-cost attitude' that has permeated sport in recent years. All too often significant studies gather dust on shelves and recommendations are too soon forgotten. For example, William R. McMurtry, *Investigation and Inquiry into Violence in Amateur Hockey* (Ministry of Community and Social Services Under the Public Inquiries Act, 1971 and Under the Athletics Control Act, R.S.O. 1970, 1974, Chapter 35) has not impacted on the National Hockey League, where violence is most prevalent. Amateur hockey is trying to eliminate violence; but with the professional model provided, it is very difficult for youth to comply.

[83]The use of anabolic steroids by athletes in international competition appears to have been first detected in 1954. Their widespread use, which some writers have expressed as having reached 'epidemic proportions', was demonstrated in 1983 in the Pan-American Games in Caracas, Venezuela, when 19 competitors were

disqualified after their drug-use was detected. As reported, dozens more of the athletes voluntarily withdrew from the Games, apparently in fear of the stringent drug-testing techniques.

[84]Philip Goodhart M.P. and Christopher Chataway, *War Without Weapons* (London: W.H. Allen, 1968).

[85]Body-building clubs report increased interest in and purchase of anabolic steroids by men using their facilities since the Seoul Olympics.

[86]For a detailed discussion of the development of amateurism, see, for example: Bruce Kidd, *The Political Economy of Sport* (Ottawa: CAHPER, n.d.), pp.54–7; Alan Metcalfe, *Canada Learns to Play The Emergence of Organized Sport, 1807–1914* (Toronto, McClelland and Stewart Limited, 1987), pp. 99–132; Lord Killanin and John Rodda, *My Olympic Years*; Harold J. VanderZwaag, 'Amateurism and the Olympic Games' in P.J. Graham and Horst Ueberhorst (eds.), *The Modern Olympics* (Cornwall, N.Y.: Leisure Press, nd.), pp. 83–106.

[87]'The International Athletic Congress', *The Times* (London), 23 June 1894, p. 9.

[88]Ibid.

[89]Ibid.

[90]'Report of the Conference held by Delegates of the International Sports Federations with the Committee on Amateurism Nominated in Vienna', *Official Bulletin*, International Olympic Committee, XII (October 1937), p. 7.

[91]Trent Frayne, *The Best of Times: Fifty Years of Canadian Sport* (Toronto: Key Porter Books), p. 51. Avery Brundage was IOC vice-president and member of the IOC from the United Sates, not president, as Frayne suggests; however, these sentiments were often expressed while Brundage was president.

[92]*The Olympic Games, Fundamental Principles, Rules and Regulations, General Information* (Lausanne, 1956), p. 77.

[93]C. Thayer, 'A question of soul', *Sports Illustrated*, 15 August 1960, p.7 4.

[94]Circular, no. AB/M/487, to IOC members, 26 April 1969, Box 71, University of Illinois, Archives, Avery Brundage Collection, 1908–1975.

[95]For the 1960 Rome Games the total television rights were sold for approximately $1.2 million. In 1968 ABC paid $2 million for the competition at Grenoble. The television rights for the 1972 Munich Olympics cost ABC $13.5 million and NBC $6.4 million. American rights to the 1976 Games in Montreal were $25 million; ABC Sports spent $40 million to televise them. NBC paid the Moscow Organizing Committee $85 million for the two-week Moscow spectacle. The United States television rights to the 1984 Summer Olympics in Los Angeles sold to ABC for $225 million. International rights garnered another $80 million approximately. NBC paid $300 million for the Seoul Games and ABC paid a record $309 million for the US broadcasting contract for the 1988 Calgary Games. NBC guaranteed $401 million (US) for the Barcelona Olympics in 1992. The media have played an important role in assisting the IOC to strengthen its own coffers, but they have also determined the 'best' viewing time for events from a sponsorship perspective and have tried to control scheduling. NBC had difficulty at the Seoul Olympics in 1988 because of the time difference between Seoul and the American viewers, and sponsors were guaranteed a refund.

[96]See Metcalfe, op. cit., pp. 99–132, for a thorough discussion of the development of amateurism in Canada. He argues that the amateur concept was supported, promoted, and protected in Canada by male members of the upper middle class at the expense of participation opportunities for the lower-economic-class workers and women.

[97]The classification of Canadian athletes—by means of an A, B, or C card-system, depending on performance relative to international standings—was devel-

oped by the Canadian Olympic Association in 1973. In 1986–7 all carded athletes received a basic $450 monthly allowance. An additional high-performance payment of $100 and $200 was made to B- and A-card Olympic athletes respectively.

12. GOVERNMENT INVOLVEMENT IN FITNESS AND AMATEUR SPORT

[1]Government of Canada. House of Commons Debates. Official Report, Fourth Session, Twenty-fourth Parliament, Volume VIII, 1960–1961. Introduction to Bill C-131: 28 September 1961, p. 8461; Amendment of Wording of Resolution: 20 September 1961, p.8601; First Reading: 22 September 1961, pp. 8716–39; Second Reading: 25 September 1961, pp. 8832–65; Third Reading: 26 September 1961, pp. 8873–5.

[2]C. Westland, *Fitness and Amateur Sport in Canada, The Federal Government's Programme: An Historical Perspective* (Ottawa: Canadian Parks and Recreation Association, 1979).

[3]M. F. Rogers, on behalf of the Canadian Sports Advisory Council, Brief Concerning the Problems Arising from Physical Fitness Deficiencies in Canada (Ottawa: 1958), p. 17.

[4]Duke of Edinburgh, speech delivered to the Canadian Medical Association, Toronto, 30 June 1959.

[5]J.F. Kennedy, 'The Soft American', *Sports Illustrated*, 26 December 1960, pp. 15–17.

[6]T. K. Cureton, 'The Case for Physical Fitness', *Think*, September 1958, pp. 22–5; Government of Canada. *Canadian Physical Efficiency Tests: manual for the use of persons conducting the tests* (Ottawa: Fitness and Consultant Services of the Department of National Health and Welfare and R.C.A.F. Recreation and Physical Fitness Branch of the Department of National Defence, 1958); Government of Canada, *5-BX Plan for Physical Fitness* (Ottawa: Royal Canadian Air Force Publication. Pamphlet 30/1, 1958); Government of Canada. *X-BX*

Plan for Physical Fitness (Ottawa, Royal Canadian Air Force Publication, pamphlet 30/2 1960).

[7]Government of Canada. House of Commons Debates, 27 May 1958, pp. 517–18.

[8]Donald Macintosh et al., *Sport and Politics in Canada: Federal Government Involvement Since 1961* (Kingston and Montreal: McGill-Queen's University Press, 1987), pp. 13–14.

[9]Government of Canada. House of Commons Debates. op. cit; Government of Canada. Debates of the Senate. Fourth Session, Twenty-fourth Parliament, 1960–1961. First Reading of Bill C-131: 26 September, 1961, p. 1174; Second Reading: 26 September 1961, 1177–84; Third Reading: 27 September 1961, p. 1201.

[10]Government of Canada, House of Commons Debates, p. 8718.

[11]Government of Canada. House of Commons Debates, op. cit., p. 8719.

[12]Government of Canada. An Act to Encourage Fitness and Amateur Sport. Acts of the Parliament of Canada. Fourth Session, Twenty-fourth Parliament, Part I, Public General Acts, 1960–1961, pp. 421–4.

[13]Ibid.

[14]It was surprising to hear at local CORB meetings, for example, referees who had previously willingly conducted refereeing clinics, now demanding from their sport organization a *per diem* rate and honorarium for doing the same work they had previously given freely. In many ways it assisted those women who previously could not afford to participate to become involved, but at the same time it also put money in the pockets of those who didn't need or expect to be paid.

[15]Westland, op. cit., pp. 40–1.

[16]Canadians in university Physical Education departments enrolled in large numbers in American universities to pursue masters and doctoral programs because these were not well developed in Canada. The University of Western Ontario began its masters program in 1963

and the University of Alberta its doctoral program in 1967.

[17]Research facilities were established at the University of Toronto, the University of Montreal, and the University of Alberta.

[18]Hallett, op.cit., p. 599.

[19]J. Munro, 'Canadian Sports Potential', *Journal of the Canadian Association for Health, Physical Education and Recreation*, 35, no. 2, p. 7.

[20]Westland, op.cit.; Macintosh, op. cit.; National Advisory Council on Fitness and Amateur Sport. Review of Past Achievements 1961–1976 (undated); Government of Canada, *HI-History Buffs from Health and Welfare Canada and from Amateur Sport* (period up to 1976) (Ottawa: Health and Welfare Canada undated); Fitness and Amateur Sport Branch, 'A Brief History', *Fitness and Amateur Sport Branch Annual Report for 1977–78*, pp. 6–7;

[21]National Advisory Council on Fitness and Amateur Sport, 'A Look at the Future in Fitness and Amateur Sport' (Ottawa: Department of National Health and Welfare, Minutes of the NAC, 1968).

[22]W. H. Rae, P.W. Desruisseaux, N. Greene, *Report of the Task Force on Sports for Canadians* (Ottawa: Queen's Printer, Catalogue H21–5269E, 1969).

[23]Government of Canada, *Leisure in Canada*. Proceedings of the Montmorency Conference on Leisure (Ottawa: Department of National Health and Welfare, 1969).

[24]P. A. Ross, and Associates, *A Report on Physical Recreation, Fitness and Amateur Sport in Canada*. (Ottawa: Department of National Health and Welfare, 1969).

[25]J. Munro, 'A Proposed Sports Policy for Canadians' (Ottawa: Department of National Health and Welfare, 1970).

[26]J. Munro, 'Sport Canada, Recreation Canada', speech delivered to the National Advisory Council on Fitness and Amateur Sport, 7 May 1971 (Ottawa: National Health and Welfare, 1971).

[27]Fitness and Amateur Sport Directorate.

'The 1972 Master Plan for Physical Action in Physical Recreation and Sport Excellence'.

[28]Government of Canada, Proceedings of 1972 National Conference on Fitness and Health (Ottawa: Health and Welfare Canada, 1974).

[29]Fitness and Amateur Sport Branch, 'Game Plan', 1973.

[30]Government of Canada, *A New Perspective on the Health of Canadians (Lalonde Report)* (Ottawa: National Health and Welfare Department, 1974).

[31]Government of Canada, Fitness and Amateur Sport Branch, *Report of the National Conference on Employee Fitness in Canada* (Ottawa: Health and Welfare Canada, 1975).

[32]Government of Canada, Fitness and Amateur Sport Branch, *Report of the National Conference on Women and Sport* (Ottawa: Health and Welfare Canada, 1975).

[33]I. Campagnolo, *Toward a National Policy on Amateur Sport: A Working Paper* (Ottawa: Fitness and Amateur Sport Branch, 1977).

[34]I. Campagnolo, *Toward a National Policy on Fitness and Recreation* (Ottawa: Fitness and Amateur Sport Branch, 1979).

[35]I. Campagnolo, *Partners in the Pursuit of Excellence: A National Policy on Amateur Sport* (Ottawa: Fitness and Amateur Sport Branch, 1979).

[36]G. A. Regan, *A Challenge to the Nation: Fitness and Amateur Sport in the 80's* (Ottawa: Fitness and Amateur Sport Branch, 1981).

[37]J. Munro, op.cit.

[38]Report of Task Force . . ., op.cit., p. 47.

[39]Munro, op.cit., 1970, pp. 27–8.

[40]The National Centre for Sport and Recreation was renamed 'Place R. Tait McKenzie, National Sport and Fitness Administrative Centre' when it opened at 1600 James Naismith Drive, Gloucester, in January 1989. McKenzie (1867–1938) was a Canadian-born surgeon, educated at McGill, who for twenty-six years (1904–30) was Director of Physical Edu-

cation at the University of Pennsylvania, but became renowned as a sculptor, specializing in physically accurate depictions of athletes, as in his frieze *The Joy of Effort* (in the wall of the Olympic Stadium at Stockholm), his war memorial *The Call* (Edinburgh), and The Plunger (University of Toronto).

[41]Interview with Cor Westland, March 1986.

[42]'Participaction Packs a Punch', *Financial Post*, May 1978.

[43]'Fitness Goes to Work', *Financial Post*, 1980.

[44]*Financial Post*, op.cit.

[45]Marc Lalonde, *A New Perspective on the Health of Canadians–A Working Document* (Ottawa: Department of National Health and Welfare, 1974).

[46]PARTICIPaction. *1971–1981, A Decade of Action. 10th Anniversary Report*, 1981, p. 18.

[47]Fitness Canada. *A User's Guide to CFS Findings*,The Canada Fitness Survey (Ottawa, Fitness Canada, 1983),.p. 29; *Fitness and Lifestyle in Canada*. A Report by Canada Fitness Survey (Ottawa: Fitness Canada, 1983), p. 67; *Canadian Youth and Physical Activity*, A Report by Canada Fitness Survey (Ottawa: Fitness Canada, 1983), p. 58; Barry McPherson and J. Curtis, *Regional and Community Type Differences in the Physical Activity Patterns of Canadian Adults*. A Canadian Fitness Survey Report (Ottawa: Fitness Canada, 1986), p. 47; *Changing Times: Women and Physical Activity*. A Report of the Canada Fitness Survey (Ottawa: Fitness Canada, 1984), p. 46; *Physical Activity Among Activity-Limited and Disabled Adults in Canada*. A Report of the Canada Fitness Survey (Ottawa: Fitness Canada, 1986), p. 38.

[48]Canadian Fitness and Lifestyle Research Institute,1986. Annual Report, p. 21.

[49]D. Macintosh, 'Federal Government and Voluntary Sports Associations' in *Not Just A Game*, eds. Jean Harvey and Hart Cantelon (Ottawa: University of Ottawa

Press, 1988), p. 131.

[50]Brian Mulroney's Conservative government defeated John Turner's brief Liberal government in September 1984.

[51]Sport Canada, *Women in Sport: A Sport Canada Policy* (Ottawa: Sport Canada, 1986).

[52]Canada improved its position from twenty-first in 1972 in Munich to eleventh in Montreal in 1976, and to fourth in the Los Angeles Olympics in the unofficial medal count. Sport Canada, the sport-governing bodies, and the Canada Olympic Association spoke with pride on the planning initiatives undertaken and the supplementary resources made available to assist these endeavours.

[53]Macintosh, op. cit., 1988, pp. 121–40.

[54]Government of Canada, 'Sport Canada: Athlete Assistance Program Policies and Guidelines, 1986–87' (Ottawa: Ministry of Supply and Services, July 1986).

[55]During the Dubin Inquiry many suggested that it may have been owing to the pressures to meet performance expectations, established for the athletes by their National Sport Organizations and by Sport Canada, that forced them to turn to drugs and cheating to achieve their goals and retain and/or improve their funding levels.

[56]Bruce Kidd, 'The Élite Athlete', in *Not Just a Game*, op.cit., pp. 297–300.

[57]Government of Canada, Fitness and Amateur Sport Branch, *Annual Report 1984–85* (Ottawa: Division Supplies and Services, FAS 7666, 1985), p. 5.

[58]Government of Canada, Fitness and Amateur Sport Branch. *Annual Report 1985–1986* (Ottawa: Division of Supply and Services. FASS 7713,1986).

[59]Federal/Provincial-Territorial Task Force Report on Fitness (unpublished paper, May 1987).

[60]Government of Canada, Fitness and Amateur Sport Branch, *Fitness Fits! Report of the Canadian Symposium on Youth Fitness* (Ottawa: Fitness Canada (undated)).

61Government of Canada, *Fitness . . . the Future. Summary Report of the Canadian Summit on Fitness, June 1986* (Ottawa: Fitness Canada (undated)).

62 'Jasper Talks: Strategies for Change in Adapted Physical Activity in Canada', *CAHPER Journal.* 53 Sept.-Oct 1987, p. 5.

63Fitness Canada, *The Future and Fitness* (unpublished paper, April 1986). Fitness Canada, 'Task Analysis. Minister's Committee on Fitness' (unpublished paper, January 1987).

64Government of Canada, Fitness and Amateur Sport Branch, *Fitness . . . the Future! Achieving the Vision* (Ottawa: Fitness Canada, August 1987).

65I had the pleasure and challenge of serving as President of the Fitness Summit, which included (i) a cross-Canada visit, beginning in Newfoundland and concluding in Vancouver, to talk with people involved in the fitness movement to ascertain the issues facing them and their ideas of future recommendations to enhance the involvement of all Canadians in physical activity; (ii) focus-group testing and distribution of a questionnaire to many Canadians both involved and not involved in fitness activities; (iii) planning, organizing, and conducting a three-day national conference to explore the future of fitness (the size of the conference was established at 200, as large as the budget would permit and as large a group as was thought to be manageable and capable of communicating together); and (iv) producing a substantive report.

66Government of Canada. *Fitness . . . The Future. Summary Report of the Canadian Summit on Fitness. June 1986* (Ottawa: Fitness Canada (undated)), p. 4.

67Charest met with the fitness community quickly after assuming his leadership role and advised them that the government would not be 'privatizing' fitness. This met with wide approval.

68*Toward 2000: Building Canada's Sport System*, the Report of the Task Force on National Sport Policy, with an overview by the Honourable Jean J. Charest, Minister of State Fitness and Amateur Sport, August 1988.

69Ibid., pp. 19–22.

70Commission of Inquiry Into the Use of Drugs and Banned Practices Intended to Increase Athletic Performance established by Prime Minister Mulroney with Justice Charles Dubin as Commissioner. It opened in November 1988.

71From October 1988 to March 1989 the Dubin Inquiry had cost $1.4-million in the 1989 budget estimates; for 1989–90 expenditures an addition $2.33 million was budgeted. The Ministry of Fitness and Amateur Sport, in the same budget presentation, had a decrease of 7%. The Director of Sport Canada Abby Hoffman said that the NSO would have to determine carefully how their money would be used but did not believe that many sports would be eliminated from federal funding as a result of the decrease in Sport Canada's budget.

72Each drug test costs approximately $200. If all national, university, and provincial-level athletes were to be tested regularly, the $52 million (1986–7) Sport Canada budget would have few dollars to fund their élite programs. The COA at its Annual Meeting in April 1989 established a policy requiring NSOs to implement random unannounced testing of athletes and also advised them that all Canadian Olympic athletes would have drug tests before leaving for future Games.

73 'Sports funds cut less than expected:officials', the *Hamilton Spectator*, 29 April 1989. Government funding was reduced by 7%, Sport Canada from $58-million to $55-million (4%), but funding for doping control was doubled to $1-million.

Index